D0207474

Creative Women in Medieval and Early Modern Italy

Creative Women in Medieval and Early Modern Italy

A Religious and Artistic Renaissance

Edited by
E. Ann Matter
and John Coakley

University of Pennsylvania Press
Philadelphia

Printed in the United States of America

Library of Congress Cataloging-in-Publication Data

Creative women in medieval and early modern Italy : a religious and artistic renaissance / edited by E. Ann Matter and John Coakley.

p. cm.

Papers presented at a conference held at the University of Pennsylvania, Sept. 1991.

Includes bibliographical references and index.

ISBN 0-8122-3236-4

1. Women in Christianity—Italy—History—Congresses. 2. Italy—Church history—Congresses. 3. Italy—Intellectual life—Congresses. 4. Sex role—Religious aspects—Christianity—History of doctrines—Congresses. I. Matter, E. Ann. II. Coakley, John Wayland.

BV639.W7C69 1994

274.5'05'082—dc20

94-27864
CIP

For Caroline Walker Bynum

Contents

Illustrations

Preface and Acknowledgments

This book grew out of the conference "Creative Women in Medieval and Early Modern Italy" held at the University of Pennsylvania in September of 1991. Collegiality was the key word of this gathering. Many of the participants are friends and colleagues who have long worked together on topics having to do with the history of Italy; some met for the first time at the conference "Women, Religion, and the Arts in Early Modern Europe," organized by Craig Monson at Amherst College in the spring of 1990; others met for the first time in Philadelphia. But, however we came to know one another, many of us are now involved in joint projects that began at the conference. The excitement of the intellectual exchange we experienced is reflected in the essays gathered together here.

As John Coakley explains in the introduction, the chapters of this book focus on the special creativity of women over an extremely rich and changeable period of the history of Italy, the dawning of what we understand as the modern period. The intellectual and societal changes that took place between the thirteenth and the seventeenth centuries did not bring unqualified good to women. Especially for women of intellectual, spiritual, and artistic gifts, few (and perhaps increasingly fewer) avenues of artistic expression were open. Religion was the one realm in which women did manage to carve out a niche, however cramped and small, for self-expression. All the contributions to this volume deal with Italian religious life or religious patronage or religious control—simply because the life of religion was the one place where women's creativity found a viable context.

It is, nevertheless, obvious that there were many different and contrasting experiences of self-actualization in this context, just as there are many contrasting ways in which the stories presented here can be told. This volume is, by design, multidisciplinary and multicultural. Quite aside from the nuances of each particular historical problem treated, there are striking differences in the treatments. The nationality and academic discipline of each author creates some obvious differences: philosophers see things differently from art historians, literary scholars read a document differently from social historians, American and Italian scholars often have different perspectives on similar issues. It is the hope of the editors and contributors of this volume that these differences in scholarly approach will be as instructive and interesting as the lives of the women they uncover to the modern reader's gaze.

Three of these essays were originally presented at the conference in Italian. Thanks are due to Sue Brotherton, who translated those early versions for the benefit of the non-Italian-speaking audience. The final versions of these essays were translated by Anne Jacobson Schutte (Zarri), Robert Kendrick (Riccardi), and E. Ann Matter (Fumagalli Beonio-Brocchieri).

We are grateful to all those whose financial support made the 1991 conference possible, including the Consulate General of Italy in Philadelphia; the AMICI of the Center for Italian Studies; the departments of History of Art, History, Music, Religious Studies, and Romance Languages; the Humanities Council, the Center for European Studies; the Center for Cultural Studies, the Committee on Medieval Studies; and the Women's Studies Program of the University of Pennsylvania. Most of all, we would like to thank the Center for Italian Studies at the University of Pennsylvania, and especially its enthusiastic and generous director, Stuart Curran, for support of both the conference and this volume.

This book is dedicated to Caroline Walker Bynum, teacher, colleague, and inspiration to so many of the contributors to this volume, and a force to be reckoned with for anyone who works in the fields of the history of women and the history of Christianity.

E. Ann Matter
Philadelphia
June 1993

John Coakley

1. Introduction: Women's Creativity in Religious Context

Communal Italy in the period from the thirteenth century to the seventeenth holds, in anyone's reckoning, a preeminent place in the cultural history of the West. And although the Italian Renaissance may not have had quite the central role Jakob Burkhardt claimed for it in the creation of the self-expressive "individual," no one can doubt that this was a period of conspicuously self-expressive individuals, especially in the fields of art, government, and humanistic scholarship. That most of these figures were male has seemed so self-evident, and conformed to assumptions so deeply rooted in us, that no one particularly called attention to the fact until recent decades. Then in the first wave of the new feminist scholarship, the question whether there had even been a "Renaissance" for women was raised and answered in the negative: recent scholarship has tended to present the period, especially in its later phases, as one in which women's lives became not less but more restricted, as public space was increasingly denied them and their voices were increasingly obscured by the voices of men.[1] The essays in the present volume do not fundamentally take issue with that assessment; indeed at many points they support and illustrate it. But while they do not ignore or minimize the restraints placed on women's opportunities to find their own space and voice, the essays nonetheless demonstrate remarkable creativity among Italian women of the period.

It is especially in the religious life of the period that the authors of these essays find the evidence of such creativity. By "creativity" I mean, broadly, people's use of the materials available to them—the circumstances and opportunities of their lives and their culture's repertory of ideas, assumptions, conflicts, and images—to express themselves in some new way. To say that women displayed such creativity especially in the religious life is not to deny that some women also did so in secular realms; there were indeed female rulers as well as secular female artists and humanists, who are now receiving deserved scholarly attention.[2] These examples, however, were relatively few, since the opportunity of those fields was most often unavailable to women. By contrast, women's involvement in the religious life was extensive, especially in monastic institutions both cloistered and non-cloistered. This involvement made available to them in abundance the resources and possibilities of the religious imagination as well as certain unique, if often unofficial, opportunities to speak and be heard.[3] These opportunities constituted, to be sure, a two-edged sword, for religious life could exact a high price of restriction for the modicum of freedom it offered. But the freedom was real nonetheless, and the essays in this volume explore a variety of ways in which women used it. The importance of religious themes and institutions therefore calls first for some reflections here on women and the religious life in this period. The essays themselves will then be introduced and surveyed in the light of those reflections.

* * *

Beginning roughly in the thirteenth century in the urban centers of Italy and elsewhere in Europe, and specifically in the context of the religious life, individual women begin to be visible to us in greater numbers than in any previous period, as the amount of writing about and even by women increased.[4] A crucial factor in this development was the powerful evangelical movement of the time, which underlay the mendicant orders as well as the widespread heresies, and in which women had a very large part, as Herbert Grundmann has shown. The women came into contact especially with the mendicant friars, and even though, as Grundmann has made clear, the friars did not spawn this female piety, nonetheless they assumed a crucial role in channeling it into forms acceptable to the ecclesiastical hierarchy.[5] The friars also served as major agents in establishing saintly women in new prominence, so that the proportion of female saints among saints overall in the period from the thirteenth to the fifteenth century was notably high.[6] Furthermore, as André Vauchez has pointed out, quite apart from that relatively high proportion of female saints, the most prominent of the mendicant-supported saints were female.[7]

From these women's cults in particular came the documentation that tells us most of what we know about devout women in this period: canonization processes and dozens of vitae of saints, including often their quasi-first-hand revelations and sometimes material indisputably coming from themselves. These materials allow historians a glimpse of their experience, of the way they understood themselves and brought themselves to action, and this glimpse has helped clarify some broad historical issues that concern their creativity. Three interrelated questions may serve to introduce these issues. First, in what ways did the severe restriction of women's roles within the church, and their subjection to largely male authority, affect the form and content of their self-expression? Second, what was distinctively female about these female lives and voices? And third, who were their audiences (so to speak) and how were they understood?

To begin: the restrictedness of women's roles, and their subjection to male ecclesiastical authority, are fundamental facts that no study of these women can ignore. The exclusion of women from the priesthood, and even from preaching, was firm.[8] Furthermore, as Grundmann has pointed out, for the Middle Ages the "religious life" was by definition a life lived under the monastic disciplines and structures that were part of the Church's total order. Consequently the story of the "movement" of women's piety in the High Middle Ages, when viewed as a whole, becomes almost inescapably an account of how women were incorporated into those disciplines and structures; thus Grundmann's still-essential study of the subject is as much about the male orders and the papacy, who were principals in that process of incorporation, as about the groups of women themselves.[9] The incorporation process was substantially complete by the late thirteenth century, and so established the responsibility of the mendicant friars in particular for directing both the temporal and the spiritual affairs of great numbers of convents under their care, as well as of untold numbers of non-cloistered women who were members of the mendicant Third Orders. Friars and other clerics also had a strong hand in establishing the reputation of women of extraordinary piety or spiritual gifts. The late-fourteenth-century chronicler Luca Dominici of Pistoia, for example, wrote of the clergy of the Tuscan shrine of Santa Maria a Cigoli, who, eager for pilgrims, organized a procession around a miracle-working shepherd girl whose prophecies had reportedly called people to the shrine: "When she wants to say something or ask for silence she says it to a preacher who accompanies them and he repeats it and preaches."[10] This dynamic whereby clerics mediated between holy women and their public is in fact at work, albeit more subtly, in most hagiographical writings about women of the period, since with few exceptions the writers were clerics with some stake in the saint's cult.[11]

These comments must suffice to suggest the strictures within which pious women led their lives. Our question is how those strictures affected female voices as we hear them in our sources. In other words, how was women's creativity related to the constraints imposed on them? Scholars are not of one mind in answering this question. The recent work of two scholars who answer it in strikingly different ways may serve to illustrate what is at stake here: the studies by Rudolph Bell and Caroline Walker Bynum of the phenomenon of extreme fasting among medieval holy women, which, as they both point out, figured almost not at all in the lives of their male counterparts. The constraints on women occupy an important place in both scholars' analyses of this phenomenon of fasting, but whereas for Bell those constraints constitute an almost exclusive factor explaining the terms of the women's behavior, Bynum sees a variety of factors at work.

Bell applies psychoanalytical insights to construe the women's extreme fasting as strategies to achieve an "autonomy," a control over themselves which they strongly needed and which was otherwise not afforded them. Drawing on what, in Bell's account, are implicitly dualistic notions in the Christian ascetic tradition—that "the flesh cannot be tamed and therefore must be obliterated"—each of these women waged an internal "war against her body" so as to gain control of her own salvation. At the same time, she waged an external war on the "patriarchy that attempts to impose itself between the holy anorexic and her God," in the sense that by controlling her own intake of food in a way that she believed God willed, she could in effect both define herself and, in the name of a higher power, defy the constraints of family and ecclesiastical authority.[12] (It is this goal of control of self through self-starvation, which these medieval women share with modern anorexic ones, that prompts Bell to call them "holy anorexics"—although he stresses that, emerging as they did in very different cultural contexts, "holy anorexia" and "anorexia nervosa" are not identical.[13]) Catherine of Siena, the best known of the many figures Bell discusses, may serve as an example. Catherine, says Bell, had an "enormous capacity for faith and a very strong need for autonomy," attributable (on slim evidence, it must be said) to her infantile experience of breastfeeding and weaning.[14] Accordingly, out of her conviction that she had a privileged relationship to Christ, she used her fasting and other austerities to manipulate her family into acceding to her desires to remain unmarried and become a Dominican tertiary, and later, once her confessors became convinced of her divine privilege, she managed through similar means to attain a "position of enormous strength" with ecclesiastical authorities as well.[15]

For Bell, "holy anorexics" did indeed achieve something, but both their individual stories and their collective story are tragic. As for their achievement, they "did in fact break out of the established boundaries within which a male hierarchy confined female piety, and thereby established newer and wider avenues for religious expression by women more generally."[16] How they opened the way for other women is not made clear, but it is at least clear that the "anorexia" itself had an important role in securing for Catherine of Siena, Angela of Foligno, or Margaret of Cortona the recognition and hearing they otherwise would not have had. But the price was high; for most of the women he discusses, with the significant exception of those who submitted to the moderating discipline of the cloister, the end of the story was death by starvation. And the end of the whole story of "holy anorexia" is somber, too. After 1500 or so, male clerics tended to withdraw even what acceptance they had previously (and in Bell's account rather grudgingly) afforded to such women, so that, although they continue to appear in the sources through the seventeenth century, it is almost always in a context of suspicion, for example of witchcraft or deceit. Thus in Bell's telling, although extreme fasting was a successful weapon in certain late medieval women's hands in the struggle for autonomy, their victory was at best temporary, partial, and costly.

Bynum discusses many of the same holy women as Bell, but she places them in a broader cultural context. Instead of presenting a set of dramas moved along by psychological factors, she illuminates the women's behavior by presenting a web of assumptions and convictions that were part of the fabric of the culture in which the women lived. Specifically, she explores various ways in which food held religious significance for women and in which the culture associated women uniquely with food. In such a context, Bynum can show that accounts of devout women, when compared with those of men, were much more likely not only to describe fasting behavior but also to show them distributing food to the poor, and most particularly to associate them with that quintessential food of Christians, the eucharist, which had a disproportionately large place not only in the women's devotion but also in their miracles and visions.[17] Underlying this association of women with food, moreover, she finds a deep-seated tendency in late medieval culture to associate the female with the humanity of Christ. "Both men and women described Christ's body in its suffering and its generativity as a birthing and lactating mother and may at some almost unconscious level have felt that woman's suffering was her way of fusing with Christ because Christ's suffering was 'woman.'"[18] Accordingly the women's fasting and other austerities, no less than their eucharistic devotion, held strong power to signify their uniquely female connection with Christ: "women found it very easy to identify with a deity whose flesh, like theirs, was food. In mystical ecstasy, in communion, in ascetic *imitatio*, women ate and became a God who was food and flesh."[19]

For Bynum, then, the stories of fasting women do not have quite the air of tragedy that they do for Bell. This is not to suggest that she ignores or underplays the structures of patriarchy as they affected the women, nor does she imagine that the women had the freedom of movement or the expressive diversity of ecclesiastical roles that were available to men.[20] Like Bell, moreover, she recognizes the role of fasting and other food practices in helping women achieve "control of self" and "control of circumstance." She points out how women's privileged association with the eucharist could serve effectively to criticize, bypass, or even challenge outright the authority of clerics—as when Marie of Oignies vomited the host consecrated by an unworthy priest, or Alice of Schaerbeke received the eucharist directly from Christ, or Gertrude of Helfta saw a vision affirming the validity of the absolution she conveyed to her nuns before mass in the absence of their confessor.[21] But Bynum cautions against seeing these women as "aping" the clergy or even, for the most part anyway, seriously questioning their authority (although they certainly criticized them). The women themselves, as well as others, understood their powers as charismatic and prophetic—a role different from, but not necessarily in conflict with, men's authority of office.[22] Consequently Bynum does not construe female roles and behaviors as primarily challenging male ones in the sense of seeking to supplant them, but rather as coexisting with them in a complementary and interconnected way, within the rather complex system of meanings that the culture attached to gender. In this sense Bynum hears the women's voices more as expressions *of* those principles and assumptions that ordered their culture, than as protests against them.

In considering the essays in this volume, the reader may do well to bear in mind these two contrasting perspectives on the relationship between women and the structures of society within which they moved. In Bell's perspective, the struggle against the repressive forces that would deprive women of a voice is the primary reality that fuels the essential drama of these women's lives. In Bynum's perspective, while the existence of those repressive forces is not denied, the essential drama arises rather from the women's use of the resources the culture made available to them, within the realm of the subtle and complex set of assumptions about gender they shared with that culture. Perspectives similar to each of these may be discerned among the present essays. The latter view is perhaps better represented than the former; nonetheless both are here, and if there is an implicit tension between the two, this is perhaps no unhealthy thing. It may also be that the experience of sixteenth- and seventeenth-century women is more conducive than that of their late medieval counterparts to an analytical approach centered, like Bell's, on the effects of constraints and repression, as the reader may begin to judge from the summaries given later on in this introduction.

The first of our three questions has already anticipated the other two. As for the question of what was distinctively female about these women's lives and voices, enough reference has already been made to the work of Bynum to suggest that part of women's distinctiveness surely lay in their gender-specific association with food and with the body, and thereby in a deeper sense with the incarnate Christ.[23] Another distinctive characteristic was their visionary experience; as several studies have shown, visions, as well as mystical ecstasies and paramystical phenomena associated with them such as levitation or the stigmata, were much more likely to be reported of women than of men.[24] When they wrote, moreover, women characteristically wrote of their visions. As Elizabeth Petroff, writing from a perspective similar in this respect to Bell's, has put it, women who wrote of their visions were asserting their own drive to express their personal experience "in the face of pervasive institutional misogyny" that in fact did not encourage them to write.[25] This was surely so. On the other hand, it is worth noting that women's association with visions, like their association with fasting, may indicate not only their reaction to the restraints placed on them but also elements in the system of interrelated meanings that men as well as women attached to gender. André Vauchez, for example, has noted that among the saints officially promoted by the male mendicant orders, a neat divide exists between female saints, who were noted for their mysticism, and male saints, who were noted for their learning.[26] Catherine Mooney similarly has shown in her study of thirteenth-century Tuscan saints' vitae that, whereas the male saints pursued this-worldly knowledge, the female saints are "portrayed consistently as living on the boundary as it were between this world and the other world. As conduits for God's word to this world, women function as bridges between these worlds."[27]

These words of Mooney, referring as they do to images of women conveyed in texts by men, may serve to introduce the third question, that of the meaning of women for their "audience." The overwhelming majority of the texts that witness to women's experience were written by men. It is becoming increasingly apparent that male interest in holy women was anything but casual, and could be extremely appreciative; the male clerical hagiographers who wrote about women, at least before 1500, rarely adopted a detached or inquisitorial stance, but rather displayed an intense fascination and admiration.[28] This seems to have been the case in part at least because of their sense of the limits and inadequacy of their own office and learning, and their perception of the women as "other," embodying in particular a connection with the divine that they did not find in themselves.[29] One thinks, for instance, of Catherine of Siena's learned and highly placed Dominican confessor, Raymond of Capua, who related that he once saw Catherine's face become God's own face—her presence in effect becoming no less than God's presence for him.[30] But, as Karen Scott notes in her essay in this volume, Catherine's understanding of herself could be quite different from Raymond's understanding of her; and in general the sense of "otherness" that comes across so strongly in men's accounts of women is not surprisingly lacking in those few cases where we can observe women writing about themselves or each other.[31] Karen Glente's comparison of the work of two late medieval hagiographers, one male (Thomas of Cantimpré) and one female (Katherine of Unterlinden), shows, for instance, how, in describing female saints' levitation, the man emphasized their inimitable miraculous separation from the earthly circumstances around them, whereas the woman saw the miracle as a sign of something imitable, namely the enlightenment and passionate devotion the saints were in fact sharing with those around them.[32] It is clear, then, that the gender of the hearers had much to do with the meanings attached to women's voices.

This is not the place to explore all the implications of these differences of perception. Suffice it to say that to listen to the "voices" of women in this period we must pay attention not only to what those voices said but also to how they were heard. And we need, in particular, to develop an ear for the culture's assumptions about gender, which helped to define and finely tune the social relations within which these women lived. Those were assumptions that did, indeed, restrain women's self-expression in important ways, although in other ways they condoned and even fostered it.

* * *

Let us turn now to the essays in this volume. They are grouped in three sections. The essays in the first section deal with women's religious expression in the period from the thirteenth to the fifteenth century; those in the second similarly focus on women's religious expression, but in the sixteenth and seventeenth centuries. The third group of essays concerns artistic, rather than specifically religious, expression among cloistered religious women in the sixteenth and seventeenth centuries. The writers represent several disciplines and the essays cover a wide territory. Without attempting to survey all their important implications for their various fields of specialty, I wish here to place them in the context of the themes of gender and religion just discussed.

In the essays of the first group, these themes are especially apparent. Mariateresa Fumagalli Beonio-Brocchieri, for instance, applies to texts of the mystics Clare of Assisi, Umiltà of Faenza, and Angela of Foligno the question of what is characteristically female in their voices. Although she does not stress food imagery in particular, her answer is reminiscent of Bynum in calling attention to a common emphasis on imagery related to the body and sensuality, combined with suffering—what she calls a "painful physicality."

A concern with women's "audience," and specifically with the distinction and interplay between male and female perceptions of women, also surfaces prominently in the essays of the first group. The mystical *Libro* of Angela of Foligno is usually treated straightforwardly as Angela's own work, in part because "Brother A.," the scribe who wrote it down, seems to present it as such. Catherine Mooney, however, argues here from an examination of the scribe's interpolations and comments that he himself had a considerable role in shaping the text. This conclusion does not imply that the book ceases to be substantially Angela's book; it does suggest that what we are "hearing" in this text is not simply Angela's voice but rather the product of her interaction with, as it were, an individual male audience, whose perceptions have affected her in various ways. The involvement of audiences in the production of texts is also a major concern of Katherine Gill's essay. In this case the audiences were female and the voices—those of the fourteenth-century devotional writers Domenico Cavalca and Simone de Cascina—were male. Gill in effect stands on its head the conventional wisdom that women's voices are usually not purely accessible to us because we hear them only through men's mediation, and suggests that the voice of the male author is also not purely his own; it may be shaped by the perceptions of women who constituted his audience and entered his text in significant ways, and who thereby become accessible to us within it. In the work of Simone de Cascina in particular, Gill sees devout women providing clerical men a "sentimental education" through an experience-based religious expressiveness that they and the men appear to have considered distinctively female.

Along with their interest in the intertwining of medieval author and audience, the authors of the first group of essays also display a tendency to emphasize the aspects of religious women's environment that were hospitable to their self-expression. This is the case in Gill's demonstration of her male authors' attentiveness to their female audience. It is also the case in Karen Scott's essay here on Catherine of Siena. Scott shows that, although one might never suspect so from Catherine's vita by Raymond of Capua, in which she is portrayed in heroic relief against critics who thought it inappropriate for a virgin to cut such a public figure, her letters make no mention of any gender-based objections to her apostolate, about which she appears quite confident.[33] From other evidence too, such as documents from the circle of Catherine's near-contemporary Giovanni Colombini, the Sienese founder of the Gesuati, Scott suggests that a positive model of a socially committed spirituality was available for laypeople including women in Catherine's Siena, which in general provided a "nurturing environment" for her self-expression. (Scott's estimation of Catherine's relationship to her environment thus contrasts sharply with that of Bell, discussed earlier.) The essay by Ann Roberts points, in effect, to another such environment, and one that receives more attention later in the volume: the cloister. Roberts examines the works of art commissioned for the Dominican convent of San Domenico in Pisa during the tenure of the prioress Chiara Gambacorta (who was to become a saint herself, and had Catherine of Siena as her sometime mentor) in the early fifteenth century. Her findings suggest that the influence of Chiara on these works was strong and coherent, constituting in itself a form of religious expression.

In comparison with the essays in the first group, those in the second, which move into the early modern period, tend to suggest a less hospitable response to women's voices. Carolyn Valone studies three noblewomen who made substantial donations for the support for new Jesuit institutions in sixteenth-century Rome. Valone finds that, although the influence of one of these in particular, Giovanna d'Aragona, may be discerned in some of the art at the Jesuit novitiate San Vitale, still the Jesuits underplayed the important contribution of these women, which has since "largely been forgotten." The seventeenth-century Venetian women Ann Jacobson Schutte discusses in her essay also experienced a markedly hostile environment. These were young women who, unable to realize their desire to become nuns, came under the influence of male confessors whose perceptions became the "mirrors" in which they saw and fashioned an image of themselves. The image they fashioned was that of the holy woman, characterized by extreme fasting, frequent communion, and revelations. But this self-fashioning had disastrous consequences: the Inquisition condemned them as fakes. In her analysis of these women, Schutte emphasizes the hostility of their surroundings (thus creating a picture of women's religious experience reminiscent more of Bell than of Bynum), and the spiritually impoverishing effect of their reliance on male confessors for their self-image. She contrasts them with female painters of self-portraits in this period, who, on the basis of interactions with a wider variety of people, appear to have had rather healthier views of themselves.

These essays of the second group suggest also that the arena for women's religious self-expression came to be more confined within the strict limits of institutional monasticism. Thus the stories Schutte relates could well have functioned as cautionary tales for women who tried to fulfill religious aspirations outside the monastery.[34] As for nuns themselves, Ann Matter's study of the commentary on the Rule of Saint Clare of Assisi by the seventeenth-century Capuchin nun Maria Domitilla Galluzzi calls attention to a certain trade-off the convent represented for women. She notes that Maria Domitilla's work, advocating a strict observance of the Rule, is essentially a "conservative defense of a conservative view of women's religious lives." Why such enthusiasm for an obviously restrictive institution? Because "the obvious disadvantages of Maria Domitilla's life—enclosure, subservience, poverty, hunger—were compensated for by the advantages of a spiritual tradition, credibility, space, a voice." In other words, although strict monastic enclosure and discipline exacted a price, they could give a woman an opportunity and a context for self-expression which in this period she would not otherwise have had. It is germane to this insight that Maria Maddalena de' Pazzi, whose teachings Antonio Riccardi discusses here, was a cloistered Carmelite, although her mysticism may remind us of her noncloistered predecessor Angela of Foligno, both in its scope and broadly in its "corporeality."

That the cloister was not, however, the only institutionalized monastic option for women in this period becomes clear from Gabriella Zarri's study of the iconography of the sixteenth-century Company of Saint Ursula, founded by Angela Merici. The Ursulines, whose calling was to be not nuns in the cloister but rather "virgins at home" in service of church and family, were nonetheless organized almost militarily, with the high sense of institutional self-awareness and missionary purpose typical of the new orders of the sixteenth century (and not necessarily characteristic of the medieval female tertiaries who were otherwise their counterparts in serving "at home").

The third and final group of essays explores the artistic activities of some sixteenth- and seventeenth-century Italian nuns. In part, they show cases in point of that female religious trade of subservience for "a space, a voice," to which Matter has earlier called attention. Thus Elissa Weaver shows that in the biblical play *Jacob the Patriarch* by the Florentine Franciscan nun Maria Clemente Ruoti (1637) there was a "conflict of ideologies": the play approvingly portrays women's obedient submission to the authority of men but at the same time complains of their subjection. At the heart of the work is a "didactic purpose: to teach women how to live together" in the monastery given this paradoxical situation. At any rate, it was the convent that provided Ruoti the dramatist invaluable resources that she would not have had outside it, namely "a convent literary tradition, women writers and actresses, an informed, demanding audience, and the encouragement, even the obligation to participate in the tradition." Similarly Craig Monson writes of the Bolognese composer and nun Lucrezia Orsina Vizzana that her opportunity to create music was probably greater in the cloister than it would have been in secular society.

The essays in the third group also strongly demonstrate that cloister walls were far from impermeable; an artistic nun who had submitted herself in obedience did not entirely give up communicating with the creative world beyond the cloister. Thus, according to Weaver, another play of Ruoti, *The Birth of Christ*, was aimed at an audience beyond the convent, and shows much evidence of contact with the surrounding city. Monson likewise shows that Vizzana's music responded to changes in musical culture outside the convent, and displays evidence of influence of composers such as Adriano Banchieri, Ottavio Venizzi, and possibly Claudio Monteverdi. Finally, Robert Kendrick, in his study of perceptions of Milanese nuns' music, presents a nuanced view of artistic nuns' relationship with the world outside, especially with authoritative male clerics, whose attitudes varied. At one extreme was the view of the archbishop Carlo Borromeo, who after a visitation of the Franciscan convent of Sant'Apollinare in 1571, reprimanded the nuns for contact with a male music-master and for possessing "madrigals and amorous sonnets," and thus displayed a restrictive stance toward women that perhaps does not surprise us. But Carlo's cousin and successor Federigo Borromeo, who seems to have taken a special interest in the experience of religious women, actually encouraged nuns' musical activity. The evidence of other witnesses, at any rate, shows that activity to have been lively throughout the period.

* * *

Taken together, what do these essays tell us about the creativity of women in the period of the thirteenth to the seventeenth centuries, especially as it pertains to those matters of gender and religion discussed at the outset?

The essays prompt a comparison between the late medieval and early modern situations in which women's voices were heard. They suggest, in the first place, a discontinuity between two situations in the matter of the restrictions placed upon women. In the earlier period, there appears to have been more opportunity for women's religious expression outside the cloister, and more direct interaction with the world. There also is much evidence in the earlier era of a positive and sympathetic interest in women's voices among the men who were in the position of mediating these to a broader audience. In the later period, the arena for women's self-expression seems to have been more restricted to institutional, especially cloistered, contexts. But it is important not to exaggerate this overall discontinuity, for there are also points of continuity. On the one hand, it hardly needs saying that elements of restrictiveness can be observed in the earlier period as well. Furthermore, the advantages of the cloister as a "space" for women's self-expression were not peculiar to the later period, as the case of Chiara Gambacorta indicates. On the other hand, the admiring interest of male clerics in religiously expressive women, of which there are many famous examples in the earlier period, can appear in the later period as well, for instance in the person of Federigo Borromeo.

More fundamentally, in these essays taken together, along with other recent work, a vision begins to cohere of a history not just of women in this period, but more broadly of gender relationships within the pattern of the culture's creative energy. We are beginning to comprehend something of the complexity of people's understandings of maleness and femaleness, and of the ways in which those understandings were at work in the social relationships out of which emerged the creative women to whom the following pages are devoted.

Notes

1. Joan Kelly-Gadol, "Did Women Have a Renaissance?" in *Becoming Visible: Women in European History*, ed. Renate Bridenthal, Claudia Koonz, and Susan M. Stuard (Boston: Houghton Mifflin, 1977), pp. 139–64, 2d ed., pp. 175–201. For an overview of recent pertinent work in social history, see the editors' Introduction in *Rewriting the Renaissance: The Discourses of Sexual Difference in Early Modern Europe*, ed. Margaret W. Ferguson, Maureen Quilligan, and Nancy J. Vickers (Chicago: University of Chicago Press, 1986), pp. xv–xxxi. For a comprehensive treatment of the subject see now Margaret L. King, *Women of the Renaissance* (Chicago: University of Chicago Press, 1991).

2. See King, *Women of the Renaissance*, pp. 157–239.

3. David Herlihy has argued that, although in most respects women's position in society was diminishing in this period, the period offers abundant examples of an "alternate route to personal fulfillment and social leadership" for women through "charisma" as distinct from "office and authority." David Herlihy, "Did Women Have a Renaissance? A Reconsideration," *Medievalia et Humanistica* n.s. 13 (1985): 1–22.

4. On the "proliferation" of female writers of the period, see Peter Dronke, *Women Writers of the Middle Ages: A Critical Study of Texts from Perpetua (d. 203) to Marguerite Poreto (d. 1310)* (Cambridge: Cambridge University Press, 1984), p. 202.

5. Herbert Grundmann, *Religiöse Bewegungen im Mittelalter*, 2d ed. (Hildesheim: Olms Verlagsbuchhandlung, 1961), pp. 208–318.

6. Donald Weinstein and Rudolph Bell call this the "era of female sanctity," since the percentages of saints in the authors' large sample who were female in those centuries are 22.6 (thirteenth century), 23.4 (fourteenth century), and 27.7 (fifteenth century)—figures obviously not representing majorities but significantly larger than for the preceding and succeeding centuries (11.8 for the twelfth century, 18.1 for the sixteenth). Donald Weinstein and Rudolph M. Bell, *Saints and Society: The Two Worlds of Western Christianity, 1000–1700* (Chicago: University of Chicago Press, 1982), p. 220.

7. André Vauchez, *La sainteté en occident aux derniers siècles du moyen âge, d'après les procès de canonisation et les documents hagiographiques* (Rome: École Française de Rome, 1981), p. 245. For a more extended discussion of this phenomenon, see John Coakley, "Friars, Sanctity and Gender: Mendicant Encounters with Saints, 1250–1325," in *Medieval Masculinities*, ed. Clare Lees (Minneapolis: University of Minnesota Press, 1994).

8. Francine Cardman, "The Medieval Question of Women and Orders," *Thomist* 42 (1978): 582–99.

9. Grundmann, *Religiöse Bewegungen*, pp. 5–6, passim.

10. Daniel Bornstein, "The Shrine of Santa Maria a Cigoli: Female Visionaries and Clerical Promoters," *Mélanges de l'École Française de Rome: Moyen Âge, Temps Modernes* 98 (1986): 219–28; quotation from Luca, p. 225.

11. On the role of male clerics in producing hagiographical texts about women, see Catherine Mooney, "Women's Visions, Men's Words: The Portrayal of Holy Women and Men in Fourteenth-Century Italian Hagiography," Ph.D. dissertation, Yale University, 1991.

12. Rudolph M. Bell, *Holy Anorexia* (Chicago: University of Chicago Press, 1985), pp. 115–16.

13. Bell, *Holy Anorexia*, pp. 19–20.

14. Bell, pp. 51, 29–35.

15. Bell, pp. 35–45, 116.

16. Bell, p. 117.

17. Caroline Walker Bynum, *Holy Feast and Holy Fast: The Religious Significance of Food to Medieval Women* (Berkeley: University of California Press, 1987), pp. 73–149.

18. Bynum, pp. 260–61.

19. Bynum, p. 275.

20. Bynum, pp. 1–30.

21. Bynum, pp. 227–32.

22. Bynum, pp. 235–37. See also John Coakley, "Friars as Confidants of Holy Women in Medieval Dominican Hagiography," in *Images of Sainthood in Medieval Europe*, ed. Renate Blumenfeld-Kosinski and Timea Szell (Ithaca, NY: Cornell University Press, 1991), pp. 222–46.

23. See Sharon Farmer, "Softening the Hearts of Men: Women, Embodiment and Persuasion in the Thirteenth Century," in *Embodied Love: Sensuality and Relationship as Feminist Values*, ed. Paula M. Cooey, Sharon A. Farmer, and Mary Ellen Ross (San Francisco: Harper and Row, 1987), pp. 115–33.

24. See Bynum, *Holy Feast*, pp. 25–26; Peter Dinzelbacher, "Europäische Frauenmystik des Mittelalters: Ein Überblick," in *Frauenmystik im Mittelalter*, ed. Peter Dinzelbacher and Dieter Bauer (Ostfildern bei Stuttgart: Schwabenverlag, 1985), pp. 11–23; Weinstein and Bell, *Saints and Society*, pp. 228–29.

25. Elizabeth Petroff, *Medieval Women's Visionary Literature* (New York: Oxford University Press, 1986), p. 4. She cites in this connection the observation of Peter Dronke (*Women Writers of the Middle Ages*, p. 4) that "the women's motivation for writing at all, for instance, seems rarely to be predominantly literary: it is more often urgently serious than is common among men writers; it is a response springing from inner needs, more than from an artistic, or didactic, inclination. . . . Hence the women . . . show excellingly a quality (literary, but also 'metaliterary') of immediacy: they look at themselves more concretely and more searchingly than many of the highly accomplished men writers who were their contemporaries."

26. Vauchez, *La sainteté*, p. 409. See also idem, "Les pouvoirs informels dans l'Église aux derniers siècles du moyen âge: Visionnaires, prophètes et mystiques," *Mélanges de l'École Française de Rome: Moyen Âge, Temps Modernes* 96 (1984): 281–93.

27. Catherine Mooney, "Women's Visions in Fourteenth-Century Italian Spiritual Texts," paper given at the 1990 Berkshire Conference on the History of Women, p. 23.

28. See Coakley, "Friars as Confidants."

29. John Coakley, "Gender and the Authority of Friars: The Significance of Holy Women for Thirteenth-Century Franciscans and Dominicans," *Church History* 60 (1991): 445–60.

30. *Acta sanctorum Aprilis*, vol. 3 (Paris, 1866), p. 884, par. 90.

31. Caroline Walker Bynum, "Women's Stories, Women's Symbols: A Critique of Victor Turner's Theory of Liminality," in *Anthropology and the Study of Religion*, ed. Robert L. Moore and Frank E. Reynolds (Chicago: University of Chicago Press, 1984), pp. 110–18.

32. Karen Glente, "Mystikerinnenviten aus männlicher und weiblicher Sicht: Ein Vergleich zwischen Thomas von Cantimpré und Katherina von Unterlinden," in *Religiöse Frauenbewegung und Mystiche Frömmigkeit im Mittelalter*, ed. Peter Dinzelbacher and Dieter Bauer (Cologne and Vienna: Böhlau, 1988), pp. 260–62.

33. Raymond's treatment of Catherine, incidentally, thus appears to display the same tendency Glente has pointed out in Thomas of Cantimpré (see above n. 32)—to underscore a female saint's "otherness" by alienating her from her natural environment.

34. For a different view of religious possibilities for women outside the cloister, on the basis of fifteenth- and sixteenth-century sources, see Katherine Gill, "Open Monasteries for Women in Late Medieval and Early Modern Italy: Two Roman Examples," in *The Crannied Wall: Women, Religion, and the Arts in Early Modern Europe*, ed. Craig Monson (Ann Arbor: University of Michigan Press, 1992), pp. 15–47, especially the conclusion, p. 35.

Part I

Women's Religious Expression: Thirteenth to Fifteenth Centuries

Mariateresa Fumagalli Beonio-Brocchieri

2. The Feminine Mind in Medieval Mysticism

The title of this essay immediately forces us to ask an imperative question. Is there something that defines and characterizes the mental process, the *forma mentis*, of medieval mystical texts in a feminine, as distinct from a masculine, sense? The answer, which deserves more than the limited examination I propose here, demands that we all have a clear idea (the same idea) of the meaning of terms such as "mind," "mysticism," and even "medieval."[1] I will explore this question by means of a *via media*, first indicating pragmatically the meaning of the terms used in this discussion.

By "mind" I mean the definition established first by sociology and then by the French new historicism: the attitudes, dispositions, and behavior of a group selected to characterize the group itself.[2] More simply, the term "mind" in the title indicates those characteristics that are statistically more frequent in the texts of the authors to whom I shall refer. These characteristics make one suppose, if not a structure, at least an attribute which can be isolated and studied in depth.

With regard to the term "mysticism," the problem is greater and more profound. It cannot be addressed without acknowledging the entire *querelle* which underlies it and which cannot be considered in depth here.[3] Nevertheless, let us pause briefly on the inner dialectic of the concept: the distinction between a "negative" aspect of mystical thought that tends toward the annihilation of the individual in the "ocean of the divine," and a positive aspect that instead underlines the fulfillment and realization of the individual in God. Mysticism can have as an axiom the affirmation of the impossibility of reaching God through the ordinary processes of the human mind. In contrast, yet at the same time and in a complementary way, it can have another axiom which says that there is an intimate relationship of origin between God and human beings on the basis of which humans can turn to God and be reunited in ecstasy, *excessus*, or deification.

Translated by E. Ann Matter.

Let us consider an example from Christian antiquity which, although distant, may have reached the Latin world in a thousand ways and then, through sermons, preaching, and citations, reached the minds of the most simple and unlettered people. I refer to the presence of the *homoiōsis theou* that returns with insistence in the *Protrepticus* and the *Paedagogus* of Clement of Alexandria.[4] I do not mean to indicate Clement as a clear source, but rather to suggest that this is an idea which was well diffused in the classical world, but which probably appears in Clement for the first time in a Christian context.

Inside the mystical inquiry (for mysticism is essentially an inquiry) we can also note the progressive gradations of access to the divine. Bonaventure, for example, distinguishes between thought (*cogitatio*), meditation (*meditatio*), and, highest of all, contemplation (*contemplatio*).[5] Another conception of mysticism is as an unregulated, sudden rush. In a third way, and perhaps even more revealing, we can distinguish between the model of ascent, of being taken up into the third or the seventh heaven (as in Paul or Augustine),[6] and, the model of the descent of God, almost like an invasion into the depths of the mystical soul. The drawing near and communion between humans and God can take place, on the one hand, by means of sound, hearing the Voice, or (more rarely and apparently more intellectually) according to sight, in a *visio*. Examples of both ways are found in Augustine.

Turning to the excellent work of Alain de Libera on philosophy and mysticism[7] reveals another distinction, or rather a dialectic internal to mystical experience. This is a dialectic between a mysticism that tends toward an absolute separation from the body and a mysticism that moves irresistibly through "bodily madness." And then again, the difference between mystical experience as it is lived and mystical experience as it is narrated should also be considered. Certainly a relationship of a total, physical, sensible, intellectual, and emotive experience is much different from and more problematic than a relationship expressed as an intellectual theory and its oral or written expression.

It is important to bear in mind from the start that in the Middle Ages the term "mystical" is used neither for the state of a soul nor for an experience, even less for a person, man or woman. In medieval parlance, "mystical" refers only to theology, as seen in the title of a famous work by Dionysius the Pseudo-Areopagite, *The Mystical Theology*.[8] Indeed, in a certain sense, only God is "mystical," that is, hidden. Dionysian theology shows by means of a succession of affirmations and negations how to arrive at nonknowing (*agnosia*) of and union (*enosis*) with God without images (*afairesis*). Ignorance (that is, unknowability) and union are not attributes of the soul as much as they are attributes of God. God is unknowable, and essentially one with humanity and with all of reality.[9]

But let us return to the historiographical problem of the term "mystical." Our observations have all tended to indicate the variety and the richness—in a word, the unexplainable nature—of mystical experience in a general sense. This brings into greater focus the individual and creative signature of every individual mystical account.

A historian of philosophy is irresistibly attracted (often, perhaps, with negative results) to the valorization of the traditions into which the author studied is inserted. From this comes the execrable proliferation of "isms" (realism, empiricism, and so on) that become almost entities unto themselves and then force the scholar into painful interpretative acrobatics to make individual cases fit into general categories. But it seems that the scholar of treatises of religious mysticism runs the opposite risk, the overvalorization of the single case, which can lead to an excessive pyschologism and to the exaggeration of the exceptional quality of the text in question. Continual comparisons, study of the terminology and the historical context can serve as correctives to this tendency; these are tools that permit us to contextualize the language of a single mystical experience and to evaluate the language used in the narration of the experience itself.

Now we come to the subject I hope to develop in this brief essay: the examination of a few (in my opinion, significant) texts of three mystical women of thirteenth-century Italy. Bearing in mind that certain terms and locutions used by these authors are also present in "high" culture we can suggest some connections between philosophical culture and doctrinal culture (*cultura magistrale*). The latter, in turn, can give us other tools by which to judge the linguistic creativity of our mystical authors and their relationship with the world around them so we can explore how an illiterate woman of Siena or a young widow of Foligno was able to live, not knowing how to transcribe this language, but only how to listen to it and dictate it to others.

First, let us consider a text of the "little plant," the *plantucula* of Francis of Assisi, Clare: her letter of 1234 to Agnes of Prague. Clare writes:

> When you have loved [Him], You shall be chaste; when You have touched [Him], You shall become pure; when You have accepted [Him], You shall be a virgin.
>
> Whose power is stronger,
> Whose generosity is more abundant,
> Whose appearance more beautiful,

Whose love is more tender,
Whose courtesy more gracious.
In Whose embrace You are already caught up.
Who has adorned Your breast with precious stones,
And has placed priceless pearls in Your ears
and has surrounded You with sparkling gems
as though blossoms of springtime
and placed on Your head a golden crown
as a sign [to all] of your holiness.

Therefore, most beloved sister, or should I say, lady worthy of great respect: because You are the spouse and the mother and the sister of my Lord Jesus Christ [2 Cor. 11:2; Mt. 12:50], and have been adorned resplendently with the sign of inviolable virginity.[10]

What are the concepts to which Clare returns with over-precious insistence? The words are explicit and strong in their immediacy: caresses, possession, sexual union, virginity, and also the physical and material beauty of the body and its ornaments. This passage, like others of her other writings, emphasizes an imagination concentrated on a model of a nuptial and loving relationship, with a strong emphasis on physical beauty and the radiant pleasure this union evokes from Clare's bewildered soul. The simultaneous presence of the concepts of maternity, spousal union, and virginity is especially notable.[11] This combination shows beyond question the transfer of meaning from a physical plane to the realm of the symbolic.

But then why does the text speak of "spouse," "virgin," and "mother" all at the same time? The subject in relation to these terms is always the same: Christ, in his most tender humanity. The erotic and conjugal relationship does not here seem sufficient, for, from another point of view in this dialogue with the divine, we are made aware of a feminine quality that is in itself holy and assured of purity: that is, virginity. Here, maternity is understood, after the example of the Virgin Mary, as another type of deeply physical union.

Surprisingly, mother (not father) is the term used for the Christ who is, subtly and implicitly, the playful love (*amore giocondo*) of Umiltà of Faenza. Umiltà, whose real name was Rosanna, was born of a noble family in 1226. She was first a wife, then a nun, then a hermit. Umiltà had a vision that urged her to found a community dedicated to John the Baptist. Like Hildegard of Bingen (although unlike most mystics) she lived a long life and died at the age of 84.

In Umiltà's writings, touch and smell as well as intoxicated sight become part of the visionary experience. Against all the rules of Christian-Platonic asceticism, these are the physical instruments chosen for the elevation of the sensible and loving soul. Umiltà writes:

> Just as God entered into the closed womb of the Virgin, so he can show himself in any form to holy people. . . . These search for him and find him in any form, speaking with him and touching him. . . . The soul contemplates God through the great desire of divine love, they approach him and touch him and speak with him. . . . And the Lord does not only allow himself to be touched by these, but also lets them kiss his feet and his most holy breast. . . . How the soul is restored and how it is beautiful when it finds itself in the presence of such a most beautiful youth. And it can embrace him and take in his most fragrant odor.[12]

Of a splendid physicality is Umiltà's metaphor of a lamb, in which can be perceived a very special intellectual capacity and cultural awareness:

> And this little lamb bleating with hunger who calls for a pasture to fatten it up is the soul which wants to remain with Christ, who is its pasture. And it wishes to go where the grass is new, it wishes to gather only flowers and contemplate the beauty of its dear love and with this desire it fills its breasts with the milk of charity, to enter into the garden of its true love, to choose red and white roses. . . . I am the pilgrim lamb for your love: you know the grass which I grazed in my pasture, you know if my life is sweet or bitter. You should not marvel if I ask only love from you . . . love in your wholeness . . . the most delicious honey.[13]

But Umiltà, as has already been suggested, has another characteristic that makes her similar to the "Sibyl of the Rhine": the need to communicate to others the truth taught to her by God. Her language remains that of the most simple and sensory experience, but, like Hildegard, Umiltà is one of the few cases of females who were learned in an academic sense.[14]

In the same century, we find Angela of Foligno, who, like Umiltà, knew the state of matrimony. As is well known, Angela remained completely alone after the death of her mother and her husband. Around 1290, in absolute poverty after having given away all her possessions, she entered the Third Order of the Franciscans. Her spiritual autobiography is known as the *Memoriale* of the friar Arnaldo, the Franciscan who collected her confidences little by little (since Angela probably knew how to read but not how to write) and actively intervened with his own observations on this confessional dialogue. Angela died in 1309.

The texts of Angela of Foligno have been amply studied by a number of scholars;[15] I limit myself here to pointing out a few aspects of her writings that can give a sense of a "feminine" quality (in the sense discussed earlier) of her mystical experiences.

Angela affirms that her soul "experiences God," or rather, that it "feels" him; and she is aware, partly because of the continual objections of Fra Arnaldo, that this experience has to do with a God different from that of the *pagina sacra*, the Bible, even the Gospels. This is the first point that distinguishes her text from the other two mystical texts we have considered here, those of Clare and Umiltà, and it can be ascribed to a singular attitude: her violent passion and strength, which leads her often to highlight the contradictory aspects of her experience. Angela does not seek accord or conciliation. We can divide her mystical experience into three "moments" or levels: love, nothingness, and resurrection.[16]

Let us pause for a closer look at the first two of these "moments." With regard to the first, Angela says:

> Suddenly while I was engrossed in this effort and desire, a divine sword sounded in my soul: "My love for you has not been a hoax." These words struck me a mortal blow. For immediately the eyes of my soul were opened and I saw that what he had said was true. I saw his acts of love, everything that the Son of God had done, all that he had endured in life and in death—this suffering God-man—because of his inexpressible and visceral love. Seeing in him all the deeds of true love, I understood the perfect truth of what he had said, that "his love for me had not been a hoax," but that he had loved me with a most perfect and visceral love. I saw, on the other hand, the exact opposite in myself, because my love for him had never been anything but playing games, never true. Being made aware of this was a mortal blow and caused such intolerable pain that I thought I would die.[17]

It is striking that this move overturns the sequence of the love relationship that usually exists between the mystical lover and God. Paradoxically, Angela is the desired woman, sought and loved more than she loves. The divine love does violence to her, she is not immediately able to respond fully. Is this closer to a model of courtly love than to the *excessus* of Bernard of Clairvaux? Perhaps. But the entire movement of love and reference to any sort of code are then overturned in a leap of love which slips away even from these models.[18]

But notice the first moment of the passage from the "moment" of passionate love to nothingness:

> For when love is pure, you consider yourself as worthless, see yourself as dead and as nothing, and present yourself to God as dead and putrid.[19]

Angela refers to a type of humility very different from that which left her happy and fulfilled: "this humility is accompanied with countless ill effects";[20] she sees herself damaged, she sees no remedy and "not even a small window through which I could escape."[21] Every consolation is excluded, as is every remembrance of divine graces received. Angela becomes "non-love," and sees God in the darkness. But just at the moment of the most profound "non-love," in "this most efficacious good seen in this darkness now resides my most firm hope, one in which I am totally recollected and secure."[22] The vision then becomes most elevated because it is secret:

> But when God is seen in darkness it does not bring a smile to the lips, nor devotion, fervor, or ardent love; neither does the body or the soul tremble or move as at other times; the soul sees nothing and everything; the body sleeps and speech is cut off. And all the signs of friendship, so numerous and indescribable, all the words which God spoke to me, all those which you ever wrote—I now understand that these were so much less than that which I see with such great darkness, that in no way do I place my hope in them, nor is there any of my hope in them. Even if it were possible that all these previous experiences were not true, nonetheless, that could in no way diminish my hope—the hope that is so secure and certain in the All Good which I see with such darkness.[23]

When she lies in this state of "desolate quiet" Angela does not distinguish the human form from the divine: "I see all and I see nothing."[24]

> When I am in the God-man, my soul is alive. And I am in the God-man much more than in the other vision concerning the God-man. The vision with darkness, however, draws me so much more that there is no comparison.[25]

Thus the union with God is regained in returning up from the undifferentiated abyss, and Angela once again knows joy, the joy of "being in the divine bed." Thinking back on her ecstasy, Angela brings into focus these two diverse states:

> In the first state, God presents himself in the inmost depths of my soul. I understand not only that he is present, but also how he is present in every creature and in everything that has being, in a devil and a good angel, in heaven and hell, in good deeds and in adultery or homicide, in all things, finally, which exist or have some degree of being, whether beautiful or ugly.
>
> Another mode of God's being present to my soul is much more special . . .

this presence of God alone, without any other gifts, is that good . . . my words blaspheme and make hash of what they should express.[26]

From a philosophical point of view, two details of Angela's visions are especially worthy of note, namely, the God who is everywhere, even "beyond" moral categories, and the idea of darkness and nothingness. These bring to mind Meister Eckhart, a philosopher who was also a great mystic. Instead of referring to one of the works of Eckhart, let us make a comparison instead to a text very close to his thought, a simple, linear treatise from a woman's voice: *Also waz Schwester Katrei*. This was written in the community of Beguines at Strasbourg, and is almost a manifesto of the sect of the Free Spirit.[27]

This is the account of an experience and of the relation of the experience; the protagonists are a young woman and her confessor, just as in the case of Angela of Foligno. Katrei, like Angela, is opposed to an official, "high," magisterial culture, and is aware of her opposition:

> It seems to some, and it appears very possible, that the flower and the kernel of beatitude are found in the knowledge through which that spirit knows that it knows God. But I assure you that it is not so. I say that the noble person receives and holds God only through God's being, life and beatitude, after God and in God, and not at all though knowing, contemplating, or loving God.[28]

And Katrei adds proudly:

> God wishes that this [knowledge of God through contemplation] not be my beatitude. It could be enough for another to have it, but I pity him.[29]

Elsewhere Katrei equates "the noble man" with "the poor man" and "the ignorant man" as opposed to the theologian.

Katrei exclaims to her confessor: "Rejoice with me, for I have become God."[30] Between this deification and a return to life, Katrei places death, thereby reproducing the path of Christ, who is born, dies, and returns to life. Katrei also experienced the void, nothingness: nothing more to be done, no interior exercise, no effort, no word, reducing herself to nothing.

Eckhart had written about the "death" of the soul in the Trinity, losing its own nothingness and being thrown into the deity, where it discovers the "divine void." If we think of the equation of nothingness with evil of the Platonic-patristic tradition (nothingness as body and sensible sin) it is evident that the concept of nothingness in Eckhart is another thing entirely; his linguistic model is, once more, Dionysian or Eriugenian. Eckhart quotes Pseudo-Dionysius, from chapter 2 of the *Celestial Hierarchies*: "negations about God are true, but affirmations are unsuitable." In this sense, God is not essence, or goodness, or any other positive attribute. And so he alludes to God by means of dissimilar figures, rather than by means of positive and somehow similar figures.[31] Eriugena notes that the idea of a similitude of God runs the risk of assuming that language and imagination could reach and exhaust the divine reality, which is impossible.[32] Another text which may help us to understand this point is the *Compendium de humilitate* (an anonymous treatise inspired by the circle of Bonaventure), which says that by "gathering nothingness from all creatures, man separates the spirit from every vanity of existence."[33]

Therefore, the void, negation, nonbeing, be it in a metaphysical or a moral sense, opens a vista into the indefinite and indefinable space on the other side of existence and being, into mystery. Angela of Foligno's "blasphemy" is thus the equivalent of Eriugena's monstrous images, for example, the calf covered with feathers in his *Celestial Hierarchies*.[34]

Without any conscious awareness of philosophical terms, women such as the Beguines of the Low Countries and Angela of Foligno, women on the margins of the institutions of high culture, had a learned culture of their own. This culture was replete with a language rich in emotion and specific meanings, irreplaceable, a language that cannot, of course, be found in contemporary magisterial and scholastic treatises. This could also be said of Hildegard of Bingen, who has recently been studied as a philosopher.[35] To an attentive reader, Hildegard's writings reveal diverse traditions of high culture, even, strictly speaking, a philosophical culture, including apocalyptic and evangelical metaphors, hermetic ideas,[36] and Dionysian and Eriugenian concepts. Hildegard was a cultured woman, and (unlike Clare, Umiltà, and Angela) she was a Benedictine nun, in whom the culture of the monastery, "the culture of silence and the desire for God,"[37] was at once strong, peculiar, and consolidated.

But as for herself, Hildegard is a woman who claims to have received "visions" that unveiled for her some divine truths; this brings her close to the mystical women we have considered in this essay. We cannot pause here to consider Hildegard's superb treatises of cosmological visions in which the learned nun traced patterns not unlike those of her contemporaries, the *magistri* at Chartres and Paris. Like Adelard of Bath, she scrutinizes the earth, the trees, jewels, and sky as the habitat of human beings and the fountain of medicine.[38] Hildegard is often far from the emotivity and the individual mystical relationship with God shown by her contemporary Elisabeth of Schönau.[39] It seems fair to say that Hildegard's interests exceed her individual life, expanding into that "different air" from which she observed the cosmos and the passage of time in the atemporal embrace of God. But other aspects of Hildegard's writings are of greater interest to us.

As is well known, the writings of Hildegard include a clear appreciation of the pleasures of love, of that particular hot, fiery wind of desire "which issues from the marrow and descends to the loins, warming the blood with the taste of pleasure."[40] Might these be details of confidences gathered from conversations with and letters from other women who appealed to her for help and counsel?[41] Probably, but they are confidences that also recall biblical and classical texts certainly not unknown to a twelfth-century abbess. Love, Hildegard observes, spreads through all the limbs and burns sweetly in women, but is more concentrated and powerful in men.[42] In other places, Hildegard used with great delicacy the image of the joy of a child who, after forlorn weeping, finds once again the nurturing maternal breast of the Church or of Christ, an image used to suggest a happiness that is entirely spiritual.[43]

This positive estimation of physical love is not unique in medieval culture, although it is certainly rare.[44] For Hildegard, sexual love—like all things material and therefore inferior—preserved traces of an unforgettable immaterial beauty. On the other hand, we know that Hildegard's "visions" were not a loss of consciousness (since she always spoke of seeing with open eyes and in a waking state), nor hardly ever a cause of physical pain or loss. Instead, she speaks of an exalted visionary state, losing every anxiety, taking on a girlish bloom, and losing her look of age. It seems that her "mystical emotions" were totally immaterial, full of celestial beatitude. But side by side with these images are other passages from her writings that remind us of that amorous, painful physicality of Angela of Foligno and Umiltà of Faenza: a marvelous mystical vision in which the visionary loses consciousness and is struck in the depth of her bowels; a vision of a beautiful and loving man (not explicitly identified with Christ) who infuses her womb with the perfume of balsam, and to whom Hildegard exults in the infinite joy and desire to continue to gaze at him. The atmosphere here is very similar to that of the writings of unlearned visionaries. The model that we have called "nuptial," a mixture of emotion and biblical culture, is found even in the writings of the rational and learned Hildegard.[45]

In conclusion, we can verify that, even if we are still not able to answer our ambitious opening question, we can draw some conclusions from the juxtaposition of different texts, seen through the lens of the history of philosophy. On the one hand, we have seen that the ideas of what we might call (at least for the sake of convenience) "high culture" circulated in simplified forms in the texts of women mystics. On the other, the all-involving emotionality and affectivity of our women mystics was doubtless more intense, but not different from, the expressions of Bernard of Clairvaux or Meister Eckhart, not to mention the archetype of religious emotion, Augustine. The implicit and widespread concept that the theologian is male and the mystic is female does not seem well based. One marked characteristic does, however, distinguish the works of Clare, Umiltà, Angela, and even Hildegard: the consciousness of "not having gone to school." This is a sociological fact, not a cultural one. Several of the authors discussed here were, in fact, cultured in the sense of having full possession of the rhetoric of the age; in the delight in elegant, sometimes even affected, writing; in the knowledge of biblical citations; in the echoes of philosophical readings. The paths of culture did not belong exclusively, even then, to the schools; nor should we forget that the direct or indirect knowledge of Augustine alone, an influence that can be verified in the writings of many mystical women, was already a vehicle of philosophical culture.

I repeat: "not having gone to school" is a sociological fact; it is not the natural condition that our women, under the influence of the prevailing (but not the only) tradition that linked original sin to the consequent inferiority of women, thought it to be.[46] But the painful consciousness of marginalization led these women, even the learned and powerful ones like Hildegard of Bingen, to mention repeatedly the fact that they had not gone to school and were therefore "poor little women." This is a sign of a suffering minority, a sign that could become an obsession.

To what tradition, what model of expression and communication, could women authors and mystics who had "not gone to school" and thus did not possess the patrimony of *topoi* of the masculine, scholastic, world then turn? For an answer, we should not look to an idea of female nature (a concept that could be understood as indefinable and even "mystical") but to the female condition, existential and historical.

The women I have considered in this essay could make use of only one unique, concrete, and common experience, the basis of every metaphor of their language: the amorous or conjugal and/or the maternal relationship. This was a relationship which many of them (Angela, Umiltà) actually lived, and which others (Hildegard) learned from the confidences of other women. And it cannot be denied that this relationship was marked on their biological structure and their natural truth by a singular quality, a quality I define as "painful physicality."

Notes

1. See the discussion of the term "medieval" in Mariateresa Fumagalli Beonio-Brocchieri and Massimo Parodi, *Storia della filosofia medievale* (Bari: Laterza, 1989), pp. vii–xviii.

2. Georges Duby, "Histoire de la mentalité," in *Histoire*, ed. H. Parrain (Paris: Gallimard, 1973).

3. See A. Lalande, *Vocabulaire technique et critique de la philosophie*, 10th ed. (Paris: Presses Universitaires de France, 1968), and *Dictionnaire de la théologie catholique* (Paris, 1899).

4. Clement of Alexandria, *Protrepticus*, ed. O. Staehlin, 2d ed. (Leipzig: Hinrichs'sche Buchhandlung, 1936); *Paedagogus*, ed. H. I. Marrou, 3 vols. *Sources Chrétiennes* 70, 108, 158 (Paris: J. Vrin, 1960–70). English translations of both texts by G. W. Butterworth, Loeb Classical Library (New York: G. P. Putnam's Sons, 1919).

5. Bonaventura da Bagnorea, *Itinerarium mentis in Deum*, ed. Ad Claras Aquas (Rome: Quaracchi, 1882), vol. 1; English trans. José de Vinck (Paterson, NJ: St. Anthony Guild Press, 1960).

6. Paul: 2 Cor. 12; Augustine, *Confessions* IX, 10, 24.

7. Alain de Libera, *Penser au Moyen Âge* (Paris: Éditions du Seuil, 1991), pp. 299ff.

8. Dionysius the Pseudo-Areopagite, *The Mystical Theology*, PG 3, English trans. Colm Luibheid in *Pseudo-Dionysius: The Complete Works* (New York: Paulist Press, 1987).

9. Dionysius the Pseudo-Areopagite, *The Divine Names*, PG 3, trans. Luibheid.

10. "Quem cum amaveritis casta estis, cum tetigeritis mundior efficiemini, cum acceperitis virgo estis; cuius possibilitas fortior, generositas celsior, cuius aspectus pulchrior, amor suavior et omnis gratia elegantior. Cuius estis iam amblexibus astricta, qui pectus vestrum ornavit lapidibus pretiosis et vestris auribus tradidit inaestimabiles margaritas, et totam circumdedit vernantibus atque coruscantibus gemmis atque vos coronavit aurea corona signo sanctitatis expressa. Ergo, soror carissima, immo donna veneranda nimium, quia sponsa et mater estis et soror Domini mei Jesu Christi, virginitatis inviolabilis et paupertatis sanctissimae vexillo resplendentissime insignita." Clare of Assisi, *Epistola prima ad beatam Agnetem de Praga*, ed. Marie-France Becker, Jean-François Godet, and Thadée Matura. Sources Chrétiennes 325 (Paris: J. Vrin, 1985), pp. 84–86; trans. John Vaughn, *Francis and Clare: The Complete Works* (New York: Paulist Press, 1982), p. 191.

11. This combination is also found in the writings of Hildegard of Bingen;

see especially Barbara Newman, *Sister of Wisdom: Saint Hildegard's Theology of the Feminine* (Berkeley: University of California Press, 1987).

12. "Come Dio entrò nel chiuso grembo della vergine così può in qualunque forma mostrarsi ai santi . . . in qualsiasi forma lo cercano, lo trovano, parlando con lui, guardandolo e toccandolo. . . . L'anima contempla il Signore . . . per il grande desiderio del amore divino gli si avvicina lo tocca e parla con lui. . . . D'altra parte il Signore non solo permette di essere da lei toccato ma anche che gli siano baciati i piedi e il santissimo petto . . . come é ristorata l'anima e quanto é beata quando si può trovare davanti a un simile bellissimo giovane e può abbracciarlo e appropiarsi del suo frangantissimo odore." "Sermone I: Nel natale del Signore," in *Scrittici mistiche italiane*, ed. Giovanni Pozzi and Claudio Leonardi (Genoa: Marietti, 1988), pp. 98–99.

13. "E questa pecorella belante per fame, che invoca in una pastura che la ingrassi, é l'anima fedele che vuol rimanere con Cristo, che è la sua pastura. E vuole andare dove c'è l'erba novella vuol cogliere solo i fiori e contemplare la bellezza del suoi diletto amore e con il desiderio riempire le mammelle del latte della carità, entrare nel giardino del suo amore verace, scegliere rose bianche e rosse. . . . Io sono la pecora pellegrina per amore tuo: tu conosci l'erba che brucai nel mio pascolo, tu sai se la mia vita é dolce o amara. Non ti devi meravigliare se chiedo soltanto amore . . . amore nella sua interezza . . . il miele saporoso." "Sermone VI: In onore di Gesù Cristo," ed. Pozzi and Leonardi, p. 101.

14. Pozzi and Leonardi, p. 94.

15. I will mention here only a recent scholarly conference: *Angela da Foligno: terziaria Francescana*, Atti del convegno storico nel VII centenario dell'ingresso della beata Angela da Foligno nell'Ordine Francescano Secolare (1291–1991), Quaderni del Centro per il Collegamento degli Studi Medievali e Umanistici nell'Università di Perugia, 27, ed. Enrico Menestò (Spoleto: Centro Italiano di Studi sull'Alto Medioevo, 1992).

16. Pozzi and Leonardi, p. 135.

17. "E mentre me ne stavo così, all'improvviso udii nell'anima una voce che mi disse—Non ti ho amata per scherzo—. Questa parola mi colpì come un dolore mortale; subito, infatti, gli occhi della mia anima si apirono e compresi com'erano vere quelle parole. E vedevo le opere di questo amore. Vedevo quanto aveva fatto il Figlio di Dio per questo suo amore. Scorgevo tutte le prove che questo Dio e uomo passionato aveva sostenuto in vita e in morte per quel suo indicibile e smisurato amore. E come vedevo in lui tutti i segni del vero amore e comprendevo anche l'assoluta verità di quella parola, poiché Gesù mi amò non per scherzo, ma con un amore perfetto e totale, così vedevo che in me c'era tutto il contrario, poiché Io amavo per scherzo e non sinceramente. E questa constatzione m'era divenuta una pena mortale, un dolore così intollerabile che mi pareva di morire." "Istruzione XXIII," ed. Pozzi and Leonardi, p. 138; trans. Paul Lachance, *Angela of Foligno: Complete Works* (New York: Paulist Press, 1993), p. 280.

18. See Étienne Gilson, "St. Bernard and Courtly Love," in *The Mystical Theology of St. Bernard* (Kalamazoo, MI: Cistercian Publications, 1990), French ed. (Paris: J. Vrin, 1980).

19. "quando l'amore è puro, l'anima non ha alcuna stima di sé, si vede morta

e un nulla, e morta e disfatta si rimette in Dio." *Memoriale*, chap. 7, ed. Pozzi and Leonardi, p. 150; trans. Lachance, p. 193.

20. "questa umiltà invece non mi arreca che mali innumerevoli." *Memoriale*, chap. VIII, ed. Pozzi and Leonardi, p. 154; trans. Lachance, p. 200.

21. "né feritoia attraverso cui poter scappare." *Memoriale*, chap. VIII, ed. Pozzi and Leonardi, p. 154; trans. Lachance, p. 201.

22. "In questo bene, così potente che mi rivela nella tenebra, sta ora la mia speranza, incrollabile, tutta raccolta in sé, e sicura." *Memoriale*, IX, ed. Pozzi and Leonardi, p. 156; trans. Lachance, p. 202.

23. "Ma la visione de Dio nella tenebra non reca né riso sulle labbra né devozione né fervore, né amore appassionato, poiché non tremano né si muovono il corpo né l'anima, come sono soliti; ma l'anima nulla vede e tutto scorge; il corpo è come assopito e la lingua è senza vita. E tutte le numerose e indicibili prove di amicizia che Dio ha voluto concedermi, e tutte le parole dettemi finora da lui, e tutto ciò che tu hai scritto fino ad oggi, capisco che sono cose talmente inferiori a quel bene che vedo con tanta tenebra, e non ripongo la mia speranza, né essa tende verso quelle gioie. Anzi, se fosse possibile che tutte quelle passate esperienze non fossero vere, questo fatto in nessun modo diminuirebbe o attenuerebbe la mia speranza radicata, che è sicura in quel bene totale che vedo con tanta tenebra." *Memoriale* IX, ed. Pozzi and Leonardi, p. 157; English trans. Lachance, p. 204.

24. "tutto vedo e nulla scorgo." *Memoriale* IX, ed. Pozzi and Leonardi, p. 158; trans. Lachance, p. 205.

25. "E in questo stare nel Dio-Uomo, l'anima vive; e in questo Dio-Uomo sto molto di più che in quello con la tenebra, l'anima è viva; ma il Dio della tenebra l'attrae molto di più." *Memoriale* IX, ed. Pozzi and Leonardi, p. 158; English trans. Lachance, p. 205.

26. "Nel primo modo si manifesta nell'intimo dell'anima mia: e allora sento la sua presenza e capisco come è presente in ogni creatura e in ogni cosa che possieda in sé l'essere: nel demonio e negli angeli buoni, nel paradiso e nell'inferno, nell'adulterio e nell'omicidio e in ogni buona azione, e in ogni cosa che esista o sommunque possieda l'essere, tanto se bella quanto se brutta.

"Nel altro modo Dio si presenta all'anima mia in modo più speciale . . . che questa sola presenza di Dio, senza altri doni, costituisce quel bene . . . poichè la mia parola allora è più capace di devastare e bestemmiare che esprimere." *Memoriale* IX, ed. Pozzi and Leonardi, p. 161; English trans. Lachance, pp. 212–13.

27. The text has been edited by F. J. Schweitzer, *Der Freiheitsbegriff der deutschen Mystik: Seine Beziehung zur Ketzerei der "Brüder und Schwestern vom Freien Geist," mit besonderer Ruucksicht auf den pseudoeckhartischen Traktat "Schwester Katrei"* (Frankfurt and Berne: P. Lang, 1981). This discussion is based on de Libera, *Penser au Moyen Âge*, pp. 309–16.

28. De Libera, p. 310.

29. De Libera, p. 310.

30. De Libera, p. 311.

31. Meister Eckhart, *Commentary on Exodus*, chap. 78 in *Meister Eckhart: Teacher and Preacher*, trans. Bernard McGinn, Frank Tobin, and Elvira Borgstadt (New York: Paulist Press, 1986), p. 70.

32. John Scotus Eriugena, *Expositiones in hierarchiam coelestem*, II, 3, ed. J. Barbet, CCCM (Turnholt: Brepols, 1975), p. 33.

33. Pseudo-Bonaventure, *De humilitate*, discussed in de Libera, *Penser au Moyen Âge*, pp. 319–21. See also B. Distelbrink, *Bonaventurae scripta authentica, dubia, vel spuria critica recensita* (Rome: Istituto Scientifica Franciscalia, 1975), pp. 101–102.

34. *Expositiones in hierarchiam coelestem*, II, 3 (ed. Barbet), p. 35.

35. Mariateresa Fumagalli Beonio-Brocchieri, *In una aria diversa* (Milan: Mondadori, 1992), chap. 2.

36. Fritz Saxl, *La fede negli astri* (Milan: Boringhieri, 1965).

37. Jean Leclercq, *The Love of Learning and the Desire for God*, trans. Catherine Misrahi, 3d ed. (New York: Fordham University Press, 1982).

38. Fumagalli Beonio-Brocchieri, *In una aria diversa*, pp. 88ff.

39. For Elisabeth, see Anne L. Clark, *Elisabeth of Schönau: A Twelfth-Century Visionary* (Philadelphia: University of Pennsylvania Press, 1992).

40. Newman, *Sister of Wisdom*, p. 129, quoting from the *causae et curae*, p. 69.

41. Michela Pereira, "Maternità e sessualità nell'opera de Ildegarda da Bingen," *Quaderni Storici* 44 (1980): 564–79.

42. Newman, *Sister of Wisdom*, pp. 129–31.

43. Newman, pp. 234–35.

44. Peter Brown, "From Apostle to Apologist: Sexual Order and Sexual Renunciation in the Early Church," in *The Body and Society: Men, Women and Sexual Renunciation in Early Christianity* (New York: Columbia University Press, 1988), pp. 33–64.

45. Fumagalli Beonio-Brocchieri, *In una aria diversa*, chap. 1.

46. Peter Brown, "To Undo the Works of Women: Marcion, Tatian, and the Encratites," in *The Body and Society*, pp. 83–102.

Catherine M. Mooney

3. The Authorial Role of Brother A. in the Composition of Angela of Foligno's Revelations

One of the central questions under discussion in current research on medieval religious women regards their portrayal in medieval documents. Do the portraits of these women reflect the actual lives of the women themselves, or do they more aptly convey ideals of female sanctity fostered and propagated by medieval writers, the large majority of whom were male clerics? One obvious approach to solving this dilemma is to turn to the writings of the women themselves. But here the historian confronts another problem: many of these women's writings reach us only indirectly through the pens of scribes, confessors, and editors whose interpretive ears may, wittingly or not, change or even skew a woman's own thoughts and deeds. This is, of course, a problem affecting not only women, but also men whose lives are similarly depicted in texts authored by others. In the case of religious women, however, the dilemma is particularly critical since so many of their texts, the total number of which is far smaller in any case than those of their male counterparts, have been mediated by the guiding hand of a male authority. If scholars are to say anything definitive about women's lives and spirituality—if they are, in short, to give them a "voice"—then an attempt must be made to disentangle their voices from those of their male scribes and editors.

Brief mention of just a few medieval religious women whose dictation and writings have been influenced by the collaborative efforts of their male contemporaries suffices to suggest the magnitude of this challenge. Elisabeth of Schönau's brother Ekbert played a pivotal role in recording most of her visions and spiritual pronouncements, influencing especially her later works through his arrangement and thematic unification of her visionary experience.[1] Mechthild of Magdeburg's work, which she composed herself in Low German on loose sheets of paper and in response to a request by Henry of Halle, her Dominican confessor, is known to us only through a Latin version attributed to Henry or other Dominicans of Halle and a High German version made by Henry of Nördlingen.[2] Margery Kempe relied first on the scribal help of an unnamed Englishman who had lived in Germany and who seemed to write neither English nor German well. She then procured the aid of a priest who was so anxious to represent the eccentric Margery in an orthodox light that he is suspected of having rephrased portions of her story.[3] Scholars are still debating the extent to which Birgitta of Sweden's dictation has been edited, rearranged, and freely interpreted by her spiritual guides, Master Matthias of Linköping and Peter of Alvastra among others.[4] None of the prolific Catherine of Siena's writings have survived in her own hand and some scholars doubt that she ever learned how to write. She depended instead on numerous scribes, a few female but most male, and was known to dictate at times to two or three at a time.[5]

Since the extent to which scribes and editors actually influenced women's dictation and writing varies dramatically from one case to the next, each text must be examined on its own merits. This essay, through analysis of Angela of Foligno's relationship with her male scribe as revealed in her revelations, highlights some strategies that may be useful in separating out other women's words from those of their male interpreters.

The few facts known about Angela of Foligno's life virtually all derive from scattered comments included in the text of her renowned revelations.[6] She was born about 1248[7] in Foligno, a town then of a few thousand inhabitants and situated about ten miles southeast of Assisi. Like many other celebrated Italian holy women of this period, Angela was married and the mother of several children when she embarked on her spiritual journey in about 1285. Since familial ties customarily precluded a primary commitment to the religious life, it is not entirely surprising to learn that Angela felt consoled when her mother, husband, and children all died within a brief span of time, an event for which she had in fact prayed.[8]

Shortly thereafter, perhaps in 1290 or 1291 when Angela was about forty-two, she felt free to dedicate herself wholly to a life of piety and to associate herself with the Franciscan order. Her religious life was in many respects self-styled, unencumbered by detailed regulation, and refreshingly free from formal ecclesiastical supervision. Be that as it may, her spiritual legacy reaches us only through the scrim of the male-mediated and male-authorized text that recounts her spiritual journey. In this respect, Angela is representative of myriad late medieval women whose spiritual insights and life stories unfold in texts composed under the guiding influence—or sometimes controlling authority—of male patrons, superiors, confessors, scribes, translators, and editors.

Angela's revelations were recorded in a lengthy text that has traditionally been depicted as her own dictated account. It has been tellingly described by scholars with epithets such as "a true spiritual diary,"[9] her "spiritual autobiography,"[10] and "a true and authentic 'author's text.'"[11] One influential edition entitled the work "The Autobiography and Writings of Blessed Angela of Foligno."[12] Her scribe has been depicted as her "mouthpiece."[13] The implication of such language is that Angela is the undisputed and sole author of the text—this in spite of the fact that all scholars recognize that a Franciscan friar actually *wrote* the text.

Angela purportedly dictated her revelations over the course of at least four and perhaps up to six years to a Franciscan who identifies himself to us only once in the text. He calls himself "Brother A.," traditionally identified as Brother "Arnaldo," a name still employed by many scholars despite the fact that there is no meaningful evidence to support this claim.[14] Ludger Thier and Abele Calufetti, the scholars responsible for the critical edition published in 1985, divide the work into two main sections of approximately equal length, the *Memorial*[15] and the *Instructions*.[16] With critical apparatus, the two parts, together entitled *The Book of Blessed Angela of Foligno*, amount to some 300 pages of Latin text.

The thirty-six *Instructions* are discrete texts composed by a number of anonymous writers, quite likely devotees of Angela, who wrote both during her life and after her death in 1309.[17] Until further research more precisely establishes the relationships joining these texts to Angela and to the sundry writers self-presenting as her scribes, readers should eye with caution scholarly attempts that draw on the instructions to illuminate Angela's thought or to substantiate, complement, or elaborate information provided in the *Memorial*.

The *Memorial*, the focus of this essay, was recorded by Brother A., who was both relative and confessor of Angela. Most scholars agree that he began writing in late 1291 or in 1292, shortly after he and Angela had returned to their native Foligno from Assisi, where he had encountered her in an excited state of spiritual turmoil. He probably continued writing until about 1296 or 1297, after which time the *Memorial* was approved by Cardinal John Colonna and eight other theologians.[18] The most likely date of death suggested so far for Brother A. is 1300.[19] It is generally agreed that he wrote in Latin, basing his text on what Angela spoke to him in her own Umbrian dialect.

As Table 1 indicates, the *Memorial* has nine chapters, which proceed chronologically through the twenty-six steps of Angela's spiritual journey. Chapter 1 describes the first nineteen steps, or, as Angela once designates them, "transformations" her soul experienced.[20] Brother A. introduces the twentieth step before abruptly ending this first chapter. While the steps themselves are arranged in the chronological order in which they were experienced by Angela, Brother A. is at pains to make clear that the chronology of the text's composition began not with the first step but with the twentieth. It was during Angela's experience of this step in Assisi and then back in Foligno that Brother A. made the momentous decision to write her spiritual account, which at that point he ingenuously expected to amount to no more than the few jottings he then made regarding the spiritual turmoil he had witnessed in Assisi. Only later did he grow curious about her experiences prior to this, recounted in steps 1 through 19 and subsequently fashioned into chapter 1, which concludes with the introduction of step 20.

TABLE 3.1. Brief Outline of the Structure of the *Memorial*

Chapter	*Content*
1	Steps 1 through 19, and the beginning of step 20
2	Brother A.'s explanation regarding how he began to write, and a brief overview of chapters 3 through 9
3	First supplementary step or revelation[1] (This is the continuation and end of the twentieth step, which Brother A. now renames and renumbers as the first step or revelation. This chapter includes the first notes he recorded.)
4	Second supplementary step (= step 21)
5	Third supplementary step
6	Fourth supplementary step
7	Fifth supplementary step
8	Sixth supplementary step
9	Seventh supplementary step

[1]The term "supplementary" is not Brother A.'s but has been added by modern editors to distinguish these last seven steps from the first nineteen steps.

Chapter 2 constitutes a kind of pause in the *Memorial* composed only after Brother A. had been listening to Angela and writing for several years: he presents an overview of chapters 3 through 9, each of which is devoted to one of the final seven steps of her journey, that is, steps 20 through 26 (which he renames as steps 1 through 7, to be discussed below); and he tells us how he came to compose the *Memorial*. Chapter 3, the record of her twentieth step, thus contains the earliest notes made by Brother A. when he first questioned her about what had happened in Assisi and immediately thereafter. Chapters 4 through 9 represent his efforts to present the steps that she experienced after step 20, the period in which the two had forged their writing relationship and during which they met periodically for Angela to continue her narration and Brother A. his writing.

To complicate the picture yet more, the editors of the critical edition posit that there were two major redactions of the *Memorial*, a hypothesis they advance with a detailed exposition of the text's manuscript and redactional history.[21] They theorize that Brother A. is responsible for both the briefer *minor* account, which they argue he wrote first, and also the expanded *maior* account.[22] Questions raised by several scholars regarding Thier and Calufetti's double-redaction theory make it clear that further research is required before it can be confidently accepted or rejected.[23] Internal evidence clearly indicates that each redaction underwent a development of its own, each showing signs that the author reordered various passages, added certain comments, and so forth. Although a number of the assertions made by Thier and Calufetti regarding this intricate and often enigmatic text remain open to challenge and require further scholarly investigation, their study nonetheless stands as the most exhaustive analysis to date.

Throughout this essay I will provisionally adopt the conventional point of view, which has yet to be discredited, that the same person is responsible for both redactions, since the redactor/s self-present/s as a single writer who is solely responsible for the evolution of the text, an evolution the writer discusses at various points within the course of the narrative. The existence of multiple redactors could resolve some of the problematic features of the text, but such a hypothesis is uncorroborated conjecture at this point. It is especially important to note that the main points of my argument regarding the relationship of Angela's own words with those of the written text stand, with minor adaptations, regardless of the number of redactors or the chronological order of the *minor* and *maior* accounts.

A straightforward reading of the text suffices to show that Brother A. attentively assembled his numerous conversations with Angela, rearranging, revising, and amplifying them to produce the ordered text as it now appears in the critical edition. Unlike so many other narrators and "scribes," the chatty Brother A. is immediately accessible to the reader. He frequently interpolates his own comments among Angela's to indicate, for example, under what circumstances he learned certain incidents, when he wrote them down, how Angela appeared as she spoke to him, and how he reacted to some of her teachings and revelations.

Virtually all the scholarly literature about the *Memorial*, with the exception of a few discussions of its complicated manuscript history, focuses on Angela of Foligno herself: her theology, her visions, her ecstatic encounters with the divine.[24] This is hardly surprising: her words and experiences, at least as they are given to us by Brother A., constitute the major portion of the text. She is the celebrated protagonist of both the *Memorial* and the *Instructions*. Her intimate knowledge of God imbued her with charismatic religious authority: a sizable circle of followers, both men and women, clergy and laity, gathered around Angela even during her lifetime.

Although Brother A. identifies himself as Angela's relative and confessor, he is most obviously—even in his own self-understanding—just another of these devotees. He describes himself repeatedly throughout the *Memorial* as her "brother secretary" and regularly portrays himself as unworthy of the task.[25] This is more than a simple modesty topos. Brother A.'s avowals regarding his own reluctance to meddle with the transmission of Angela's message are so frequent and candid that no scholar to date has significantly questioned his honest intentions. Describing his first attempts to record Angela's experiences, he writes:

> Since at that time I experienced in myself a special and new grace from God, one I had never before experienced, I wrote with great reverence and fear so as to add nothing of my own, not even a single word unless I had heard it straight from the mouth of the one telling me, nor did I want to write anything after I left her. Rather, when I wrote seated near her, I would make her repeat again and again the words which I should write.[26]

A number of scholars have seized on this avowal to conclude that Brother A. wrote *only* when seated beside Angela and that he never altered her words.[27] Although his profession of fidelity to her words is unambiguous, the context of his remarks and their precise literal meaning could qualify their import. This comment occurs in his second chapter in a passage explaining why he initially began to record the divine secrets revealed to Angela. It is possible that he is reminiscing specifically about his first attempts to record Angela's words rather than making an observation about his writing relationship with her in general, although elsewhere in his text he makes claims that similarly underline his fidelity to her words. Perhaps more important, it should be noted that he states merely that he did not *want* to write after he left her.[28] In the last chapter of the *Memorial*, Brother A. incidentally reveals that he did occasionally write when she was not with him, albeit reluctantly: "From the beginning until the end I scarcely wrote anything except when she was speaking to me in person."[29]

Brother A.'s testimony that the words imputed to Angela by him are utterly accurate reflections of her message has been accepted with scant qualification by all the principal scholars commenting on Angela's life and revelations.[30] Sporadic traces such as the above passage of Brother A.'s own authorial role are all but lost on the reader, thickly embedded as they are within his frequent and emphatic protestations of fidelity to Angela's words. Brother A. is, in his own mind, a simple secretary, *frater scriptor*, "brother scribe" as his self-description is often rendered, a mere conduit putting to page another's dictation. Scattered throughout his lengthy report of what he claims to have heard Angela say, however, are myriad clues about his own relationship with Angela and his involvement in committing her story to page. If we ignore the central themes of the *Memorial*—Angela's visions and spiritual teachings—and focus only on the scattered remarks revelatory of Brother A.'s hand in the composition, we can uncover abundant evidence that Brother A. was not simply an insignificant accessory, slavishly repeating what Angela told him: indeed, he was an active and energetic collaborator in authoring the *Memorial*.

The most conspicuous clue, perhaps, is his forthright acknowledgment of his own deficiencies as a scribe. Indeed, his frequent and detailed confessions of ineptitude, which go well beyond conventional claims to modesty, merit at least as much credence as his assertions regarding his attempt to report Angela's words faithfully. He acknowledges at the outset of the narrative, in setting forth his reasons for writing the *Memorial*:

> In truth, I could grasp so little which I could then write regarding [Angela's divine secrets] that I considered and perceived myself to be like a sieve or sifter which does not retain the fine and precious flour, but only the most coarse. . . .
>
> And this will show the extent to which I was incapable of grasping her divine words except in the roughest manner: once, when I was writing the

words just as I understood them straight from her own mouth, and I was reading back to her the words I had written so that she could continue her dictation, she told me in amazement that she did not recognize them. And another time when I was reading back to her so that she could see if I had written correctly, she replied that my expression was dry and insipid; it astonished her. Another time she put it this way: "Your words remind me of what I said to you, but the writing is quite obscure because the words you read to me do not convey the intended meaning; for that reason, your writing is obscure." Similarly, another time she said: "What is inconsequential and meaningless you have written, while concerning the precious experience of my soul, you have written nothing."[31]

Brother A.'s candid admissions of his inadequacy as a scribe, which are among the few remarks of his cited regularly by researchers, are winsome in a way. They have understandably persuaded most scholars that Brother A. was an honest and sincerely intentioned secretary. More enigmatic is the fact that many of the same researchers who choose to believe in the scribe's sincerity, choose not to believe his recurrent assertions that he was incapable of grasping and articulating Angela's message.[32] One should bear in mind, of course, that a prominent motif running throughout the *Memorial* is Angela's own inability to express the ineffable. Nonetheless, although one should recognize that the divine nature of Angela's experience accounts in part for the scribe's inability to capture her experience in human words, his avowed ineptitude is, in his own telling, owing also to his own insufficiency as a scribe.[33] Thus the critical reader must consider carefully the extent to which Brother A.'s lack of understanding may have influenced his presentation of Angela's own narrative.

A second striking indication that the words we read are not Angela's is the fact that Brother A. translated her spoken Italian into his own stiff, scholastic Latin, a problem perhaps hinted at by Angela herself in the previously cited quotation in which she informed Brother A. that his writing was dry and insipid. Elsewhere, he similarly reports:

> Christ's faithful one told me the above-stated things in other words, certainly more copious, efficacious, and illuminating. . . . For that reason, when I read [what I had written] back to her, she said that I had written it not fully, but on the contrary dryly and incompletely, although she would later confirm that what I had written was true.[34]

Third, even were one to grant that large portions of Brother A.'s text may be generally accurate renderings in Latin of her Italian words, we know that he shifted the perspective of many of her remarks. He wrote, for example:

> She spoke concerning herself in the first person, but it sometimes happened that I would write in the third person on account of my haste, and I still have not corrected it.[35]

This comment appears in the very last paragraphs of the *Memorial*, where Brother A. alludes to various aspects of the compositional process underlying the text. While most of these comments form part of the briefer *minor* redaction, this comment occurs only in the lengthier *maior* redaction. Although Brother A. perhaps once intended to transpose all of Angela's words back into her own voice and possibly succeeded in doing so on occasion, he appears to have abandoned the plan by the time he added this comment.[36] This is true whether or not the editors of the critical edition are correct in their hypothesis regarding the chronology of the *minor* and *maior* accounts: both occasions on which the scribe informs the reader that he had intended to return Angela's words to her own first-person voice but did not succeed in doing so are, from internal evidence alone, reflective comments added only after the major portion of his text had already been composed.[37]

Even more significant than the technical point that he does not accurately render Angela's own first-person voice is the fact that Brother A.'s use of the third person strongly suggests that he wrote as an *outside* listener. He is not a mere conduit allowing Angela's words to flow unaltered through his rote transcription to the written page; rather, as an author, he is conscious that he is receiving an*other* person's report, someone he thinks of most naturally as "she." His position as outside listener is confirmed when one considers that it takes longer to write "she said that she . . ." than it does to write "I . . ." Nevertheless, according to his own account, Brother A. automatically falls into the lengthier, third-person voice when compelled to write in haste. This suggests that the portions of narrative that appear in Angela's own first-person voice may also not be simple, straightforward transcriptions of her words. Rather, in these less pressured moments, the scribe had the time to move in his own mind from his own position as outside listener first hearing "I," then thinking "she," and finally managing to shift back to "I" in his attempt to be faithful to Angela's own words. Brother A.'s brief remarks concerning his use of pronouns indicate that he is a third party, a sympathetic one to be sure, intervening between Angela and her words, and, as I argue later, selecting and interpreting some of her expressions.

Brother A.'s use of the third person touches on yet another thorny issue, since much of the *Memorial* remains in the third person. We can only surmise as to how much of this third-person narrative properly belongs to Brother A., providing us with his interpretive view of Angela, and how much belongs more properly to Angela but was simply never transposed back into her first-person narrative voice.

Fourth, further evidence of Brother A.'s active collaboration in composing the *Memorial* may be suggested by the very existence of two redactions that are both attributed to him, one substantially lengthier than the other. If the editors of the critical edition are correct in their assertion that the *maior* redaction was composed after the *minor*, then it is probable that substantial portions of the lengthier text, including numerous passages that purport to quote Angela's own words, were composed by Brother A. relying on either memory or his own insight into Angela's experience rather than on her guiding presence.[38] This would surely undermine his claims to have written virtually only when at her side, scrupulously avoiding any additions or alterations to the words he himself heard from her own mouth, claims made, it should be noted, in both redactions.[39] Moreover, there are indications in the text that both redactions underwent certain revisions consisting of additions or rearrangements of material.[40]

A number of reservations should be noted regarding each of the four points just made indicating that Brother A. actively collaborated in authoring the *Memorial*. Regarding the first point, it is worth noting that his free admissions that he often did not understand Angela ironically serve also to enhance his credibility since they underscore his forthright manner.

Regarding the second point, an argument, albeit a somewhat strained one and contrary to the judgment of most scholars, could be made that the *Memorial* was first composed in Italian before being translated into Latin. It might thus be conjectured that at one time, in a now lost text, Brother A.'s text more accurately approximated Angela's own language.

Regarding the third point, a review of the scholarly apparatus of the critical edition reveals, on balance, few transpositions of either third-person narratives about Angela back into her own first-person voice or alterations in the opposite direction. This is true whether one is comparing the *minor* and *maior* accounts or analyzing variations among the several manuscript families of the *maior* redaction. In the absence of more conclusive evidence of scribal alterations, one might posit a host of theories absolving Brother A. from significantly altering Angela's voice through his reliance on third-person narrative: perhaps relatively few passages were ever in need of "correction," to use Brother A.'s own terminology, back into the first person; perhaps one of the now lost exemplars posited by the critical editors would demonstrate that he had succeeded in adapting the most relevant passages and that only a few were left in the third person; perhaps even those passages remaining in the third person were nevertheless generally reliable reports of Angela's own dictated narrative.

Regarding the fourth point, the existence of two redactions, one considerably longer than the other, does not in and of itself establish that Brother A. departed significantly from Angela's words. If, for example, it could be established that the *maior* account actually preceded the *minor* account, in contradistinction to the position taken by the editors of the critical edition, then one might view significant portions of the *maior* as a generally reliable report of Angela's words, written with her vigilant supervision, and the *minor* as a subsequent abridgment of the original text. This was, in fact, the opinion of Martin-Jean Ferré, an important editor and translator of Angela's work, and it has received recent support from other scholars.[41]

Finally, Brother A.'s confessed inability to grasp Angela's message must be read within the context of several other passages that declare the general truth of his text. On one occasion, as has been noted, Angela tells him (he tells us) that, although his writing was dry and terse compared to her more elaborate and feeling discourse, his text was, nonetheless, true. In fact, she continued, his text had received divine authorization that very day. Angela reported to him that the voice told her:

> Make sure, at the conclusion of the words you speak, that the following is written, namely, that thanks should be rendered to God for all the things which you have written.[42]

Angela received this locution in what would be the equivalent of the twenty-first step, designated by Brother A. as the second of the final seven steps of her spiritual journey. This step, the first to follow their pivotal encounter in Assisi, took place in 1291 or at the beginning of 1292 shortly after he had begun to record her divine revelations, certainly an opportune moment to receive divine confirmation of the recently initiated text.

In the last chapter recording the last step of Angela's journey, which according to Ferré was written about four-and-a-half to five years later, Brother A., in ready obedience to the divine command, made sure to insert the words spoken by God to Angela.[43] He understandably was careful to reiterate the divine authorization as well within passages in which he detailed his deficiencies as a scribe, thereby pointing out to the reader that his text, although incomplete and defective, contained no lies and was in fact true. Brother A. also reports that God informed Angela that he would sign the text himself.[44] Such confirmations of divine authorship are standard stock within the texts of medieval women's revelations. Although these formulaic comments suggest the sincere intentions and devout belief of both Angela and Brother A., they do not lessen the import of so many other relatively unique, non-stereotypic passages that suggest the significant distance separating Brother A.'s writing from Angela's words, to say nothing of God's words to her. What is minimally true from a reading of all Brother A.'s comments regarding the relative merits and defects of the text is that it falls far short of Angela's own spoken message, owing not only to its divine ineffable nature, but also to Brother A.'s human deficiencies as a scribe.

Analysis of the compositional construction of the text offers evidence yet more critically suggestive of Brother A.'s collaborative hand in authoring the *Memorial*. This evidence is apparent from a consideration of three clues beyond the four discussed above: fifth, how and why Brother A. began the *Memorial*; sixth, his choice of subject matter as revealed through his questions, abbreviations, omissions, selections, and points of disagreement with Angela; and seventh, how he structured the work and positioned himself within it relative to Angela's experience.

A fifth indicator, then, of Brother A.'s authorial role emerges from the fact that the *Memorial* was initiated at his behest and in response to his own doubts. He informs the reader repeatedly that he compelled Angela to speak to him about her spiritual experience. As noted above, Brother A. began to record Angela's revelations during step 20 of her spiritual journey. He had encountered her screaming and shrieking in the town of Assisi, at the doors of the church of Saint Francis. Brother A. was visiting the Franciscan friary there; Angela was on pilgrimage to the town made holy by Francis of Assisi, the saint for whom the church was named. He writes:

> The true motive and reason why I began to write is, for my part, the following. On one occasion, Christ's faithful one had come to the church of Saint Francis in Assisi where I was dwelling in the convent. While she was sitting in the entrance of the doors to the church, she began to scream. It was for this reason that I, who was her confessor, relative, and still her principal and only advisor, was greatly ashamed, especially since many brothers, who

> knew both me and her, had come to that place to see her screaming and shrieking. . . . So great was my pride and my arrogant shame that out of embarrassment I did not go up to her; rather with shame and indignation I waited a little for her screaming to cease and I remained at a distance. Even after she ceased from that noisy crying, arose from that door, and came over to me, I could scarcely speak calmly to her. I told her that never again was she to dare to return to Assisi, the place where this evil had befallen her, and I told her companions that they should never bring her there.[45]

Brother A. suspected that an evil spirit was the source of Angela's fit, so when they were both back in Foligno he forced her to tell him what had happened. He writes:

> Since I wanted to know the reason for the aforesaid crying I began to compel her [*coepi cogere eam*] by every means I could that she make known to me why she had screamed and cried like that so much.[46]

And elsewhere:

> When I, brother, had returned from Assisi to our land, the homeland of Christ's faithful one, I began to question and to force her [*cogere*] with all my powers and by means of all the ways in which I knew she was obliged to me, that she recount to me thoroughly the reason and motive for her screaming and shrieking in [the church of] Saint Francis. And thus constrained by me [*coacta a me*] . . . she began to relate [what had happened].[47]

He intended to submit her account in writing to a wise and spiritual man for expert evaluation.[48] It is abundantly clear that Brother A., not Angela, instigated the recording of her experiences by compelling her to speak. The *Memorial* was his idea and the subject matter of Angela's first dictated entry was determined by his particular interests.

For her part, however, Angela was hardly reluctant to speak. Indeed, she quickly alerted the scribe that he would need many pages to record her account. Brother A. writes:

> I began by carelessly jotting down brief notes, as a sort of "memorial" for myself, on a small scrap of paper since I thought I would have little to write. A little while after I had forced her to begin talking, it was announced and revealed to Christ's faithful one that I should use not a single small sheet for writing, but a large notebook. However, since I did not really believe her, I wrote on two or three small blank pages which I was able to find in my little book. Afterwards I was indeed forced to make a notebook of fine paper.[49]

Angela's apparent readiness to respond to Brother A.'s interests and her advice to him that he would be writing quite a bit more than he had at first anticipated may well suggest her own interest in telling her story. At the same time, her status as a woman and especially as confessee to the priest Brother A. undoubtedly inclined her and possibly even frightened her to respond fully to his demand, particularly in light of his suggestion that the source of her spiritual experience was an evil spirit.

In fact, the doubt Brother A. inspired in Angela regarding her own experience illuminates not only the inception of Brother A.'s and Angela's writing relationship, but also various aspects of their ongoing relationship throughout the *Memorial*. In order to meet the scribe's demand that she disclose what had happened to her at Assisi, Angela recounted her experience leading up to the screaming incident. She informed Brother A. that the Holy Spirit had been conversing quite intimately with her on her journey to Assisi, remarking at length about many subjects. He continued this colloquy until after she had reached Assisi and entered the church of Saint Francis for the second time. Angela repeated to Brother A. many of the Holy Spirit's comments to her: "My daughter, my delight, my temple"; "I love you more than any woman in the valley of Spoleto"; "I am the Holy Spirit who has come to you to give you a consolation you have never tasted"; "Ask for whatever grace you wish for yourself and your companions and for whomever you like"; "I am the Holy Spirit who enters into your inner self."[50]

In the course of their colloquy, Angela reveals herself to be a personality inclined to doubt the truth of her own experience, a characteristic evident throughout the entire *Memorial*. Angela oscillates back and forth between experiences of intense doubt and stalwart certitude. At one moment, she doubts herself, a revelation she has received, or some other divine experience; in the next, having been reassured by a divine consolation or other heavenly confirmation, she effusively alleges unwavering faith. But such declarations of confidence, except at the very close of the *Memorial*, are always followed by new experiences of doubt. This tendency to vacillate between doubt and certitude is already apparent in the early narrative of her encounter with the Holy Spirit. While on the road to Assisi, she had asked Saint Francis in prayer to help her acquire a number of graces. Shortly thereafter, the Holy Spirit initiated his colloquy with her:

> You prayed to my servant Francis, but I did not want to send any other messenger. I am the Holy Spirit and I come to you to give you a consolation you have never before tasted.[51]

The Holy Spirit promised to remain with her until the second time she was to enter the church of Saint Francis; he professed his deep love for her and even suggested he might favor her more than he had favored Francis of Assisi. Such forceful praise filled Angela with doubt:

> I began greatly to doubt these words and my soul said to him, "If you were the Holy Spirit, you would not say this to me because it is inappropriate and I am a frail person who might become vainglorious."[52]

Angela then recounts an intense interchange in which the Holy Spirit relentlessly endeavored to rid Angela of her doubt, she all the while resisting his attempts with protestations of her unworthiness. Although the Holy Spirit's words filled her with joy, she only acknowledged full faith in the divine presence when he withdrew from her on her second entrance into the church of Saint Francis. It was at that moment that she began to shriek, drawing the embarrassed attention of Brother A. and others. She reports:

> Then, after he had withdrawn, I began to scream loudly and to cry out. I screamed and shrieked throughout shamelessly saying this very phrase, "Love unknown, why do you leave me?" What is more, I could not and did not say anything else, but I kept shouting without shame the aforesaid phrase, namely, "Love unknown, why, why, why?" However, my voice so mangled the phrase that it was unintelligible. Then he left me with a certainty, without any doubt, that this had surely been God.[53]

So overwhelmed with consolation was she after this intense and prolonged encounter that she lay speechless, languishing in her bed for eight days. During this period she was again accompanied by the divine presence, identified three times by a voice speaking to Angela's companion as the Holy Spirit.[54] At this point, Angela concludes her lengthy description to Brother A. of the circumstances surrounding the screaming episode in Assisi. She emerges as someone inclined to doubt and in need of continual reassurance.

Brother A.'s suspicion regarding her experience probably did more than compound Angela's anxieties; it quite likely influenced his portrayal of her by underlining the themes of doubt and certitude, issues we know were important in his own mind as well. For example, while Brother A.'s doubt served as the catalyst for her story of encounter with the Holy Spirit, it also moved the account in a definite direction. He quickly singles out the one aspect of her story he finds troubling:

> I, brother, who, unworthy, wrote these divine words, interrogated her asking how she had been told in the preceding revelation "I am the Holy Spirit,"

and then shortly afterward been told "I am the one who was crucified for you."[55]

In Angela's entire account, she had never mentioned the Trinity, although she did remark that the Holy Spirit had blessed her and her companion in the name of the Father and the Son and the Holy Spirit.[56] It had not occurred to Angela to doubt the theological correctness of her religious encounter with the Holy Spirit until her more educated and doctrinally oriented confessor and scribe suggested it.[57] Brother A. continues:

> After this interrogation, she returned home. Later, she came back to me and responded thus: "After I went home I began to think because I had a doubt about what you asked me. Since I know that I am entirely unworthy, whenever a doubt is suggested to me, then I doubt. And while I was thus doubting, I heard this answer: "Ask him, Brother A., why what was spoken to you has already come into you, that is, the Trinity."[58]

The ensuing passage, a somewhat strained and even confusing commentary on the Trinity, clearly owes as much if not more to Brother A.'s own guiding hand as it does to Angela's personal experience.[59]

There are plentiful clues elsewhere in the *Memorial* that show the theme of doubt and certitude to be a concern as central to Brother A. as it was to Angela. He presses her, for example, for a detailed explanation of how she could know "truly" that her experience of God was authentic.[60] On another occasion, long after the scribe had exchanged his role of skeptical inquisitor for that of faithful devotee, he writes:

> One time Christ's faithful one, as was her custom, confessed to me, brother, with such perfect awareness of her sins and with so much contrition and weeping from the beginning of her confession until almost the end, and with so much truth that I wept, and in my heart I regarded it most certain that, even if the whole world were deceived, God would not permit a person of such rectitude and truth to be deceived. And I pondered this judgment in my heart since the exceptional greatness of the things I had heard from her had amazed me, prompting some little doubt and testing my credulity.[61]

It seems reasonable to suggest that Brother A.'s own concerns about belief and doubt, apparent at the very inception of the text, inclined him to accentuate these themes in his retelling of Angela's own experience; the precise extent to which this is so necessarily remains an open question.

A sixth feature that highlights Brother A.'s role as author of the

Memorial emerges from a study of numerous, often subtle markers throughout the text that indicate the constant choices he made throughout the compositional process. Tracking his choices entails careful scrutiny of myriad minor, sometimes barely perceptible remarks regarding the questions he posed and the subjects he highlighted, abbreviated, or passed over in silence. These comments, often inadvertent on his part, can yield significant evidence about his interests, interests which surely helped determine the overall shape of the *Memorial*.

Paul Lachance is one of few scholars to recognize explicitly the important role played, for example, by Brother A.'s questions. He writes of Brother A. (whom he and some scholars call Arnaldo):

> Throughout the *Memorial* we find [the scribe] constantly questioning, pressing for clarity, and even at times using Scripture, reprimanding his penitent (rarely is the role reversed). Arnaldo's faithful and demanding masculine presence thus served as a significant catalyst in Angela's development, calling on her to discriminate and focus inner meanings, as well as to articulate and name more clearly and precisely what she was experiencing.[62]

With this insight, quite unfortunately expressed in terms of gender bias, Lachance treads a careful line. On the one hand, he generally concurs with the majority of scholars who emphasize Brother A.'s scrupulous fidelity as a scribe. "It is difficult," Lachance writes,

> to ascertain to what extent Arnaldo, as spiritual director, influenced the practice of Angela's daily life or her thinking. . . . As to his immediate influence on her thinking—and surely there was some—there is little direct external evidence of it in the dialogues recorded in the *Memorial*. As Giorgio Petrocchi points out, "In the stronger moments, marked by raw narrative realism, the interventions of Arnaldo must have been none, or almost none." Clearly, throughout the narrative, Angela's personality dominates and Arnaldo remains in the background.[63]

On the other hand, Lachance's explicit recognition that Brother A.'s role was more than that of mere conduit for Angela's words is significant. Although Lachance's earlier work recognized "no direct external evidence" of Brother A.'s influence, his most recent work has moderately revised this view, recognizing instead some "little direct external evidence."[64] There he quite rightly alludes, albeit briefly, to the scribe's abbreviations of Angela's message, his transposition of her language into Latin, and his internal organization of the text. While still clearly emphasizing the dominance of

Angela's personality and mystical experience within the *Memorial*, he recognizes Brother A. as "a co-protagonist of her communications from God." Lachance's brief allusions to these important subjects warrant further elaboration.

Interspersed throughout the *Memorial*, for example, are numerous allusions to questions Brother A. posed to Angela.[65] Once, focusing on how a troubled conscience could thwart his scribal fidelity, he inadvertently slips in a phrase suggesting that he *regularly* questioned Angela during their meetings. He writes that before they would meet

> I took pains to confess my sins, knowing that if, on whatever topic God inspired me to question her, all ended in an orderly fashion, it would be by divine grace.[66]

Elsewhere he similarly reveals that questioning her formed part of his standard practice:

> Since Christ's faithful one used to receive a new grace every time she received communion, I, brother, just as I usually did on other occasions, asked her if this communion had brought her contentment.[67]

It is worth noting that Brother A. refers to many of his inquiries in a haphazard, almost offhand way. For example, he begins a sentence,

> And then she responded to me, the brother scribe questioning her, by saying the following . . .[68]

The text that follows is sometimes so engrossing that the reader easily overlooks (as virtually all the scholarship bears out) the fact that the scribe recording her teachings and experiences instigated the discussion in the first place. So, even granting that the scribe was doing his best to present Angela's own words, would she, if left to her own devices, ever have raised the subject under consideration? We see the other side of this coin in another passage, where Brother A. notes unobtrusively at the end of a passage that once when she was unable to answer his questions regarding how God can be known in his creatures, he simply quit writing:

> When I, brother scribe, inquired about this knowledge, she responded to me that not only were her previous remarks fragmentary, but also that other things about which I was inquiring were also incomplete, as it seemed to me too, and so at that point I quit writing.[69]

While a detailed analysis of all the passages in which Brother A. questioned Angela lies beyond the purview of this essay, a general review supplies unmistakable signposts pointing the reader toward Brother A.'s preferred issues. Many of the specific questions he posed concerned her visions per se or, less often, emerged within the context of or initiated a discussion of Angela's visionary experience.[70] His own interest in her visions is obvious as he relentlessly presses her to reveal the details of her supernatural experiences:

> After I had given her communion, before she had departed, I pressed her to tell me if God had bestowed any grace upon her. She said, "Before I received communion, when I was just about to receive, this was spoken to me: 'Beloved, the all good is within you and you are going to receive the all good.' And then it seemed to me that I saw the omnipotent God." I, brother writer, asked her if she had seen something with any form. She responded, "No, I did not see anything with any form." I, brother, pressed her further, and she responded to me, "I saw a plentitude, a beauty, wherein I saw the all good."[71]

It is a well-known fact that visions formed a prominent part of many late medieval women's experience.[72] This is corroborated not only by reading their own texts, but also the more numerous texts about them by male hagiographers. In the Italian context, where visionary experiences are especially pronounced in male hagiographic texts about women (in contrast to male hagiographic texts about men), this emphasis is clearly related to late medieval clerical distrust of word-based, human knowledge. These writers delight in contrasting unlearned women's ineffable visionary knowledge with mere human knowledge. Philosophical and theological learning, acquired from schools and books, vehicles of learning conventionally associated with men, were the subject of intense scrutiny and growing skepticism within intellectual circles. Philosophers and theologians themselves debated the very nature and value of human knowing, underscoring the radical limits of human logic and language, tools too finite to comprehend religious truths.[73] Given the fact that so many women's texts were penned under the guiding hand of male confessors, scribes, and editors, it is worth asking whether or not the prominence of visions even in women's own writings is owing in part to male patronage of women visionaries, women who were, in essence, sources of supernatural knowing. After all, many women's religious texts have survived until today owing to their promotion and approval by powerful male supporters.

In light of this late medieval skepticism, it is no surprise to find that a dominant theme throughout the *Memorial* concerns the superiority of Angela's supernaturally infused knowledge over the knowledge of theologians, preachers, and even scripture scholars. Brother A.'s specific interest in her visionary activity, highlighted by many of the questions he put to her, reflects the clerical concerns of his age. His willingness to labor painstakingly over a period of years to record Angela's frequent encounters with the supernatural (despite Franciscan gossip about his relationship with her) surely tells us as much about him as it does about her.

The *Memorial* is rife with other markers besides Brother A.'s questions that yield valuable clues to the scribe's own interests. On a number of occasions, he specifically names issues or incidents which Angela reported to him, but which he then omitted or abbreviated in his account.[74] Even when extenuating circumstances such as lack of time force him to eliminate or condense material, one might ponder his method of choosing what to omit or abbreviate and what to include. On three occasions, for example, he passes over or abbreviates Angela's descriptions of harsh penances or bodily sufferings, while in another passage he says he paid little attention to Angela's narration of Christ's torments and sufferings.[75] Indeed, bodily suffering, a prominent theme in late medieval women's writings and in texts about them, plays a relatively moderate role in the *Memorial*, despite the fact that intermittent remarks within the text reveal that Angela did indeed endure bodily illness and suffering.[76] The extent to which this theme has been tempered by the scribe's own interests, his difficulty understanding Angela's descriptions of her suffering, or other circumstances is representative of the types of issues that can be illuminated through close scrutiny of his omissions and abbreviations.

In passing remarks, he similarly notes that he sometimes selectively chose his subjects from among those recounted to him.[77] The selections include a dream or vision in which Angela's own supernatural experience is shown to be more powerful than meditating on the words of scripture or listening to preachers, an erotic description of her lying in ecstasy alongside Christ in the sepulcher, and a graphic description of a vision of love moving toward her like a sickle. Brother A.'s own editorial choices appear elsewhere in the *Memorial* as well. Angela was once recounting to him her experience of seeing the Christ child in the host. Probably recalling that Brother A. had undertaken to write her experiences in order to subject them to the judgment of a wise and spiritual man, she continues:

> [This vision] was a source of such joy that I do not believe I will ever lose it. It filled me with so much certitude that I do not doubt it in any respect or in any way; accordingly, it is not necessary that you write it down.[78]

Angela may not have objected to the scribe's decision to include the incident anyway, but in another instance, we find Brother A. directly opposing her wishes, recording a passage she vehemently denounced as inaccurate. He writes:

> This revelation of the passion of the Lord recorded here at the beginning of this fifth step on divine union and love was, through my orders, first written in the vernacular by a certain young boy. This was because my brothers had forbidden me, brother writer, to speak to Christ's faithful one for the purpose of recording [her words]. As a consequence, it was very incompetently and badly written, so much so that when I read it to Christ's faithful one once, I heard her say that I should destroy it rather than transcribe it in that state. But since I, brother, did not have time to correct it with Christ's faithful one, I translated it into Latin just as I found it, adding nothing, on the contrary, painting, as it were, as does a painter since I could not understand it. What follows, therefore, is just as I found it written in the vernacular.[79]

Brother A. resists Angela's suggestions or disagrees with her on other occasions as well.[80] It is notable that several of these incidents once again set scripture, the spoken word, and bookish questions in inferior positions vis-à-vis Angela's own felt supernatural knowledge of God.

Although the import of each of Brother A.'s questions, abbreviations, omissions, selections, and disagreements varies and must be evaluated within the context of the entire *Memorial*, it seems clear that a careful and cumulative analysis of all these minor, seemingly insignificant pieces of evidence can yield a mine of information about the role of Brother A. as writer and his relationship with Angela.

The seventh and final feature indicative of Brother A.'s authorial role regards the very structure of the *Memorial*. Brother A.'s first notes recorded Angela's explanation of her screaming episode at the church of Saint Francis in Assisi. He incorporated this account into chapter 3 of the *Memorial*, a chapter devoted entirely to this Assisi event. This is the twentieth step of Angela's spiritual journey, known also, as indicated in Table 1, as the first supplementary step.[81] Brother A. then proceeded to record Angela's account of the nineteen steps previous to their meeting in Assisi, which became chapter 1; his account of how the book began, which became chapter 2; and all her experiences subsequent to their meeting in Assisi, which became chapters 4 through 9.

It is important to recall that Brother A. begins a new numbering system after he introduces step 20 in the first chapter, identifying it and subsequent steps as steps 1 through 7. Scholars have designated these last steps as "supplementary" steps in order to distinguish them from the preceding nineteen steps. Yet this clearly conflicts with his opening statement in chapter 1, where Brother A. writes:

> [Angela] reported that when she conversed about God with a [female] companion, she had, based on her own experience, designated thirty steps or transformations which the soul makes as it advances in the penitential journey.[82]

Brother A. concludes this first chapter with a brief introduction to the twentieth step and devotes his second chapter to an overview of the remainder of the *Memorial*. He candidly opens this chapter:

> It should be noted at this point that I, brother writer, with the help of God, diligently tried to make the content of this narration continuous from the first step to the twenty-first step. . . .
>
> From that point, however, I did not know how to organize the material, because thereafter I was only rarely and sporadically able to speak with her to write anything down. Moreover, since I was not certain how to number and distinguish any of the steps after the nineteenth step, I have tried my best to organize the rest which follows under seven steps or revelations. I have enumerated these steps according to the states of divine grace I saw Christ's faithful one in or my knowledge of her growth in the gifts and charisms of grace, and also according to what seemed most appropriate and convenient to my thinking.[83]

In essence, Angela's experiences and her words have been reorganized in chapters 3 through 9 to accord with Brother A.'s theological understanding of the various states of grace. He thus reduces her thirty steps to twenty-six and, acknowledging his rearrangement of her material, renumbers the last seven of these as steps 1 through 7, to which he then devotes the major portion of the text.

Brother A.'s new divisions and numbering for the last steps, which honestly reflect his reworking of her spiritual itinerary, is symbolically significant as well, for it was Brother A. who interpreted the Assisi event as a critical, central turning point in her spiritual journey. The nineteen steps leading up to that moment are briefly summed up and relegated to the first chapter, not only because he learned about them retrospectively, but because they pale in significance beside the steps she experienced after he began to write. He tellingly refers to these latter steps as "revelations,"[84] a term he does not apply to any of the steps before they initiated their writing relationship. Yet a number of these earlier steps, even as briefly described, easily qualify as revelations: in step 10 God appeared to her many times; in step 13 the heart of Christ was shown to her; in step 17 she received numerous visions, was granted a qualitatively new faith in God and began to experience his sweetness continually; by step 18 Angela had become so inflamed with God's love that she screamed at the mere mention of his name; and in step 19 she was overcome with delight, lost her power of speech, and appeared to be dead, surely a description of an ecstatic state.[85]

These first nineteen steps are clearly demarcated from the last seven not only because Brother A., in his ignorance, has been forced to rearrange and renumber the latter, but because he inadvertently exalts all of Angela's experiences subsequent to his entrance into the intimate details of her spiritual life. Despite the fact that he and Angela could meet but rarely and irregularly shortly after he began to record her experiences, he manages to devote a lengthy chapter to each of the last seven steps or "revelations."[86] Although evidence can be adduced that Angela's progress in the spiritual life, despite her constant oscillations between doubt and faith, may have carried her to new heights toward the end of her religious journey,[87] it seems insufficient to explain the imbalance Brother A. establishes between her spiritual life prior and subsequent to his work as her confidant and scribe.

If any feature at all significantly distinguishes step 20, when Brother A. came upon her in Assisi, from the preceding and subsequent steps, it is the presence of the Trinity, that is, the very doctrinal point Brother A. elicited from Angela through his first doubt-inspiring interrogation. He further magnifies the relevance of the Trinity and builds expectations around it as a theme by apprising the reader, in each of the first two chapters, of Angela's eventual experience with the Trinity in Assisi.[88] If it is true that the *minor* account preceded the *maior* account, these advance references become particularly meaningful, for both belong only to the longer account and thus would have been added only after Brother A. had forced Angela to identify her Assisi experience explicitly as an encounter with the Trinity.

Chapter 2, Brother A.'s presentation of himself as humble and faithful scribe, interrupts not only the narrative sequence of the twenty-six steps (see Table 1), but also the critical twentieth step itself, which he began at the end of chapter 1 and takes up again only in chapter 3. Brother A. has at once placed himself at the center of this pivotal spiritual experience and at the beginning of her most momentous "revelations," now renumbered as if to mark a qualitatively new stage in her spiritual itinerary. Although the sincerely intentioned scribe was perhaps unaware of his self-positioning within the narrative, it seems a strange coincidence that Angela's spiritual life should take such a dramatic swing toward the sublime, begin again as it were, at just the moment when he happened to ask her about it. My point, in short, is that the entire structure of the *Memorial* is built out from the perspective of Brother A. He inadvertently casts the day he intruded into her inner thoughts as a central turning point in her experience, and he correlates the beginning of their writing relationship with what he represents as the genesis of her most significant religious experience.

In assessing the relative contributions of Angela of Foligno and Brother A. to the creation of the *Memorial*, the weight of scholarly opinion has consistently tipped the scales heavily toward Angela as virtually the sole author of the *Memorial*, even while recognizing that she dictated her spiritual experiences to the Franciscan scribe, Brother A. This essay attempts to tip the scales away from Angela and toward her collaborator, Brother A. If the fascinating tale of her spiritual revelations and teachings has been somewhat neglected in the process, it is by no means to obscure or undervalue her inestimable contribution to the creation of the *Memorial*. Indeed, my point is precisely to recognize the collaborative nature of the writing relationship shared by Angela and Brother A. While she supplied and inspired her scribe with her own sublime experiences, his hand enfleshed her voice in written words, providing us with the physical text that is virtually our only trace of the thoughts of either author. Of course, delineating precisely the boundaries of each author's contribution to such a collaborative effort is not only impossible, it also ignores the nature of medieval religious authorship, which frequently lacked the individualistic cast so evident in modern writing and which emphasized instead collective truths shared by a community of believers. Fortunately for the modern reader interested in ascertaining the distinctive contributions of Angela of Foligno and Brother A., the scribe has left myriad clues throughout his text which provide at the very least revelatory evidence of his own authorial role and interests in writing the *Memorial*. Scholars may be able to speculate more knowledgeably about the individual voices of Angela of Foligno and Brother A. by carefully weighing the plentiful evidence of Brother A.'s authorial role against major motifs of the text that appear to belong more singularly to Angela. In the final analysis, however, the *Memorial* remains a collaboratively authored text. Each author uncannily seems to have recognized this fact in a virtually unique passage that jointly identifies both Angela and Brother A. as speakers and writers of the *Memorial*. A divine voice commands them both:

> Make sure, at the conclusion of the words you [plural] speak, that the following is written, namely, that thanks should be rendered to God for all the things which you [plural] have written.[89]

I gratefully acknowledge the Women's Studies in Religion Program of the Harvard Divinity School, which supported me as a Research Associate during the year I researched this chapter. My thanks also to Constance H. Buchanan, program director, and my fellow research associates, Frances Foster, Deborah Hertz, Teresia Hinga, and Elizabeth V. Spelman for their insightful comments.

Notes

1. Anne L. Clark, *Elisabeth of Schönau: A Twelfth-Century Visionary* (Philadelphia: University of Pennsylvania Press, 1992).

2. Frances Beer, *Women and Mystical Experience in the Middle Ages* (Woodbridge, England: Boydell Press, 1992), pp. 78–108; Mary Jeremy Finnegan, *The Women of Helfta: Scholars and Mystics* (Athens: University of Georgia Press, 1991), p. 20.

3. Clarissa W. Atkinson, *Mystic and Pilgrim: The Book and the World of Margery Kempe* (Ithaca, NY: Cornell University Press, 1983).

4. Tore Nyberg, Introduction, in Birgitta of Sweden, *Life and Selected Revelations*, ed. Marguerite Tjader Harris (New York: Paulist Press, 1990); Jésus Berdonces and Tore Nyberg, "Brigida di Svezia, santa," *Dizionario degli Istituti di Perfezione*, ed. Guerrino Pellicia and Giancarlo Rocco (Rome: Edizione Paolini, 1974), 1: cols. 1572–78.

5. Suzanne Noffke, Introduction, in *The Letters of Catherine of Siena*, ed. Noffke, Medieval and Renaissance Texts and Studies, 52 (Binghamton, NY: Medieval and Renaissance Texts and Studies, 1988).

6. *Il libro della Beata Angela da Foligno (Edizione critica)*, ed. Ludger Thier and Abele Calufetti, 2d ed. (Grottaferrata [Rome]: Collegii S. Bonaventurae and Claras Aquas, 1985), pp. 25–103; this work will be cited hereafter as *Il libro*, without

the editors' names when I am referring to the body of the text, and with the editors' names when I am referring to commentary belonging to the editors. On Angela's life and spirituality, see Paul Lachance, *The Spiritual Journey of the Blessed Angela of Foligno According to the Memorial of Frater A.* (Rome: Pontificium Athenaeum Antonianum, 1984); Clément Schmitt, ed., *Vita e spiritualità della Beata Angela da Foligno* (Perugia: Serafica Provincia di San Francesco, 1987); *Sante e beate umbre tra il XIII e il XIV secolo: Mostra iconografica* (Foligno: Edizioni dell'Arquata, 1986); Enrico Menestò, ed., *Angela da Foligno: Terziaria Francescana*, Atti del Convegno storico nel VII centenario dell'ingresso della beata Angela da Foligno nell'Ordine Francescano Secolare (1291–1991), Foligno, 17–18–19 novembre 1991 (Spoleto: Centro Italiano di Studi sull'alto Medioevo, 1992).

7. On the dating of major events in her life, see Thier and Calufetti, *Il libro*, pp. 25–39; and Martin-Jean Ferré, "Les principales dates de la vie d'Angèle de Foligno," *Revue d'Histoire Franciscaine* 2 (1925): 21–33.

8. *Il libro*, chap. 1, p. 138, ll. 89–93.

9. Antonio Blasucci, "L'itinerario mistico della B. Angela da Foligno," in Schmitt, *Vita e spiritualità*, p. 207.

10. Abele Calufetti, "La B. Angela da Foligno e l'Eucaristia: Visioni, esperienze, insegnamenti," in Schmitt, *Vita e spiritualità*, p. 333; Enrico Menestò, "Beate e sante dell'Umbria tra Duecento e Trecento: Una ricognizione degli scritti e delle fonti agiografiche," in *Sante e beate umbre*, p. 69; Salvatore Aliquò, Introduzione, in *L'esperienza di Dio amore: Il "Libro,"* trans. Aliquò (Rome: Città Nuova, 1973), p. 8; and see Carole Slade, "Alterity in Union: The Mystical Experience of Angela of Foligno and Margery Kempe," *Religion and Literature* 23 (1991): 114.

11. Romana Guarnieri, Preface, in *Angela of Foligno: Complete Works*, trans. Paul Lachance (New York: Paulist Press, 1993), p. 7.

12. *L'autobiografia e gli scritti della Beata Angela da Foligno*, ed. Michele Faloci Pulignani, trans. Maria Castiglione Humani (Città di Castello: Il Solco, 1932).

13. Thier and Calufetti, *Il libro*, p. 48.

14. *Il libro*, chap. 3, p. 190; see also Instruction 26, pp. 628–30.

15. *Il libro*, pp. 126–400; the *Memorial* is so named because Brother A. once comments that he first began to write brief notes about Angela's experiences as a sort of "memorial": *Il libro*, chap. 2, p. 166, l. 86.

16. *Il libro*, pp. 404–742.

17. Thier and Calufetti, *Il libro*, pp. 41–51, 108–15.

18. "Testificatio," *Il libro*, pp. 126–28.

19. Thier and Calufetti, *Il libro*, pp. 50, 113; Lachance, *Complete Works*, p. 50; and see *Il libro*, Instruction 26, pp. 628–30, ll. 45–59.

20. *Il libro*, chap. 1, p. 132, l. 5.

21. Thier and Calufetti, *Il libro*, pp. 43–73, 108–13, 117.

22. Thier and Calufetti, *Il libro*, pp. 43–51, 108–13.

23. Menestò, "Problemi critico-testuali nel 'Liber' della beata Angela," in idem, *Angela da Foligno: Terziaria*, pp. 171–75; idem, "Beate e sante dell'Umbria," in *Sante e beate umbre*, pp. 69–72. See also Giovanni Pozzi, *Il libro dell'esperienza* (Milan: Adelphi, 1992), pp. 236–37, 246, who questions the double-redaction theory but without detailing his objections; Martin-Jean Ferré, *Le livre de l'expéri-*

ence des vrais fidèles (Paris: Éditions E. Droz, 1927), pp. xvi–xxviii. For critiques concerning other aspects of Thier and Calufetti's critical edition, see Menestò, "Problemi critico-testuali nel 'Liber,'" pp. 161–79; Pozzi, *Il libro dell'esperienza*, pp. 236–47.

24. Bibliography may be consulted in *Il libro*, pp. 9–22; Sergio Andreoli, "Bibliografia sulla Beata Angela da Foligno (1248/49–1309)," *L'Italia Francescana* 60 (1985): 75–92; and idem, "Angela da Foligno: Bibliografia (1984–1987)," *L'Italia Francescana* 63 (1988): 185–200.

25. *Il libro*, chap. 1, p. 156, l. 305; chap. 3, p. 190, l. 181.

26. *Il libro*, chap. 2, pp. 170–72, ll. 134–39; see also chap. 1, p. 134, ll. 33–38; chap. 9, pp. 398–400, ll. 495–532. All translations are mine. I would like to thank Paul Lachance for graciously making available to me his draft English translation of the *Book*. In my own translations, in which I have sometimes favored literal renderings to a more congenial English translation, I have had the scholarly luxury of consulting Lachance's own interpretation and choice of English vocabulary, now published as Angela of Foligno, *Complete Works*.

27. Martin-Jean Ferré, "Les oeuvres d'Angèle de Foligno," *Revue d'Histoire Franciscaine* 2 (1925): 481; Augusta Merzagora, "Il libro della B. Angela da Foligno," *Vita e Pensiero* 35 (1952): 248, cited in Thier and Calufetti, *Il libro*, p. 46, who seem to concur.

28. See also *Il libro*, chap. 9, p. 400, l. 523.

29. *Il libro*, chap. 9, p. 400, ll. 517–19. Further evidence that he wrote sometimes when he was not with her might be adduced from chap. 5, p. 248, ll. 195–97.

30. Giorgio Petrocchi, "Astrattezza e realismo nel *Liber* di Angela da Foligno," in *Ascesi e mistica trecentesca* (Florence: Felice le Monnier, 1957), pp. 1–19, is possibly the first scholar to broach at any length the subject of the literary relationship between Angela, Brother A., and the scribes (*transcrittori*) subsequently responsible for the *Instructions*. He argues that a certain diversity of style inevitably separates the lively vernacular expressions of Angela from the more sober and dry Latin of her scribes, but still concludes that her language undeniably grounds that of her scribes; cf., however, Mauro Donnini, "Appunti sulla lingua e lo stile del 'Liber' della beata Angela da Foligno," in Menestò, *Angela da Foligno: Terziaria*, pp. 181–213, who details the lexical and stylistic similarity of Angela and her scribes. Pasquale Valugani, in the introduction to a translation of Angela's revelations published for a popular audience, refers to the principal role of Brother A. in the composition of Angela's revelations; see *L'esperienza mistica della beata Angela da Foligno nel racconto di Frate Arnaldo*, trans. Maria Castiglione Humani (Milan: Biblioteca Francescana Provinciale, 1964). Valugani's work, which I have been unable to consult, is reviewed with harsh comments for his designation of Brother A. as author of the revelations by Innocenzo Colosio, "Una nuova edizione delle opere della Beata Angela da Foligno," *Rivista di Ascetica e Mistica* 10 (1965): 189–93. More recently, reviewers of Lachance's *The Spiritual Journey* have noted the need to address the "problem of contaminated authorship" in the *Book*, and to attempt "to unravel what is Angela's in the spirituality of the *Book* and what is contributed by Brother A."; respectively Rudolph M. Bell, in *Studia Mystica* 11 (1988): 73–75; and Caroline Walker Bynum, in *Church History* 57 (1988): 359–60.

31. *Il libro*, chap. 2, pp. 170–72, ll. 132–34, 143–52. See also chap. 4, p. 222, ll. 257–60.

32. See, for example, *Il libro*, chap. 2, pp. 159–60, ll. 6–17; pp. 170–74, ll. 132–73; chap. 4, p. 222, ll. 257–60; chap. 7, p. 310, ll. 258–59; chap. 8, p. 336, ll. 9–15; chap. 9, p. 358, l. 39; p. 368, ll. 170–73; p. 400, ll. 522–27; see also chap. 4, p. 218, ll. 210–18.

33. Thier and Calufetti cite material difficulties surrounding the scribe's listening and writing task and the ineffability of Angela's experience to account for the scribe's failings; they discount his repeated admissions of incompetence by attributing them to his humility, *Il libro*, pp. 45–46.

34. *Il libro*, chap. 4, p. 222, ll. 258–60.

35. *Il libro*, chap. 9, p. 400, ll. 516–17.

36. For examples of transpositions from the third person back to the first person, assuming that the *maior* redaction followed the *minor* redaction, see *Il libro*, chap. 3, pp. 190–94, ll. 190–216; chap. 7, p. 304, l. 182.

37. For the other comment, see *Il libro*, chap. 2, p. 172, ll. 140–42.

38. Menestò, "Beate e sante dell'Umbria," in *Sante e beate umbre*, p. 71; idem, "Problemi critico-testuali nel 'Liber,'" in idem, *Angela da Foligno: Terziaria*, p. 175.

39. *Il libro*, chap. 1, p. 134, ll. 33–38; chap. 9, p. 400, ll. 511–27; and see chap. 2, p. 170, ll. 134–42, 153–54.

40. See *Il libro*, chap. 1, p. 134, ll. 33–38; p. 140, l. 118; chap. 3, p. 180, ll. 46, 50–51, 57; chap. 7, l. 273 through chap. 9, l. 150; and see chap. 7, p. 310 n. 21.

41. Menestò, *Angela da Foligno: Terziaria*, pp. 171–75; Pozzi, *Il libro dell'esperienza*, pp. 236–47, especially 236–37, 246. Lachance, *Complete Works*, pp. 53–54, also does not express unqualified support for Thier and Calufetti's double-redaction theory, although he does not explicitly specify his reservations.

42. *Il libro*, chap. 4, p. 222, ll. 261–62; see also chap. 2, p. 162, l. 35.

43. *Il libro*, chap. 9, p. 370, ll. 179–80. On dating, see Ferré, "Les principales dates," *Revue d'Histoire Franciscaine* 2 (1925): 25–26.

44. See Brother A.'s closing remarks, chap. 9, pp. 388–400, ll. 495–510, especially 508–10; and also chap. 2, p. 172, ll. 161–62.

45. *Il libro*, chap. 2, pp. 168–70, ll. 97–103, 109–14.

46. *Il libro*, chap. 2, p. 170, ll. 116–18.

47. *Il libro*, chap. 3, p. 176, ll. 10–16; for further evidence that Brother A. compelled her to speak, see chap. 2, p. 166, ll. 87–88; p. 170, l. 123.

48. *Il libro*, chap. 2, p. 170, ll. 123–25.

49. *Il libro*, chap. 2, pp. 166–68, ll. 85–91.

50. For the Holy Spirit's colloquy with her, see *Il libro*, chap. 3, pp. 178–86, ll. 30–128. It is interesting to note that the divine voice of God individually informed several other women that each was the best-loved woman in the valley of Spoleto. He apparently kept them all in ignorance of the others' similarly singular status.

51. *Il libro*, chap. 3, p. 178, ll. 35–37.

52. *Il libro*, chap. 3, p. 180, ll. 52–54.

53. *Il libro*, chap. 3, p. 184, ll. 109–15.

54. *Il libro*, chap. 3, p. 188, ll. 165–67.

55. *Il libro*, chap. 3, p. 190, ll. 181–84.

56. *Il libro*, chap. 3, p. 188, l. 154.

57. Angela also calls Christ "more than an earthly father," chap. 5, p. 238, l. 93. The fluidity Angela brought to her understanding of God can be found in the texts associated with other female contemporaries, such as Margaret of Cortona.

58. *Il libro*, chap. 3, p. 190, ll. 184–91.

59. An opinion supported by Thier and Calufetti, *Il libro*, chap. 3, p. 190 n. 24; chap. 1, p. 154 n. 29; Lachance, *Complete Works*, p. 370 n. 33.

60. See, for example, *Il libro*, chap. 4, pp. 226–28, ll. 317–28.

61. *Il libro*, chap. 7, p. 306, ll. 208–15.

62. Lachance, *Complete Works*, p. 51; and see Lachance, *The Spiritual Journey*, p. 121.

63. *Complete Works*, p. 51, citing Petrocchi, "Astrattezza e realismo nel *Liber*," in *Ascesi e mistica trecentesca*, p. 8; see also Lachance, *The Spiritual Journey*, pp. 121–22. It is worth remarking that Lachance's suggestion that it was Brother A. who pushed Angela to clarify her thinking and express herself more precisely, despite his admissions regarding his own ineptitude, is eagerly underlined by some reviewers of *The Spiritual Journey*; N. Bériou, in *Revue des Sciences Philosophiques et Théologiques* 72 (1988): 453–54; Arm. Toubeau, in *Nouvelle Revue Théologique* 107 (1985): 913; and cf. the more astute comments of Bell, in *Studia Mystica* 11 (1988): 73–75. Bériou attempts to enhance further the clerical sources of Angela's language and teaching by hypothesizing that she drew vocabulary and a "grammar" to describe her conversion from contemporary preachers.

64. Respectively Lachance, *The Spiritual Journey*, p. 121; and idem, *Complete Works*, p. 51; see also Lachance, "The Experience of God in the Spiritual Journey of the Bl. Angela of Foligno," in Schmitt, *Vita e spiritualità*, p. 248.

65. *Il libro*, chap. 2, pp. 164–66, ll. 71–73; p. 170, ll. 116–18; chap. 3, p. 176, ll. 11–14; p. 184, ll. 104–5; p. 190, ll. 181–84; pp. 194–96, ll. 233–35; chap. 4, p. 204, ll. 53–54; p. 208, l. 112; p. 210, ll. 124–25; p. 212, l. 140; p. 226, ll. 317–18; p. 226, ll. 319–20; chap. 5, p. 240, ll. 109–15; p. 248, ll. 202–3; p. 250, ll. 219–21; p. 250, ll. 224–25; chap. 6, p. 274, ll. 203–4; pp. 278–80, ll. 275–78; p. 286, ll. 341–45; chap. 7, p. 302, l. 177; p. 306, ll. 219–20; p. 306, ll. 223–24; p. 306, l. 225; p. 310, ll. 263–64; p. 312, ll. 273–75; p. 312, l. 279; p. 320, l. 362; chap. 9, p. 356, ll. 19–28; p. 360, ll. 84–86; pp. 362–64, ll. 107–8; p. 372, ll. 219–20; p. 378, ll. 283–85; p. 378, ll. 289–90; see also chap. 4, p. 218, ll. 210–12. For a question Brother A. posed to Angela's companion, see chap. 7, p. 320, l. 371.

66. *Il libro*, chap. 2, p. 174, ll. 164–67.

67. *Il libro*, chap. 9, p. 372, ll. 217–20.

68. *Il libro*, chap. 4, p. 212, l. 140.

69. *Il libro*, chap. 5, p. 250, ll. 219–20.

70. *Il libro*, chap. 3, p. 184, ll. 104–5; pp. 194–96, ll. 233–35; chap. 4, p. 204, ll. 53–54; p. 210, ll. 124–25; p. 212, l. 140; p. 226, ll. 317–18; p. 226, ll. 319–20; chap. 6, pp. 278–80, ll. 275–78; p. 286, ll. 341–45; chap. 7, p. 302, l. 177; p. 306, ll. 219–20; p. 306, ll. 223–24; p. 306, l. 225; chap. 9, p. 356, ll. 19–28; p. 360, ll. 84–86.

71. *Il libro*, chap. 7, pp. 306–8, ll. 218–27.

72. Peter Dinzelbacher, *Mittelalterliche Visionsliteratur: Eine Anthologie*

(Darmstadt: Wissenschaftliche Buchgesellschaft, 1989), pp. 28–30; Dieter R. Bauer, "Diskussionsüberblick," in *Frauenmystik im Mittelalter*, ed. Peter Dinzelbacher and Dieter R. Bauer (Ostfildern bei Stuttgart: Schwabenverlag, 1985); Elizabeth Petroff, *Medieval Women's Visionary Literature* (New York: Oxford University Press, 1986); André Vauchez, *La sainteté en occident aux derniers siècles du moyen âge, d'après les procès de canonisation et les documents hagiographiques* (Rome: École Française de Rome; Paris: Diffusion de Boccard, 1981), pp. 437–40; Donald Weinstein and Rudolph M. Bell, *Saints and Society: The Two Worlds of Western Christendom, 1000–1700* (Chicago and London: University of Chicago Press, 1982), pp. 181, 228–29, 232.

73. Catherine M. Mooney, "Women's Visions, Men's Words: The Portrayal of Holy Women and Men in Fourteenth-Century Italian Hagiography," Ph.D. dissertation, Yale University, 1991.

74. *Il libro*, chap. 1, p. 134, ll. 33–38; p. 140, ll. 116–19; chap. 2, p. 174, ll. 168–73; chap. 4, p. 216, ll. 197–99; chap. 5, pp. 234–36, ll. 63–65; p. 248, ll. 193–97; chap. 8, p. 336, ll. 9–15; chap. 9, p. 368, ll. 170–74; and see chap. 2, pp. 158–60, ll. 6–10; p. 172, ll. 154–55; chap. 4, p. 222, ll. 257–60.

75. *Il libro*, chap. 1, p. 134, ll. 33–38; chap. 1, p. 140, ll. 116–19; chap. 8, p. 336, ll. 9–15; chap. 5, pp. 234–36, ll. 63–65; see also chap. 4, pp. 218–20, ll. 206–24, where Brother A. abbreviates several subjects, including Angela's commentaries on God as doctor bringing the medicine of his blood to sick souls and the [spiritual] infirmities of the various members of her own body.

76. See notably, chap. 8, pp. 336–46, ll. 9–126. Brother A. here notes his difficulty in understanding her sufferings and the fact that they seemed to dissipate toward the end of this step in her journey; p. 336, ll. 14–15; p. 346, ll. 117–20.

77. *Il libro*, chap. 1, pp. 148–50, ll. 219–47; chap. 3, p. 178, ll. 17–21, 30–33; chap. 7, p. 296, ll. 98–111; pp. 298–300, ll. 115–39; and see chap. 3, pp. 188–90, ll. 165–78 for selections the scribe may have made from stories recounted to him by Angela's companion.

78. *Il libro*, chap. 3, p. 198, ll. 262–64.

79. *Il libro*, chap. 7, p. 288, ll. 8–17; the passage transcribed from the vernacular into Latin continues until p. 296, l. 95.

80. *Il libro*, chap. 5, p. 240, ll. 116–21; chap. 7, p. 314, ll. 302–7; pp. 318–20, ll. 349–56; pp. 322–24, ll. 403–15; chap. 9, pp. 356–58, ll. 19–49.

81. *Il libro*, chap. 3, p. 178, l. 30 through p. 188, l. 156; and see p. 158 n. 2.

82. *Il libro*, chap. 1, p. 132, ll. 4–6.

83. *Il libro*, chap. 2, pp. 158–60, ll. 6–7, 11–17.

84. *Il libro*, pp. 158–60, ll. 6–17; he here refers to all seven steps as revelations, although his lengthy exposition of the sixth step in chap. 8 does not explicitly refer to it as a revelation.

85. *Il libro*, chap. 1, pp. 140, 142, 148–56.

86. *Il libro*, chap. 2, pp. 158–60, ll. 6–12.

87. Lachance, *The Spiritual Journey*, pp. 123–392.

88. *Il libro*, chap. 1, p. 154, ll. 286–87; chap. 2, p. 160, ll. 21–23.

89. *Il libro*, chap. 4, p. 222, ll. 261–62; see also chap. 9, p. 370, ll. 179–80; and chap. 2, pp. 158–60, ll. 6–10.

Katherine Gill

4. Women and the Production of Religious Literature in the Vernacular, 1300–1500

Exchanging Words

Preaching and vernacular religious literature constitute a key site of literary innovation in the late Middle Ages. Sermons, original compositions in *volgare*, and vernacular translations also represent the principal vehicles for the exchange of religious ideas and the expression of religious attitudes. Preaching and translating were complementary enterprises. Not only did preaching often consist of extemporaneous translation of Latin texts to a non-Latin-speaking audience, but the success of this mediation created an appetite and hence a market for religious literature. This demand prompted translations, often quite free, of Latin devotional classics and saints' lives, texts that could then serve as matter for sermon composition or for private reading after the preacher's voice fell silent. The importance of preaching as a stimulus for translations and, consequently, the development of the vernacular as a literary language has been described by the literary historian Carlo Delcorno:

> In the age of the Mendicants, preaching was transformed into a refined instrument of pedagogy, stimulating in the minds of listeners new horizons of expectations both on a religious and cultural plain. It is here that the feverish productivity of translators finds its full significance. The interrelatedness of translation and preaching illustrates the dynamic of revival, operating through the vertical transmission of (textual) content, which characterizes medieval culture.[1]

Here Delcorno, following Hans Robert Jauss, includes the audience's "horizon of expectation" as an important element in the dynamic of literary innovation.[2] We can place that image of the audience, expectant or disinterested, both before and after the moment of a sermon's composition and delivery. For the horizons and interests of an audience are not simply created, by a preacher, translator, or author; they are also something with which a text's composer creates. These expectations can direct choices of subject, genre, style, and language. The audience can, therefore, play an important part in the genesis of a work, as well as in its public life.

Hence the social history of a text extends backward and forward from the moment of writing, embracing the initiatives of patrons, oral phases of gestation, intended audience, and actual audience response. Moreover, *Volgarizazzione*—at once translation, interpretation, and popularization—is among the most social of literary activities, the one most profoundly determined by interactions between translators and their audiences.[3] This acknowledgment of the social dimensions of texts has encouraged literary historians to revise anachronistic notions of authorship or replace them with concepts such as "textual communities" (highlighting the collective and colloquial dimensions of a work's gestation[4]) or "literary institutions" (emphasizing the many stages, many interventions, many accommodations a literary work undergoes as it moves unstably toward its public life[5]). We have seen, then, a general shift of attention away from questions that privilege the role of an author, toward unnervingly expansive and more open-ended ones. "Where (in the broadest sense) does a work come from? How is it circulated? Who controls it?"[6]

Urging a rigorous renunciation of modern notions about the ways written texts come into existence and how they function once they join their readers (or listeners) in a social life, literary theorists have provided a stimulus for new lines of questioning and research. If "the historical life of a literary work is unthinkable without the active participation of its addressees,"[7] we must now seek information that will enable us to envision how an audience did or might participate. If a full recognition of the collaborative nature of literary works requires that we see them in terms of multiple phases of production, with multiple hands and interests involved, we need to chart those phases, find those hands, and identify those interests. If translation is transaction, "il banco di cambio dello spirito," what did each party give and gain?[8]

When we bring the expectation that audiences determine the genesis, the meanings, and the fortunes of texts to the subject of religious literature in the vernacular, our questions immediately begin to involve women. A proliferation of vernacular works written or translated for women, commissioned or purchased by women, copied or illustrated by women can be documented to varying degrees in every region of late medieval Europe.[9] Over fifty years ago Herbert Grundmann highlighted the relationships between women and mendicant friars as primary to the emergence of interest and initiative in developing religious prose, a development with strong impact on vernacular literature in general.[10] In Italy, this vernacular impetus has been characterized as "un movimento . . . oceanico di traduzione," markedly propelled by women's religious communities, tertiaries, more or less informal groups of penitents, and confraternities.[11] The prominence of women in the *volgare* market for religious books joins a high level of female literacy and a broad range of religious initiatives by women as factors that flag Italy as a promising site to test theories of premodern literary production and the female audience.[12]

Nevertheless, despite the acknowledged presence of women near the site of composition, in the audience, and in the manuscript traditions of the most popular examples of Italian vernacular literature, the significance of these coincidences remains, for the most part, unexplored. If the written text represents but one stage in a process, how are we to envision those other stages and the role of women in them? Much of the answer lies latent and diffuse, scattered in colophons, in dedicatory remarks, on flyleaves, in testaments and contracts, in account books, in old and modern inventories, in the footnotes to antiquarian studies of a single author, text, or institution. Thus the first task of this essay is to illustrate women at work in some of many dimensions of literary production and consumption.[13] In order to bring women's more invisible roles into sharper focus, I will not here consider works incontestably attributed to female authors.[14] Instead, I will look at what Jerome McGann would call the "literary institution," whose various elements (audiences, author/composers, translators, secretaries, scribes, editors, patrons, promoters, distributors, censors) shaped religious literature in the vernacular.[15]

These collective components of the "literary institution" very often coincide with a variety of religious institutions, whose character is the second focus of this essay. I will look especially at women's religious life and at some traditional assumptions about that life that have blocked recognition of the possibility of female collaboration and agency. By relating contemporary religious practices and social arrangements to some of the most popular early Italian devotional texts, I hope to shed some light on motives animating both texts and collective religious life.[16] Among my literary sources, the early fourteenth-century translation of the *Vitae patrum* by

Domenico Cavalca (d. 1342) and the *Colloquio spirituale* by Simone da Cascina receive special attention.

Production and Distribution

I begin with the most material aspect of manuscript and book production: scribal activities and commercial exchange. The surviving account books and chronicles from a number of fifteenth-century women's religious communities show their members acting as scribes, illustrators, and distributors of manuscripts. In addition to executing various stages of production themselves, they also arranged for and paid others to carry out different steps. A fifteenth-century register of *entrate e uscite* from the Perugian Franciscan convent of Monteluce, notes payments received from abbesses, uncloistered religious women (designated as *bisoche* or *pinzochere*),[17] secular persons of both genders, and friars acting as agents for at least one other conventual scriptorium, Santa Lucia in nearby Foligno.[18] A diverse central Italian clientele acquired breviaries, books of hours, and antiphons executed by various nuns at Monteluce. Members of this Perugian convent, which numbered seventy-odd women in the mid-fifteenth century, also copied and disseminated biographies and writings by Franciscan holy women, notably Angela of Foligno, Catherine of Bologna, and Eustochia of Messina. In addition, the nuns contracted out certain stages of production—binding to a nearby monastery of Franciscan friars at Monteripidio, illustration to lay miniaturists. Finally, we learn from the account books that Monteluce was, unsurprisingly, an avid consumer of manuscripts (and later printed books), purchasing them from friars, monks, and laypersons, keeping them to copy, designating them for the use of the community, or selling them again to others. At Monteluce in Perugia, as with a conspicuous number of fifteenth-century Clarissan monasteries affiliated with the Observant reform movement, writing and commissioning literary works accompanied this busy production and consumption of manuscripts and books.[19]

The complex interrelations that characterized the production of manuscript versions of devotional texts emerge even more clearly when we turn to the account books of a community that ran one of the first printing presses in Italy, San Jacopo di Ripoli in Florence, a convent that began as an association of recluses.[20] Their *entrate e uscite* from the 1470s throw into relief the participation of many parties in the process of book production.

The capital to acquire type matrices came from a generous lay woman, a loan from the prioress, and the gift of a bushel of flour from a Sister Costanza. Sisters were paid as compositors and, together with traveling preachers, laypersons, and street hawkers, acted as "middle persons" in the sale and distribution of their books. Payments record transactions with Italian and foreign illuminators, of both secular and clerical status. In a manner analogous to the arrangements of the nuns at Monteluce in Perugia, the sisters of San Jacopo worked in partnership with a nearby community of friars (San Marco) and responded to a "vulgar" market that included other nuns, *pinzochere*, monks, and laypersons. For example, they produced 1,300 copies of a *Libro da compagnia ovvero fraternità dei Battuti*, sold 1,000 *Lives* of Saint Margaret to a street singer, and supplied a diverse public with a constant stream of penitential psalms in both Latin and the vernacular.[21]

In its industriousness San Jacopo was not unique. The women of Corpus Domini, Catherine de Vegri's convent in Bologna, immediately availed themselves of the first printing press that came to town (in 1470) to publish the first in series of editions of Catherine's *Le sette armi spirituali*, making it a fifteenth-century best-seller.[22] The extremely elegant breviary copied and illuminated in 1453 by Maria Ormani (leaving us her portrait on f. 89), makes clear that whatever community she belonged to fostered a high level of skill and learning.[23] The Paradiso and Santa Caterina al Monte (alias San Gaggio) were likewise literary centers in the fifteenth century, Santa Caterina was so in the fourteenth as well.[24] Moreover, the provenance of a number of fourteenth-century manuscripts indicate that, at least for Monteluce and San Jacopo, the fifteenth-century interest in texts was an amplified extension of earlier traditions.[25] In 1600 the Index of Prohibited Books produced lists of books owned by monastic women which demonstrate that Monteluce, Santa Lucia, and Sant'Anna did not quickly lose their literary character.[26]

The account books of women's religious communities are, of course, just one type of source displaying the transfer of manuscripts and books to and from women. Testaments and inventories of monastic libraries and confraternities, some of which loaned out manuscripts, supplement the evidence of the account books.[27] In 1435 Fra Augustino, the bishop of Gonessa and a prominent member of the Augustinian Order, left all his books to his sister Maria. In 1439 Jacobella de Tostis, the member of a Roman magnate clan and also of a group of *pinzochere*, gave a house which was to be sold to buy a breviary worth one hundred florins; the breviary, together with two other prayer books, were designated for the use of members of her penitent community.[28]

Three testaments connected to Santa Lucia in Foligno are particularly revealing. In 1447, near the end of her life, having left her miserable twenty-year marriage with Galeazzo di Maletesta, Lord of Pesaro, for the religious regimen of Santa Lucia in Foligno, Battista da Montefeltro drew up a testament in which she charged her granddaughter Constantia, wife of Duke Alexander Sforza, with the transfer of her "librictum sermonum Iacobi de Vorragine, factum ad reverentiam gloriose virginis Marie" to Dominican friars in Foligno. In addition, Battista, now Sister Girolama, left her copy of Saint Jerome's letters to the Observant Franciscans in Pesaro. The rest of her private library went to Santa Lucia.[29] Not long before Girolama made her bequests, the erudite nineteen-year-old daughter of a Perugian jurist, Elena Coppoli, had fled her unconsummated marriage and turned over all her possessions (which certainly included books) to Santa Lucia, where she took the religious name Cecilia. Sister Cecilia's mother, entering Santa Lucia about five years later, sacrificed one of her breviaries to her deceased husband's illegitimate son, a friar, before following in her daughter's footsteps.[30]

A healthy presence of aristocratic patronage assisted the volume and velocity of production and acquisition at Monteluce, Santa Lucia, and Sant'Anna (known since the fourteenth century, and despite its lay status, as *lu munisterio delle Contesse*). Alliance with the ascendant Observant Franciscans added, at least initially, to their range of patronal channels and connected these Umbrian communities with a network of newly created or newly revived monasteries throughout Italy.[31] But testaments and other forms of legal documentation confirm similar patterns of interest and exchange through a wide social spectrum.[32] In the 1363 testament of Bernardo Guidonis of Assisi we perceive the hope that his concubine is not pregnant and that his daughter Nina will remember his soul as she uses the psalter he leaves her.[33] In 1448, Margarita "domini Honofrii de Perusio," the *ministra* (administrative head) of a thriving but nonaristocratic penitent community in Perugia, San Antonio de Padua ("vulgariter nuncupati el monasterio de le poverelle da Fuligne"), ("commonly called the monastery of the poor sisters of Foligno"), in her eagerness to acquire manuscripts, had the misfortune to buy a missal and breviary recently stolen from the sacristy of San Rufino in Assisi.[34] About the same time in

Florence, a former prostitute was compelled to give her book of hours to her pimp, a compromise arranged by the city priors, in order to gain the freedom to enter a women's community.[35]

Literary and Devotional Salons

Almost all the Italian vernacular authors and translators had some sort of close connection with religious women.[36] Thus one finds with new texts, as with new saints in this period, that when you scratch one you find immediately a community, or a nexus of communities. Such is the case with three related Florentine communities: Santa Catherina al Monte, often called San Gaggio (or, colloquially, Cajo) in Florence, together with two communities founded by and for former courtesans, prostitutes, and, I suspect, clerical concubines.[37] All three trace their origins back to the sermons and the organizational support of Simone Fidati of Cascia (d. 1348), an itinerant Augustinian preacher, translator, and author of religious texts.[38] To the milieu of these communities we owe a number of important texts and translations. These include those authored by Simone himself: *Ordine della Vita Cristiana* (1333), the Latin *De Gestis Domini Salvatoris* (a Gospel paraphrase), and a number of letters;[39] a translation of the *De Gestis* by Simone's literary and pastoral protégé, Giovanni da Salerno; a *Regola* attributed to Saint Augustine, framed by Giovanni for *convertite*;[40] and Giovanni's translation of an *Esposizione della Regola del San Agostino* from a Latin version attributed to Hugh of Saint Victor. Simone also composed a *Regola o Dottrina ad una Figliuola Spirituale*, addressed to a woman in Rome. The women of San Gaggio managed to acquire the most important codices of Giordano da Pisa's *Quaresimale* as well as good copies of the works of other preachers and translators throughout the fourteenth and fifteenth centuries. In the last quarter of the fifteenth century, Domencio Scarperia, hermit at the monastery of Santo Spirito in Florence, translated the *Sermones* of St. Bernard, as well as a large collection of Pseudo-Augustinian works for the San Gaggio community.[41]

Simone Fidati composed his Latin *De Gestis* at the request of Tommaso Corsini, a prominent Florentine who renounced an immense fortune to live out his days in a small house adjacent to San Gaggio. This community was founded—about a decade after the establishment of the convertite houses in 1344—by Monna Nera, a young widow of the notable

Manieri clan, with the support of Simone and additional funding by Corsini.[42] While Tommaso lived, his service efforts on behalf of the community were so marked that Santa Caterina/San Gaggio earned the further soubriquette of "le donne di messer Tommaso." When Monna Nera died (1376), Tommaso's wife, Monna Ghita, took over the leadership of the community. A confraternity associated with the church of Santo Spirito, an institution important for both Dante and Boccaccio, also sponsored San Gaggio. The confraternity of Santa Maria Novella (Dominican) and of Orsanmichele (a lay oratory) were also involved at various times in the maintenance and legal representation of San Gaggio and Santa Elisabetta, as well as other women's groups.

Monna Nera's community and the convertite houses, like the texts they requested, received, or conserved, were born of friendship and a sense of partnership shared by diverse individuals and groups. Acknowledging an otherwise unknown Florentine woman in the prologue to his *Arbor vitae crucifixe Jesu*, Ubertino da Casale wrote:

> She [Cecilia] taught me the whole process of the highest contemplation of the life of Jesus and the hidden things in my heart and many other things as well.[43]

Even though the texts themselves repeatedly signal reciprocity in the writer's relationship to an immediate audience, we tend to forget the alliances between institutional and literary history.

> Remembering your request, I have tried, my sister, to write for you this *Ammonizione*, as you have asked . . . because I know your mind's passion for divine scripture and that you try to live according to what you read. [I know that] I do not profit from doing what your charity has taken care to ask; but if through this work you advance in divine love, and then I will have a part of your profit.[44]

To establish the contribution of women to the contents of religious texts, even those addressed directly to them, is more difficult than the task of documenting their ownership of manuscripts or their role as scribes and typesetters. We have to probe a variety of sources to begin to imagine their inclusion in the authorial role (what Foucault would call the author-function) or to identify points at which female intervention might have shaped the ideas transmitted by sermons, translations, or new literary compositions. Looking first at the work of preachers, we find that chance indications do survive. In fact, *exempla* and sermons appear to have been quite permeable to women's voices and interests. The notes of a thirteenth-century preacher reveal that his conversations with Parisian Beguines shaped the sermons he addressed to them.[45] *Gli Assempri* of the Sienese Augustinian prior Filippo degli Agazzari (d. circa 1422) cites women as sources for some of his edifying true stories, signing off with footnotes like "le sopra dete cose udi da due antiche e venerabigli donne" ("I heard these things from two old and venerable ladies").[46] A letter of March 1496 shows how Caterina Rucellai prevailed on a friar of San Marco, to have Girolamo Savonarola retract a proposal he made during the course of a sermon.[47] Likewise, Savonarola's own letters indicate the powerful effect the censorship of a Pisan abbess had on him.[48] In the case of Giordano da Pisa (d. 1311) we have strong circumstantial evidence in the knowledge that a number of his vernacular Lenten sermons were delivered immediately after he had dined with members of women's religious communities; that the most important manuscript edition of Giordano's sermons was owned by the female community of Santa Caterina al Monte; that other copies of his sermons were owned and copied by women; and that his preaching was supported with at least one woman's testamentary bequest.[49]

For most literary historians, this kind of evidence has remained merely circumstantial. In fact, faced with the ubiquitousness of religious women in the manuscript traditions and even in the rubrics of sermon collections, Delcorno concludes that religious women were among the first to copy the *reportationes*, or notes, taken from sermons, because their isolated enclosure excluded them from the preacher's public.[50] Moreover, while he insists that the merchants, artisans, and bankers who recorded Giordano's sermons "were not passive secretaries," but "intervened in the transmission process, shortening, amplifying and commenting on the sermon heard,"[51] he grants religious women only the role of readers and conservators of manuscripts. Delcorno's occlusion of religious women from the most active sites of exchange derives from a somber projection of post-Tridentine ideals onto Trecento women's communities and a forgetfulness of the frequency of preaching, teaching, and discussion within women's communities. With such a view, it is difficult to imagine religious women as the manuscript producers (in the sense that a movie is produced) that we know they were; and it is even harder to begin to imagine collaborative authorship.

The City a Desert

It should be clear by now that the activities already described took place in a field in which religious women were not tightly segregated from religious men or lay society. Following the movement of women through the movement of books, we have glimpsed the variety of communities and relationships that could express an individual's religious identity. "So you would have liked to have entered a religious community," wrote Simone Fidati in his *Regola ovvero dottrina a una sua figliuola spirituale*, addressed to a woman in Rome, "but things did not work out that way, at least not with a habit and entrance into a monastery."[52] Things did not work out that way for many women in the later Middle Ages. Others did not desire a religious vocation until later in life. Moreover, many who elected a religious life did not choose a cloistered or strictly regulated context. Religious culture in Due- and Trecento Italy was deeply marked by what historians today term the "penitential movement," a set of attitudes and a cultural disposition favoring experimentation, dramatic conversions, and quiet ad hoc arrangements.[53] Hermits gathered in the grottos above the hilltown; clusters of recluses settled at the city gates; permanent clerical and clairvoyant guests resided in the affluent household; pilgrims journeyed in search of new beginnings; charismatic itinerant preachers, often recent converts, dramatically disconnected their listeners from material and familial ties.

I would like now to look closely at one work of translation, one closely tied to preaching imperatives, and to explore what might be called its "social history." A translation of "lives and sayings of desert fathers" was executed by Domenico Cavalca together with a team of collaborators at the Dominican monastery of Santa Caterina at Pisa during the early decades of the fourteenth century.[54] These consisted of rather free translations of Latin texts, most of which had been culled in turn from Greek collections memorializing figures associated with eremitic and communal experiments of the third and fourth centuries.[55] The title "Lives of the Holy Fathers" (*Vite dei santi padri*) is rather misleading, for on almost every page we find famous and forgotten holy women: Mary Magdalene, the elder and younger Melania, female hermits, women's communities, converted prostitutes, as well as sisters, sponsors, and clients of the masculine desert "fathers."[56] Cavalca's translation (or better, version) of the *Life* of the Magdalene illustrates well the tone and spirit of the works emanating from Santa Caterina in this period.[57]

Citing Jerome as his source, Cavalca begins his version by informing his audience that the Magdalene had been betrothed to John the Evangelist, who then jilted her on their wedding night in order to withdraw to the desert. Their wedding, he continues, was the very marriage at Cana where Jesus turned the water into wine. The Gospel writers frequently omit details like this, explains the narrator, because, as here, everyone would have known who the bride and groom were. Furthermore "they had too much to write to include everything, so we have to fill in the gaps. In any case," he adds genially, "I like to think this is how it happened." Mary, very much in love with John, was utterly distraught after her abandonment. In dishonor she returned to confinement in her family's house, confused and stunned because "the man to whom she had given all her love had given himself to a love she herself did not yet understand." ("I bring this up," intervenes the narrator, "because worldly people have too much blamed Mary for the bad life she lived for a short time.") Mary Magdalene had "too much spirit" to stay cooped up at home. So she spent her days socializing, in order to ease her desperation and "to keep herself from dying of inner pain." The narrator explains that this is how the Magdalene acquired the reputation as a loose woman and came to be called a prostitute, which is the way people in those old-fashioned times referred to women who were too socially visible. It was rather an undiscriminating way of talking, the narrator admits, "but that's how they were back then. I have often thought that the unrestrained behavior of many women today would make them seem worse than prostitutes to the ancients."

This excerpt, abridged and paraphrased from the *Life of the Magdalene*, illustrates how colloquial Cavalca's work can be, in both its language and its form. Here, more markedly than in almost any other *Life*, his audience is congenially present to him, as he makes himself and his views frankly available to the audience. "Io mi penso, che . . ." begins many a sentence. It is a strategy that imitates and enhances the twice-told quality of his core sources, the anecdotes and pithy aphorisms with which early monks and hermits remembered their heroes and advised their followers. Translation and interpretation are closely intertwined. He makes the adjustments which, in his view, textual lacunae and cultural difference demand. As with the well-known *Le meditazioni sulla Vita di Gesù Cristo*, remembering and imagining flow seamlessly together.[58] Shifting his focus continually from the past to the present, from the indirect discourse of narrative to direct address, Cavalca weaves the storyteller and audience into a single perspective, regarding with edified charity the life of Mary Magdalene.

Along with his literary activities, Cavalca was involved in the life of several women's religious communities. In 1299 he intervened on behalf of the convent of Sant'Anna al Renaio, on the southern outskirts of Pisa, so that it might be released from some of the constraints of strict enclosure. He was also confessor and troubleshooter for a Pisan women's confraternity, the Misericordia. By 1334 this confraternity had assumed a residential character, having settled into houses belonging to a Pisan merchant and adjacent to a chapel dedicated to Santa Viviana. Assisted by Cavalca, the women of the Misericordia merged in 1342 with a group of *convertite*, a term usually rendered "reformed prostitutes," but, as in Cavalca's ancient world, so in his contemporary one many a life situation might reside behind the words *meretrice*, *convertite*, and their synonyms.[59] After uniting, both groups embraced a more formal modus vivendi. The combined community was soon known as the nuns of Santa Marta. Numerous bequests in Cavalca's testament, directed to communities other than Sant'Anna, the Misericordia, and Santa Marta, indicate an extensive network of female clients, friends, and supporters. After Cavalca's death in 1342, religious women maintained a vigorous connection with his literary corpus. The provenances of the most reliable manuscript editions of his works, as with Giordano da Pisa, are communities of nuns and *pinzochere*.[60]

The character of Cavalca's female audience and clientele highlights something very important to our understanding of his audience and vernacular works. The religious women in his immediate circle were not predominantly cloistered nuns, but lay women or uncloistered religious women living privately or communally. Pisa in the late Due- and early Trecento was typical of many Tuscan and Umbrian towns in that it harbored a multitude of persons who sought to conduct a religious life outside traditional institutions: hermits, recluses, reformed prostitutes.[61] The deregulated convent, the woman's confraternity, the merchant's house-made-monastery, these are consistent with the data from archives and saints' *vitae* in a period marked more by conversion than by profession.[61] Moreover, fluidity and malleability were characteristic not only of the religious associations and institutions, but also of the *itinera* of many pursuing a religious vocation. This was particularly true for women. The spiritual itineraries of many Italian saints and beata convey these women in and out of diverse vocations and affiliations: laywoman, recluse, pilgrim, hospital worker, foundress, abbess, oblate, confraternity sister, and so on.[62] For example, as a penitent, the former concubine Margaret of Cortona successively worked as a birthing assistant, founded a hospital, and lived as a recluse in a well-to-do woman's house. Stability of categories was not a strong feature of women's religious life on either the individual or the institutional level. Cavalca's decision to translate stories and letters which reflect the unsettled, pre- or proto-monastic period of the early church was certainly to some extent informed by the extra-institutional character of religious aspiration and activity he observed around him.

In forging a sort of *Winesburg Ohio* set in a Tuscanized Egypt or Palestine, in renewing his Latin texts with downhome interjections and armchair cultural anthropology, Cavalca created not only a literary monument and new syllabus for vernacular readers, but also a refracted image of his own society. The attractive inclusiveness and entertaining eccentricities of the motley population we meet in his "short stories of the desert"[63] would have lent a legendary strength to the institutionally ambiguous position of his spiritual friends and professional charges. In this spirit, an anonymous successor knit together Cavalca's vernacular *vite* and *detti* ("sayings"), making a work meant to serve women living a religious life outside a monastery, dedicating it to Paula and Eustochium, and passing it off as a work of Saint Jerome. Cavalca's work would also have served others, who, like himself, were called on to teach or manage affairs for such precarious enterprises as houses for reformed prostitutes and uncloistered women. His translations offer a kind and venerable mirror to contemporary individual and collective efforts to sustain a monasticism without walls.[64]

However Cavalca's pastoral and literary interests might have intertwined, he gained a wide and varied audience. A widowed mother commissioned an edition of *Vite* "per consolatione dell'anima sua e secondariamente a chonsolazione delle sue figliuole."[65] Among the notations of borrowed wigs, beards, and hats in the record books of confraternities, whose sacristies often functioned as a cross between theatrical warehouses and lending libraries, we can find reminders like the following: "Io antonio di ser Agniolo ebbe in presto il livero di vita patruum començando da Santo Pavolo primo romito."[66] Moreover, the frequency with which Cavalca's translations of desert anecdotes and aphorisms appear in subsequent vernacular works, especially in exchanges between spiritual friends, suggests a complementary oral currency.[67] Even before Cavalca translated the *Vite*, Dominican preachers of the Duecento had been making on-the-spot translations to serve as *exempla* in their sermons.[68] The desert lives were, in fact, recommended reading for preachers in training.[69] In a manner analogous to the use and transmission of *exempla* by preachers, the little stories popularized by Cavalca became a way in which men and women talked to each other about the struggles and goals of spiritual life. Angela of Foligno quotes and paraphrases from the sayings of Evagrius translated in the *Vite dei santi padri*.[70] The telegraphic form and colloquial style of the recently popularized ancient apothegmata also found imitators. For example, an admirer of a *converso* named Fra Silvestro framed his memorial to this saintly laybrother in the form of *detti*, each beginning, "He was accustomed to say . . ."

> The good old ancients gave themselves as breasts, for their contemporaries and for modern people; they have given themselves to be suckled, to be food, to sustain. . . .
>
> If someone wants to take up the religious life, give [the person] help, not advice.[71]

In his *Reggimento e costumi di donna*, the moralizing Francesco Barberino, who gives nothing but advice, writes disapprovingly that female *converse* profer their own *detti*, conducting themselves as "philosophers or teachers."[72] He also observes, with his usual critical spin, that women will believe the words of a female recluse more often than they will believe a master in theology. Nevertheless, collections of *detti* circulated under the names of both Angela of Foligno and Clare of Montefalco. So too, the *vite* and canonization processes of female saints portray their subjects as counselors and conveyors of timely wisdom. Finally, more than a hundred years after Cavalca, the Franciscan charged with spiritual services—including the acquisition of manuscripts, for the newly revived Perugian community of Monteluce—composed for the sisters his own *detti*. Among them we find the following authorization:

> Speak in charity and you will speak theologically. One may understand the Scriptures without *grammatica*, namely by a certain light from God. *Grammatica* is nothing but a language.[73]

The case of Cavalca and his translation enterprise illustrates the interplay between audience and text both before and after the moment of writing. We can see in his translations a mirror of the social and religious situations of an audience and the provision of matter from which its members might gather sources for the construction of their own authority. This kind of interplay also occurs in texts giving evidence of men's use of women's words and stories. For example, women's stories did much to make the reputations of local saints, giving momentum to cult, backbone to canonization process, and, ultimately, more matter for preaching. Women make up significant proportions of the witnesses giving testimony for the canonization processes of Clare of Montefalco, Nicolà of Tolentino, Bernardino of Siena, and Francesca of Rome. When, in composing liturgical offices for the recently canonized Bernardino and the recently translated Saint Monica, the curialist Mafeo Vegio drew primarily from female testimony.[74] Additional evidence of vertical translation from the popular to the official is offered by some preachers, who, mixing contemporary "true stories" with edifying *exempla* taken from long-standing literary authorities, indicate female informants. The *Assempri* of the Sienese Augustinian, Filippo degli Agazzari, are an outstanding example of this practice.

In these oral and written exchanges, reciprocal acts of quotation, we can glimpse the creation of a shared religious culture. With *detti*, as with real life and legendary *exempla*, those who thought in the vernacular as well as those who thought in Latin could, together, *raggionare*, think about religious things—or argue about them. In the 1330s, in a public disputation staged to discredit him, the itinerant Dominican preacher Venturino da Bergamo was presented with the question: Did the evil angel sin in the first instant of his creation? Venturino responded with the following anecdote from the popular *Vitae patrum*. A young monk read in the Epistle to the Hebrews that Melchizedek had no parents. He grew anxious, wanting to know the name of the priest's father, and took his worry to an old monk, who responded, "One does not embrace the religious life to investigate *vana et curiosa* but what is valuable to ourselves and others."[75] Although he appears to have trumped the scholars here, Venturino's predicament and response suggest some of the tensions that fissured religious culture and plagued vernacular efforts, even in these most favorable centuries.

Grammatica Is Nothing but a Language

Several varieties of ambivalence organize the rhetoric of vernacular literature written for women as a genre. The two most sensitive issues were gender and language.[76] Translation of religious writing, early associated with suspect religious groups, had been explicitly associated with women, and the friars' relationship to them, in 1242, when the Dominican General explicitly forbade translation in the context of *cura monialium*.[77] At the beginning of the fourteenth century, a time when Latin loan words were rapidly enriching vulgar usage, the preacher Jacopo Passavanti appears grammatically and intellectually frustrated as he complains about the difficulties of expressing religious ideas in the vernacular.[78] Yet in Latin or in vernacular the preachers themselves show us the female audience and the unnervingly autonomous religious culture they desire to reach. Sermons irritably represent women busily engaged in private devotions performed before images or with rituals of holy water.[79] Giordano da Pisa, only slightly older than Cavalca, mocks crazy men and women who withdraw into cells, seeking the desert, and bemoans the gravity of the offense when artisans and women discuss and interpret scripture—"especially grave when these are women, because women are much farther from the Scripture and the letter than men." Yet at the same time, he urges women to learn to read and acquire "buoni libricciuoli."[80] Giordano, whose imagery is often rigidly hierarchical, borrowing the structures of Pseudo-Dionysius, reserved special outrage for women who preached, even in the city that produced blessed Umiltà and copies of her sermons.[81] Despite the best credentials, Giovanni da Salerno met with objections to the translations he made for the *convertite* of Santa Elisabetta: "There are some people to whom it does not seem a good thing that I have done this, especially at the request of women."[83] Giovanni reminds his detractors of Saint Jerome. He defends himself by saying his translations are really nothing more than written versions of what a preacher or confessor would offer.[83] So the scuffles continued, and so too the production of vernacular works.

At stake in these arguments was not simply the proper role for religious women or lay spiritual circles. The role of the clergy, of confessors, of preachers was equally on the line. Giovanni Bonvisi's statement that "*grammatica* is nothing but a language," leveling the linguistic playing field as it does, would have represented a shocking demotion for scholastically trained Jacopo Passavanti or Giordano da Pisa. The popularity of Saint Jerome in late medieval Italy is symptomatic of the ambivalence aroused by vernacular language usage and the relationships between religious men and women. Jerome the penitent also represents the desire for a shared religious culture[84]: "Helpless, I cast myself at the feet of Jesus, I watered them with my tears, I wiped them with my hair."[85]

The ascendency of Jerome points us immediately to the practice of spiritual direction, which, like preaching, was closely bound up with the production of religious literature in the vernacular. Most authors of devotional literature were also confessors or spiritual mothers, sisters, sons, or fathers. Jerome the penitent, the desert pilgrim, the translator and correspondent was just the kind of authority for a new vernacular age, with its emphasis on preaching, translating, and spiritual direction. He proved especially useful in authorizing literacy and religious relations between men and women. "Translations," he wrote, "must address the whole human race," not a specialized audience.[86] That nonspecialized audience, which confronts any reader of Jerome's translations, but most notably the biblical books, was largely female.

At the beginning of the fourteenth century, the authentic Jerome was known primarily through his prologues to and commentaries on the books of the Bible, the majority of which are addressed to Paula, Eustochium, or both. But to have a true sense of Jerome as fourteenth-century Italy knew, promoted, and imitated him, one must turn to his *doppelganger*, Pseudo-Jerome, and volume 30 of the *Patrologia Latina*. In volume 30 we meet Pseudo-Jerome, pre-Erasmian Jerome, the "chaperone" of apocryphal texts.[87] His work and identity would expand even more when he began to write in vernacular Italian,[88] and his authentic and pseudonymous voices could blend so much more subtly in translation.

Jerome's authentic corpus provided grounds for authorial usurpation. "Of the letters to Paula and Eustochium, the number is infinite: I write them every day."[89] This professed infinity, backed by his Vulgate disclosures, created a literary possibility that medieval writers proved unable to resist. Over time authors with his nom de plume supplied the authoritative account of the Assumption of Mary.[90] One composed, others elaborated an abridged psalter, which from the eleventh century formed the core of many prayer books owned by the laity, especially women.[91] Jerome's real and invented responses to his female correspondents also worked their way into the liturgical setting through the *Martyrologium Hieronymianum* and similar collections, where they provide a conversational frame to feast day readings.[92] As in the thirteenth-century apse mosaic in Santa Maria Maggiore in Rome, these inquisitive groups perch in the cornices of legends and liturgical sources, chatting informatively.

To Jerome's authentic letters reporting the hospitals, hospices, house monasteries, intellectual efforts, and pilgrimages of early Christian Roman women, new letters were slowly added, like the one to Celantia, a busy household administrator. Gathered as they were in medieval manuscripts, these letters functioned as small charters for women for whose diverse endeavors, talents, interests, and religious experiences did not match the limited *ad status* sermon format or formal ecclesiastical legislation. They also authorized, even glamorized, male involvement with and sponsorship of women's religious interests.

> After you gave up all to God,
> Unmarried, married, celibate women
> You illuminated with splendid words.[93]

This verse from a fourteenth-century *laude* would have traveled with the soulful a capella voices of a confraternity through late medieval city streets. Girolamo da Siena (d. 1420), an Augustinian associated with Santo Spirito in Florence, dedicated his work to desert saints, and appealed to his patron, Jerome.[94] Giovanni Dominici (d. 1419) kept in a special register careful copies of his letters to his spiritual mothers and daughters.[95] The reforming Franciscan preacher Bernardino of Siena located the birth of his vocation with an encounter with Jerome's letters, which he turned to after the death of his foster mother, a tertiary dedicated to hospital work.[96] It becomes almost impossible to distinguish between pastoral and literary relationship: the amalgamated Jerome embraces and endorses both.

Much of the Pseudo-Jerome corpus, as with Pseudo-Augustine, consists of compositions written for women and immediately, or eventually, identified with women's religious experience.[97] We see here how audience can create author. The audience was, of course, composite. The parts that interest us here consist of women who want a religious education, of persons who might judge negatively the activity of writing for women, and of men looking for a voice with which to speak of, and to, and even in the register of women's religious experience. Like Cavalca's "Io mi penso, che," which enlarged the imaginative range within which the audience could place the Magdalene and all she might stand for, so Pseudo-Jerome helped enlarge the range of the male voice in religious literature. He also helped religious men forge a vocation that was both pastoral and literary.

Colloquy and Ventriloquy

Much has been written about confession and spiritual direction as an instrument of social and psychological control.[98] If this were the whole story we would not see the kinds of communities or vernacular texts we encounter in the Tre- and Quattrocento. In practice the position of spiritual director was not as simple, limited, or authoritarian as often imagined. Very often confessors were friends or relatives; frequently a woman's spiritual director or confessor would be significantly younger than she; a wealthy woman might be a young cleric's patron and he her protégé. "My mother, I embrace you a hundred thousand million times; may you be ardent. . . . You are to me as Christ in my heart."[99] So wrote Giovanni Colombini in two of his letters to the abbess and sisters of Santa Bonda in Siena. These are important perspectives to keep in mind when we approach vernacular writers for whom spiritual direction supplied both the context and content of their written work.

So it was with the writer to whom I now turn, Simone da Cascina, a Dominican active in the second half of the fourteenth century. Simone lived in the same monastery as Domenico Cavalca, which continued to provide spiritual services to several lay and monastic women's groups. Simone's *Colloquio spirituale* was composed about 1391 for an audience of religious women.[100] Structured as a conversation among four personae, the *Colloquio* presents a written mimesis of the oral setting of spiritual direction and friendship. Each speaker displays a different religious disposition, a different idiom, and thus a different genre of religious expression.[101] The text under discussion in the *Colloquio* is fundamentally an oral and dramatic one: the words and gestures of the mass.

The conversation of Simone's characters dramatizes an ideal of instruction and friendship. The first speaker is Caterina, a religious woman of unspecified status, whose questions prompt the responses of the other three speakers and generate the text. The second speaker is Simone, the author's homonynm, a master in theology, who offers to brighten Caterina's penitential mood with an explanation of the theological symbolism of the liturgical ritual. The third speaker, the Fraticello, is a companion of Simone, perhaps a lay brother or preacher, or both. He displays a zest for complex allegorical schemes, schemes both he and the others refer to as "belle fantazie." The final speaker, the Monachetta, is a passionate mystic. The interaction of these figures is marked by affability and mutual appreciation.

> Good point sister . . . I am glad you added that, maestro. . . . What's on your mind, Fraticello? . . . Thank you Fraticello and I [Caterina] ask that when *belle fantazie* come into your mind that you not remain quiet. . . . Well said.[102]

Moreover, the characters clearly have an impact on each other. At the onset, Caterina's rueful *contemptus mundi* provokes Simone's theological explication of the Mass. This inspires the mystical outpouring of the Monachetta, which near the end brings the Fraticello to a sober, penitential frame of mind and tempers his impulse to construct ever more elaborate cathedrals of symbols.

The expressive foursome offer a conversational gloss on a text, the Mass, which is not primarily a written document, but a performance to which they all have equal access. Each character is involved in a process of responding to the liturgy, of making it his or her own, of elaborating on it in a particular idiom: penitential and meditational, theological, allegorical, mystical. None of these modes of response is autonomous; the characters respond to each other as well as to the Mass.

After Simone explains the meaning of the priest's vestments, he exhorts Caterina to enact her own ritual of vestment as she approaches the altar, mentally and psychologically putting off certain attitudes and putting on others.[103] A theological comprehension of ritual objects and gestures (Simone's expertise) is insufficient—Caterina must invent and enter her own imaginative ritual. Implicit is the expectation that the *Colloquio*'s audience, like the interlocutors, will engage in several levels of translation, appropriating various perspectives, participating in the imaginative processes set out for them, and translating the Mass into the words and images of their own idiom.

As the plot reaches the point of the elevation of the host, the Monachetta bursts out with a vernacular paraphrase of the *Adoro te devote*, demonstrating how well she has understood both the meaning of the mass and the Latin responsory hymn attributed to Thomas Aquinas.[104] The contemplative Monachetta also reproduces at appropriate moments passages from Pseudo-Augustinian texts, which comprised the standard reading for religious women in the late Middle Ages. Thus she introduces her own paraliturgical practices into the liturgical performance. At the point of the Monachetta's most effusive and linguistically inventive outpouring, the Fraticello responds with the awed declaration: "Those are not the words of a woman."[105]

The expectation that an audience would make texts their own, perform their own translations, and become in some sense living media for texts is both implicit and explicit in the *Colloquio*. While Simone encourages acts of translation and personal interpretation during the course of the *Colloquio*—Caterina's appropriation of the priest's vesting rituals, the Fraticello's allegorical excursuses, the Monachetta's vernacular reproductions of hymns and devotional readings—he is seized at the last moment with anxiety for the public life of their collaborative text.

> "Before we part, [he says,] let's first pray to the true Judge of all things that our colloquio doesn't fall into the hands of bad intentioned persons. . . ." The Fraticello responds, "Don't worry, maestro, about whom it reaches. Persons of ill-will are not always believed." "I know," concedes Simone, "But because of their cleverness and dissimulation there is still a danger." "I have good hope for this our colloquio," reassures the Fraticello. "It will defend itself from the misinterpretation and deprecation of charlatans." "So let it be then," concludes Simone.[106]

The *Colloquio* demonstrates, even dramatizes, the importance of the role of an audience in the mind of an author. The inclusion of female voices signals the instrumentality of female religious experience to a work that, in turn will be offered to them. Simone de Cascina has assumed what Michael Baxendall has described as the role of a fifteenth-century religious painter: he has produced the work of a professional visualizer.[107] He executes in a textual medium what the audience practices imaginatively.

More clearly than in most religious writing addressed to women, Simone da Cascina demonstrates how the audience is not an entity that can be placed objectively and discretely outside the text. The female audience is a presence in the mind of the writer. This presence creates a certain kind of imaginative and hence textual possibility, enabling the writer to express thoughts and sentiments that might be deemed inappropriate for another destination. Here Simone da Cascina works through female personae to express the sorrowful emotions of a penitent, curiosity and puzzlement in the face of divine truths, spontaneous prayer, and mystical speech. He effects a kind of ventriloquy, or scribal transvestism. In their letters, other religious writers of the period express emotion, or talk about its importance, and explore the themes of meditation and contemplation more frequently in letters addressed to women than in those to men.[108] For instance, for all his professions that he intends to instruct, the rhetoric of Giovanni Dominici is more expressive than didactic or informative.[109]

Giovanni Boccaccio offers another example of this literary maneuver in *The Elegy of Lady Fiammetta*, in which he makes a feminized audience and a female voice the condition and vehicle of expression. At the start, Fiammetta addresses her audience: "I wish to recount my story to you, noble ladies . . . consider these things . . . and feel them with a woman's heart."[110] The subject is love. The ideal speaker and audience are thus female. Religious experience, like love, is also a gendered experience. "The consolation that I seek is that I may become a true *sister* of Christ," writes

Giovanni Colombini to his sisters in Christ, the religious women of Santa Bonda.[111] Elsewhere he emphasizes his delight at being transformed by love into another.[112] With Simone de Cascina, as with many of the male writers of letters addressed to women, voice and authorial persona appear to be modulated by a gendered "horizon of expectation." A female audience may elicit, permit, even authorize a rhetoric or a range of expressiveness that the writer might otherwise not have attempted. With Simone in his *Colloquio* this rhetoric is imitative, an attempt at literary echoing; it enlarges the readers' affective and intellectual experience of the text, and of the Mass.

By highlighting the oral, social (and sociable) context of the production of texts and translations, I have aimed to show how, if clerics offered women a theological education, women offered men a sentimental education in the widest sense. As Cesare Segre said, vernacularization is a state of mind before it is a language act.[113]

The audience of vernacular texts addressed to women has typically been envisioned as made up of institutionally constrained, rather isolated women with an interior focus. This has reduced the cultural import and influence ascribed to both the texts and the female readers. At stake is not so much the ordering of days and minds of legally dead women. Rather, choices of authority, voice, and genre addressed to religious women are engaged with issues pertaining to the professional identity of religious men as well as women. In the late fifteenth and sixteenth centuries these choices increasingly hinged on ideas about the proper ordering of civic, ducal, and ecclesiastic domains.[114]

Although it is a regular literary practice to doubt the authenticity of texts ascribed to medieval women authors, hypothesizing instead degrees of debt to male scribes, secretaries, and promoters, the same practice has rarely been applied to texts attributed to male authors. Perhaps, with a clearer perception of the dynamism that characterized women's social and religious roles, we can now begin to apply the same critical habits to works that carry the names of men and to their female collaborators.

Notes

1. Carlo Delcorno, "Predicazione volgare e volgarizzamenti," *Mélanges de l'École Française de Rome, Moyen Âge, Temps Modernes* 89 (1977): 679–89, at p. 683; see also pp. 688–89.

2. Hans Robert Jauss, "Theory of Genres and Medieval Literature," in *Towards an Aesthetic of Reception*, trans. Timothy Bahti (Theory and History of Literature 2) (Minneapolis: University of Minnesota Press, 1982), pp. 76–109, esp. 90–95, 99–101.

3. Gianfranco Folena, "'Volgarizzare' e tradurre': Idea e terminologia della traduzione dal Medio Evo italiano e romanzo all'Umanismo europeo," in *La traduzione: Saggi e studi*, ed. Giuseppe G. Petronio (Trieste: LINT, 1973), pp. 57–120; see especially 64ff. Also pertinent is Folena's "Textus testis: caso e necessità nelle origini romanze," in *Concetto, storia, miti e immagini del Medio Evo*, ed. V. Branca (Florence: Sansoni, 1973), pp. 483–507; see p. 507 for the cultural impact of mendicant preaching and translation. More laypersons preached and translated than Folena or Delcorno acknowledge. Thus they give too stark an impression of high/low and clerical/lay segregation.

Cesare Segre has emphasized *volgarizazzione* as a state of mind, one that precedes any act that might be called literary; see his *Lingua, stile e società* (Milan: Feltrinelli, 1974), and *Volgarizzamenti del Due e Trecento* (Turin: Unione tipografico-editrice torinese, 1953).

4. Michel Foucault, "What Is an Author?" in *Rethinking Popular Culture: Contemporary Perspectives in Cultural Studies*, ed. Chandra Mukerji and Michael Schudson (Berkeley: University of California Press, 1991), pp. 446–64; Brian Stock, *The Implications of Literacy: Written Language and Models of Interpretation in the Eleventh and Twelfth Centuries* (Princeton, NJ: Princeton University Press, 1983).

5. Jerome J. McGann, *A Critique of Modern Textual Criticism* (Chicago: University of Chicago Press, 1983). "Authority is a social nexus, not a personal possession; and . . . the initiation [of each new work] takes place in a necessary and integral historical environment of great complexity. Most immediately . . . it takes place within the conventions and enabling limits that are accepted by the prevailing institutions of literary production" (p. 48). In the modern age "literary institutions" include author, editor, publisher, illustrator, printer, distributor. One task of this chapter is to block out and illustrate aspects of the literary institutions shaping vernacular religious texts in late medieval Italy.

6. Foucault, "What Is an Author?" p. 462.

7. Jauss, "Literary History as a Challenge to Literary Theory," in *Towards an Aesthetic of Reception*, p. 19.

8. "The spiritual exchange bank." Giuseppe de Luca, *Scrittori di religione del Trecento: Testi Originali* (Milan and Naples: Riccardo Ricciardi, 1954; Turin: Einaudi, 1977), vol. 2, p. 368.

9. Abundant evidence testifies to the importance of religious literature in the individual and collective life of women in the fourteenth and fifteenth centuries. Susan Groag Bell provides a good orientation to this subject in "Medieval Women Book Owners: Arbiters of Lay Piety and Ambassadors of Culture," in *Sisters and Workers in the Middle Ages*, ed. Judith M. Bennett, Elizabeth A. Clark, Jean F. O'Barr, B. Anne Vilen, and Sarah Westphal-Wihl (Chicago: University of Chicago Press, 1989), pp. 135–61, which originally appeared in *Signs* 7/4 (Summer 1982). For a general catalogue of European didactic literature addressed to women,

see Alice A. Hentsch, *De la littérature didactique du Moyen-Âge s'addressant spécialement aux femmes* (Cahors, 1903; rpt. Geneva: Slatkine, 1975). Ruth Kelso in her *Doctrine for the Lady of the Renaissance* (Urbana: University of Illinois Press, 1956) gives a bibliography of didactic literature and treatises addressed to women, pp. 326–462.

On use of manuscripts in women's religious communities, particularly in a liturgical (or paraliturgical) context, see Jeffrey F. Hamburger, "Art, Enclosure and the *Cura Monialium*: Prolegomena in the Guise of a Postscript," *Gesta* 31/2 (1992): 108–34, especially pp. 118–20, and his voluminous notes. For books of hours one may turn to the recent article by Virginia Reinburg and the bibliographies in *Time Sanctified: The Book of Hours in Medieval Art and Life*, ed. Roger Wieck (New York: George Braziller and the Walters Art Gallery, 1988). For Italy in particular see below nn. 11 and 12. Bibliographic directions to printed editions of works treated in this essay are supplied by F. Zambrini, *Le opere volgari a stampa dei secoli XIII e XIV* (Bologna, 1884; with S. Morpurgo's *Supplemento e indici*, Bologna, 1929).

10. Herbert Grundmann, in his study of twelfth- and thirteenth-century religious movements, was the first to insist that the relationship between religious men and women was crucial to the development of the vernacular prose literature and hence the vernaculars as literary languages. This literary and religious alliance was not, Grundmann notes, a natural outgrowth of the administrative imperatives of new (male) religious orders—on the contrary it ran counter to them—but rather developed from women's relationships with friars. See chapter 8 of the revised edition of Grundmann's *Religiöse Bewegungen im Mittelalter: Untersuchungen über die geschichtlichen Zusammenhänge zwischen der Ketzerei, den Bettelorden und der religiösen Frauenbewegung im 12. und 13. Jahrhundert und über die geschichtlichen Grundlagen der Deutschen Mystik* (Berlin: Everings Historische Studien, Band 268, 1935; rev. ed. Darmstadt: Wissenschaftliche Buchgesellschaft, 1961). I have used the Italian translation by Maria Ausserhofer and Lea Nicolet Santini, *Movimenti religiosi nel Medioevo: Ricerche sui nessi storici tra l'eresia, gli Ordini mendicanti e il movimento religioso femminile nel XII e XIII seiolo e sui presupposti storici della mistica tedesca*, (Bologna: Mulino, 1980). See also Grundmann's "Die frauen und die Literatur im Mittelalter," *Archiv für Kulturgeschichte* 26 (1936): 129–61. Grundmann focused on what he classified as "mystical literature."

11. "An oceanic movement of translation," Giuseppe de Luca, *Letteratura di pietà a Venezia dal '300 al '600*, Saggi di "Lettere italiane" III (Florence: Olschki, 1958), pp. 17–18. Even more valuable are de Luca's four-volume *Scrittori di religione del Trecento: Volgarizzamenti* (Milan and Naples: Riccardo Ricciardi, 1954; Turin: Einaudi, 1977); and his simultaneously published two-volume *Scrittori di religione del Trecento: Testi originali*. See his Introduction in *Testi Originali*, vol. 2, pp. 358–86 (printed identically in *Volgarizzamenti*, vol. 4, pp. 761–90), for a thoughtful overview of vernacular religious literature. His short prefaces to each text selection frequently note female patronage, ownership, and execution and often offer valuable manuscript information as well.

With a catalogue of sixty Italian manuscripts containing translations of an immensely popular set of Pseudo-Augustinian texts, Geneviève Esnos lends weight and specificity to de Luca's assertion of female interest in religious literature in her

"Les traductions médiévales françaises et italiennes des *Soliloques* attribués à Saint Augustine," *Mélanges d'Archéologie et d'Histoire* (École Française de Rome) 79 (1967): 299–370.

12. For literacy see Franco Cardini, "Alfabetismo e cultura scritta nell'éta comunale," in *Alfabetismo é cultura scritta* (Perugia: Università degli studi di Perugia, 1978), pp. 147–86. Women's leadership in religious life is discussed later. There are four recent articles that treat vernacular works addressed to women in the period under consideration here. All the authors focus on didactic works and, with the exception of Gabriella Zarri, tell us more about male attitudes and literary convention than about women or context. The first is a misleadingly entitled article by Anna Benvenuti Papi, "Devozioni private e guide di coscienze femminili nella Firenze del Due-Trecento," *Ricerche Storiche* 16 (1986): 565–601; reprinted as "Padri Spirituali" in her collected essays, *In castro poenitentiae: Santità e Società femminile nell' Italia medievale*, Italia Sacra 45 (Rome: Herder, 1990), pp. 205–46.

Gabriella Zarri lists sixty early printed works addressed to women, in her "La vita religiosa femminile tra devozone e chiostro," in *Le sante vive: Cultura e religiosità femminile nella prima età moderna* (Turin: Rosenberg and Sellier, 1990), pp. 21–50; for further discussion see her "Note su diffusione e circolazione di testi devoti (1520–1550)," in *Libri, idee e sentimenti religiosi nel Cinquecento Italiano*, collected papers from the conference of the same title, 3–5 April 1986, sponsored by Istituto di Studi Rinascimentali (Ferrara: Edizioni Panini, 1987), pp. 131–54. Although principally concerned with early printed books, the notes and observations in Zarri's articles are especially valuable.

Finally, there is Geneviève Hasenohr Esnos's meticulous study of prescriptive rules authored by clerics, "La vie quotidienne de la femme vue par l'église: l'enseignement des 'journées chrétienne' de la fin du moyen âge," in *Frau und Spätmittelalterlicher Altag: Internationaler Kongress Krems an der Donau 2. bis 5. Oktober 1984*, Veröffentlichungen des Instituts für mittelalterliche Realienkunde österreichs 9 (Philosophisch-Historische Klasse Sitzungsberichte, 473) (Vienna: Österreichischen Akademie der Wissenschaften, 1986), pp. 19–102. Likewise, the masculine point of view is the real subject of her bibliographically useful "Modèles de vie féminine dans la littérature morale et religieuse d'Oc," in *La femme dans la vie religieuse du Languedoc (XIIIe–XIVe s.)*, Cahiers de Fanjeaux 23 (Fanjeaux: Privat, 1988), pp. 152–70.

13. For women as the owners and producers of the best editions of works of the most famous preachers and vernacular writers of the Trecento, see Carlo Delcorno, *Giordano da Pisa e l'antica predicazione volgare*, Biblioteca di Lettere italiane, vol. 40 (Florence: Olschki, 1975), pp. 79–80; Giordano da Pisa, *Quaresimale Fiorentino 1305–1306*, ed. Delcorno (Florence: Sansoni, 1974), p. lxxiii n. 5; and Delcorno, Preface to Simone da Cascina, *Colloquio Spirituale*, ed. Fausta Dalla Riva (Biblioteca di Lettere italiane, Studi e Testi 26) (Florence: Olschki, 1982), pp. 11–13.

14. The following anthologies provide useful introductions to female religious writers: *Scrittici mistiche italiane*, ed. G. Pozzi and C. Leonardi (Genoa: Marietti, 1988); *Medieval Women Writers*, ed. Katharina M. Wilson (Athens: University

of Georgia Press, 1984); and *Women Writers of the Renaissance and Reformation*, ed. Katharina M. Wilson (Athens: University of Gerogia Press, 1987).

15. See McGann, *Critique of Modern Textual Criticism*, pp. 51–54, for the idea of "literary institution" as developed for the eighteenth century. I am grateful to Anthony G. Grafton for directing me toward what has proven to be a useful organizing concept.

16. My approach follows that of Natalie Z. Davis, "Printing and the People," in *Society and Culture in Early Modern France* (Stanford, CA: Stanford University Press, 1975). Davis suggests that the "the combined effort of author and reader" in the world of the early printed book can best be understood "first, if we supplement thematic analysis of texts with evidence about audiences that can provide context for the meaning and uses of books; second, if we consider a printed book not merely as a source for ideas and images, but as a carrier of relationships" (p. 192).

17. *Bizoche* or *bisoche* and *pinzochere* are terms for uncloistered religious women; Romana Guarnieri, "Pinzochere," *Dizionario degli Istituzioni di Perfezione* (Rome: Edizione Paolina, 1980), pp. 1721–49.

18. For production and exchange of books at Monteluce, my principal sources are: Ugolino Nicolini, "I minori osservanti di Monteripido e lo 'scritorium' delle clarisse di Monteluce in Perugia nei secoli XV e XVI," *Picenum Seraphicum* 8 (1971): 100–130; *Memoriale di Monteluce: Cronaca del monastero delle clarisse di Perugia dal 1448 al 1838*, ed. Chiara Augusta Laniati, with an introductory essay by Ugolino Nicolini (Assisi: Santa Maria degli Angeli, 1983) (see especially the inventory of books, pp. xxii–xxxvi); and Ignazio Baldelli, "Codici e carte di Monteluce," appendix to "Un Formulario di Cancelleria Francescana tra il XIII e XIV secolo," by Giuseppe de Luca, *Archivio italiano per la storia della pietà* (Rome: Edizioni di Storia e Litteratura, 1951), vol. 1, pp. 387–93.

Baldelli notes evidence for thirteenth- and fourteenth-century manuscript use, p. 387. The extensive documentation provided by Cesare Cenci in his *Documentazione di vita assisiana, 1300–1530*, 3 vols. (Grottaferrata [Rome]: Editiones Collegi S. Bonaventura ad Clara Aquas, 1974–76) offers several examples of friars and members of confraternities assisting in the acquisition of religious manuscripts and images (see n. 67 below). For German friars acting as artistic and literary agents, procuring commissions, see Hamburger, "Art, Enclosure," 120.

19. The scribal activity of Monteluce and Santa Lucia was accompanied by much literary activity, compositions, and translations both by sisters and by Franciscan friars with whom they had close ties. Both produced chronicles of their communities, wrote biographies of notable women within their communities and their order, and composed spiritual writings and poetry. See *Ricordanze del monastero di S. Lucia osc. in Foligno (cronache 1424–1786)*, ed. Angela Emmanuela Scandella, with an appendix on other Umbrian women's communities by Giovanni Boccali (Assisi: Edizioni Porziuncola, 1987), pp. xii–xiii, for collaboration with Monteluce and writings by sisters.

20. For the publishing activities at San Jacopo, which began in 1476, see P. Bologna, "La stamperia fiorentina del monastero di S. Jacopo di Ripoli e le sue

edizione," *Giornale Storico della Letteratura Italiana* 20 (1892): 349–78; 21 (1893): 45–69; E. Nesi, *Il diario della stamperia di Ripoli* (Florence: B. Seeber, 1903); and M. A. Rouse and R. H. Rouse, *Cartolai, Illuminators, and Printers in Fifteenth-Century Italy* (Los Angeles: Department of Special Collections, University of California Research Library 1988), especially pp. 38–60, 72–93.

21. Rouse and Rouse, *Cartolai*, p. 36 (payments to sisters as compositors); p. 38 (acquisition of matrices); pp. 45–47 (marketing); p. 59 (collaboration with illuminators).

22. Serena Spanò Martinelli, "La canonizzazione di Caterina Vegri: Un problema cittadino nella Bologna Seicento," in *Culto dei santi, istituzioni e classi sociali in età preindustrialie*, ed. Sofia Boesch-Gajano and Lucia Sebastiani (L'Aquila and Rome: Japadre, 1984), pp. 719–34, see p. 722 for printing.

See also Spanò Martinelli's "Per uno studio su Caterina da Bologna," *Studi Medievali* ser. 3, 12 (1971): 712–59, especially pp. 756–59; and idem, "La biblioteca del 'Corpus Domini' bolognese: l'inconsueto spaccato di una cultura monastica femminile," *La Bibliofilia* 88 (1986): 1–23.

23. National Library of Vienna, 1923 [Theol. 729]; described by Hermann Julius Hermann in *Die Handschriften und Incunabeln der italienischen Renaissance* 4 vol. (Leipzig: K. W. Hiersemann, 1930–33), pp. 11–17.

24. The Florentine women's community known as Paradiso, a Brigittine foundation, was founded by Niccolaio degli Alberti, friend of the humanist Coluccio Salutati. One of its fifteenth-century members was Suor Orsola, daughter of Feo Belcari, translator of religious texts and author of a vita of Giovanni Colombini (d. 1367). Colombini, the Sienese leader of a religious movement that sent shock waves of dramatic conversions through Tuscany and resulted in a new religious order for men, the Gesuati, left a corpus of passionate letters between spiritual friends. On the Paradiso and manuscripts, see R. Piattoli, "Un capitolo di storia dell'arte libraria ai primi del Quattrocento: Rapporti tra il monastero fiorentino del Paradiso e l'Ordine francescano," *Studi francescani* 29 (1932): 1–21. For the Gesuati as sponsors of religious literature and the monastery of the Paradiso, see Georg Dufner, *Die "Moralia" Gregors des Grossen in ihren italienischen Volgarizzamenti*, Miscellanea Erudita 2 (Padua: Antenore, 1959), pp. 71–72; and Esnos, "Les Traductions." A codex containing one of the best versions of Domenico Cavalca's *Frutti della lingua* belonged to Fra Zanobi, the procurator of the Paradiso, and later to the sisters of the Annunciata, also in Florence (Florence: Biblioteca Centrale Nazionale, *Conventi soppressi* F.3.1372).

25. For San Jacopo's conservation of sermons, see De Luca, *Testi originali*, Preface to Giordano da Pisa. Earlier in the fifteenth century, Sister Angelica of San Jacopo di Ripoli in Florence copied Domenico Cavalca's *Specchio di Croce*, signing off with an echo of Catherine of Siena in her self-reference "indegna serva e schiava di Jesú Christo," see Florence, Biblioteca Riccardiana, cod. 2102, cited in Carlo Delcorno, "Cavalca Domenico," *Dizionario biografico italiano* (Rome: Società Grafica Romana, 1979), pp. 577–86, at p. 584. For the same work copied at Sant'Anna in Foligno, see Rome, Biblioteca Casanatense cod. 404 (fifteenth century), with the annotation: "Questo libro e chiamato lo specchio della croce e delle donne de santa anna de fuligno." On Monteluce's fourteenth-century library, see Baldelli,

"Codici e carte di Monteluce." Studies that complement and expand Baldelli's brief observations about the copying habits at Monteluce, with reference to southern Italian convents, are those of Virginia Brown, "*Flores Psalmorum* and *Orationes Psalmodicae* in Beneventan Script," *Medieval Studies* 51 (1989): 424–66; idem, "The Survival of Beneventan Script: Sixteenth-Century Liturgical Codices from Benedictine Monasteries in Naples," in *Monastica: Scritti raccolti in memoria del XV centenario della nascità di S. Benedetto (480–1980)*, Miscellanea Cassinese 44, vol. 1 (Monte Casino: Pubblicazione Cassinese, 1981), pp. 237–355.

26. Biblioteca Apostolica Vaticana (BAV), Vat. lat. 11315, ff. 95v–101r, "Inventario delli libri che sono dentro il Monastero di Monte lucido di Perugia fatto alle 13 d'Aprile 1600," indicates that Monteluce's library remained well-stocked. Relevant to the discussion below, it is worth noting the early printed editions of Domenico Cavalca's *Pungilingua* and *Specchio della Croce*, a work entitled *Sermoni del b. Ephrem*, pseudonymous and authentic works of Augustine and Jerome, and in *Vite de santi padri descritte da S. Hieronymo et altri Autori* (most likely translated by Cavalca). Similar inventories in BAV, Vat. lat. 11315 for the "monache dette le murate della Città di Castello" (11v–114r), Santa Cecilia in Città di Castello (114r–116r), the "monasterio del paradiso" also of Città di Castello (116r–118r), and San Antonio of Padua in Perugia (101v–103v) indicate shared tastes in other Umbrian women's communities.

In BAV, Vat. lat. 11286, 375r–380v, the list of "libri expurgati" from religious communities in Perugia adds more to our picture of literary strength in Perugian women's communities by showing us what four more of Monteluce's neighbors (all of them initially penitent communities) lost. The lists are unspectacular. Books of unknown authorship and vernacular Scripture or Scripture commentary (even the penitential psalms) were prime targets. The only faintly heretical text shows up in several copies of a Venetian edition of Heinrich Herp's *Specchio di perfezione*, a work written between 1455 and 1460 at the request of a devout widow and confidante, which drew from Margherite Porete's (d. 1310) condemned *Mirror of Simple Souls*. On this work see Romana Guarnieri, *Il movimento del libero spirito: Testi e documenti* (Rome: Edizioni di Storia e Letteratura, 1965), p. 478.

27. Susan Groag Bell made good use of testaments in her "Medieval Women Book Owners." For Beguine testaments in Belgium, see Michel Lauwers and Walter Simons, *Béguines à Tournai au Bas Moyen Âge: Les communautés béguinales à Tournai du XIIIe au XV siècle* (*Torncacum: Études interdisciplinaires relatives au patrimoine culturel tournaisien*, vol. 3) (Tournai: Archives du Chapitre Cathédral and Louvain-la-Neuve: Université Catholique de Louvain, 1988), especially p. 33.

28. For Maria and Jacobella, see Rome, Archivio Generalizio Augustiniana (AGA), C.3 *Pergamena*, nn. 2 and 5; 9.

29. Cesare Cenci, "Il testamento della b. Cecilia Coppoli da Perugia e di Battista (Girolama) di Montefeltro," *Archivum Franciscanum Historicum* 69 (1976): 219–31, especially pp. 225–31. For Battista's life, see A. Fattori, "Battista da Montefeltro," *Picenum Seraphicum* 2 (1916): 225–35, 337–45. For her literary corpus, including letters, *laude* (including one on Saint Jerome), sonnets, and sermons (including one delivered before Pope Martin V), see A. Fattori, "Rime inedite di Battista da Montefeltro," *Picenum Seraphicum* 3 (1917): 337–51; and P. O. Kristeller,

Iter Italicum, I–II (Leiden: Brill, 1965–67), under "Malatesta Battista, Jeronima." Jerome represented for Battista not only a literary and spiritual patron, but also, as we know from her gifts to the Hieronimite community in Pesaro, an institutional client; see Cenci, "Il testamento," p. 222 n. 4. For the literary-monastic milieu in which Battista moved, see A. Fantozzi, "La riforma osservante dei monasteri delle clarisse nell'Italia centrale," *Archivum Franciscanum Historicum* 23 (1930): 361–82, 488–550.

30. Cenci, "Il testamento," p. 223 n. 2; A. Fantozzi, "Documenti intorno alla beata Cecilia Coppoli clarissa (1426–1500)," *AFH* 19 (1926): 212.

31. The communities of Santa Lucia, Monteluce, Sant'Anna, and Corpus Domini shared a number of features in addition to production, collection, and dissemination of texts. Except for Monteluce, which seems to have shifted its status (de facto if not de jure) several times, all had been until the mid-fifteenth century informally organized lay communities. At this point, they allied themselves with the Observant branch of the Franciscan Order and accepted a stricter rule. In the decades before this alliance and throughout the fifteenth century, they attracted a notable number of women from regionally powerful families. For a brief period the interests of the male Observants and the well-educated religious women appear to have harmonized, yielding, among other things, a lively literary culture extending through a network of women's communities. Both the books and the religious ideas of the women of Monteluce traveled as various sisters moved throughout central Italy reforming, reviving, or refounding communities for women. For this reform movement see, most fundamentally, Fantozzi, "La riforma osservante"; idem, "Documenti," 194–225, 334–84; Nicolini, *Memoriale*, pp. xx–xxi; and the essays in *La beata Angelina da Montegiove e il movimento del Terz'Ordine regolare francescano femminile: Atti del convegno di studi Francescani, Foligno, 22–24 settembre 1983*, ed. Raffaele Pazzelli and Mario Sensi (Rome: Analecta Tertii Ordinis Regularis Sancti Francisci, 1984).

32. The account books of Monteluce indicate inexpensive and moderately priced manuscripts.

33. Cenci, *Documentazione di vita assisiana*, vol. 1, p. 145. In addition, Bernardo's testament left money so that the pier next to his burial spot in San Francesco would be painted with a crucifix flanked by Mary, John the Evangelist, Francis, and the Magdalene. Bernardo's daughter Nina was a sister in the community of San Paolo of Assisi.

34. Cenci, *Documentazione de vita assisiana*, vol. 1, p. 591. San Antonio was a group of Franciscan penitents who, unlike the similar communities of Santa Lucia and Sant'Anna, resisted the Observant friars.

35. Gene Brucker, *The Society of Renaissance Florence: A Documentary Study* (New York: Harper and Row, 1971), pp. 211–12.

36. The principal male, vernacular, religious writers of this period include Domenico Cavalca, Giovanni dalle Celle, Gentile da Foligno, Simone Fidati da Cascia, Giovanni da Salerno, Simone da Cascina, Giovanni Colombini, Giovanni Dominici, Girolamo da Siena, Tommaso Caffarini, Pietro Arrivabene, and Girolamo Savonarola. These are the best-known writers and translators of the Tre- and

Quattrocento whose activities, letters, dedications, and manuscript traditions connect them with religious women.

37. Accounts of the history of these interrelated communities are not wholly consistent. For a brief, clear account based on antiquarian sources see the notes of Benvenuti Papi, "Devozioni private," pp. 219–25. Benvenuti Papi also discusses Santa Caterina al Monte alias San Gaggio and its neighboring women's institutions in "Donne religiose nella Firenze del Due-Trecento: Appunti per una ricerca in corso," in *Le mouvement confraternel au moyen âge: France, Italie, Suisse* (Rome: L'École Française de Rome, 1987), pp. 62–68. Mary Germaine McNeil, the only author who tries to reconcile source discrepancies, gives a good account of the foundation of Santa Caterina in her *Simone Fidati and His "De Gestis Domini Salvatoris,"* Ph.D. dissertation, Catholic University of America, Studies in Medieval and Renaissance Latin Language and Literature XXI (Washington, DC: Catholic University of America Press, 1950), pp. 27–29. A fuller but more confusing presentation is proffered by Nicola Mattioli, *Il beato Simone Fidati da Cascia, dell'Ordine Romitano di S. Agostino e suoi scriti editi e inediti . . .*, Antologia Agostiniana, 2 (Rome: Tipografia dei Campidoglio, 1898), p. 1. Mattioli published excerpts from the chronicles of San Gaggio, as did G. Bacchi in "Il Monastero di 'S. Elisabetta delle Convertite," *Bollettino Storico Agostiniano* 7 (1931): 145–47, 234–38; 8 (1932): 150–52, 182–83; and Bacchi, "S. Caterina da Siena e le Agostiniane di S. Gaggio-Firenze," *Bollettino Storico Agostiniano* 3 (1927): 148–49.

38. The works of Simone Fidati and their translations by Giovanni da Salerno are either edited or described in the following studies by Nicola Mattioli: *Il beato Simone Fidati*; id. *Fra Giovanni da Salerno dell'Ordine Romitorio di S. Agostino del secolo XIV e le sue opere volgare inedite . . . con uno studio comparativo di altre attribute al P. Cavalca*, Antologia Agostiniana, 3 (Rome: Scuola Tipografia Salesiana, 1901); *Gli Evangeli del b. Simone da Cascia esposti in volgare dal suo discepolo fra Giovanni da Salerno*, ed. Mattoli, Antologia Agostiniana 4 (Roma: G. d'Antonis, 1902).

39. Arrigo Levasti, ed., *Mistici del Due e del Trecento* (Milan: Rizzoli, 1960); *L'Ordine della Vita Cristiana*, or simply *Vita Cristiana*, is edited on pp. 609–82; a summary of the life and works of Simone occurs at pp. 1004–5.

40. *Convertite* is a term designating penitent women, often those who had lived previously as concubines or prostitutes.

41. David A. Perini, "Scarperia (fr. Domenico de)," in *Bibliographia augustiniana*, 4 vols. (Florence: 1929–38), 2: 170–72.

42. This information is found in the community's late-fourteenth-century chronicle. For nine years before the foundation, Monna Nera, after having entrusted her children to her mother-in-law, had lived a religious life in her own home together with a circle of friends and followers. During this time she maintained a close relationship with the itinerant Simone Fidati. See Mattioli, *Il beato Simone Fidati*, p. 83; and McNeil, *Simone Fidati and "De Gestis,"* pp. 27–29.

43. Ubertino da Casale, *Arbor vitae crucifixe Jesu*, ed. Charles T. Davis (Turin: Bottega d'Erasmo, 1961) at p. 4: "Nam ad provintiam Tusciae veniens sub titulo studii, inveni in multis viris virtutis spiritum Jesu fortiter ebulire. Inter quos

vir Deo plenus Petrus de Senis, pectenarius, et devotissima Cecilia de Florentia, sic me introduxerunt ad arcana Jesu qui stupendum esset si scriberetur perspicitas ipsius eorundem. Nam prefata virgo . . . totum processum superioris contemplationis de vita Jesu et arcana cordis mei et alia multa de parvulo Jesu saepissime me instruxit." The Florentine communities of San Gaggio and Santa Elisabetta were linked, like Ubertino, to the literary and religious culture of the Spiritual Franciscans and the legacy of Angelo Clareno, who was Simone Fidati's teacher and spiritual guide.

44. An anonymous fourteenth-century writer put these words into the mouth of Saint Jerome, under whose name he published a series of *exempla* taken from the *Vite dei santi padri*; quotation is from the prologue of *Il libro dell' Ammonizione di Santo Ieronimo a Santa Paula*. See the similar statement by Giovanni da Salerno, Mattioli, *Fra Giovanni da Salerno*, p. 311: "Et per ciò, suore et figliuole in Christo, la cui charità per vostra pura ed affamata fede mi constrense a trascrivere in vulgare alcune parole di questo tesoro evangelico et christiano." ("And so, sisters and cherished daughters in Christ, love of your pure and intense devotion impels me to translate into vernacular some words from this apostolic and Christian treasure.")

45. Nicole Bériou, "La prédication au béguinage de Paris pendant l'année liturgique 1272–1273," *Recherches Augustiniennes* 13 (1978): 105–229. Bériou shows, through attention to marginal notes in a preacher's manuscript, that Pierre Limoges composed some of his sermons to Beguines on the basis of conversations with the Beguine *magistra*; see pp. 121–22, 194.

46. Filippo degli Agazzari, *Gli Assempri*, ed. Piero Misciattelli, 2d ed. (Siena: Edizioni Cantagalli, 1972), p. 80 for the venerable ladies. Confession was a rich source of exemplary tales for the preacher Filippo, who collected them firsthand or through the medium of colleagues who also heard confessions. Filippo (c. 1339 to c. 1422) was a friar at Lecetto, a hermitage linked closely to the efforts and promotion of Catherine of Siena, before he became prior of San Agostino in Siena. The manuscript preface to his *Assempri* gives a composition date of 1397.

47. Fran W. Kent, "A Proposal by Savonarola for the Self-Reform of Florentine Women (March 1496)," *Memorie Domenicane*, n.s. 14 (1983): 335–41.

48. *Le lettere di Girolamo Savonarola, ora per la prima volta raccolte e a miglior lezione ridotte*, ed. Roberto Ridolfi (Florence: Olschki, 1933). See especially pp. 31–38 for Savonarola's response to the "admonizione" of the prioress of San Domenico in Pisa, dated Florence, 10 September 1493.

49. Delcorno, *Giordano da Pisa*, pp. 79–81. Rubrics accompanying Giordano's sermons contextualize the delivery or note Giordano's other activities of the day: "Sunday morning at the *donne convertite*, in the garden"; "to the women of San Domenico in Cafaggio"; "to the women at San Gaggio"; and with the date March 13, 1305, "dopo mangiare, al le donne da Ripole, [predicato] in platea." As for the material support of preachers by women, we know that in her testament of 1301, Betecca, widow of Enrico Villani, left Giordano da Pisa 100 soldi; see Delcorno, *Giordano da Pisa*, p. 104 n. 3. See later for bequests to the preacher and translator Domenico Cavalca n. 54.

50. Delcorno, *Giordano da Pisa*, pp. 79–80. With regard to the rubrics, Delcorno points out that the Italian *a* can mean either "to" or "at." For him the rubric "al le donne da Ripole" indicates simply that the sermons were given geographically *near* that community, not *to* the women. Two sermons delivered in women's religious houses are published by de Luca, *Testi Originali*, vol. 1, pp. 5–13; a third at Santa Maria Novella, the devotional center for *larvae* of male and female penitents who had colonized the surrounding neighborhood, a fourth to the confraternity of Orsanmichele, one of whose responsibilities was the legal representation of convertite communities. De Luca, observing the same marginal notes and rubrics as Delcorno, concludes that the women's communities provided the setting and auditors.

As for women making copies of sermons, see Delcorno, "Cavalca Domenico," pp. 577–86, at p. 584.

For Bonaventura's sermons for the sisters of Santa Chiara, see G. Cantini, "S. Bonaventura da Bagnorea 'Magnus Verbi Dei Sator,'" *Antonianum* 15 (1940): 69. Another indication of textual exchange between the recluses of San Damiano, the Franciscan Order, and ultimately wider religious culture is the fact that Clare's breviary appears to have provided a model for liturgical practice at the Roman curia. See Augustine Cholat, *Le Bréviaire de saint Claire conservé au Couvent de Saint-Damien à Assisi et son importance liturgique* (Opuscules de Critique Historique, fasc. VIII) (Paris: Fischbacher, 1904), pp. 34–49; and Michel Andrieu, "L'Ordinaire de la chapelle papale et le Cardinal Jacques Gaétani Stefaneschi," *Ephemerides Liturgicae* 1/4 (1935): 230–60.

51. Delcorno, "Predicazione volgare e volgarizzamenti," p. 684.

52. *Regola ovvero dottrina a una sua figliuola spirituale*, as found in BAV, *Reginensis* 1744, ff. 1r–79r; see Mattioli, *Il beato Simone Fidati da Cascia*, pp. 226–42, at pp. 230–31.

53. Italian scholars, whatever their regional focus, use one word most frequently to describe the effects and concrete manifestations of the penitential movement among the laity in the late Middle Ages; that word is "vast." Vast, too, is the scholarly literature on the categories of religious behavior associated with the penitential sensibility (reclusion, pilgrimage, confraternities, penitent communities, hospital foundations, and so on). Giovanna Casagrande has written a very useful review article, which serves as a guide to recent research: "Il movimento penitenziale nei secoli del basso medioevo: Note su alcuni recenti contributi," *Benedictina* 30 (1983): 217–33. Pertinent here too is her "Forme di vita religiosa femminile nell'area di Città di Castello nel sec. III," in *Il movimento religioso femminile in Umbria nei secoli XIII–XIV: Atti del convegno internazionale di studio: Città di Castello 27-28-29 ottobre 1982*, ed. Roberto Rusconi (Perugia: Regione dell'Umbria; Florence: La Nuova Italia, 1984), pp. 125–57. See also Anna Benvenuti Papi, "Penitenza e penitenti in Toscana: Stato della Questione e Prospettive della Ricerca," in *Ricerche di Storia Sociale e Religiosa* 17–18 (Rome: Edizioni di Storia e Letteratura and Editrice Ferraro, 1980), pp. 107–21; and idem "Donne religiose," pp. 41–82. At p. 112 n. 23 of "Penitenza e penitenti," Benvenuti Papi lists forty-four Florentine penitential women's communities, "corpuscoli semimonastici," for which the ear-

liest surviving documentation falls between the thirteenth or early fourteenth centuries.

54. The popularity of Cavalca was enormous, accelerating through the fourteenth century and reaching its peak in the fifteenth. Over 500 manuscripts containing one or more of his original or translated works survive; over two hundred of these contain significant clusters of his *Vite dei santi padri*. The best edition of the *Vite* and the one used here is that edited by Bartolomeo Sorio with A. Racheli (Trieste: Lloyd Austriaco, 1858).

Fundamental for the life and work of Cavalca is Delcorno's richly informative "Cavalca Domenico," pp. 577–86. For a descriptive census of Florentine manuscripts containing the *Vite* see idem, "Per l'edizione delle *Vite dei santi padri* del Cavalca: La tradizione manoscritta: i codici delle biblioteche fiorentine," *Lettere Italiane* 29 (1977): 265–89, and 30 (1978): 47–87. Although his principal interest is to note the influence of Guillaume Peyraut's (d. c. 1271) *Summa de vitiis et virtutibus* on Cavalca's *Frutti della lingua*, Renzo Lotti provides a useful summary of the state of Cavalca research in his "Sui *Frutti della lingua* del Cavalca," *La Columberia* 51, n.s. 37 (1986): 109–209, at pp. 110–21. Lotti's chronology of Cavalca's work, however, is less complete than Delcorno's in "Cavalca Domenico," at p. 578.

Cavalca's other translations include the *Dialogo* of Saint Gregory (c. 1329), Letter 22 of Saint Jerome (addressed to Eustochium), and the *Atti degli apostoli*. After completing his translations, Cavalca seems to have turned to compilations or treatises which drew heavily from his earlier translations together with translated passages from other popular Latin texts. In probable chronological order, these include: *Specchio di Croce* (in over 100 surviving manuscripts, his most original and popular composition); *Medicina del cuore ovvero trattato della Pazienza*; *Specchio dei peccati* (1333); *Pungilingua*; *Frutti della lingua*; *Disciplina degli spirituali*; *Trattato delle trenta stoltzie*; *Esposizione del Simbolo degli Apostoli*. Delcorno credits Cavalca with about 50 verse compositions which accompany his prose works; despite the density of *vite* and *detti* in the *Epistola di san Girolamo ad Eustochio* (or *Libro dell Ammonizione*), a work that was quickly attributed to Cavalca, Delcorno remains unpersuaded. See Delcorno, "Cavalca Domenico," p. 578.

55. On the sources of *Vite dei santi padri*, which include Jerome, Athanasius, Timothy of Alexandria as translated by Rufinus, Palladius, Evagius Ponticus, Pope Pelagius's collection of *Verba Seniorum*, Sulpicius Severus, Cassian, and James of Voragine, see Delcorno, "Cavalca Domenico," p. 580. Or, for more detail, Guy Philippart, "Vitae Patrum: Trois travaux récents sur d'anciennes traductions latines," *Analecta Bollandiana* 92, fasc. 3–4 (1974): 353–65.

56. Cavalca concentrates on the accounts of the most famous desert mothers in his fourth and last section, assisting those later copyists and commissioners who wanted only female saints; for example, Rome, Biblioteca Nazionale Centrale, Fondo San Pantaleo, 29 (dated July 2, 1455).

57. Cavalca's version of the Magdalen's life is one of his longest *Vite* and is found in *Vite dei santi padri*, ed. B. Sorio, pp. 329–86. I paraphrase from pp. 329–30. A comparison with James of Voragine's version in the *Golden Legend*, an utterly different reading, reveals Cavalca's charitable ease with both textual and social deviance.

58. *Le meditazioni sulla Vita di Gesù Cristo*, dated to the early fourteenth century and attributed to Giovanni de Caulibus, is a devotional work addressed to a woman associated with a Franciscan milieu in Umbria or Tuscany. See Isa Ragusa and R. B. Green, *Meditations on the Life of Christ: An Illustrated Manuscript of the Fourteenth Century (Bibliothèque Nationale, Paris, Ms. Ital. 115)*, trans. I. Ragusa (Princeton, NJ: Princeton University Press, 1961).

59. For convertite, especially in Florence, of a later period, see Sherrill Cohen, "Asylums for Women in Counter-Reformation Italy," in *Women in Reformation and Counter-Reformation Europe: Public and Private Worlds*, ed. Sherrin Marshall (Bloomington and Indianapolis: Indiana University Press, 1989), pp. 166–88; Sherrill Cohen, *The Evolution of Women's Asylums Since 1500* (New York: Oxford University Press, 1992). For Milan, see Ruth Liebowitz, "Prison, Workshop and Convent: A House of Convertite in Counter-Reformation Milan," paper presented at the Sixth Berkshire Conference on the History of Women, Northampton, Massachusetts, 1 June 1984. Studying the depositions of 142 women interviewed by Carlo Borromeo's vicar in a 1579 apostolic visit conducted at Santa Valeria in Milan, Liebowitz notes the compulsory and degrading quality of sixteenth-century policies toward *convertite*, which left the women without freedom and without social or spiritual status.

For an attempt at functional specialization, see Richard Trexler, "A Widow's Asylum of the Renaissance: The Orbatello of Florence," in *Old Age in Preindustrial Society*, ed. Peter N. Sterns (New York: Holmes and Meir, 1983), pp. 119–49. For convertite and Rome, see Pamela Askew's very thoughtful chapter, "The Casa Pia: The Magdalen," in her *Caravaggio's Death of the Virgin* (Princeton, NJ: Princeton University Press, 1990), pp. 84–107. For institutions for girls at risk in early modern Rome, see Maria Elena Vasaio, "Il tessuto della virtù: Le zitelle di S. Eufemia e di S. Caterina dei Funari nella Controriforma," *Memoria* 11–12 (1984): 53–64.

60. For Cavalca's testament and the disputed date of death, see Delcorno, "Cavalca Domenico," p. 579. The previously cited inventories of Monteluce, Santa Lucia, Sant'Anna, and Corpus Domini all testify to the popularity of Cavalca in women's communities, especially his *Vite* and his *Specchio di croce*. See also the Roman manuscript *Casanatense* 404 (fifteenth century): "Questo libro e chiamato lo specchio della croce e delle donne de santa anna de fuligno."

61. Delcorno's article "Per l'edizione delle *Vite dei santi padri* " offers a detailed census of Florentine manuscripts containing the *Vite*. From this list a number of fifteenth-century manuscripts can be securely connected to female use; as numbered by Delcorno they are #7, *Redi* 157 #16, Florence, Biblioteca Nazionale Centrale, II i 115 (*Magl.* XXXVIII, 2), "questo libro è delle monache di sancta Marta a montughi"; #18 Florence, BNC, III iii 89 (Magl. XXI, 123), "Questo libro à fatto scrivere mona ghostantia donna fu dj benedetto cicciaporci el quale libro à ffatto fare per consolatione dell'anima sua e secondariamente a chonsolazione delle sue figliuole " (subsequently owned by Constantia's daughters); #29, Florence BNC (*Magl.* XXXV, 217) bequeathed to the sisters of San Miniato ad Monte (Benedictine) by Monna Lionardo, who retained the use of it for her lifetime. To these we can probably add Rome, Biblioteca Nazionale Centrale, *San Pantaleo* 29,

dated July 2, 1455, which contains lives of holy women only. Even more examples are provided by Delcorno in "Cavalca Domenico." To these we may add the manuscript cited in Mattioli, *Fra Giovanni da Salerno*, p. 212, texts: "Iste liber est sororis Antonie filie olim domini Donati de Acciaolis Monialis istius monasterii sancti petri majoris de florentia."

The fifteenth-century Augustinian tertiary of Udine, Helen Valenti (d. 1458), was praised in a funeral oration by the Augustinian theologian Simon of Rome for always carrying with her a copy of Cavalca's *Specchio di croce*. For the oration, see BAV, Rossiano 48, ff. 1a–26r; quoted by David Gutierrez, *The Augustinians in the Middle Ages, 1357–1517* (Villanova, PA: Augustinian Historical Institute, Villanova University, 1983), p. 215.

62. For experimentation and improvisation in response to a desire to live a religious life in Tre- and Quattrocento Umbria and Tuscany, see Mauro Ronzani, "Gli ordini mendicanti e le istituzioni ecclesiastiche presenti a Pisa nel Duecento," *Mélanges de l'École Française de Rome: Moyen Âge, Temps Modernes* 89, 2 (1977): 667–77; idem, "Penitenti e ordini mendicanti a Pisa sino all' inizio del Trecento," *Mélanges de l'École Française de Rome: Moyen Âge Temps Modernes* 89, 2 (1977): 733–41. See also Anna Benvenuti Papi, "Fonti per la storia dei penitenti a Firenze nel XIII secolo," in *L'ordine della penitenza di San Francesco, d'Assisi nel secolo XIII: Atti del convegno di studi francescani*, ed. O. Schmucki (Rome: Istituto Storico dei Capuccini, 1973), pp. 279–301; idem, "I frati della penitenza nella società fiorentina del Due-Trecento," in *I frati penitenti di San Francesco nella società del Due-Trecento: Atti del secondo convegno di studi francescani: Roma, 12–14 ottobre 1976*, ed. Mariano D'Alatri (Rome: Analecta T.O.R., 1977), pp. 191–200; idem "Frati mendicanti e pinzochere in Toscana: dalla marginalità sociale al modello di santità," in *Temi e problemi della mistica femminile trecentesca: Atti del XX convegno storico internazionale del Centro di Studi sulla spiritualità medievale: Todi, ottobre 14–17 1979* (Rimini: Maggioli, 1983), pp. 107–35; and, "Le forme comunitarie della penitenza femminile francescana: Schede per un censimento toscano," in *Prime manefestazioni di vita comunitaria maschile e femminile nel movimento francescano della penitenza (1215–1447): Atti del convegno di studi francescani: Assisi, 30 giugno–2 lùglio 1981*, ed. Raffaele Pazzelli and Lino Temperini (Rome: Commissione Storica Internazionale T.O.R., 1982), pp. 389–450. Additional bibliography can be found in n. 54 above.

63. Anna Benvenuti Papi presents the variety of religious forms of life in the late medieval period as confused and yielding "anarchy"; see n. 61 above and her essays in *"In castro poenitentiae": Santità e società femminile nell'Italia medievale*. I am more in sympathy with the assessment of Giovanna Casagrande, who views this as a period of energy, institutional creativity, and conscientious lay leadership; see especially her Introduction to *Chiese e conventi degli Ordini Mendicanti in Umbria nei secoli XIII e XIV: Inventario delle fonti archivistiche e catalogo delle informazioni documentarie: Gli archivi ecclesiastici di Città di Castello*, ed. Giovanna Casagrande (Archivi dell'Umbria: Inventari e Ricerche, no. 12) (Perugia: Regione dell'Umbria and Editrice Umbra Cooperativa, 1987). Here, on pp. xxvii–xxviii, in contrast with Benventuti Papi, Casagrande characterizes the collective experiments of late medieval Italy as continuous and dynamic "una situazione incostante movimento." See also Casagrande's "Forme di vita religiosa," where, in contrast to

Benvenuti Papi, she concludes that through lay communities women found more room to maneuver: "un loro spazio e margini di autonomia" (p. 157).

64. Delcorno, "Cavalca Domenico," p. 580: "Lo stile del Cavalca coglie adeguatamente la dolcezza fiabesca che emana da queste 'short stories' del deserto."

65. As the vita of a Marie d'Oignies or an Umiliana da Cerchi might serve as a model and substitute as a rule for religious women living outside a traditional institution, so Cavalca's translation could also function as both apology and model for extramural monasticism. His work, however, seems to me to stand in contrast to the hagiographies of holy women which "clericalized" women's religiosity with their focus on asceticism, the eucharist, and obedience. For a discussion of male-authored hagiography as an effort to control through models see, among others, André Vauchez, *La sainteté en occident aux derniers siècles du moyen âge, d'après les procès de canonisation et les documents hagiographiques* (Rome: École Française de Rome; Paris: Diffusion de Boccard, 1981), pp. 435–49, 472–79; and Anna Benvenuti Papi, "Umiliana dei Cerchi: Nascita di un culto nella Firenze del Dugento," *Studi Francescani* 77 (1980): 87–117. A more subtle reading of clerical authors and their female subjects is offered by John Coakley in, among other articles, his "Friars as Confidants of Holy Women in Medieval Dominican Hagiography," in *Images of Sainthood in Medieval Europe*, ed. Renate Blumenfeld-Kosinski and Timea Szell (Ithaca, NY: Cornell University Press, 1991), pp. 222–46; and Coakley, "Gender and the Authority of Friars: The Significance of Holy Women for Thirteenth-Century Franciscans and Dominicans," *Church History* 60 (1991): 445–60.

66. Delcorno, "Per l'edizione," manuscript #18.

67. "For the strengthening of her soul and, secondarily the spiritual fortification and comfort of her daughters (by blood or affection)." R. Guèze, "Confraternite di S. Agostino, S. Francesco e San Domenico," in *Il movimento dei disciplinati nel VII centenario dal suo initio (Perugia–1260), Convegno internazionale: Perugia, 25–28 settembre 1960, Bollettino della Deputazione di Storia Patria per l'Umbria, Appendice 9* (1962), pp. 597–623, at p. 621. The intense interest of Italian confraternities in vernacular translations is seconded by Esnos, "Les traductions."

68. BAV, Vat. lat. 11259 contains a collection of 18 letters of spiritual encouragement (16 addressed to women) dating from the first half of the fifteenth century. These are laden with quotations from Cavalca. On this collection see the excellent study by Geneviève Hasenohr Esnos, "Un recueil inédit de lettres de direction spirituelle du XVe siècle: le manuscrit Vat. lat. 11259 de la Bibliothèque Vaticane," *Mélanges d'Archéologie et d'Histoire* (École Française de Rome) 82 (1970): 401–500.

69. Delcorno, *Giordano da Pisa*, pp. 241–88, where the author gives a list of seventy *exempla* extracted from Giordano's sermons, a notable number of which derive from the *Vitae patrum*. Other examples of the use of the *Vitae* can be found in the sermons published by Carla Casagrande, *Predice alle donne del secolo XIII: Testi di Umberto da Romans, Gilberto da Tournai, Stefano di Borbone* (Milan: Bompiani, 1978). Raymond Creytens, "L'instruction des novices dominicains au XIII siècle," *Archivum Fratrum Praedicatorum* 20 (1950): 149 n. 110.

70. Sergio Andreoli, "Gli esempi della B. Angela nel Memoriale di fr. Arnaldo," *L'Italia Francescana* 58 (1983): 435–52.

71. De Luca, *Volgarizzamenti*, 3: 528. "Diceva: I buoni antichi deono essere poppe degli altri e de' novelli; deonli lattare e nutrire, e sostenerli con benignità e dolcezza." . . . "Diceva: Quando uno si vuol far frate, dàgli aiuto, e non consiglio." Another example is Fra Silvestro, who worked in the kitchen of a monastery: "Noi siamo dentro come la cipolla, che levato l'uno scolio, si trova l'altro" (ibid.). *Scolio* (or *spolia*) can have here the sense of either earthly husk or protective and resistant armor.

72. Francesco da Barberino, *Reggimento e costumi di donna*, ed. G. Sansone (Torino: 1957), Loescher-Chiantore 202 (work completed 1318–20). See also the passage from Ubertino da Casale's *Arbor vitae crucifixe Jesu*, cited in n. 43 above. For holy women as advisors: Benvenuti Papi, "Umiliana dei Cerchi," idem, "Margarita filia Jerusalem: Santa Margherita da Cortona ed il superamento mistico della crociata," in *Toscana e Terrasanta nel Medioevo*, ed. F. Cardini (Florence: Sanson 1982), pp. 117–38; idem, "Velut in sepulchro: Cellane e recluse nella tradizione agiografica italiana," in *Culto dei santi, istituzioni e classi sociali in età preindustriale*, pp. 414–27.

73. "Parla per carità e parlerai per teologia. Sensa grammatica se intende la Scriptura, cioè per uno certo lume di Dio. La grammatica non è altro se no uno lenguaggio." See Nicolini, "I minori osservanti di Monteripido," p. 122, where he publishes "The sayings of beato Giovanni Bonvisi da Lucca."

74. Paris, Bibliothèque Nationale, Latin 3341, ff. 229r–235r (St. Monica), ff. 240r–247r (St. Nicolà of Tolentino), and ff. 277r–293r (St. Bernardino); BAV, Vat, lat. 2110, ff. 124–28 (St. Bernardino); BAV, Ottoboniano lat. 903, ff. 19–33 (St. Bernardino); BAV, Ottoboniano lat. 1253, ff. 71–119 (St. Monica and St. Nicolà of Tolentino); and BAV, Urb. lat. 59, ff. 307–14 (St. Monica).

75. Clara Gennaro, "Venturino da Bergamo e la peregrinatio romana del 1335," in *Studi sul Medioevo Cristiano offerti a Raffaele Morghen* (Rome: Istituto Storico Italiano per il Medioevo, 1974), pp. 376–406, at pp. 400–401.

76. Vittorio Coletti, *Parole dal pulpito: Chiesa e movimento religiosi tra latino e volgare nell'Italia del Medioevo e del Rinascimento* (Casale Monferrato: Marietti, 1983), see especially pp. 73–80, where the author provides a multitude of quotations demonstrating anxieties of preachers and translators about the dangers of giving (or even attempting to give) vernacular speakers an expanded vocabulary for religious thought and formulations.

77. Grundmann, pp. 407–8.

78. Delcorno, "Predicazione volgare e volgarizzamenti."

79. For example, the *ad status* model of Humbert of Romans: *Predice alle donne del secolo XIII: Testi di Umberto da Romans, Gilberto da Tournai, Stefano di Borbone*, ed. Carla Casagrande (Milan: Bompiani, 1978), p. 53. For similar annoyed observations by Giordano of Pisa regarding womens' disinterest in preachers, see Delcorno, *Giordano da Pisa*, p. 52.

80. See Delcorno, *Giordano da Pisa*, pp. 49–51, 224, for institutionally indifferent or hostile religious groups who have created their own religious subculture. For women as mediators and readers of Scripture, see pp. 51, 70.

81. See Giordano's sermon in Orsanmichele, the home of the confraternity

that supported female penitent communities throughout the fourteenth and fifteenth centuries (11 April 1305): "E però non si dee fare ogni uomo predicatore; a chi predica, e no gli è commesso, e non essendo da ciò, pecca gravemente. Non è commesso ad ogni uomo l'ufficio del predicare; ché innanzi innanzi, a tutte le femine è vietato in tutto e per tutto." De Luca, *Testi originali*, vol. 1, p. 23.

82. "Sono alcune persone a le quali forse che non pare ben fatto ch'io abbia facto questo spetialmente a pettitione di femine. Alle quali (persone) si potrebbe rispondere per molti modi chi volesse disputatre, contendere et litigare. Ma queste cotali persone non pare che sappiano o vero non pensano che in alcune contrade è volgarizzata tutta la Bibbia et molti libri di sancti et di dottori. Et sancto Jeromimo molte scripture translatò da una lengua ad un altra per consolatione di alcune sue figliuole. Et Christo nostro salvatore, non credo che abbia meno caro le femine che gli uomini, e credo che saranno salve tante femine quanti huomini, et quanto la persona è piu ignorante et fragile, tanto con maggiore compassione dee essere aiutata se desidera l'aiutorio et vuollo." Mattioli, *Fra Giovanni da Salerno*, p. 309.

83. Giovanni argues that if Simone Fidati, who prepared Latin versions of what Giovanni translated, were still alive he would be doing in person what Giovanni does in writing. Giovanni avers that he is not a good preacher, so he must replace the oral translation of preaching, with the written *volgarizzamento*. See Mattioli, *Fra Giovanni da Salerno*, pp. 304–12.

84. For the following section I am especially indebted to Daniel Russo's *Saint Jerome en Italie: étude d'iconographie et de spiritualité XIII–XVI siècles* (Rome and Paris: École Française de Rome, 1987); additionally, Eugene F. Rice, Jr., *Saint Jerome in the Renaissance* (Baltimore: Johns Hopkins University Press, 1985). The increased interest in Jerome in Italy radiated out from the Dominican *studia*, and takes us back again to Cavalca. For Russo's discussion of this "rediscovery" as a competitive response to Franciscan preaching and information relevant to Cavalca, see *Saint Jerome en Italie*, pp. 42–50.

85. Jerome, Epistle 22, 7, *The Principal Works of St. Jerome*, trans. W. H. Fremantle, with G. Lewis and W. G. Martley, in the Select Library of Nicene and Post-Nicene Fathers of the Christian Church, 2d series, vol. 6: *St. Jerome: Letters and Select Works* (Grand Rapids, MI: William B. Eerdmans, 1989, rpt. from 1892 ed.).

86. Jerome, Epistle 48, 4.

87. The epithet "chaparon d'apocryphes" comes from Pierre Salmon, *Analecta Liturgica: Extraits des manuscrits liturgiques de la bibliothèque Vaticane, contribution à l'histoire de la prière chrétienne* (Vaticano City: Biblioteca Vaticana, 1974), p. 81; for Jerome and the abridged psalter, see pp. 76–82.

On the related career of Pseudo-Augustine see, in addition to Esnos, "Les traductions," André Wilmart's fundamental "Les méditations sur le Saint-Esprit attribuées à saint Augustin," in *Auteurs spirituels et textes dévots du Moyen Âge Latin: études d'histoire littéraire* (Paris: Bloud et Gay, 1932), pp. 415–56.

For more evidence of the frequency with which popular religious texts originate in a female religious context, see D. M. Shepard, "Conventual Use of St. Anselm's Prayers and Meditation," *Rutgers Art Review* 9–10 (1988–89): 1–15; see also n. 97 herein.

88. For example, see the immensely popular *Ammonizione* addressed to Eustochium (and sometimes Paula, too), which proffered a series of masculine desert models taken from Cavalca's *Vite*.

89. So recorded Jerome, when he set about cataloging his own literary corpus in *De viribus illustris*; see *Principal Works*, p. xxviii.

90. B. Capelle, "La Fête de l'Assomption dans l'histoire liturgique," *Ephemerides Theologicae Lovanienses* 3 (1926): 33–45; and A. Ripberger, *Der Pseudo-Hieronymus-Brief IX "Cogitus me": Ein erster marianischer Traktat des Mittelalters von Paschasius Radbert* (Fribourg: Éditions Universitaires Fribourg, 1962); A. Ripberger, ed., *De assumptione Santae Mariae Virginis*, Corpus Christianorum. Continuatio Mediaevalis, 56C (Turnholt: Brepols, 1985).

91. See Salmon, *Analecta Liturgica*, for the abridged psalter attributed to Saint Jerome, pp. 76–82. The earliest Vatican manuscript dates from the eleventh century. The abridged psalter, with the incipit *Verba mea auribus*, was initially faithful to biblical text in its selections; increasing liberties were taken with the texts of later manuscripts.

Like Jerome, Augustine had a powerful pseudonymous presence in the medieval literary imagination, shaped largely by texts addressed to women.

92. "Martyrologium Hieronymianum," ed. Henri Quentin and Hippolyte Delehaye in *Acta sanctorum*, Novembris II.ii (Brussels, 1931).

93. A pocket-sized scroll, a long strip of parchment now in the Newberry Library, displays the verses of a fourteenth-century *laude*, one of which reads:

Poscia el tuo tucto a dio donasti
Vergini, coniugate et continente
Con splendida doctrina illuminasti.

(Chicago: Newberry Library, Ms. 122, dated 1350–1400). My thanks to Paul Gehl for calling my attention to this new acquisition.

94. Petrus Brocardo, *Gerolamo da Siena O.S.A. (1335–1420): la vita–le opere–la dottrina spirituale*, partial publication of dissertation, Theological Faculty of the Gregorian University in Rome (Turin: Pontificia Universitas Gregoriana, 1952).

95. Giovanni Dominici, *Lettere spirituali*, ed. M. T. Casella and G. Pozzi, Spicilegium Friburgense 13 (Fribourg: Éditions Universitaires Fribourg, 1969).

96. Maria Ludovica Lenzi, *Donne e madonne: L'educazione femminile nel primo Rinascimento italiano* (Turin: Loescher Editore, 1982), p. 165.

97. On Pseudo-Augustine, see Wilmart, "Les méditations sur le Saint-Esprit"; idem, "Deux préfaces spirituelles de Jean de Fécamp," *Revue d'Ascétique* (1937): 3–44, 394–403; and J. Leclercq and Jean Paul Bonne, *Jean de Fécamp* (Paris: J. Vrin, 1946).

98. For examples and additional bibliography, see Roberto Rusconi, "De la prédication à la confession: transmission et contrôle de modèles de comportement au XIIIe siècle," in *Faire croire: modalités de la diffusion et de la réception des messages religieux de XIIe au XVe siècle* (Rome: École Française de Rome, 1981), pp. 67–85; Lester K. Little, "Les Techniques de la confession et al confession comme technique," in *Faire croire*, pp. 87–99; Benvenuti Papi, "Umiliana dei Cerchi"; and, at great length, Jean Delumeau, *Sin and Fear: The Emergence of a Western Guilt Culture, 13th–18th Centuries*, trans. Eric Nicholson (New York: St. Martin's, 1990).

99. De Luca, *Testi Originali*, vol. 1, pp. 109, 104.

100. Simone da Cascina, *Colloquio spirituale*, pp. vi, 1–7.

101. For dialogue as a non-authoritarian and ideologically inclusive literary genre, see Jon R. Snyder, *Writing the Scene of Speaking: Theories of Dialogue in the Late Italian Renaissance* (Stanford, CA: Stanford University Press, 1989), esp. chap. 1. Another example of a work written by a friar for a women's religious community and framed as a dialogue that includes a member of its audience as one of the interlocutors is *Il trattato di Terra Santa e dell'Oriente di fr. Francesco Suriano*, ed. G. Golubovich (Milan: Tipografia Editrice Artigianelli, 1900). Francesco Suriano, originally of Venice, wrote up his travels to the Holy Land at the request of the women of Santa Lucia in Foligno, one of whom was his sister Suore Sista, who propels the narrative with her questions. Women at Santa Lucia also copied and disseminated this work.

A similar work and similar conditions are represented by the *Itinerario in Terra Santa*, addressed to the community of San Bernardino in Padua by Gabrielle Capodilista. The convent of Corpus Domini in Bologna, an Observant Franciscan community like San Bernardino and Santa Lucia, had a copy of Capodilista's *Itinerario in Terra Santa*; see Spanò Martinelli, "La biblioteca del 'Corpus Domini,'" p. 3 n. 5 and p. 16, where she notes that many Observant women's communities owned this work either in manuscript or in the popular incunabulum edition published in Perugia by Johann Wyndenast, Pietro di Colonia, and Giovanni di Bamberg (c. 1475).

One has to wonder at the coincidence of the appearance of these popular travel accounts in women's communities, all of which were formerly unenclosed, during a period in which the Observant friars were working hard to impose cloister on all Third Order Communities. Pilgrimage had been a very prominent feature of the female penitential life throughout the preceding two centuries.

102. Simone da Cascina, *Colloquio spirituale*, pp. 35–40 and passim.

103. Simone da Cascina, *Colloquio spirituale*, pp. 32–35.

104. Simone da Cascina, *Colloquio spirituale*, p. 171. On this liturgical prayer, which was gaining in popularity just as Simone da Cascina was writing, see André Wilmart, "La tradition littéraire et textuelle de l'*Adoro te devote*" in *Auteurs spirituels et textes dévots*, pp. 361–414; and a response by F. J. E. Raby, "The Date and Authorship of the Poem *Adoro te devote*," *Speculum* 20 (1945): 236–38.

105. Simone da Cascina, *Colloquio spirituale*, pp. 175–77. Here the Fraticello attempts to efface gender with what can be read as a reflexive move to grant authority to the Monachetta's words. This is interesting since mystic speech is so frequently associated with women. This disassociation of speaker from speech, together with the fact that the Monachetta here does not speak to her audience but lets them overhear a contemplative conversation, corroborates the anxieties of gender and strategies of representation noted by John Coakley; see above, note 65.

106. Da Cascina, *Colloquio spirituale*, p. 220.

107. Michael Baxendall, *Painting and Experience in Fifteenth Century Italy: A Primer of the Social History of Pictorial Style* (Oxford: Oxford University Press, 1972), esp. chap. 2.

108. See the letters of BAV, Vat. lat. 11259, and those of Giovanni dalle Celle,

Giovanni Colombini, Giovanni Dominici, and Girolamo da Siena. Both Colombini and Dominici indicate at several points that their female audience offers them the opportunity to express thoughts and feelings that offer at least as much "consolation" to the writer as to the women addressed.

109. Coletti, *Parole dal pulpito*, pp. 101–6.

110. Giovanni Boccaccio, *The Elegy of Lady Fiametta*, ed. Mariangela Causa-Steiner and Thomas Mauch (Chicago: University of Chicago Press, 1990), p. 1.

111. De Luca, *Testi Originali*, vol. 1, p. 110.

112. De Luca, *Testi Originali*, vol. 1, p. 104.

113. See note 3 above.

114. Gabriella Zarri, "Le sante vive," in *Le sante vive* (note 12 above), pp. 87–164.

Karen Scott

5. Urban Spaces, Women's Networks, and the Lay Apostolate in the Siena of Catherine Benincasa

Holy women in late medieval and Renaissance Italy enjoyed a number of options and choices. While some worked on behalf of the sick and the poor, participated in the often turbulent lives of their cities, exercised religious leadership, and thus had access to complex urban spaces, others flourished as recluses or as nuns in cloistered communities and moved relatively freely only within the infinite world of the spirit.[1] Still others, like Saint Catherine of Siena (1347–80), found creative ways to combine the active and the contemplative lives. The hagiographical texts and her own abundant writings show that Catherine's career exemplified both the mystical and apostolic opportunities available to lay women in fourteenth-century Siena, as well as the limitations these women encountered.[2]

A dyer's daughter who developed extraordinary mystical gifts in early childhood, Catherine fasted, saw visions, and experienced deep union with God. After joining the "Sisters of Penance" (or *mantellate*, lay tertiaries) associated with the Dominican order, she spent several years of isolation and prayer in her home, and then left that secluded state to care for the sick and the poor. She also served as spiritual advisor and peacemaker in her native Siena. Catherine's mystical gifts continued to develop, and in the last six years of her life her activities on behalf of her neighbors took on unprecedented forms. Between 1374 and 1380 she traveled about Italy and southern France as a kind of female apostle, preaching peace and salvation to whoever would listen. As a lay consultant to ecclesiastics, she advised two popes about organizing a crusade, ending a war with a league of Tuscan cities, and reforming the church. In 1376 she contributed to resolving the "Babylonian Captivity" of the papacy, and shortly before her death she set out to help end the Great Schism. Catherine maintained a vigorous correspondence with popes, kings, city governments, and her many friends and disciples. Her theological talents and understanding of the spiritual life are evident in the nearly four hundred letters she dictated, as is her concern to tailor each message to its recipient. Catherine's creativity was characterized by travel, bold speech, loving care for people, and a desire to affect the prominent institutions of her day.

Catherine's career would be considered unusual in any age, but her public action is especially remarkable for a late medieval uneducated lay woman of the artisan class, and it needs explaining. Though her own self-perception, cultural formation, and theological assumptions are essential parts of the explanation,[3] the context of Sienese women's religious experience she encountered during the formative period of her life, roughly in the 1360s and early 1370s, was essential to her development, too. As many scholars have shown, the gender role expectations that women faced in medieval and Renaissance Italy were generally quite restrictive, and they were probably becoming increasingly so in the Trecento.[4] The environment in which Catherine grew up must have profoundly affected her, both by imposing obstacles she sought to overcome and by providing social patterns she could exploit or use in her own way.[5]

The *Legenda Maior* is the main hagiographical source about Catherine's life and the obstacles and social patterns she encountered in Siena. Written by her former confessor Raymond of Capua to promote her canonization by the church, this text has most often been read for evidence about Catherine's asceticism and mystical experiences.[6] Yet it also offers several clues about how the environment of fourteenth-century Siena affected this one significant woman's access to the public realm. Because Raymond was particularly attentive to providing reliable references for his biographical information, he carefully put together a compendium of what all the witnesses had to say. He recorded all the gossip he heard about her and he mentioned the written documents he had read, especially the detailed notes about Catherine's life taken by her first confessor, Tommaso della Fonte.[7] Finally, Raymond also specified which episodes he had witnessed personally and which ones Catherine had told him about in private conversations or in confession.[8] The result is a complex picture of the saint's varied reputation within her own city. In detailing how both hostile and devoted onlookers viewed her mystical and apostolic life, in narrating how the Sienese reacted to what they could see of her activities as she moved about the city, the *Legenda* provides a topography of late medieval holy women's options. In particular, Raymond maps out how expectations about domestic and urban space could affect the choices women made.

Raymond of Capua made a great point of stressing the opposition and persecution Catherine encountered during her lifetime. Initially, he said, her family caused her the greatest difficulties. Her extreme ascetic and mystical behavior and her habit of giving away household belongings to the poor brought her "impediments" from everyone in the house, especially her mother.[9] As Catherine's charitable activities took her increasingly out of her secluded room and into the public streets, hospitals, and churches of her city, many ordinary citizens and religious superiors also grew critical of her behavior. As Raymond described it, all significant components of Sienese society were hostile to Catherine's special vocation. Though she was eventually able to overcome these obstacles with patience, charity, and perseverance, the people she encountered brought her much pain and anguish: "It was difficult for her to practice any act of devotion in public without suffering calumnies, impediments, and persecutions, especially from those people who should have supported her the most," that is, her early confessors and some members of the Dominican Sisters of Penance.[10] "The ancient tortuous serpent," Raymond said emphatically, "incited almost everyone against Catherine, both the spiritual and carnal, the religious and the secular."[11]

From Raymond's account one can deduce that the aspect of Catherine's life that provoked the most hostility was her visible religious presence in the midst of the city. Instead of being an anchorite or a cloistered nun whose contemplative practices were restricted to enclosed spaces and could be known only to a small group of people, Catherine found union with God in streets, neighbors' houses, and churches.[12] "The Lord began to show Himself to His spouse not only in secret places, as He had been accustomed to doing, but also in public places, openly and intimately, wherever she went."[13] The fact that her ascetic, visionary, and mystical experiences could be seen by everyone made her vulnerable to the witnesses' skepticism or misinterpretation. Raymond said that she was accused of seeking popularity, self-importance, and "singularity." For example, some devotees were seen "genuflecting" to Catherine when she was in ecstacy; when she did not stop them, hostile "murmurers" viewed this as proof that she was enjoying the public acclaim more than any holy person should.[14] Further, other slanderers suggested that her fasting and visions were a "fiction" she constructed out of vainglory. Raymond too was skeptical at first about the authenticity of Catherine's visions, because of women's propensity, he said, to "vacillate in the head."[15] The *Legenda* recounts how unfriendly witnesses tested the genuineness of her ecstacies by removing her violently from the church, by kicking her, or by thrusting needles into her leg.[16] Others suspected that her visions were inspired not by God but by the devil.[17]

More serious even than these accusations of hypocrisy and pride, which could have been directed against any unusually visible mystic, was the charge that Catherine's public life in Siena and her apostolic travels outside her own city were unacceptable religious activities because she was a woman. According to Raymond, Catherine once told him, "Father, many of our citizens and their wives, and many even of the sisters of my order have taken no small scandal at what they see as this excessive running about. . . . They say that it is not proper for a religious virgin to travel here and there in this way."[18] Other slanderers asked, "What does she go traipsing about for? She is a woman. Why doesn't she stay in her cell, if she wants to serve God?"[19] Raymond said that because of the breadth of her social contacts Catherine was unjustly accused of loose living. Some detractors even went so far as to suggest, both "secretly and publicly," that she had lost her virginity.[20] Surrounded by such attitudes, it is not surprising that Catherine entertained some doubts about her apostolate as well. According to the *Legenda*, she wondered whether her "sex was against" such a life of service to souls, "because people have contempt for it [her sex], and because for honor's sake it is not proper for this sex to keep company with the other sex."[21]

The assumption underlying these negative statements was that spiritually inclined women are unable to preserve their virtue, especially their chastity, unless they are properly "cloistered" in their homes or in monasteries.[22] It was Catherine's freedom of movement and "affable" social manner that made her particularly vulnerable to scandal and gossip.[23] Raymond himself admitted that a mission which took a member of the "weaker sex" consistently outside of her house and into public urban spaces was a "novelty," "beyond the custom of all other women."[24] He also came back several times to the point that women have to be especially careful about maintaining their reputation: "A virgin's good name is a tender thing, and a young girl's purity is a very delicate matter."[25] To most of his and Catherine's contemporaries, Raymond realized, a woman's sanctity was simply incompatible with publicity.

If the Sienese context was so inimical to Catherine's leading a spiritual life in the world, how then did Raymond explain that she succeeded in directing her creative energies into the apostolate? Far from implying that Catherine developed her talents within an entirely hostile context, the *Legenda* suggested there were at least two positive forces that boosted her self-confidence: God and the network of her close neighborhood. First and most important, Raymond asserted that Catherine was answering a divine call: God explained to her why her detractors were wrong, gave her the power to overcome obstacles and work at saving souls, converted the scandalmongers, and attracted friends to her side. Second, Raymond suggested that Catherine's apostolate in Siena followed a specifically female pattern in that it drew strength from her participation in neighborhood networks.

Though Raymond knew how disturbing this explanation would be for his audience, he attributed to Catherine's dangerous female apostolate the highest authorization possible, that of God Himself. He asserted that it was God who asked her "to forget her sex" and "to seek the company of both men and women."[26] As for her more distant travels, God successfully countered Catherine's—and her contemporaries'—objections with arguments like the following:

> The salvation of many souls requires that . . . you not inhabit your cell any more. You must leave even your own city for the salvation of souls. I will always be with you, and I will lead you forth and I will bring you back. You will carry the honor of My name and My spiritual warnings to the small and the great, as much to lay people as to clerics and religious. And I will give you a mouth and a wisdom that no one will be able to resist. I will take you also before pontiffs and before the rectors of churches and of the Christian people, so that in my customary way I might confound the pride of the strong through what is weak.[27]

In this passage Raymond defended Catherine's female apostolate by relying on the common medieval conception that women are naturally "weak," receptive, and empty vessels. Their weakness becomes a source of strength if they allow themselves to be filled entirely with divine grace. In particular, God empowers prophetic women to utter effective warnings to church leaders.[28] The *Legenda* unobtrusively takes this familiar *topos* a step further in that Raymond employed it not only to explain Catherine's prophetic role in general, but also and especially to legitimize her unusual call to leave her secluded cell and go out into her city and world. Raymond asserted that God subscribes to this theology linking the apostolate to female weakness, and that God convinced Catherine to accept it as her own, too.

Therefore, while Raymond emphasized that she encountered constant criticism for her apostolic travels and that Siena was a hostile environment for her to practice her public vocation, the message he wished to convey was that a woman's holiness could be compatible with freedom of movement, and that his saint knew this because God had told her so. His contemporaries' assumptions about female sanctity were erroneous, Raymond argued, because in fact Catherine was not corrupted by the public dimension of her life. Supported by the divine grace she received constantly, she sought neither singularity nor popularity, she was oblivious to all the human attention she received, and she did not lose her virginity. The moral of the story was that a holy woman could be trusted to move within ordinary urban society without diminishing the quality of her relationship with God.

Raymond implied also that God's power enabled Catherine to overcome all obstacles and to turn Siena into a more friendly place. Most of her detractors were converted to her cause by evident proofs of God's presence in her life: visions and miracles, as well as her humility, patience, and good will. For example, Andrea, a sick woman whom Catherine was nursing, had spread rumors doubting the saint's chastity. The woman's behavior was changed both by Catherine's perseverance in charity and by a vision in which the saint took on the appearance of an angel. Andrea finally "proclaimed with a loud voice that . . . [Catherine] was not only pure, but also holy and completely filled with the Holy Spirit," and Raymond was able to conclude that "the sacred virgin's fame thus began to shine and increase among the people."[29]

Besides God, the other positive force Raymond suggested as a possible support for Catherine's public career was the small neighborhood she lived in.[30] First, as her reputation for holiness grew, she attracted new disciples who sought out her religious guidance and helped her in her apostolates. Raymond states that the Dominican friars and tertiaries she knew and many of her disciples lived very close to her house, and he hints that these people helped her form a comfortable niche of neighborhood friends within Sienese society.

In particular, Catherine gained the friendship of a young widow named Alessia Saracini, who became a sister of penance out of admiration for Catherine's holiness. Alessia then

> left her own house and rented one in the virgin's neighborhood ["in convicinio"] so that she might enjoy her companionship more assiduously. From then on, to avoid the bustle of her father's house, the Lord's virgin began to stay frequently at Alessia's house for several days, and sometimes for weeks and months at a time.[31]

The importance of Catherine's friendship with Alessia is reflected in Raymond's description of Alessia's house as the setting for several significant stories about her Sienese apostolate. For example, it was from a window in her friend's house that Catherine saw several criminals being led down the street to their execution and that she successfully prayed for their conversion.[32] To protect Lorenza, a possessed child, from the devil's attacks, Catherine took her in as a guest in Alessia's house and performed one of her famous exorcisms there.[33] Finally, it was also at Alessia's house that Catherine miraculously made ever-increasing quantities of delicious bread out of a little moldy wheat, for distribution to the poor in a time of famine.[34] Thus Alessia's positive friendship and presence in the neighborhood encouraged Catherine to serve the poor and help save souls.

The second way in which the neighborhood assisted Catherine was by providing her with the geographical focus of much of her apostolate. Despite Raymond's statements that Catherine's moving about the city caused great scandal, most of the stories he tells about her involve places no farther than a two-minute walk away from her "father's house," which was located in the administrative *terzo* of Camollia, in the parish (*popolo*) of Sant'Antonio, in the Fontebranda district (*regio*) of Siena.[35] The framework for her activities was her close neighborhood, which was known for being one of the poorest in the city. Catherine gave clothes to a beggar in the nearby Church of San Domenico in Camporeggio.[36] She cured plague victims and cared for Palmerina, a Dominican Sister of Penance, in the Misericordia hospital, also nearby.[37] She brought food secretly to a poor widow and her children who lived in the neighborhood next to her own ("in secundo convicinio domus suae"). She cured a woman from her own neighborhood ("in ejusdem convicinio") who had fallen out of her window. She cured a sister of penance named Gemma, who lived nearby ("non remote"), of throat inflammation.[38] The people whom Catherine converted in Siena were almost all neighbors, acquaintances, or friends of friends. When she prayed for the salvation of Andrea Naddini, she called him her "neighbor and brother" ("proximum suum, convicem & fratrem suum").[39] While people in spiritual need were often referred to her by her confessors or other ecclesiastics, Catherine's female friends also brought their sons to see her at home in the hope that she would convert them.[40]

Third, the *Legenda* implies that Catherine made connections with the women of her neighborhood, strong women who resembled Catherine's own mother, Monna Lapa, in their sharp-tongued honesty, bossy instincts, taste for gossip, and basic generosity. These people were not just critical of Catherine; they could also be helpful and concerned about her. Catherine's female neighbors may have helped her in her charitable work: Raymond implied that the neighborhood gossip network informed her about which people needed her care.[41] Moreover, Raymond noted that when Catherine experienced a spiritual death (which was a temporary mystical state), her condition was witnessed by a mix of people: her female companions, especially Alessia; four Dominican friars; and finally, "almost all the women of the neighborhood, and a great crowd of acquaintances, both men and women."[42] He leaves us wondering whether these last witnesses were just curious, or whether they also felt a measure of affection and grief—probably both.

Thus the primary context for Catherine's early development of a socially based spirituality was the network of close personal bonds she found available in the small area near her home. Of course, for Raymond, Catherine's dedication to the spiritual life meant that she did not operate within her neighborhood quite in the same way ordinary women did. He tells us that she constantly contemplated God, that she talked only about God, that she avoided gossip, and that she selflessly and cheerfully served the needy despite some ill-treatment of her on their part. Despite this, her religious focus did not radically change her social behavior: it simply purified the normal pattern of neighborhood-based life. Once Catherine emerged from her years of seclusion at home, she returned to a vital social reality, to the same world she had thought she was leaving when she began her spiritual life.

Raymond implied this very clearly through the words he put in her mouth when she complained that God's call to leave her room and begin a public life would mean a "return to temporal cares" and to "the dust of the earth":

> Catherine, having heard the voice of her Shepherd and Bridegroom, understanding that she was being called from the sweetness of rest to labors, from the solitude of silence to noise, from the secrets of her room to public life, answered plaintively, "I have taken off the tunic of all temporal cares; now that I have cast them aside, how should I return to them again? I have washed

> the feet of my affections . . . clear of every stain of sin and vice, how should I sully them again with the dust of the earth?"[43]

Despite her objections, Catherine did plunge again into the ordinary corporate networks of Sienese neighborhood life, in which narrow streets and open windows ensure that nothing much remains private for long, everyone knows everyone's business, and everyone gossips about and cares for everyone else. I should like to suggest that her social spirituality based on the small neighborhood conformed to a female pattern in Trecento Siena. This becomes clearer if we compare Catherine's story to that of a slightly earlier group of Sienese men, which was characterized by an equally social religiosity.

Unlike Catherine, the converted merchant and government official Giovanni Colombini and his disciples did not conduct their earliest activities inside houses, in the vicinity of his home, or in the narrow context of a neighborhood. Two of the most important public spaces of Siena were the stage for these men's conversions: the Piazza del Campo, the main square of the town in front of the city hall, and the cathedral. Colombini wrote letters describing how he received new recruits into his informal group, or *brigata*. These were mostly wealthy and politically prominent men like himself, whose conversion meant devotion to poverty, to public foolishness, and to crying out the name of Jesus to all who would listen; they are the future Gesuati. Colombini wrote that he took them to the fountain in the Piazza del Campo, and then in a ritual of public humiliation had them remove their shoes and clothes and put on poor clothing. After singing some *laude*, they went on in a mock procession to the Duomo through the streets of the city. Colombini specified with evident satisfaction that "a good part of the city was present there" to witness the ceremony.[44] Eventually Colombini and his companions extended the public, visible, almost theatrical dimension of their behavior by traveling through central Italy and Tuscany as outrageously unconventional and fairly successful lay preachers.

Thus, while Catherine spent her formative years learning to love her neighbor through social contacts limited discreetly to the inside of homes, churches, and hospitals in a small quarter of Siena, Colombini and his friends roamed easily through the most public spaces of the city. Thus Raymond's vita suggests that the young Catherine may have been able to become a socially active holy woman because she accepted and embraced the more restricted female roles expected of her in her neighborhood.

In another way, however, Colombini's experience was similar to Catherine's. Both were lay people whose holiness was neither monastic nor reclusive, but decisively social, with an emphasis on preaching and traveling. Both were unusually ready to encourage spiritual women and men to interact with each other. Catherine's followers—her informal *famiglia*—were men and women, lay and religious. Colombini's more official *brigata* was composed only of men and became a religious order by the time of his death in 1367; but he demonstrated an unusual interest in, and respect for, spiritual women by making the female Benedictine monastery of Santa Bonda the home base of his group and befriending the abbess, Paola Foresi.[45] Colombini's positive relations with women established a pattern Catherine would later inherit.

Indeed, there are connections linking Giovanni Colombini and Catherine that suggest she may have enjoyed some special support that originated from beyond her own small neighborhood. Though the two Sienese saints probably never met, we know that they shared a common group of friends. For example, Catherine's sister-in-law and companion Lisa was a Colombini. Giovanni Colombini called the friars of San Domenico in Camporeggio "my friars," for he felt they supported him more than other Sienese friars did. Likewise, the focus of Catherine's early spiritual life was the church of San Domenico. William Flete, the Augustinian hermit at the Lecceto hermitage near Siena, befriended both Giovanni and Catherine. The first writer of a saint's life about Colombini, a Sienese notary named Cristofano Guidini, became Catherine's disciple, too.[46]

In Giovanni Colombini's *brigata*, nuns, and many friends, Catherine inherited a spiritual constituency, an audience, a group whose expectation was that strong women could and should exercise religious leadership through prayer and speech. In the most active years of her life, Catherine would take the Gesuati model one step further. Unlike Colombini's nuns, who remained in the monastery at Santa Bonda, Catherine imitated Colombini himself by becoming an itinerant preacher. Although eventually Catherine expressed her concern for the peace and salvation of her world through political and ecclesiastical apostolates of greater magnitude than anything Colombini accomplished, still she undoubtedly drew a great deal of support from the citywide networks he and Abbess Paola Foresi had helped establish.

What is it, then, that can help us explain the public creativity of a woman like Catherine of Siena? Her own genius, talent, and intelligence, her will and determination, her strong self-image, her spiritual sensitivity, her caring for people—all these personal qualities of hers were certainly important. The opposition and difficulties she encountered challenged and stimulated her as well. One can add to these factors, however, that the support of friends in her neighborhood and her city provided her with the nurturing environment she needed to grow into the influential apostle which history knows her to be.

The author is grateful to DePaul University for providing her with a summer faculty grant to conduct research, and wishes to thank friends and colleagues for their suggestions and encouragement, especially Caroline W. Bynum, Neal Clemens, Edward English, Douglas Howland, Gregory Kozlowski, Thomas Luongo, E. Ann Matter, Cynthia Polecritti, and Susan Ramirez.

Notes

1. Catherine of Genoa and Angela Merici are examples of the first type of holy woman delineated here, while Angela of Foligno, Margaret of Cortona, and Columba of Rieti are examples of the second.

2. Raymond of Capua's *Legenda Maior* is published under the title *De S. Catharina Senensi virgine de poenitentia S. Dominici*, in *Acta Sanctorum Aprilis*, vol. 3 (Antwerp, 1675), pp. 853–959 (hereafter cited as *Legenda*). A recent English translation of the *Legenda* is *The Life of Catherine of Siena*, trans. Conleth Kearns (Wilmington, DE: Michael Glazier, 1980). St. Catherine's letters are published in *Le lettere di S. Caterina da Siena*, ed. Piero Misciatelli (Florence: Giunti, 1940), 6 vols. All translations in this chapter are my own.

3. Karen Scott, "Catherine of Siena, *Apostola*," *Church History* 61 (March 1992): pp. 34–46; idem, "'*Io Catarina*': Ecclesiastical Politics and Oral Culture in the Letters of Catherine of Siena," in *Dear Sister: Medieval Women and the Epistolary Genre*, ed. Karen Cherewatuk and Ulrike Wiethaus (Philadelphia: University of Pennsylvania Press, 1993), pp. 87–121; and "'This Is Why I Have Put You among Your Neighbors': St. Bernard's and St. Catherine's Understanding of the Love of God and Neighbor," in *Atti del Simposio Internazionale Cateriniano-Bernardiniano: Siena, 17–20 aprile 1980*, ed. Domenico Maffei and Paolo Nardi (Siena: Accademia Senese degli Intronati, 1982), pp. 279–94.

4. See, for example, Joan Kelly-Gadol, "Did Women Have a Renaissance?" in *Becoming Visible: Women in European History*, 2d ed., ed. Renate Bridenthal, Claudia Koonz, and Susan Stuard (Boston: Houghton Mifflin, 1987), pp. 175–201; Margaret King, *Women of the Renaissance* (Chicago: University of Chicago Press, 1991); *Refiguring Woman: Perspectives on Gender and the Italian Renaissance*, ed. Marilyn Migiel and Juliana Schiesari (Ithaca, NY: Cornell University Press, 1991).

5. For example, female Dominican tertiaries such as herself were not

expected to engage in social work, much less in preaching or holy peacemaking; tertiaries mostly spent their days and nights in solitary prayer and penance at home. Their rule even specified that they needed to receive special ecclesiastical permission to travel outside their city. Moreover, Sienese women, like other Italian women, were excluded from participation in the political life of their city. Though the Sienese governments of the Dodici and the Riformatori in the second half of the fourteenth century were among the most open to popular participation in their day, so that several of Catherine's brothers held office, women were not allowed to take government positions or to vote.

6. Catherine's historical significance as an activist and writer has not been explored in depth in recent historical scholarship, and her life has usually been subsumed under the category of prophecy and visionary activity. For example, Rudolph Bell, Anna Benvenuti Papi, Caroline Bynum, John Coakley, Richard Kieckhefer, and André Vauchez have recently noted Catherine's extreme fasting, rigorous ascetic practices, and mystical religious experiences, and have used them to explain how she gained fame as a holy woman: see Rudolph M. Bell, *Holy Anorexia* (Chicago: University of Chicago Press, 1985), pp. 22–53; Sofia Boesch Gajano and Odile Redon, "La *Legenda Major* di Raimondo da Capua, Costruzione di una santa," in Maffei and Nardi, *Atti del simposio internazionale cateriniano-bernardiniano*, pp. 15–35; Anna Benvenuti Papi, "Penitenza e santità femminile in ambiente cateriniano e bernardiniano," in Maffei and Nardi, *Atti del simposio internazionale cateriniano-bernardiniano*, pp. 865–78, esp. p. 872; Caroline Walker Bynum, *Holy Feast and Holy Fast: The Religious Significance of Food to Medieval Women* (Berkeley: University of California Press, 1987), pp. 165–80; John Coakley, "The Representation of Sanctity in Late Medieval Hagiography: The Evidence from *Lives* of Saints of the Dominican Order," Th.D. dissertation, Harvard University, 1980; Richard Kieckhefer, *Unquiet Souls: Fourteenth-Century Saints and Their Religious Milieu* (Chicago: University of Chicago Press, 1984); and André Vauchez, "Les représentations de la sainteté d'après les procès de canonisation médiévaux (XIII–XVe siècles)," in *Convegno internazionale: Agiografia nell'occidente cristiano, secoli XIII–XV, Roma (1–2 marzo 1979)* (Rome: Accademia Nazionale dei Lincei, 1980), pp. 31–43.

7. Tommaso della Fonte was a Sienese Dominican who was also a relative of Catherine's. Presumably Tommaso got the names and places right because he was familiar with this environment and was taking notes as the events occurred, many of them around 1370, ten years before Catherine's death and several years before she emerged as preacher, peacemaker, and avid sender of letters. References to the "writings" (*scripta*) or "notebooks" (*quaternios*) left by Tommaso della Fonte include *Legenda* 113, 142, 162, 167, 181, 186, 189, 199, 202.

8. For an interesting study of Raymond's relationship with Catherine, see John Coakley, "Friars as Confidants of Holy Women in Medieval Dominican Hagiography," in *Images of Sainthood in Medieval Europe*, ed. Renate Blumenfeld-Kosinski and Timea Szell (Ithaca, NY: Cornell University Press, 1991), pp. 222–46.

9. *Legenda* 64, p. 868 col. 2: "cum multorum domesticorum impedimento"; see also *Legenda* 46, p. 865 col. 1; 167–68, p. 895 cols. 1–2. Elsewhere Raymond is careful to indicate that though everyone else in the household actively opposed Catherine's charitable activities, she obtained her father's "public mandate" to give

away food and clothing to the poor: *Legenda* 81, p. 873 col. 2; 131, p. 886 col. 1; 136, p. 887 col. 2: "Omnes de domo praeter patrem aegre ferebant eleemosynas suas."

10. *Legenda* 403–7; 405, p. 953 col. 1: "Vix poterat unum actum devotionis exercere in publico, quin pateretur calumnias, impedimenta, & persecutiones, ab his potissime, qui magis debuissent ei favere."

11. *Legenda* 172, p. 896 col. 2: "Sed antiquus serpens & tortuosus . . . cunctos quasi, tam spirituales quam carnales, tam religiosos quam seculares . . . commovit contra eam."

12. *Legenda* 30, p. 861 col. 1: "in via publica penes homines & animalia"; 132–33, 229; 39, 135, 144, 180.

13. *Legenda* 178, p. 898 col. 2: "Coepit enim Dominus ex tunc non tantum in locis secretis, ut prius consueverat, sed etiam in patentibus, palam & familiariter se ostendere sponsae suae, tam eunti quam stanti."

14. *Legenda* 151. It is significant that the earliest "portrait" of Catherine, the fresco painted by her disciple Andrea Vanni and now located in the Cappella delle Volte in the Basilica of San Domenico in Siena, shows her with a kneeling devotee kissing her hand.

15. *Legenda* 172, p. 896 col. 2: "Alii carnales & detractores notorii, dicebant esse hanc fictionem ad gloriam acquirendam, & quod non jejunabat, sed latenter optime comedebat" ("Others, carnal people and notorious detractors, said that this was a fiction intended to acquire glory and that she did not fast, but ate very well in secret."); and 87, p. 874 col. 2: "in feminis, quae agiliter vacillant in capite." See also 167, p. 895 col. 1; and 365, p. 945 col. 1.

16. *Legenda* 406–7.

17. *Legenda* 80, p. 873 col. 2.

18. *Legenda* 333, p. 937 col. 1: "Pater, plures ex nostris civibus & eorem uxoribus, & etiam ex Sororibus Ordinis mei, propter nimium ut eis videtur discursum . . . mihi scandalum non modicum sumpserunt, dicentes non decere religiosam virginem sic passim discurrere."

19. *Legenda* 365, p. 945 col. 1: "Ut quid ista gyrovagando discurrit? Mulier est. Quare non manet in cella, si vult Deo servire?"

20. *Legenda* 156–58, p. 892 col. 2. For the public as well as secret nature of the detractors' speech, see *Legenda* 405, p. 953 col. 2: "actibus ejus detrahere, tam publice quam occulte"; and 147, p. 890 col. 1: Palmerina "detrahebat ei secrete ac publice quantum poterat."

21. *Legenda* 121, p. 883 col. 2: "Sexus enim contradicit . . . tum quia contemptibilis est coram hominibus, tum etiam quia honeste cogente, non decet talem sexum con sexu alio conversari."

22. Raymond uses the word *clausura* to mean both formal monastic enclosure (*Legenda* 71) and the solitary life which Catherine voluntarily practiced at home before her apostolic call (*Legenda* 83).

23. *Legenda* 365, p. 945 col. 1.

24. *Legenda* 116, p. 882 col. 1: "ultra ceterarum mulierum consuetudinem, mittenda erat ad publicum." Raymond specified that Catherine's difficulties were caused by three factors: her "sexus fragilior, novitas notabilior, & seculi hodierni status declivior" ("her more fragile sex, the more notable novelty, and the declining state of today's age"): *Legenda* 117, p. 882 col. 1.

25. *Legenda* 408, p. 954 col. 1: "Fatentur siquidem omnes sacri Doctores, teneram esse virgineam famam, & puellarem pudorem nimis delicatum." See also 158, p. 892 col. 2.

26. *Legenda* 165, p. 894, col. 2: "Insuper erga salutem proximorum tam vehementer accendetur cor tuum, quod proprii sexu oblita, quasi ex toto conversationem praeteritam omnino immutabis, hominumque & feminarum consortium, prout assolcs, non vitabis. . . . Ex his scandalizabuntur quamplurimi." ("Besides, your heart will be kindled so vehemently for the salvation of your neighbors that, forgetting your own sex, you will entirely change your old way of life, and you will not avoid the company of men and women but will become accustomed to it. . . . Many people will be scandalized by this.")

27. *Legenda* 216, p. 906 col. 2: "Multarum animarum salus requirit . . . nec cellam pro habitaculo habebis de cetero; quin potius & urbem te propriam egredi oportebit pro animarum salute. Ego autem semper tecum ero, & ducam & reducam: portabisque nominis mei honorem & spiritalia documenta coram parvis & magnis, tam laicis quam clericis & religiosis: ego enim tibi dabo os & sapientiam, cui nullus resistere potuit. Adducam etiam te coram Pontificibus & Rectoribus Ecclesiarium ac populi Christiani, ut consueto meo modo, per infirma fortiorum confundam superbiam."

28. See also *Legenda* 122, p. 883 cols. 1–2. For an analysis of the place of these passages of the *Legenda* as a whole, see Scott, "Not Only with Words," pp. 161–81. For the view that medieval interpretations of women considered their "natural" vulnerability and weakness as the female avenue to power and strength, see Bynum, *Holy Feast*, and Barbara Newman, *Sister of Wisdom: St. Hildegard's Theology of the Feminine* (Berkeley: University of California Press, 1987).

29. *Legenda* 161, p. 893 col. 2: "Profitetur altis vocibus non modo puram esse, sed sanctam, nec non & santo Spiritu plenam. . . . Hinc coepit fama sacrae virginis inter homines clarificari & augmentari."

30. See Christiane Klapisch-Zuber, "Kin, Friends, and Neighbors: The Urban Territory of a Merchant Family in 1400," in *Women, Family, and Ritual in Renaissance Italy*, ed. and trans. Lydia Cochrane (Chicago: University of Chicago Press, 1985).

31. *Legenda* 299, p. 927 col. 2: "Proprium domus reliquiens, in convicinio ejusdem virginis domum conduxit, ut magis assidue frui posset conversatione sua. Quo facto virgo Domini coepit ad fugiendum occupationes paternae domus, frequenter in domo Alexiae commorari per dies plures, quandoque per septimanas & menses."

32. *Legenda* 228–30.

33. *Legenda* 272.

34. *Legenda* 298–99. See also Letters 271 and 277 in *Le lettere di S. Caterina da Siena*, vol. 4, pp. 158, 186–87. Catherine's correspondence with Alessia confirms Raymond's perception that the two women shared a conception of the spiritual life that involved not only silence, prayer, and seclusion but also a variety of more socially related activities. Alessia, Catherine advised, should pray, go to Mass, and do manual work about the house, but she should also care for her elderly mother and should engage in apostolic prayer, not only in general, but for quite specific political circumstances, such as the reform of the papacy or peace in Italy. Cath-

erine also showed how close a friend she felt Alessia to be: "I invite you to pray, and to get others to pray the divine Goodness that He send us the peace soon, so that God be glorified, and much evil be removed, and so that we [you and I] might be able to get together to speak together of God's admirable deeds."

35. Duccio Balestracci and Gabriella Piccinni, *Siena nel Trecento: assetto urbano e strutture edilizie* (Florence: Clusf, 1977), pp. 108–9, 127–28; and Piero Torriti, *La casa di santa Caterina e la Basilica di San Domenico a Siena* (Genoa: Sagep, 1982). Raymond of Capua provides information about the parish and district in which Catherine's house was located: see *Legenda* 39, p. 863 col. 1; 144, p. 889 col. 2.

36. *Legenda* 135, p. 887 col. 1.

37. *Legenda* 147, 245–48, 252: in addition to caring for Palmerina at the Misericordia, Catherine befriended Matteo, the Rector of the hospital, sent him patients, and cured him of the plague there. Several of her letters to Matteo have survived: Letters 58, 63, 124, 137, 210. For the location and the activities of the Misericordia, see Balestracci and Piccinni, *Siena nel Trecento*, pp. 153–54.

38. *Legenda* 131–32, p. 886 col. 1; 250, p. 915 col. 2; 260, p. 918 col. 1.

39. *Legenda* 225, p. 908 col. 2.

40. For the intervention of Tommaso della Fonte, see *Legenda* 225, 232, 272; for the intervention of William Flete, 235; for a lay woman's intervention (Rabe Tolomei), see 232–34.

41. For example, see *Legenda* 132, 251, 252 ("audivit"); 139 and 143 ("sensit"); 154 ("percepit").

42. *Legenda* 218, p. 907 col. 1: "Defunctam autem ipsam virginem pene omnes convicinae viderunt, & magis utriusque sexus notorum caterva, quae ut moris est, in tali casu concurrerat."

43. *Legenda* 118, p. 882 col. 2: "Illa vero, ex notitia vocis Pastoris sui & Sponsi, ab ille intelligens se vocata, de quietis dulcedine ad labores, de silentii solitudine ad clamores, et de cubiculi secretis ad publicum, voce querulosa respondit: Exspoliavi me tunica omnis curae temporalis jam hactenus; quomodo jam abjectam a me, iterum resumam? Pedes affectionum mearum . . . lavi ab omni sorde peccatorum & vitiorum; quomodo terrenis pulveribus illos iterum inquinabo?" See Song of Songs 5:3.

44. Letter 87, in *Le lettere del Beato Giovanni Colombini da Siena*, ed. Piero Misciattelli (Florence: Libreria Editrice Fiorentina, n.d.), p. 256: "gran parte della città vi si raccolse." See also Feo Belcari, *Vita del Beato Giovanni Colombini da Siena*, ed. Rodolfo Chiarini (Lanciano: Carabba, 1914); and more recently, Anna Benvenuti Papi, "Le donne di Giovanni Colombini," in *"In castro poenitentiae": Santità e società femminile nell'Italia medievale* (Rome: Herder, 1990), pp. 415–528.

45. Over three-fourths of Giovanni Colombini's 114 letters were sent to these Sienese women. He addressed the nuns as his "rest and delight," his "soul," and his "heart." He called the Abbess his spiritual "Mother" and became quite dependent on her affection and support. He wanted the nuns not only to pray, but also to comfort and teach people from outside their monastery. See e.g., Letters 6, 16, 22, 29, 111.

46. Belcari, *Vita del Beato Giovanni Colombini*, p. 15.

Ann M. Roberts

6. Chiara Gambacorta of Pisa as Patroness of the Arts

The role of Dominicans in the history of Italian art of the Renaissance is secure. Our histories of Florentine art would be much altered without, for example, the patronage of the friars at Santa Maria Novella, or the presence of Fra Angelico at San Marco. Nor could the history of Pisan art be written without considering the patronage and influence of the friars at Santa Caterina, who commissioned Simone Martini and Francesco Traini to execute influential images for them, and provided inspiration for several of the frescoes in the Camposanto.[1] Less often noted is the involvement of Dominican women in the commissioning and creation of works of art in the fifteenth century, which occurred despite their more limited financial means and circumscribed lives.[2]

We have been reminded of late that masculine protectors and agents were necessary parts of a nun's spiritual and economic life, and warned to take account of the roles of these men in the nuns' patronage of works of art. With a male confessor or other intermediary as the buffer between herself and the artist, what sort of impact could the religious woman have on the form or content of a work of art?[3] I hope that the objects discussed here will respond in some measure to this question. My focus will be the convent of San Domenico of Pisa, and its founding prioress, Chiara Gambacorta, whose features are recorded in the marble tomb slab created at her death in 1419 (Figure 6.1).[4] I wish to explore the impact that the prioress had on the commissioning, style, and imagery of the works of art produced during her prioracy and demonstrate how extensive her role in the creation of these works actually was.

Although not as familiar to us as some of her masculine contemporaries, Gambacorta is venerated as a Beata by the Church, as a local saint by Pisans, and as a key figure in the history of the Observant movement by the Dominican order.[5] She was born in 1362 to Pietro Gambacorta, who became the ruler of Pisa shortly after her birth. Called Tora by her family, she was married at 13 and widowed by age 15. To avoid another arranged

Figure 6.1. Marble tomb relief of Chiara Gambacorta, now in the convent of San Domenico of Pisa, Via della Faggiola. (Photo: author)

marriage, Tora surreptitiously entered a Franciscan convent in Pisa and took the name Chiara; her enraged family removed her from the convent and confined her for several months. Through Chiara's perseverance and the influence of Catherine of Siena and Alfonso Pecha da Vadaterra—the last confessor of Saint Birgitta of Sweden—Chiara's father was persuaded to consent to his daughter's profession and ultimately to build a new convent for her.

Although she had initially chosen a Franciscan house, Chiara's final profession was to the Dominican order, and when given the means to found a convent, it was to the order of preachers and their founder it was dedicated. Pietro Gambacorta obtained the grounds and buildings of a defunct convent, and Chiara and several other women installed themselves in the convent of San Domenico of Pisa in 1382, with papal approval secured in 1385. Inspired by the lessons of Catherine of Siena, Chiara devoted the convent of San Domenico to a strict observance of the letter and spirit of the Rule of Saint Augustine and the constitutions of the Dominican order. San Domenico was, in fact, the first Dominican convent of either sex which may be called "Observant." Her interpretation of the rule led to strict enclosure, austerities, a truly communal life, and careful attention to Dominican customs and liturgies. The example and mode of life chosen by Chiara Gambacorta were themselves an inspiration to the more well-known Dominican friars who led the Observant movement, including Raymond of Capua, Tommaso Caffarini, Giovanni Dominici, Leonardo Dati, and Antoninus Pierozzi.[6] Throughout the fifteenth century, the women of San Domenico were the instruments of reform in other feminine convents throughout Italy.

A strong-minded woman, Chiara was elected prioress of San Domenico in 1395, a post which she held until her death in 1419. She was renowned for her charity, piety, good counsel, and leadership. After her father was assassinated and much of her family killed or exiled, Chiara showed special kindness to the female members of the assassin's family. Her activity included an apostolate by correspondence involving, among others, Francesco di Marco Datini, the merchant of Prato, and his wife, to whom she directed spiritual instruction and prayers, as well as requests for alms. Chiara's spirituality has been analyzed in somewhat contradictory terms by modern historians; while Rudolph Bell includes her among the holy anorectics who practiced extremes of bodily mortification, Richard Kieckhefer considers her a model of moderation and sanity.[7]

With Chiara's assumption of the prioracy in 1395, the community at

San Domenico grew in numbers and in reputation. The women of San Domenico came from prominent families of Pisa, Florence, Lucca, and Genoa. The founding bull had limited the size of the community to twenty nuns, but by 1400, the community numbered closer to forty. Neither the church nor the dormitory could accommodate these numbers, and the prioress set to finding the means to build a new church and dormitory for her community. Because most of her own family had been exiled or financially ruined by the assassination of her father, Chiara solicited donations to fund these projects from wealthy families and individuals, among them the Doria of Genoa, the Medici of Florence, and the Datini of Prato. A letter dated 23 February 1396 from Chiara to Francesco di Marco Datini gives an idea of the persuasions she adopted to urge his generosity:

> My dear friend, we are building a church, of which we have great need, because the one we have, that built by Master Peter, is so small and damp that we attribute to it all our sickness. For this reason we have begun to work on that which Master Peter founded for us. It has pleased God to make this an occasion of merit to several persons. We are poor, and being poor we recommend ourselves to you for the love of Christ, that in our present need you will remember to give us whatever assistance God will inspire you to give. Alms is a good thing and this devout convent prays and will continue to pray for you, and you will participate in the fervent prayers which will be said in that church; therein will be said the Divine Office day and night.[8]

The church built as a result of this campaign still stands in Pisa, at the foot of the Corso Italia. Remodeled in the eighteenth century, suppressed in the nineteenth century, bombed in 1943, and now deconsecrated and denuded, it is only a ghost of the church Gambacorta built. Yet much of the surviving structure, the plan, and the façade date from this campaign. The façade is simple and unadorned (Figure 6.2), in contrast to the marble adornment for which Pisan structures are well known, like Santa Caterina, the church of the Dominican friars in Pisa. This simplicity may be partly a result of financial limitations, but it also is in keeping with Observant Dominican principles; a similar plainness of façade is apparent at the Dominican friaries in Fiesole and at San Marco of Florence. The church is a plain brick structure in the form of a rectangular hall divided into two distinct halves. The exterior church, which served the laity and which held the altar at which the priest said Mass, was remodeled in the eighteenth century, at which time the original wooden roof was replaced by a vault. The nuns' choir still preserves the simple trussed wood roof that originally

Figure 6.2. Façade of the Church of San Domenico, Pisa. (Photo: author)

covered both halves of the church and gives a sense of what the structure built by Gambacorta looked like (Figure 6.3). There was no access between the two churches except the grate over the altar and a communion window in the wall. This plan became rather standard in later periods, although it was but one of many plans for cloistered communities used in Trecento Italy. The church seems to have been substantially completed by 1408, although it was not consecrated until 1457. As we shall see, works of art were commissioned for it in the first decade of the fifteenth century.

Gambacorta also oversaw the building of a new dormitory wing to house the growing community. The conventual buildings already comprised two branches of dormitory, communal, and service rooms on the eastern and western perimeters of the convent. Work on the new dormitory was probably begun in 1402, and by 1409 Chiara was raising funds to roof it.[9] This structure survives also in Pisa; it was built perpendicular to the earlier conventual buildings and linked them across the northern perimeter of the convent. It consisted of two stories, the lower one arcaded, the upper articulated by simple square windows (Figure 6.4).[10]

In addition to appropriate structures, Chiara was also concerned to provide her sisters with the liturgical furnishings, books, and images that they needed to function as an Observant community. For example, her surviving correspondence details her efforts to buy books for the community, to encourage the gift of books by patrons, and to obtain the materials with which the nuns could make their own books. In this latter enterprise, she was aided by Francesco di Marco Datini, who paid for materials,[11] and Giovanni Dominici, whose efforts to obtain and illuminate books for the community of observant nuns in the convent of Corpus Domini included exchanges of books with San Domenico.[12] We know that the women of San Domenico wrote and illuminated books, but I have not been successful in locating any surviving examples of their work.

Despite (in some ways because of) the vicissitudes of suppression, confiscation, and deconsecration that mark the modern history of this and many other convents of women from the medieval period, a surprising number of paintings survive from San Domenico. The objects considered here are described very precisely in inventories taken in the early nineteenth century, when the convent was suppressed, or are otherwise traceable to San Domenico.[13] These images represent only a portion of the early fifteenth-century objects from San Domenico, but all the objects discussed here date from the time of Chiara Gambacorta's long prioracy and several bear the stamp of her personality.

Figure 6.3. Nuns' choir of San Domenico, restored after wartime bombing. (Photo courtesy of Pisa, Soprintendenza ai beni ambientali, architettonici, artistici e storici)

Figure 6.4. Dormitory on northern perimeter of cloister, San Domenico, with modern restorations. (Photo: author)

The earliest dated painting from San Domenico is a panel depicting the mystic marriage of Saint Catherine of Alexandria (Figure 6.5).[14] In a pyramidal format, the painting represents the Virgin holding her Child in her lap, while He places a ring on Saint Catherine's finger. The Virgin and Child are larger in scale than the kneeling Saint Catherine, and these three figures tower over the even smaller figure of the donor at the lower center. Without naming the donor depicted, an inscription beneath him dates the picture to April 1403 and characterizes him as a benefactor of the house.[15] In the late eighteenth century the painting hung on a wall in the nuns' choir.[16] Because the painting does not have the format typical of early fifteenth-century altarpieces, it may have been meant from the start to hang on a wall. The inscription seems to be addressed to the nuns—it exhorts them to pray for their benefactor—which would suggest that the panel was intended for a spot somewhere within the nuns' own precincts, and not for the public church.

It is significant that Catherine of Alexandria is the subject of one of

Figure 6.5. Giovanni di Pietro di Napoli and Martino di Bartolomeo, *Mystic Marriage of Saint Catherine of Alexandria*, Pisa, Museo Nazionale di San Matteo. (Photo courtesy of Pisa, Soprintendenza ai beni ambientali, architettonici, artistici e storici)

the first works commissioned for the convent. She is a patron saint of the Dominican order and her feast day was important in the Dominican liturgy. The nuns also owned a relic of the saint. Ecclesiastical geography may lie behind the choice of subject matter, too, as the principal Dominican foundation in Pisa was dedicated to Saint Catherine of Alexandria; the friars of this house served the nuns of San Domenico as confessors and protectors. Their high altar was adorned with an important polyptych by Simone Martini which gives special emphasis to Saint Catherine.[17] But unlike the image for the friars' church in which individual saints are represented in a hieratic, non-narrative image, the painting for San Domenico focuses on an episode from Catherine's life.

The moment chosen, the mystic marriage of Catherine to Christ, had special importance to nuns. As Michael Goodich has pointed out, her cult was especially appropriate for women who emulated Catherine and became brides of Christ on taking the veil.[18] The ceremony of profession was a form of marriage ceremony, which involved dressing the "bride" in a garment symbolic of her new role and placing a ring on her finger as a token of the marriage.[19] This contrasts to the ceremony of profession for friars, which, as A. H. Thomas has pointed out, derives from the medieval ceremonies of vassalage, in which the hands of the initiate are enclosed in the hands of his superior.[20] So despite the widespread use of nuptial imagery in more androgynous terms to refer to the soul, the marriage of Saint Catherine was inherently more meaningful for nuns than for friars, as the women's entry into the religious life was marked by an anagogical repetition of Catherine's betrothal. Similarly, the nuns' appropriation of the title, *Sposa di Cristo*, is as literal as it is figurative for women.[21] Some years ago, Millard Meiss demonstrated how influential the nuptial imagery surrounding Catherine of Alexandria was to the visions of her namesake, Catherine of Siena, and to other late medieval women.[22] Jeffrey Hamburger has recently explored other visual manifestations of bridal themes in the Rothschild Canticles, a work of art whose audience was probably nuns.[23]

Although neither signed nor documented as such, this painting is probably the work of the painter Giovanni di Pietro da Napoli, who was active in Tuscany in the first decade of the fifteenth century.[24] From 1402 until 1404, Giovanni di Pietro da Napoli shared a workshop with another painter in Pisa, Martino di Bartolomeo of Siena, to whom is sometimes assigned a share of this panel. The nature of the relationship among the artist (or artists), the donor, and the sisters in the convent eludes us, because we have no contract or other contemporary documentation that might explain it. It may be that the donor chose the artist (and therefore the style) of the image, but certainly the nuns and their prioress determined the subject.

No donor intervenes in another image commissioned for San Domenico of the other Catherine—Catherine of Siena—nor is the name of the artist known to us.[25] The provenance of this painting (Figure 6.6) has been obscure, but I have recently consulted documents that link it securely to San Domenico.[26] The painting has been assigned to an anonymous Pisan artist and dated anywhere from 1385 to 1450. When one considers the object in the context of the convent of San Domenico, however, both dates seem extreme, and another alternative can be proposed.

The painting has a problematic relationship to the description of Catherine's mystic marriage in Raymond of Capua's *Legenda Maior*, which was composed between 1385 and 1395 and circulated beginning in 1398.[27] While some details follow the authorized vita, other details vary. Following Raymond of Capua's text, the painting depicts Catherine's vision in which the adult Christ gives her a ring as token of spiritual marriage while several saints witness the betrothal. Although the vita says this took place in Catherine's cell at her parents' home, the architecture here, with its oratory and high walls, resembles a convent; the lily makes the wall enclose a garden, evoking the imagery of the Song of Songs and its nuptial themes. Catherine looks up to receive a ring from Christ, who appears to her in a cloud above the wall, accompanied by the Virgin and Saints Peter, Paul, and Dominic. Here again the image diverges from Raymond of Capua's account of the event; the *Legenda Maior* describes John the Evangelist and King David among the saints attending Christ, and does not mention Saint Peter. In the painting, the Virgin does not hold Catherine's hand as Christ places a ring on her finger, as is carefully described in Raymond's account. This latter detail is probably the most surprising omission, as it is common to many later images of Catherine's espousal.[28] In this early formulation of the Sienese saint's iconography for San Domenico, the Virgin's role is played down and the details are more open to interpretation. This might suggest a date for the image prior to the circulation of Raymond of Capua's definitive vita. But two of the nuns of San Domenico, Chiara Gambacorta and Maria Mancini, were correspondents and associates of Catherine of Siena, who may have had access to versions of Catherine's life other than the *Legenda Maior*.[29] The nuns may also have had their own reasons for diverging from Raymond's text; for example, the inclusion of Saint Peter may be a reference to the patron of the convent, Pietro Gambacorta, Chiara's father.

The *Mystic Marriage of Catherine of Siena* is similar in size, if not in format, to the *Mystic Marriage of Catherine of Alexandria* (Figure 6.6) and one wonders if they were meant to be companions. If so, a date during the first decade of the fifteenth century would make sense for the former image, although it is difficult to say which of the two is earlier. The possibility that the two works complement each other suggests that they be read together. Perhaps the relative lack of prominence of the Virgin in Catherine of Siena's espousal is balanced by her prominence in Catherine of Alexandria's. Both images set the event in a garden, place the *sposa di Cristo* in the same location in the composition, and give her the same gesture. This gesture, in which the left hand is held against the breast while the right hand is extended toward Christ, had already been established in images of the mystic marriage of the Virgin and the marriage of Catherine of Alexandria; its appropriation for Catherine of Siena enhances the import of the Dominican's parallel experience.[30] Her status is also elevated by the halo surrounding her head, apparently original to the painting, which anticipates her canonization by fifty or sixty years.

San Domenico's *Mystic Marriage of Catherine of Siena*, which Meiss argued was the earliest representation of an event from Catherine's legend,[31] was probably commissioned as part of the Dominican effort to have her canonized, an effort that was spearheaded by the members of the Dominican order committed to its reform. Chiara Gambacorta had a definite stake in Catherine of Siena's cult—as a Dominican, as an Observant, and as an individual whose life had been deeply affected by the Sienese saint. Her own vocation as a bride of Christ was fostered by Catherine of Siena.[32] Hence the selection of Catherine's mystic marriage, chosen from among numerous episodes in the saint's life (for example, the stigmata, the exchange of hearts with Christ, her reception of the habit from Dominic), for San Domenico's painting may be the result of Chiara's own connection to the Sienese tertiary. The painting, however, would also present the nuns of San Domenico with an important exemplar for their own religious lives.

Another painting executed for San Domenico focuses on the Crucifixion (Figure 6.7). This painting is unusual in having been painted on canvas rather than in fresco, on rather a large scale (288 × 206 cm).[33] A Latin inscription at the bottom of the image informs us that the work was painted for the monastery of San Domenico during Chiara Gambacorta's prioracy, gives the date as 1405, and tells us the name of the donor and the

Figure 6.6. Pisan Artist, *Mystic Marriage of Saint Catherine of Siena*, Pisa, Museo Nazionale di San Matteo. (Photo courtesy of Pisa, Soprintendenza ai beni ambientali, architettonici, artistici e storici)

Figure 6.7. Giovanni di Pietro di Napoli, *Crucifixion*, Pisa, Museo Nazionale di San Matteo. (Photo courtesy of Pisa, Soprintendenza ai beni ambientali, architettonici, artistici e storici)

name of the artist, Giovanni di Pietro di Napoli, to whom the panel of Saint Catherine of Alexandria has also been attributed.[34]

This painting does not take the form of an altarpiece, rather it was conceived as a wall decoration; the painted frame surrounding the image encloses the composition as would a frescoed frame. But why was it painted on canvas and not in fresco?[35] Was this medium chosen as a less expensive alternative? Was it intended for some spot in the convent still under construction in 1404? I have not been able to identify the original location intended for this painting within the convent, although its large size suggests that it was meant for some communal gathering spot. It may have been painted for the refectory as it was Dominican practice to place an image of the Crucifixion there.[36]

For this painting, we know the name of the donor, and something of his association with San Domenico. Stefano Lapi was a wealthy Pisan and "converso" (lay brother) of the convent, whose daughters and, eventually, wife joined the community.[37] He is depicted here with a younger man, perhaps a son. Stefano Lapi had long been a disciple of Gambacorta; according to Chiara's vita, he assisted her in disposing of her wealth before she entered the religious life. His long friendship with the prioress suggests his familiarity with her principles and his role as *converso* would have made him an executor of her wishes.[38] Although Lapi may have paid for the painting, it is likely that Gambacorta was involved in shaping its content and perhaps its form.

In its basic elements, this interpretation of the Crucifixion is familiar to us from countless versions of this theme executed throughout the Trecento, but the variations here deserve exploration. Perhaps most obvious is the presence of Saint Francis, who embraces the cross and kisses the feet of Christ. The participation of Saint Francis in the drama of Calvary has precedents in Franciscan imagery of the fourteenth century, for example, in Cimabue's ruined fresco in the upper church at Assisi. Despite Francis's close associations with the cross, the figure who traditionally embraces it is Mary Magdalene. A follower of Giotto depicted the Magdalene embracing the cross with Francis gesturing opposite her in a Crucifixion in the lower church at Assisi. A comparison, indeed conflation, of the two saints is implied in such images. Francis behaves with the lack of decorum usually associated with the Magdalene, and stands in her traditional role.[39] Sarah Wilk has noted that observant Dominicans also commissioned images in which Dominican friars stand in for the Magdalene and suggests it reveals the high regard in which the Observants held the Magdalene.[40] I would suggest that the women of San Domenico revered Saint Francis enough to place him in the Magdalene's traditional spot.

But why should Francis be so prominent in an image clearly intended for a Dominican convent? One cannot discount the will of the donor, who may have had his own reasons for wishing to honor St. Francis, but the Gambacorta family also had ties to the Franciscans; the family tomb was in the Franciscan church in Pisa. It should also be remembered that Gambacorta began her religious career in a Franciscan house and took the name of the foundress of the Poor Clares. Furthermore, Chiara and her sisters had a special relationship with the Franciscan order. In May of 1402, at the meeting of the Chapter General of the Franciscan order, Frate Enrico, the master of the order, confirmed that Gambacorta and all the religious of the Monastero di San Domenico of Pisa could participate in the spiritual benefits of the Franciscan order, in life as well as in death.[41] As this grace was conceded to Chiara only a few years before Giovanni di Pietro di Napoli's painting was executed, it seems likely to have been a factor in the selection of the imagery.

The composition of this image also expresses Gambacorta's adherence to Observant principles. The narrative theme is reduced to the bare essentials—there is no detail of setting or supporting cast—but includes an exemplar of the religious life. Such images occur with great frequency in works commissioned for Observant convents of different religious orders, whether Carthusian[42] or Dominican; the most familiar examples come, of course, from San Marco of Florence.

The same year that Giovanni di Pietro di Napoli painted this Crucifixion, he and Martino di Bartolomeo executed another painting for San Domenico. This is a well-preserved polyptych with the Virgin and Child at the center of a group of saints, separated by the arcades of a gold-leafed frame (Figure 6.8).[43] Here we are definitely dealing with an altarpiece, in a format Henk van Os has termed "standard" for Sienese altars of the period.[44] In the privileged spot to the right of the Virgin stands Saint Dominic with his book and lily; on the Virgin's left is John the Evangelist. Female saints are placed on the outer flanks of the altarpiece: next to Dominic is the Magdalene and next to the Evangelist is Birgitta of Sweden. The latter saint has often been misidentified in the past, as Saint Scholastica,[45] probably because she wears the habit of a nun, but her veil bears a red cross, linking her to the Brigittine order, and an inscription identifies her as "Sancta Brigita Principessa." In medallions above the standing saints are John the Baptist and Stephen. A fragmentary inscription in the center

Figure 6.8. Giovanni di Pietro di Napoli and Martino di Bartolomeo, *Altarpiece of the Virgin and Child*, Pisa, Museo Nazionale di San Matteo. (Photo courtesy of Pisa, Soprintendenza ai beni ambientali, architettonici, artistici e storici)

panel dates the painting to April 1405 (1404).[46] The altarpiece may be the object mentioned in a document from Chiara's own hand, dated 1405, which records a legacy left to the convent by Chiara's aunt, Monna Giovanna; among the gifts were funds for building the church and "la tavola dello altare."[47] Her gift may be one reason for the prominence of John the Evangelist in the painting. Chiara thus would have been involved with this commission not only as the prioress of the convent, but also as a close family member of the donor.

As Dominic, the titular of the church, stands in the position of privilege, it seems probable that this altarpiece was intended for the high altar of the newly built public church; the church was dedicated to

Dominic, the Virgin, and Saint John the Baptist, all of whom are depicted. In 1402, only a few years before this altarpiece was painted, the nuns had received the gift of a relic of Saint Dominic from the Duke of Milan, through the intermediary of Giovanni Dominici.[48] The gift of the relic and the imminent completion of the church would be reason enough to commission an altarpiece for the high altar, but they had also contracted for memorial masses on the feast days of the Magdalene, Birgitta, John the Baptist, Dominic, and the Virgin.[49] For this altarpiece to have served this purpose, it must have been in the public church.

As such, the altarpiece publically proclaims the spiritual affiliation of the convent. Not only the choice of saints, but their depiction in full length flanking the Virgin results in a static, nonnarrative image of a sort the Dominican order seems especially to have preferred, at least for the high altars of their churches. The enthroned Virgin, representing the queen of this celestial court and the Church itself, is thoroughly conventional. As Joanna Cannon has pointed out, the role of the Virgin in the history of redemption is a recurring theme in Dominican patronage.[50]

Yet this description of the altarpiece from San Domenico is incomplete. The polyptych originally had a predella, which Miklos Boskovits has identified with five predella panels in the Gemäldegalerie in Berlin.[51] (It may also have had three gable figures, which would conventionally have depicted the Annunciation over the wings and God the Father at the center.) The predellas in Berlin are attributed on the basis of style to Martino di Bartolomeo.

These predellas have as their theme the achievements and miracles of Saint Birgitta of Sweden, the mystic and reformer who died in Italy in 1373. After her death, her visions and prophecies were edited by her confessor, Alfonso Pecha da Vadaterra, Bishop of Jaen, who circulated copies of the *Liber Celestis Revelationum* all over Europe. Birgitta also founded a monastic order, based—like the Dominicans'—on the rule of Saint Augustine; the order flourished in the fifteenth century not only in her native Sweden but in Italy, the Lowlands, and England. She was canonized in 1391, and her sanctity was confirmed in 1419 by Martin V.[52] Although she was championed by powerful members of the order, her feast was not entered on the Dominican calendar. So her presence in the high altarpiece for the church of San Domenico cannot be linked to the order's own liturgy.

As reconstructed, the predellas depict from left to right: Birgitta writing down the words of an angel (Figure 6.9); Birgitta writing down what Christ and the Virgin dictate (Figure 6.10); the Nativity of Christ as

Figure 6.9. Martino di Bartolomeo, Birgitta taking dictation from an angel, from the predella, Figure 6.8, Berlin-Dahlem, Gemäldegalerie. (Photo courtesy of the Museum)

Figure 6.10. Martino di Bartolomeo, Birgitta taking dictation from Christ, from the predella, Figure 6.8, Berlin-Dahlem, Gemäldegalerie. (Photo courtesy of the Museum)

Birgitta experienced it in a vision in Bethlehem (Figure 6.11); her appearance in the dream of a Swedish princess standing on a column with red and white roses pouring from her mouth (Figure 6.12); and her delivery of pilgrims from a shipwreck (Figure 6.13). Thus the two images of the Swedish saint in her cell appear at the left of the predella, while two images of her miracles appear to the right. At the center is the Nativity, the most influential of Birgitta's visions; it stood directly below the Virgin and Child in the main section of the altarpiece.

The emphasis on Birgitta is surprising here. If this was the main altar of the public church, one might expect the predella to focus on Dominic, the titular, or at least to give equal space to the other saints depicted. When we examine the altarpiece in the context of the spiritual and liturgical life of San Domenico, however, the focus on Birgitta makes sense. As we have seen, Chiara Gambacorta was especially devoted to Birgitta, about whom she learned from Birgitta's own confessor and editor. Her vita reports that she owned a copy of Birgitta's *Istorie*, a gift from the bishop;[53] this was probably her Revelations.[54] There are certain parallels between their lives that may explain why Birgitta had such appeal for Gambacorta: both were widows, both were concerned with reforming the church, both had the gift of seeing into people's hearts. And Chiara Gambacorta used her considerable influence in Pisa to promote the Swedish mystic's cult. Special celebrations were held in San Domenico on the saint's feast day, and Chiara arranged for public preaching about Birgitta.[55] She seems also to have maintained close ties with the Brigittine foundation in Florence, the double monastery called Paradiso; at one point about 1395, a rumor circulated that Chiara intended to leave San Domenico and enter the Florentine Brigittine house.[56]

So the altarpiece, probably destined for the high altar of the public church of San Domenico, not only reflects Chiara Gambacorta's personal devotion to Saint Birgitta, but is part of a deliberate effort on her part to promote the cult of Saint Birgitta in Pisa. As such, the themes for the predella must have been chosen to underscore the aspects of Birgitta's life that Gambacorta felt were most important or most persuasive to an audience in Pisa. Therefore, this predella does not show the founding of her order, which is depicted in several Tuscan manuscripts of the Revelations and in altarpieces for the Florentine Brigittine house, or the transmission of her Revelations to the Kings of the Earth, which is depicted in some of the earliest manuscripts of her Revelations.[57] The predella instead emphasizes Birgitta's writing, her visions, and her miracles. Two of the images,

Figure 6.11. Martino di Bartolomeo, Birgitta's vision of the Nativity, from the predella, Figure 6.8, Berlin-Dahlem, Gemäldegalerie. (Photo courtesy of the Museum)

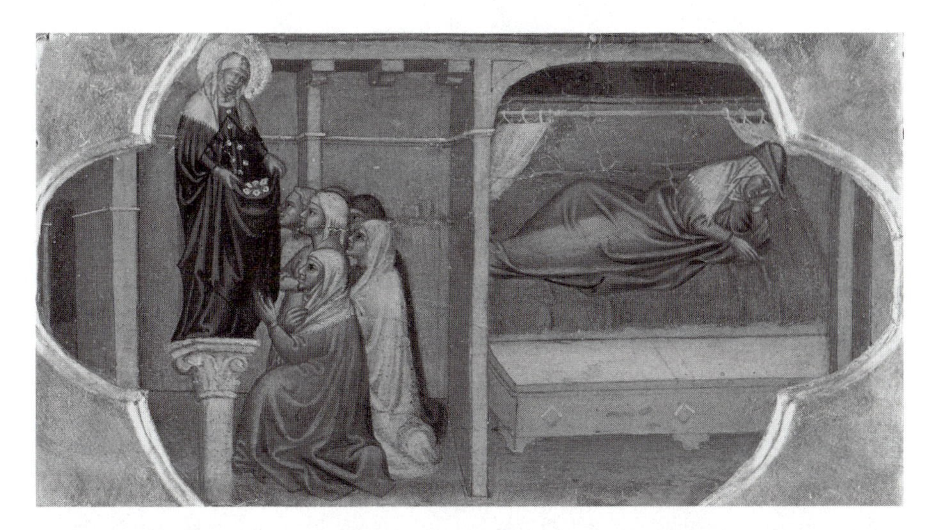

Figure 6.12. Martino di Bartolomeo, Birgitta appearing in the dream of the princess, from the predella, Figure 6.8, Berlin-Dahlem, Gemäldegalerie. (Photo courtesy of the Museum)

Figure 6.13. Martino di Bartolomeo, Birgitta interceding for shipwrecked pilgrims, from the predella, Figure 6.8, Berlin-Dahlem, Gemäldegalerie. (Photo courtesy of the Museum)

in fact, stress Birgitta's access to divine truth by representing the nun's taking dictation from an angel and from Christ and the Virgin. Rather than presenting the content of her visions, these images stress their divine source and Birgitta's active role in recording them. She is not depicted dictating the text, although her vita makes clear that her usual procedure involved a scribe. The central predella panel describes her most famous vision (about which more later), which was popularized by her writings.

The choice of miracles depicted is equally selective. Although the canonization documents describe numerous miracles of healing the blind or paralytic, or Birgitta's intervention in difficult childbirths, the predellas focus on other issues. The fourth image attests to the persuasiveness and inspiration of Birgitta's words, which fall from her mouth like roses before a spellbound audience of lay people in the dream of a Swedish princess.[58] Often in her vita and in the canonization documents Birgitta is heralded for having converted a sinner by her words. A local interest may have played a part in the selection of this event from among Birgitta's miracles; a member of the community at San Domenico, Maria Mancini, had a similar vision. Having heard about Saint Birgitta, she desired to see and hear the Swedish saint, and was blessed with a vision of the saint, who instructed her in aspects of the spiritual life.[59] The final image in the predella represents Birgitta's rescue of seafaring pilgrims, a choice certainly apposite in the seagoing culture of Pisa with perhaps a personal significance for Chiara Gambacorta, whose father had been a pilgrim to the Holy Land with Alfonso of Jaen. Birgitta is presented as learned, authoritative, mystically inspired, a potent intercessor. The predella offers the viewer in the public church of this convent not only a catalogue of qualities that Chiara Gambacorta admired in Birgitta, but qualities that the viewer could associate with the nuns in the convent of San Domenico.

Confronted with a commission to execute these scenes of a relatively new saint without a standard iconography, Martino di Bartolomeo likely looked for models in the illustrated manuscripts of Birgitta's Revelations, of which several late fourteenth-century Italian examples survive. He probably found little in the Sienese tradition to supply him with sources, as the studies of Grazia Vailati Schoenburg Waldenburg and Henk van Os seem to indicate.[60] Closer parallels may be seen in manuscripts produced in Naples (an early center of Brigittine devotion), such as Morgan Library M.498, which Carl Nordenfalk has identified as one of a series of illuminated Revelations that date shortly after Birgitta's death.[61] The frontispiece of this manuscript (Figure 6.14) depicts Birgitta seated at a desk in

Figure 6.14. Birgitta inspired by Heaven, from the *Liber Celestis Revelationum*, New York, Morgan Library, Ms. 498, f. 4v. (Photo courtesy of Morgan Library).

the lower right corner of the composition. Martino di Bartolomeo's Birgitta (Figure 6.10) sits in much the same posture, in the same direction, with a book in her lap and her hand upraised as in the Morgan miniature. A similar depiction of the saint occurs in an historiated initial on f. 8 of the Morgan manuscript.[62]

Although the Morgan manuscript may have been executed in Naples, it then traveled to Genoa as the property of Alfonso da Vadaterra, who had given a copy of the Swedish mystic's *Istorie* to Chiara Gambacorta probably in 1378. We cannot be certain that the book Alfonso gave to Chiara was decorated, but Alfonso was distributing such deluxe manuscripts all over Europe at this time and he may have given the daughter of Pisa's ruler a book rather like his own. The similarities in parts of Martino's predella to some of the images in the Morgan manuscript suggest that he was looking at something like the Morgan Revelations, for which Gambacorta would be the logical intermediary. Chiara, then, would have been important to the altarpiece not only in selecting the themes to be depicted, but in providing models from which the artist could work.

Chiara Gambacorta was probably the force behind the commission of another work of art dedicated to Saint Birgitta, an image of her vision of the Nativity at Bethelehem, also in Pisa's Museum and with a firm connection to San Domenico (Figure 6.15). This panel has been assigned to several Pisan artists, but is currently attributed to the Pisan painter Turino Vanni.[63] The theme is the same as the central predella of the high altar. In her vision, Birgitta saw the Virgin dressed in a gown of white, having cast off her outer garment and shoes, adoring the newborn Christ who lay naked on the ground. She describes Saint Joseph holding a candle whose light was outshone by the supernatural glow of Mother and Child. Popularized by her Revelations, this vision greatly influenced the iconography of the Nativity in the fifteenth century.[64]

The painting from San Domenico faithfully depicts these picturesque details in the context of an otherwise conventional Nativity scene, which includes such standard features as the ox and ass, music-making angels and the annunciation to the shepherds in the distance. The mountainous setting refers to the grotto where the vision took place. This mountain formation has three alcoves in which the figures are placed, with the Virgin and Child in the largest opening at the center, Joseph in a separate alcove on the right, and Birgitta herself in an alcove on the left. In a mandorla above the scene appears God the Father, from whom rays of light descend on Christ, the Virgin, Saint Joseph, and Birgitta herself. Birgitta is thus a

Figure 6.15. Attributed to Turino Vanni, *Saint Birgitta's Vision of the Nativity*, Pisa, Museo Nazionale di San Matteo. (Photo courtesy of Pisa, Soprintendenza ai beni ambientali, architettonici, artistici e storici)

partner in this event, equal at least to Saint Joseph; in fact, her position at the left of the composition makes her more prominent than Saint Joseph.

There was another Tuscan version of this theme current in the late fourteenth century or early fifteenth century, which has survived in a fresco at Santa Maria Novella in Florence and at least two paintings, one in the Vatican and one in the Johnson collection in Philadelphia, attributed somewhat tentatively to Niccolo di Tommaso (Figure 6.16).[65] The composition and details of the latter painting are quite different from San Domenico's: the structure of the grotto, the form of the haloes, the gesture of Saint Joseph all differ. Although the Philadelphia panel includes Saint Birgitta in the composition, she is placed outside the main space of the image in the lower right corner without the prominence she is given in the Pisan painting. If the main point of San Domenico's image is to convey the content of Birgitta's vision of the Nativity, a secondary function is to celebrate the author of the vision.

The special connection we have explored between Chiara and Saint Birgitta suggests that Chiara was again the force behind the commission. Chiara's death in 1419 would then be the *terminus ante quem* for this painting, as Birgitta's canonization in 1391 must serve as a *terminus post quem*. Little else in the documents helps to pinpoint the date for this image, and the style of Turino Vanni is not well enough understood to suggest a date on this basis. Perhaps, however, a relationship to the predella of the 1404 altarpiece may help to date this image more precisely. Both Nativities share the basic details of Birgitta's vision in a similar arrangement, although figures rendered in three-quarters view in the painting are in profile in the predella; the ox and the ass and the rendering of the Child are strikingly similar. God the Father also appears in the predella, but its horizontal format requires him to be pushed off to one side rather than appear at top center. The shared details of the two works, and the greater complexity and symmetry of the Vanni picture, suggest that it may have been one of the models consulted by Martino di Bartolomeo when he painted the predella for the altarpiece dated April 1404. If so, the painting attributed to Turino Vanni would have had to be in San Domenico before 1404.

Here again, I would suggest, the prioress took an active role in leading the artist to an appropriate model for his picture. She would thus be involved not only in the content, but in the form of the painting. Her role in the making of these images is as complex as her role in overseeing the enlargement of the conventual buildings. If she did not deal with masons or carpenters on a daily basis, she was involved in raising funds, keeping

Figure 6.16. Niccolo di Tommaso, altarpiece with Birgitta's Vision of the Nativity, Philadelphia, Philadelphia Museum of Art, Johnson Collection. (Photo courtesy of Philadelphia Museum of Art)

the projects going, and seeing them to completion. She surely made her wishes known in the works paid for by her family and supporters. It is worth noting that the paintings executed during the prioracy of Chiara Gambacorta gave special prominence to exemplars of the religious life (Catherine of Alexandria, Francis of Assisi, Catherine of Siena, Birgitta of

Sweden) and to female saints. The primary audience of several of these images—for example, the two Catherines, the Crucifixion with Francis of Assisi—was probably the nuns themselves, but the altarpiece was aimed at the public who had access to the outer church of the convent, access that the nuns did not have. Not only did this altarpiece serve the needs of the liturgy and promote to the public those saints revered by the order and the prioress, but its emphasis on the visions and miracles of Saint Birgitta demonstrated to the laity the important role that religious women played in the lives of secular men and women.

Notes

1. For the programs of the Pisan Dominicans, see Joanna Cannon, "Dominican Patronage of the Arts in Central Italy: The Provincia Romana c.1220–1320," Ph.D. dissertation, University of London, 1980. See also Millard Meiss, *Francesco Traini*, ed. Hayden B. J. Maginnis (Washington, DC: Decatur House Press, 1983); and Ellen Callman, "Thebaid Studies," *Antichità Viva* 14 (1975): 3–22. A recent study with excellent insight into the traditions of Dominican patronage is William Hood, *Fra Angelico at San Marco* (New Haven, CT: Yale University Press, 1993).

2. The only time such activity has been discussed in the past is in Dominican-authored studies of the order's artists or convents, for example, in Vincenzo Marchese, *Memorie dei più insigni pittori, scultori ed architetti domenicani* (Florence: A. Parenti, 1845–46), or Innocenzo Taurisano, *I Domenicani in Lucca* (Lucca: Baroni, 1914). These studies have been most concerned with artistic production by nuns.

3. These issues were raised in a session of the College Art Association annual meeting in February 1991, the proceedings of which, edited by Caroline Bruzelius and Constance Berman, have appeared in *Gesta* 31 (1992); and by Caroline Walker Bynum in the introduction to her essays in *Fragmentation and Redemption. Essays on Gender and the Human Body in Medieval Religion* (New York: Zone Books, 1991).

4. The tomb is now preserved at the new convent of San Domenico in Pisa, Via della Faggiola, 26. On it, see Roberto Paolo Ciardi et al., *Scultura a Pisa tra Quattro e Seicento* (Pisa: Pacini, 1987), pp. 17–18.

5. On Chiara Gambacorta, see Niccola Zucchelli, *La Beata Chiara Gambacorta: La Chiesa ed il Convento di San Domenico in Pisa* (Pisa: Tipografia Editrice Cav. F. Mariotti, 1914); and S. Ferrali, "Gambacorta, Chiara," in *Bibliotheca Sanctorum* (Rome: Istituto Giovanni XXIII nella Pontificia Università lateranense, 1965): vol. 6, cols, 23–26. The only biography of Chiara in English was written by Sister Mary Evelyn Murphy, O.P., *Blessed Chiara Gambacorta* (Fribourg: Imprimerie de l'oeuvre de Saint-Paul, 1928), but Chiara was chosen as a paradigmatic

fourteenth-century saint by Richard Kieckhefer for *Unquiet Souls: Fourteenth-Century Saints and Their Religious Milieu* (Chicago: University of Chicago Press, 1984).

6. For Chiara's role as a stimulus to the reformers, see Daniel Mortier, *Histoire des maîtres généraux de l'Ordre des frères prêcheurs* (Paris: A. Picard, 1902–1920), vol. 3, pp. 583–93; and Vincenzo Marchese, *Scritti Vari* (Florence: F. Le Monnier, 1855), pp. 32, 445–47.

7. See Rudolph M. Bell, *Holy Anorexia* (Chicago: University of Chicago Press, 1985), p. 222; and Kieckhefer, *Unquiet Souls*, pp. 44–49 and passim.

8. The text of this letter has been published in Zucchelli, *La Beata Chiara Gambacorta*, p. 346. This English translation is from Murphy, *Blessed Chiara Gambacorta*, p. 115.

9. In a letter to Francesco di Marco Datini, dated July 17, 1410 (Pisan style, thus actually 1409), Chiara writes: "This seems the opportune time to roof the dormitory, and we therefore earnestly beg you . . . to lend us what we ask of you for a few months." The letter is translated in Murphy, *Blessed Chiara Gambacorta*, p. 145.

10. The third story in this branch of the convent is a modern addition.

11. Again, Chiara's letters to Datini record the transactions made between them; in a letter of 1397, published in Zucchelli, *La Beata Chiara Gambacorta*, p. 354, Chiara writes to Francesco: "Ho ricevuto le carte, da far lo Pistolario."

12. On Dominici's activities in this area, see Creighton Gilbert, "Tuscan Observants and Painters in Venice ca. 1400," in *Interpretazioni Veneziane: studi di storia dell'arte in onore di Michelangelo Muraro*, ed. David Rosand (Venice: Arsenale, 1984), pp. 109–20.

13. These inventories are transcribed and analyzed in my forthcoming study, "Dominican Women and Renaissance Art."

14. Now in the Museo Nazionale di San Matteo in Pisa. The painting measures 163 × 78 cm. For this work, see Enzo Carli, *Il Museo Civico di Pisa* (Pisa: Pacini, 1974), p. 64; and Augusto Bellini Pietri, *Catalogo del Museo Civico di Pisa* (Pisa: Tipografia municipale, 1906), pp. 133–34.

15. The inscription reads, "Mcccciiii Aprile fu il mese preghiamo dio per chi fa le spese." The date should be translated to 1403, because the Pisan calendar is a year ahead of the common calendar.

16. It is described as such in the inventories mentioned in n. 13.

17. On which see, Joanna Cannon, "Simone Martini, the Dominicans and the Early Sienese Polyptych," *Journal of the Warburg and Courtauld Institutes* 45 (1982): 69–93.

18. Michael Goodich, "The Contours of Female Piety in Later Medieval Hagiography," *Church History* 50 (1981): 20–32.

19. See the description of the ceremony in M. Auge, "Consecrazione delle vergine," *Dizionario degli Instituti di Perfezione*, ed. Guerrino Pelliccia and Giancarlo Rocca (Rome: Edizioni Paoline, 1975), vol. 2: cols. 1613–27.

20. A. H. Thomas, "La profession religieuse des Dominicains: formule, cérémonies, histoire," *Archivum Fratrum Predicatorum* 39 (1969): 5–52.

21. For the greater tangibility of the "bride of Christ" metaphor for women than for men, see John Bugge, *Virginitas: An Essay in the History of a Medieval Ideal* (The Hague: Martinus Nijhoff, 1975), especially pp. 80–110.

22. Millard Meiss, *Painting in Florence and Siena After the Black Death* (New York: Harper and Row, 1964), pp. 111–13.

23. Jeffrey Hamburger, *The Rothschild Canticles* (New Haven, CT: Yale University Press, 1991).

24. For Giovanni di Pietro da Napoli, see Ulrich Thieme and Felix Becker, *Allgemeines Lexikon der Bildenden Kunstler von der Antike bis zur Gegenwart* (Leipzig: W. Engelmann, 1907–50), vol. 14, p. 140; Richard Offner, *Italian Primitives at Yale University* (New Haven, CT: Yale University Press, 1927), p. 42; Bernard Berenson, *Italian Pictures of the Renaissance, Central Italian and North Italian Schools* (London: Phaidon, 1986), vol. 1, pp. 182–83.

25. Now in Pisa at the Museo Nazionale di San Matteo. It measures 107 × 71 cm. See Carli, *Il Museo di Pisa*, p. 83, where it is assigned to the Pisan "Master of Saint Ursula."

26. The painting is described by Carlo Lasinio, the first keeper of the city's paintings in the Camposanto, in an 1810 inventory as being from San Domenico: "A painting on panel representing Saint Catherine of Siena, on her knees below a building, various saints in a glory, in the good style of the 1400's." The document is in the archive of the Accademia of Florence. The full documentation will appear in my forthcoming study of the convent's patronage.

27. For the text of Raymond of Capua's vita see *Acta Sanctorum* (Paris, 1866), April, vol. 3, pp. 861–986. A convenient English translation is *The Life of Catherine of Siena*, translated and annotated by Conleth Kearns (Wilmington, DE: Michael Glazier, 1980).

28. See the examples in George Kaftal, *Saint Catherine in Tuscan Painting* (Oxford, Blackfriars, 1949), pp. 46–51.

29. Meiss, *Painting in Florence and Siena*, pp. 111–113, discusses a version of Catherine's life, the *Miracoli*, written in 1374. The mystic marriage took place prior to 1362, that is, before Catherine met either Maria Mancini or Chiara Gambacorta, which was probably in 1375 when the Sienese saint sojourned in Pisa. Both women were included on Tommaso Caffarini's list of potential witnesses for Catherine of Siena's canonization *processus*, early in the fifteenth century. See Robert Fawtier, *Sainte Catherine: essai de critique des sources* (Paris: Éditions de Boccard, 1921), p. 43.

30. See Meiss, *Painting in Florence and Siena*, Figs. 99, 100, 105, 107.

31. Meiss, *Painting in Florence and Siena*, p. 113 n. 33. This conclusion depends on his acceptance of a date c. 1385, which I have argued is not likely. It must further be modified by the recent dating of a painting in the Museo Vetreria in Murano of Catherine of Siena's stigmata to the 1390's by Gaudenz Freuler, "Andrea di Bartolo, Fra Tommaso d'Antonio Caffarini, and Sienese Dominicans in Venice," *Art Bulletin* 69 (1987): 570–86. This painting, too, comes from a house of Observant Dominican women.

32. Two letters from Catherine of Siena to Chiara Gambacorta (addressed to "Monna Tora, figliola di Misser Pietro Gambacorta") encourage the newly wid-

owed girl to persist in her desire to leave the secular world. The letters are published in Zucchelli, *La Beata Chiara Gambacorta*, pp. 22–28. They are numbers CXCIV and CCLXII in Niccolò Tommaseo's edition of *S. Caterina da Siena: Le Lettere* (Siena: Giuntina & Bentivoglio, 1913–1923), v. 3, pp. 105 and 416.

33. Now in Pisa, at the Museo Nazionale di San Matteo. See Bellini Pietri, *Catalogo del Museo Civico di Pisa*, p. 134; Carli, *Il Museo di Pisa*, p. 64, mentions the picture without cataloguing it.

34. The inscription reads: "Factum fuit tenpore sororis clare priorisse istius monasterii Anno Domini M cccc v Fieri Fecit Stefanus Lapi domini Lapi Roghate Deum Pro eo Iohannis Petri de Neapoli pinsit." Again, the date 1405 may need to be rolled back to 1404, because of the idiosyncratic Pisan calendar.

35. The likeness of this painting to fresco has led many scholars to discuss it as a fresco transferred to canvas, but Bellini Pietri, *Catalogo del Museo Civico di Pisa*, p. 134, refers to this as "uno dei pochi grandi dipinti su tela dell'epoca." For a discussion of the relative costs and possible reasons for choosing canvas over panel, see Diane Wolfthal, *The Beginnings of Netherlandish Canvas Painting* (Cambridge: Cambridge University Press, 1989). See also Martin Wackernagel, *The World of the Florentine Renaissance Artist*, trans. Alison Luchs (Princeton, NJ: Princeton University Press, 1981), pp. 154–55.

36. On Dominican refectories and their adornment, see Creighton Gilbert, "Last Suppers and Their Refectories," in *The Pursuit of Holiness in Late Medieval and Renaissance Religion*, ed. Charles Trinkaus and Heiko A. Oberman (Leiden: E. J. Brill, 1974), pp. 371–402.

37. Stefano Lapi's relationship to the convent is documented in a brief vita of his daughter, Giovanna, written by Domenico da Peccioli, the convent's first confessor and a friar at Santa Caterina. The vita is published in Zucchelli, *La Beata Chiara Gambacorta*, p. 397. His earlier connection with Chiara is described in the vita of Chiara written by one of her contemporaries and published in Zucchelli, p. 371–72.

38. See R. Creytens, "Les convers des moniales dominicaines au moyen âge," *Archivum Fratrum Predicatorum* 19 (1949): 5–48.

39. Caroline Bynum notes that both Francis and the Magdalene were associated with devotion to Christ's toes; see Bynum, "The Body of Christ in the Later Middle Ages: A Reply to Leo Steinberg," *Renaissance Quarterly* 39 (1986): 437, n. 80.

40. See Sarah Wilk, "The Cult of Mary Magdalen in Fifteenth-Century Florence and Its Iconography," *Studi Medievali* ser. 3, 26 (1985): 685–98.

41. Pisa, Archivio di Stato. Diplomatico S. Domenico. 147 bis. 1402, May 17.

42. See, for example, the numerous images of Crucifixions with Carthusians at the foot of the cross which Charles Sterling has linked to the Chartreuse de Champmol in Dijon; Charles Sterling, "Oeuvres retrouvées de Jean de Beaumetz, peintre de Philippe le Hardi," *Musées Royaux des Beaux-Arts Bulletin* 4 (1955): 59–62. One such panel is in the Cleveland Museum of Art, for which see, The Cleveland Museum of Art, *European Paintings Before 1500* (Cleveland: The Cleveland Museum of Art, 1974), pp. 12–15.

43. Now in Pisa, Museo Nazionale di San Matteo. It measures 134 × 198

cm. See Carli, *Il Museo di Pisa*, p. 63 and Bellini Pietri, *Catalogo del Museo Civico di Pisa*, p. 99–100. Current scholarship sees this panel as a collaboration between Giovanni di Pietro di Napoli and Martino di Bartolomeo.

44. Henk van Os, *Sienese Altarpieces, 1215–1460: Form, Content, Function, II, 1344–1460* (Groningen: Egbert Forsten Publishing, 1990), pp. 35–64.

45. Giorgio Vigni, *Pittura del Due e Trecento nel Museo di Pisa* (Palermo: Palumbo, 1950), p. 70, calls her Scholastica, as does Berenson, *Italian Pictures of the Renaissance*, vol. 1, p. 183.

46. As best I can make out, the inscription in the center panel reads: "M CCCC V dAbrile Io H . . . . Ise Pregiamo dio . . . . :"

47. A document in the Diplomatico of San Domenico at the Archivio di Stato of Pisa records the following donations (this transcription comes from Zucchelli, *La Beata Chiara Gambacorta*, pp. 197–198): "Anno Domini MCCCCVI [stile pisano] Noi Monache del Monasterio di Santo Dominico abbiamo ricevuto da monna Giovanna donna che fu di Choscio Gambacorta fiorini CCC.[the document goes on to clarify how this sum was to be divided among monna Giovanna's heirs, the friars minor, and the convent of San Domenico] Ancora per denari ci die quando si fe la chiesa grossa limosina e per la tavola dello altare; ci oblighamo e promettemo di darci per lle e per lli sui morti tre messe la settimana."

48. Recorded by Domenico da Peccioli in his history of the convent, published as follows by Zucchelli, *La Beata Chiara Gambacorta*, pp. 88–89: "non est silentio omittendum ut rei certae notitia, transmittatur ad posteros, nec a devito gratitudinis, in quantum nobis est, per ignorantiam excusemur. Qualiter Dominus Johannes Dominicus, Monasterii et Conventus nostri valde devotus, olim referendarius in Civitate Bononiae per illustri Principe Domino Duce Mediolani ex Reliquiis B. Patris Dominici in dicta civitate existentibus, unum ex dentibus honorifice collacatum in quodam tabernaculo argenteo, ad praefatum vestrum Monasterium transmisit, quem habemus apud nos. A.D. MCCCCIII." As Giangaleozzo Visconti, the Duke of Milan referred to in the document, died in September 1402 (common style), these events must have taken place before this date; Peccioli uses the Pisan calendar.

49. These masses were contracted in honor of Manno degli Agli, an associate and friend of Francesco di Marco Datini, who died in Pisa in 1400. A stone tablet, still preserved by the nuns of San Domenico, records their obligation. The inscription, transcribed by Zucchelli, *La Beata Chiara Gambacorta*, p. 243, reads as follows: "Memoria duna limosina che Manno Degli Agli da Firenze lasso almonistero di san Domenico di pisa con condisione che le monache faccino dire ognianno nella loro chiesa cinque messe perlanima sua in perpetuo cio e lo di di santa maria Maddalena lo di di santa brigida lo di di santo johanni baptista lo di di sancto dominico lo di di sancta Maria di septembre et in quanto lassasseno questo fare lo dicto lassito lasso alla chiesa di sancta maria maggiore di firenze conditione di far dire le dicte messe nei dicti di mori di luglio mcccci."

50. Joanna Cannon, "Dominican Patronage of the Arts in Central Italy."

51. Miklos Boskovits, *Frühe Italienische Malerei Gemäldegalerie Berlin* (Berlin: Gebr. Mann, 1988), pp. 103–6.

52. See the entry by M. C. Celletti in the *Biblioteca Sanctorum* vol. 3, p. 530. The canonization documents have been published in *Acta et Processus Canonizacionis Beate Birgitte*, ed. Isak Collijn (Uppsala: Almqvist & Wiksell, 1924–31). For her iconography, see George Kaftal, *The Iconography of the Saints in Tuscan Painting* (Florence: Sansoni, 1952), pp. 218–20. Less useful is Anthony Butkovich, *Iconography of St. Birgitta of Sweden* (Los Angeles, CA: Ecumenical Foundation of America, 1969).

53. Zucchelli, *La Beata Chiara Gambacorta*, p. 373, quoting from the contemporary vita of Chiara: "li disse di Santa Brigida, et delli il libro della sua Istoria, et Ella la prese in tanta devossione, et fecela sua advocata, et da Lei ricevute molte gratie."

54. To my knowledge, no manuscript of the Revelations from San Domenico survives, but San Domenico's sister house of Corpus Domini in Venice owned a manuscript of the Revelations (in Latin), which is now in the Biblioteca Nazionale Marciana in Venice, Ms. Lat. III 225. The manuscript, dated to the early 1400s, includes the following note: "Primum volumen revelacionum beate brigide monasterii corporis christi de veneciis ordinis predicatorum." See *Sancta Birgitta Revelaciones Liber I* ed. Carl-Gustaf Undhagen (Stockholm: Almqvist & Wiksell, 1977), p. 164. It should be remembered that these two houses exchanged books for copying, so Corpus Domini's manuscript may have been made after a manuscript from San Domenico.

55. Mentioned by Kieckhefer, *Unquiet Souls*, pp. 45–46.

56. Discussed in a letter of Ser Lapo Mazzei, the notary of Francesco Datini, dated 13 November 1395: "Ben farei a dare alcuna cosa di mia mano: che so che vale quello che vi disse la Monaca da Pisa: ma voi non ve ne ricordate. Ella viene ora a entrare nel santo monistero di Santa Brisida, che fa messer Antonio," Lapo Mazzei, *Lettere d'un notaro a un mercant del secolo XIV* ed. Cesare Guasti (Florence: Le Monnier, 1880) vol. I, p. 120. See also Geneviève Hasenohr Esnos, "Un Recueil inédit de lettres de direction spirituelle au XVe siècle, Le ms. Vat. lat. 11259 de la Bibliothèque Vaticane," *Mélanges d'Archéologie et d'Histoire* 82 (1970): 420.

57. For these other images of Birgitta, see Kaftal, *Iconography of the Saints in Tuscan Painting*, pp. 218–20 and Carl Nordenfalk, "Saint Bridget of Sweden as Represented in Illuminated Manuscripts," in *De artibus opuscula XL: Essays in Honor of Erwin Panofsky*, ed. Millard Meiss (New York: New York University Press, 1961), pp. 371–93.

58. Boskovits identified the subject of this panel, the textual source for which is an eighteenth century vita of Birgitta: G. Burlamacchi, *Vita della serafica madre S. Brigida di Svezia* (Naples, 1720), p. 118.

59. This event is recorded in the life of Maria Mancini reported in Giuseppe Sainati, *Vite dei santi, beati e servi di dio nati nella diocesa pisani*, 3d ed. (Pisa, 1884), pp. 156–57.

60. Grazia Vailati Schoenburg Waldenburg, "Le Rivelazioni di Santa Brigida, Ms. I V 25/26 della Biblioteca Communale di Siena," in *La Miniatura Italiana in età Romanica e Gotica*, ed. Grazia Vailati Schoenburg Waldenburg (Florence: Olschki, 1979), pp. 553–74 and Henk van Os, *Sienese Altarpieces*, pp. 119–20.

61. Nordenfalk, "Saint Bridget," p. 373 and passim; for the Morgan manuscript, see also the description in Undhagen, *Sancta Birgitta Revelaciones Liber I*, pp. 156–60.

62. Nordenfalk, "Saint Bridget," Fig. 9.

63. The panel is now in Pisa at the Museo Nazionale di San Matteo; it measures 132 × 100 cm. See Carli, *Il Museo di Pisa*, pp. 70–80 and Bellini Pietri, *Catalogo del Museo Civico di Pisa*, p. 92. The attribution of this painting has been quite controversial over the years; it has been linked to artists from Florence, Orvieto, Lucca and Pisa. The Pisan museum currently assigns it to Turino Vanni, and I see no reason to reject this attribution. For Turino Vanni, see Thieme and Becker, *Allgemeines Lexicon*, vol. 33, p. 488; and M. Frinta, "A Seemingly Florentine, Yet Not Really Florentine Altarpiece," *Burlington Magazine* 117 (1975): 527–35.

64. Henrik Cornell, *Iconography of the Nativity of Christ* (Uppsala: A.-b. Lundequistska bokhandeln, 1924) and Erwin Panofsky, *Early Netherlandish Painting* (Cambridge, MA: Harvard University Press, 1953), pp. 125 ff.

65. For the Philadelphia panel, see *Catalogue of Italian Paintings: John G. Johnson Collection* (Philadelphia: Philadelphia Museum of Art, 1964), p. 58; and Frederick Antal, *Florentine Painting and Its Social Background* (London: K. Paul, 1948), p. 199, who assigns the Philadelphia panel to Niccolo di Tommaso, along with the Vatican panel.

Part II

Women's Religious Expression: Sixteenth and Seventeenth Centuries

Carolyn Valone

7. Piety and Patronage: Women and the Early Jesuits

In 1990 and 1991 Jesuits throughout the world celebrated the "Ignatian Year," commemorating the 500th anniversary of the birth of Ignatius of Loyola in 1491, and the 450th anniversary of the founding of the Society of Jesus in Rome in 1540. Many interesting conferences and exhibitions were devoted to this celebration, but perhaps one aspect of early Jesuit history received less attention than it deserved, and that is the extraordinary role played by women patrons of the Jesuits in the second half of the sixteenth century in Rome.

Emblematic of this problem is the church of the Gesù itself, begun in 1568 and consecrated in 1584. The role of its great patron, Cardinal Alessandro Farnese, is, of course, always remembered, partly because he had his name prominently displayed across the facade of the church. But if we consider the interior of the church, and the chapels completed by the early 1600s, it may come as a surprise to find that the two main chapels on either side of the high altar were commissioned by four closely related women, that two of the six side chapels had women patrons, that a third chapel was paid for by a wife and her husband, and that the pulpit also had a woman patron.[1]

A complete discussion of women and the early Jesuits is beyond the scope of this study; thus I would like to focus only on the women whose piety and patronage provided two of the *fundamental* Roman spaces for the newly founded Society of Jesus: the first permanent seat of the Collegio Romano, and the first permanent Jesuit novitiate for the Roman Province.

The original patron of the Collegio Romano was Marchesa Vittoria della Tolfa (Figure 7.1).[2] From the earliest years of the Society, Ignatius of Loyola had envisioned a Roman college as the seminal teaching institution for the new order.[3] During his lifetime he was unable to find a benefactor willing to undertake the financial burden of such an establishment, but in

Figure 7.1. Bust of Vittoria della Toffa, Santa Maria in Aracoeli, Rome (Photo: Giandean)

1551, with the help of Francesco Borgia, he was able to open the first College in a modest rented house at the foot of the Capitoline Hill, near the small church of Santa Maria della Strada, which had been conceded to the Jesuits by Pope Paul III in 1541.[4] For nearly ten years the College moved from one temporary location to another, usually in rented spaces in palaces of Roman families in the general area of Santa Maria della Strada. Many appeals were made to the popes to undertake the important task of founding a Roman College for the Jesuits, but Paul III, Julius III, and Marcellus II gave only stop-gap monetary donations, and the years of Paul IV Carafa (1555–59) were particularly difficult ones for the Jesuits because his unpopular war with Spain drained every Roman purse, and his own patronage was generally directed toward the Theatines, a new order he had helped found in 1524.[5] Although Paul IV's reign was not a propitious one for the Jesuits, they were to benefit from it in an unexpected manner.

Marchesa Vittoria della Tolfa was Paul IV's niece, daughter of his sister, Elisabetta Carafa. In 1553 Vittoria's husband, Camillo Pardo Orsini, died, leaving her a wealthy, childless widow. Although Orsini had lost his important properties in the kingdom of Naples because of his untimely change of allegiance from the Spanish to the French earlier in the century, he remained a gentleman of some means, but in exile from Naples, much to his wife's disgust.[6] When Camillo died, his will stipulated that the debt of 17,000 scudi owed him by Giulio della Rovere was to be used to build a chapel in Saint John Lateran and to maintain ten chaplains to carry out services there. His wife, however, had other plans. With the help of her uncle, the pope, she managed to redirect the money to quite a different pious work: the founding of a convent and church for Franciscan nuns on a site near the obelisk of San Macuto, part of which she had purchased to add to property she already had inherited from her husband and her uncle, Paul IV. She ordered that the convent be called Santa Maria della Nunziata, and that it be administered by the Company of the Annunciation, which was to admit girls without dowries into the convent in return for the marchesa's promise to make the Company heir to her own dowry for future funding.[7] Unfortunately for the nuns, this "Carafa connection" had unpleasant repercussions: when Paul IV died on 18 August 1559, the *popolo romano* unleashed its intense hatred against this pope, whose disastrous Spanish war, harsh puritanical policies, and rapacious nephews had caused tremendous hardships in the city, and the nuns felt they had to flee their new convent which was in danger of being burned and looted by the rioting crowd.[8]

According to the Jesuit manuscript entitled *Origine del Collegio Romano e suoi progressi 1551–1743*, various people, noting that the convent was now empty and conveniently close to Santa Maria della Strada, suggested that the Jesuits should take advantage of the situation to obtain such an excellent site for their College, a sentiment echoed by their new general, Giacomo Lainez, who nonetheless felt it was necessary to wait for just the right moment. This apparently arrived with the election of Pius IV in December 1559, and very quickly Lainez mobilized powerful support from Cardinals Morone, Savelli, Farnese, and d'Este to petition Pius IV for his aid in convincing the Marchesa della Tolfa that establishing a Jesuit college would be "a divine service," adding, "in any case, it does not seem that she has set her mind firmly on this or that pious work, although she has thought of some other nuns."[9] The writer of the manuscript goes on to say that the Marchesa, who was very pious, was pleased with the pope's attention and agreed to change her donation from the convent to the college. The pope responded with the generous offer to annul her previous contract with the Company of the Annunciation, leaving her free once again to dispose of her dowry as she wished.[10]

On 22 April 1560, the actual document of the donation was drawn up and notarized, describing the Marchesa's gift of property and three houses (including her own), plus the convent and the foundations of the Church of the Annunciation, with a total value of 16,000 scudi. There were certain conditions to be met. For example, the Jesuits were to complete the College Church, which was to retain its dedication to the Annunciation according to the Marchesa's wishes; the coat of arms of her husband was to be put in visible places; and certain rents were to be paid by the Jesuits, including rent for a suitable house for the Marchesa, who had relinquished to them her own palace (although later she freed them of that obligation, feeling it was unsuitable to the spirit of her gift).[11]

In less than a month the Jesuits opened their first permanent Roman college. They described it as a beautiful place, located in a most convenient part of Rome, with the Quirinal Hill to the east and the Pantheon to the west (Figure 7.2). Although they had not yet completely reorganized the space to their needs, they praised the fine portal which faced the obelisk of San Macuto, the classrooms which were separated from the dormitory by a portico, and the living area itself, with a spacious inner courtyard. They concluded that the place was most suitable to their needs, and that all eleven classrooms would soon be filled.[12]

One year later, in 1561, the Marchesa della Tolfa desired to see the fruits of her patronage and asked Pius IV for permission to enter the College, which was granted. She toured the entire place and was extremely pleased to see how well it had been organized. She was charmed by the excellent manners of the young men, the diversity of countries they represented, and their intense piety and penitence, which moved her to tears.[13]

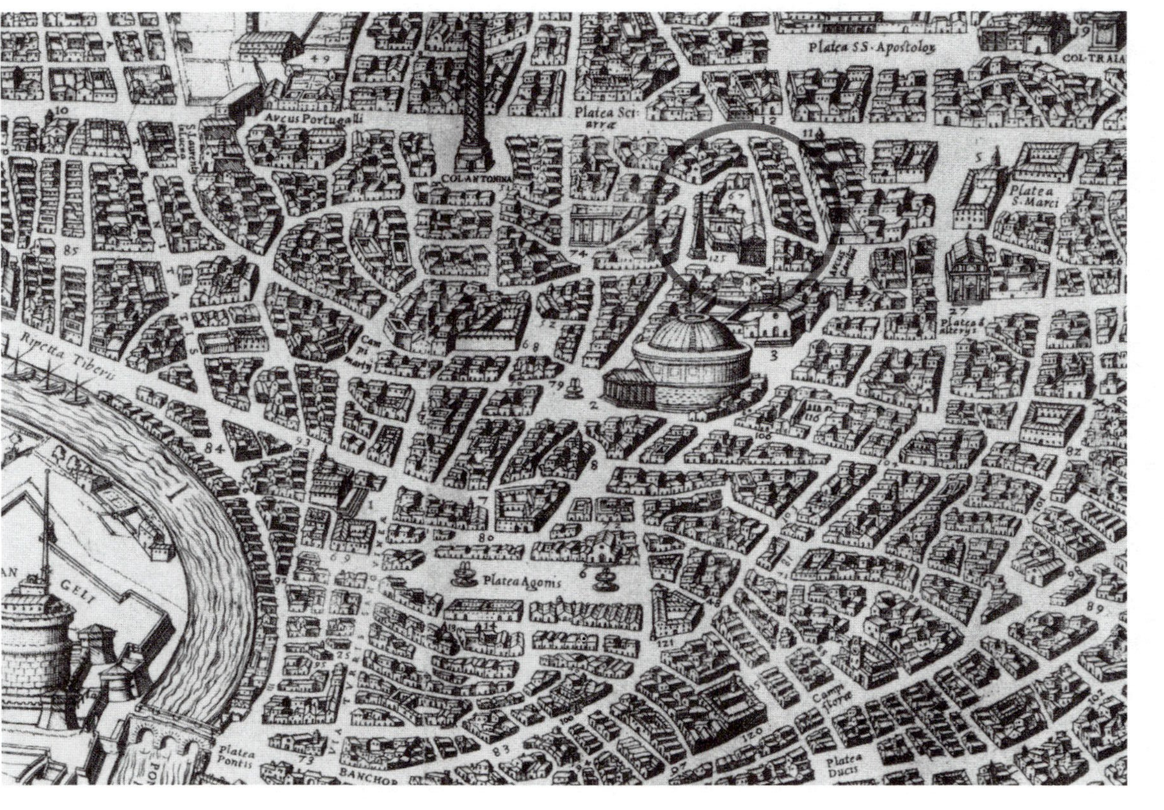

Figure 7.2. Detail of the Cartaro map of 1576, showing the Collegio Romano.

By 1579 this amicable state of affairs between the Jesuits and the Marchesa had begun to deteriorate, although in her will of 12 February 1578 she did make them the beneficiaries of certain rents from two pieces of property she owned, and the executors of her estate were Jesuit fathers.[14] However, in the first of eight codicils to her will, this one dated 12 June 1579, we hear of her discontent about the fact that her husband's coat of arms has not been properly displayed at the College, a complaint that may have been prompted by the Jesuits' campaign to enlist Pope Gregory XIII Boncompagni as their *new* patron of the Collegio Romano, which they now described as being in a miserable state and overcrowded.[15] Under the new general, Claudio Acquaviva, this campaign was crowned with success when Gregory XIII, in April 1581, agreed to provide the Jesuits not only with a large donation of money, but also with the ongoing benefice of the Abbey of Chiaravalle to fund the Collegio Romano. To show their gratitude, the Jesuits wished to name him "founder" of the College, but the pope modestly refused, indicating that there were others before him entitled to this honor, referring to the Marchesa della Tolfa, who was well known to him via her uncle, who had promoted the career of the young Boncompagni. The Jesuits were quick to reassure him that she had no claim to the title of founder for, by definition, only patrons who gave ongoing, income-producing gifts could be called founders, and so the pope agreed to accept the title. When this news came to the Marchesa's ears, continues the writer of the manuscript on the origins of the college, she immediately complained to the pope, citing all she had done for the Jesuits. The pope, not wishing to get involved, sent her letter on to the Jesuits who attempted to smooth over the situation by repeating their definition of founder, a title they never had promised to her; but they also assured her that they would always recognize their perpetual obligation to the Marchesa and her late husband, who would be known as special benefactors of the Collegio Romano.[16]

The argument was still in progress on 5 August 1581, when Padre Sardi, in a letter to one of his colleagues, wrote, "The old woman is more obstinate than ever, but let us hope everything will turn out well."[17] In this hope, the Jesuits were to be disappointed, although recent Jesuit historians have indicated that this charitable and pious woman *was* satisfied with the glorious new future of the Collegio Romano.[18] Such passive generosity, however, was not her style, and even before Sardi's letter of August 1581, she had completely disinherited the Jesuits in codicil number three of her will, dated 1 June 1581, and redirected that money to a chapel in the new Carmelite church of Santa Maria in Traspontina. She also removed all Jesuit executors from her will.[19]

The Jesuits made one last gesture in 1583, when Padre Acquaviva instructed that a lengthy inscription in black marble with gold letters be placed in the College Church of the Annunciation to commemorate the patronage of the Marchesa della Tolfa toward the Collegio Romano.[20] When that church was torn down in the seventeenth century to make way for the new church of Sant'Ignazio, this inscription was moved to an inconspicuous corner of the passage leading from Sant'Ignazio to the sacristy, where it still remains, largely unnoticed.

The Marchesa della Tolfa, however, had not played her last card. In 1592, six years after her death, the Jesuits received an unpleasant surprise: the Theatines brought a legal case against them over the property Paul IV Carafa had willed to his niece in 1545. The pope had stipulated that if the Marchesa died without legal issue, the property was to revert to the Theatines, who were now claiming it, even though the new Collegio Romano was resting on it. Finally Pope Clement VIII had to step in to resolve the problem, which ended with the Jesuits paying the Theatines 8,350 scudi to give up their claim.[21]

It is interesting to note that when Gregory XIII's splendid new Collegio Romano opened in November 1584, various inscriptions and statues proclaimed him "Fundatori et Parenti" of the College, but the institution was not called the Gregoriana.[22] The Jesuits had to wait until 1930 and the opening of their new university in Rome to confer this honor on him posthumously. In the foyer of the new Gregoriana there is a handsome inscription (Figure 7.3) listing those who contributed to the original Collegio Romano: Ignatius of Loyola, Francesco Borgia, Julius III, Paul IV, Pius IV, and Pius V.[23] Conspicuously absent is the Marchesa della Tolfa, and one wonders what happened to that "perpetual obligation" promised to her in the early 1580s.

More recently, in the catalogue of the 1990 Vatican show, entitled *Saint, Site and Sacred Strategy: Ignatius, Rome and Jesuit Urbanism*, the Marchesa's part in the establishment of the Collegio Romano is somewhat obscured by the fact that she is mistakenly called the Marchesa della Valle,[24] a shortened form of one of her husband's lost titles, Marchesa della Valle Siciliano, but also the name of one of the great Roman families, the della Valle. Thanks to the well-organized and accessible Jesuit Archives

Figure 7.3. Inscription from the foyer of the Gregoriana. (Photo: Cynthia Stollhans).

located at the Curia of the Society of Jesus in Rome, however, the seminal role of Marchesa della Tolfa as patron, if not founder, of the Collegio Romano can be retrieved.

Two other women fared much better in their claims to be recognized as founders of early Jesuit institutions; they are Giovanna d'Aragona Colonna and Isabella Feltria della Rovere Sanseverino. Numerous documents in the Jesuit Archives confirm for each of them the title of *fondatrice* for the first permanent Jesuit novitiate for the Roman Province.

Giovanna d'Aragona was praised by poets, musicians, statesmen, and churchmen alike as one of the most influential, cultured, beautiful, and pious women of the sixteenth century.[25] Her portrait (Figure 7.4) from the school of Raphael, was painted about 1518, the year she was betrothed to Ascanio Colonna, Duke of Paliano, with a dowry of 22,000 scudi.[26] They were wed on 5 June 1521, but this marriage between Neapolitan-Spanish aristocracy and Roman nobility was to prove an unhappy one. She dutifully bore seven children to the Colonna name, including the most illustrious Marc'Antonio Colonna, future hero of the great Battle of Lepanto against the Muslim Turks, but on the birth of this, her last, child in 1535 she abandoned her husband, whose uncertain political policies and unsavory way of life offended her. She withdrew to the island of Ischia to join a circle of women much influenced by the reform ideas of Juan de Valdés.[27] In spite of frequent attempts by the Jesuits to reunite the ill-matched couple, she refused to be persuaded, and even a letter in 1552 from Ignatius of Loyola himself, which listed twenty-six reasons why she should return to her husband, failed to move her.[28] She also refused to use her husband's title of Paliano, and always signed herself Duchessa di Tagliacozzo, a Colonna property where she sometimes resided.

Giovanna finally returned to Rome in triumph in 1560, after the death of her husband in a Neapolitan prison in 1557 for his suspected defection to the French, and also after the demise of Paul IV Carafa, the archenemy of both the Colonna and the Spanish.[29] In spite of the Jesuits' failure as marriage counselors, they remained in her good graces because of their leadership in Catholic reform, and also because of the strong Spanish element in the Society of Jesus. She was especially close to Francesco Borgia, who was general from 1565–72.

Giovanna owned a fine house and a large garden on the edge of the Quirinal Hill, where she often withdrew to enjoy the "good air" of the Quirinal, particularly during the hot summer months (Figure 7.5). Just to the east of her property was a small, dilapidated church called Sant'Andrea

Figure 7.4. School of Raphael, *Giovanna d'Aragona*, c. 1518, Paris, Louvre. (Photo courtesy of Cliché des Musées Nationaux, Paris)

in Monte Cavallo, which in 1565 was conceded to the Jesuits by Giovan'Andrea Croce, bishop of Tivoli (Figure 7.6).[30] In 1566, moved by the Jesuits' need for a permanent novitiate for the Roman Province, Giovanna d'Aragona resolved to found such an institution, offering part of her own house and garden, which could be joined to Sant'Andrea, plus an endowment of 6,000 scudi, which included 1,000 scudi in jewels.[31]

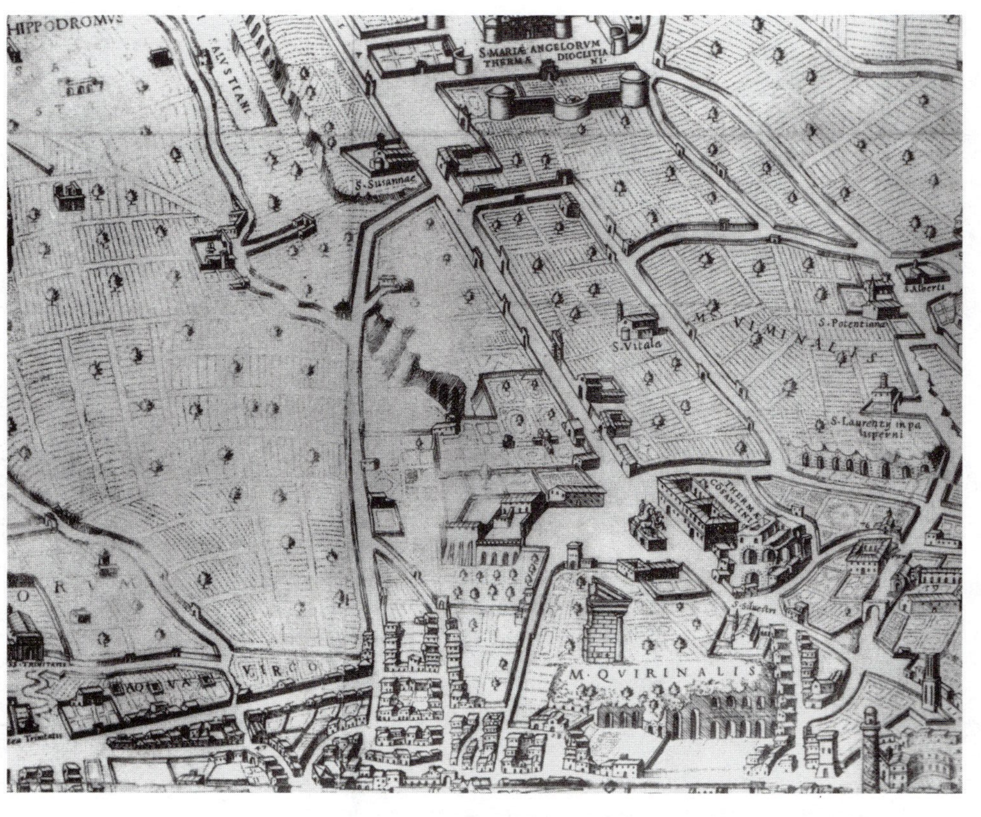

Figure 7.5. Detail of Cartaro map of 1576, showing the Quirinal Hill.

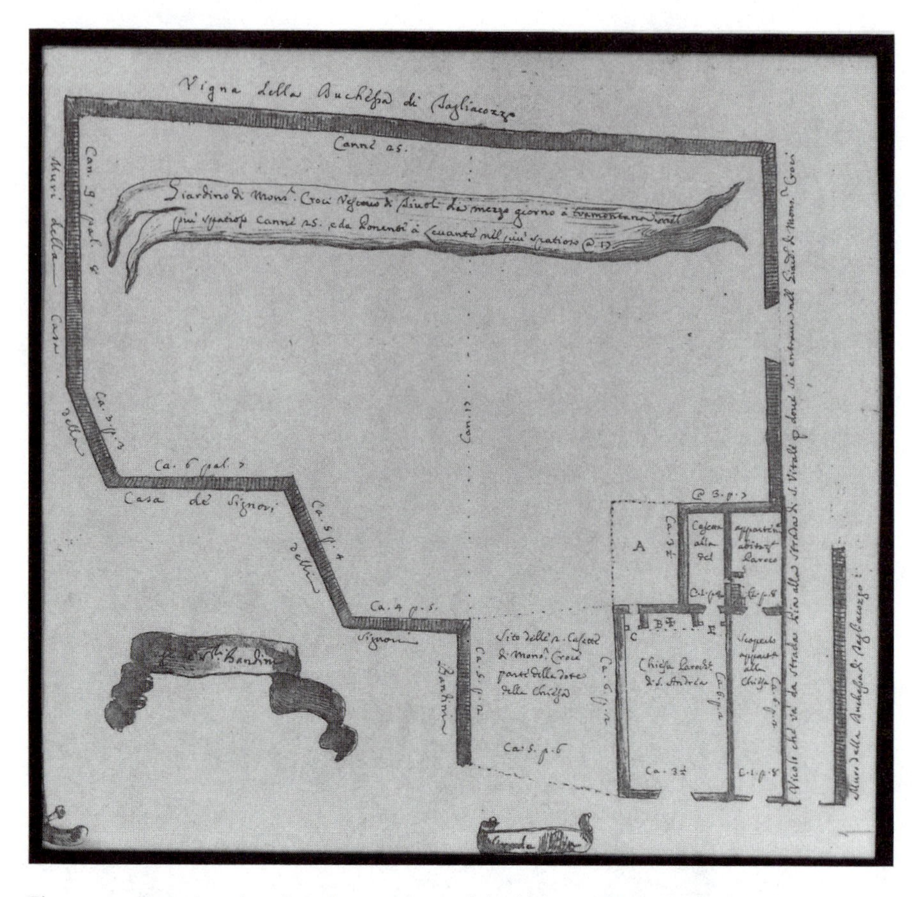

Figure 7.6. Drawing showing the property of the bishop of Tivoli, Sant'Andrea, and the property of Giovanna d'Aragona, as it would have looked in 1565. (Photo: ARSI)

On the feast of Saint Andrew, 30 November 1566, the Jesuits honored Giovanna with a sung Mass in the small church of Sant'Andrea, where they presented her with a white candle to mark her role as *fondatrice* of the novitiate. Although her gift of 6,000 scudi was considerably less than Marchesa della Tolfa's, she did conform to the Jesuit definition of founder: a person whose gift provided continuous income.

Early in 1567 the Jesuits, thanks to Giovanna's endowment, began a new church of Sant'Andrea; it used one wall of the old church and the outer wall of the duchess's house for its boundaries, thus creating a larger church but blocking the alley that had led to the gardens and to San Vitale beyond (Figure 7.7). In February 1568 the new church was consecrated by

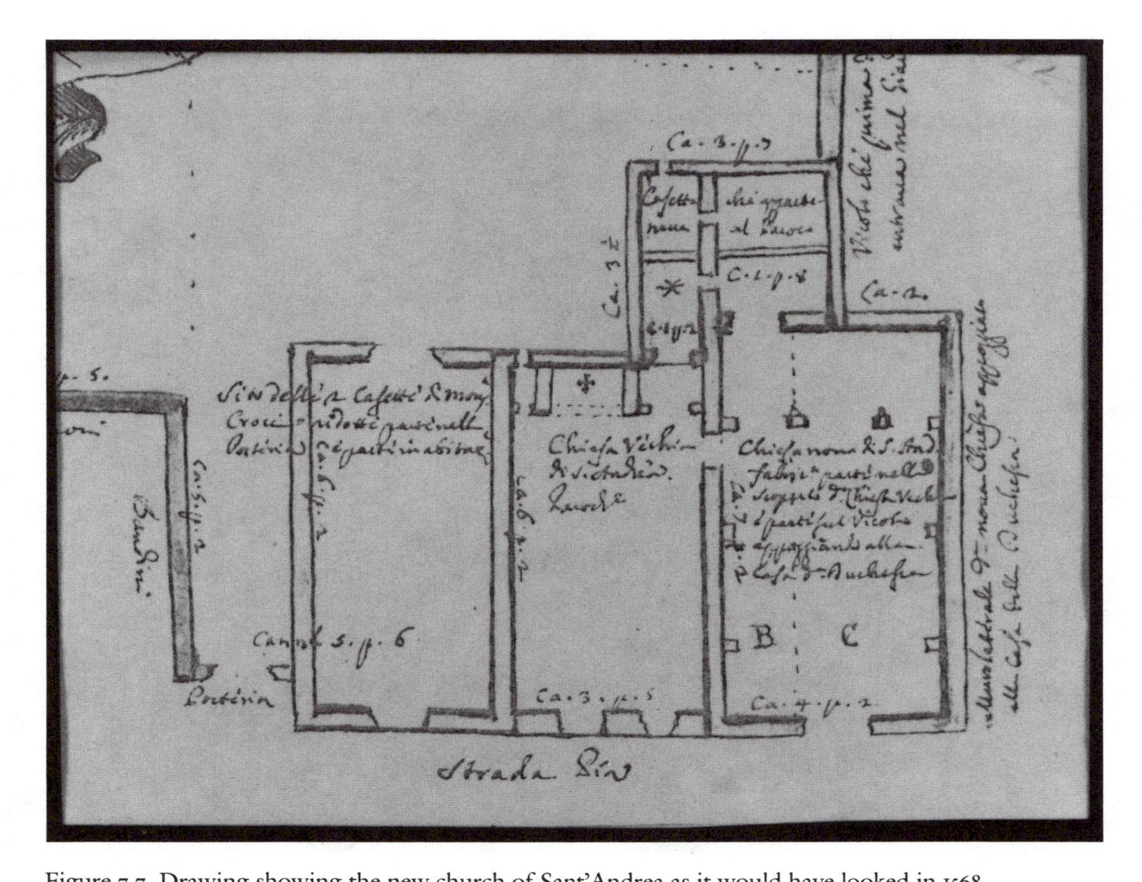

Figure 7.7. Drawing showing the new church of Sant'Andrea as it would have looked in 1568. (Photo: ARSI)

Cardinal Marc'Antonio Colonna, and Giovanna was commended for setting a good example to other wealthy patrons by establishing this holy place amidst the pleasure gardens which covered most of the Quirinal Hill in mid-century. By 1569 the novitiate was ready to receive some seventy novices. About one hundred years later this whole complex was replaced by a new novitiate centered around Gian Lorenzo Bernini's exquisite baroque church of Sant'Andrea al Quirinale.

Even Giovanna d'Aragona was not to have everything her own way with the Jesuits. She made known to Francesco Borgia that she wished to open a second-story corridor connecting her house to a balcony covered with shutters in Sant'Andrea, so she and her women and family might hear Mass there with the novices, but Borgia refused, finding her wish to be "too zealous, and lacking in discretion."[32]

The writer of the Jesuit chronicle of the novitiate may give us some hint of how Giovanna took this refusal, because he reports that she later gave the rest of her house and garden to be used as a convent for Capuchin nuns, "a paradise of angels," he writes. Subsequent documents indicate that these angelic neighbors caused the Jesuits a good deal of legal trouble with regard to boundaries, height of walls, location of windows, road use, and so on.[33] Not the least of the drawbacks was the curtailment of Jesuit expansion of the novitiate, but this problem was to be solved by another *fondatrice*, Isabella della Rovere.[34]

Behind Sant'Andrea was another church that had fallen into disrepair, the Early Christian Titulus of San Vitale (Figure 7.8), now located well below street level on the Via Nazionale. On 20 November 1595, Clement VIII, by papal bull, conferred this church on the Jesuits who were in great need of space for enlarging their novitiate.[35] Although they immediately began renovating the church and its grounds, the actual foundation of the novitiate of San Vitale took place in April 1598, when Isabella della Rovere Sanseverino, Princess of Bisignano, endowed it with the extraordinary sum of 90,000 scudi, in her own name and the name of her deceased son, Giovanni Teodoro, Duke of San Marco.[36] This sum far outstripped any other amount given to the novitiates of Sant'Andrea and San Vitale, including bequests from Gregory XIII and the king of Spain. It is thus not surprising that the Jesuits named Isabella the second *fondatrice* of the now combined novitiates, but they firmly declared that this in no way changed Giovanna d'Aragona's role as *fondatrice*, "senza mutare niente della sudetta prima fondazione " ("changing nothing of the so-called first foundation").[37]

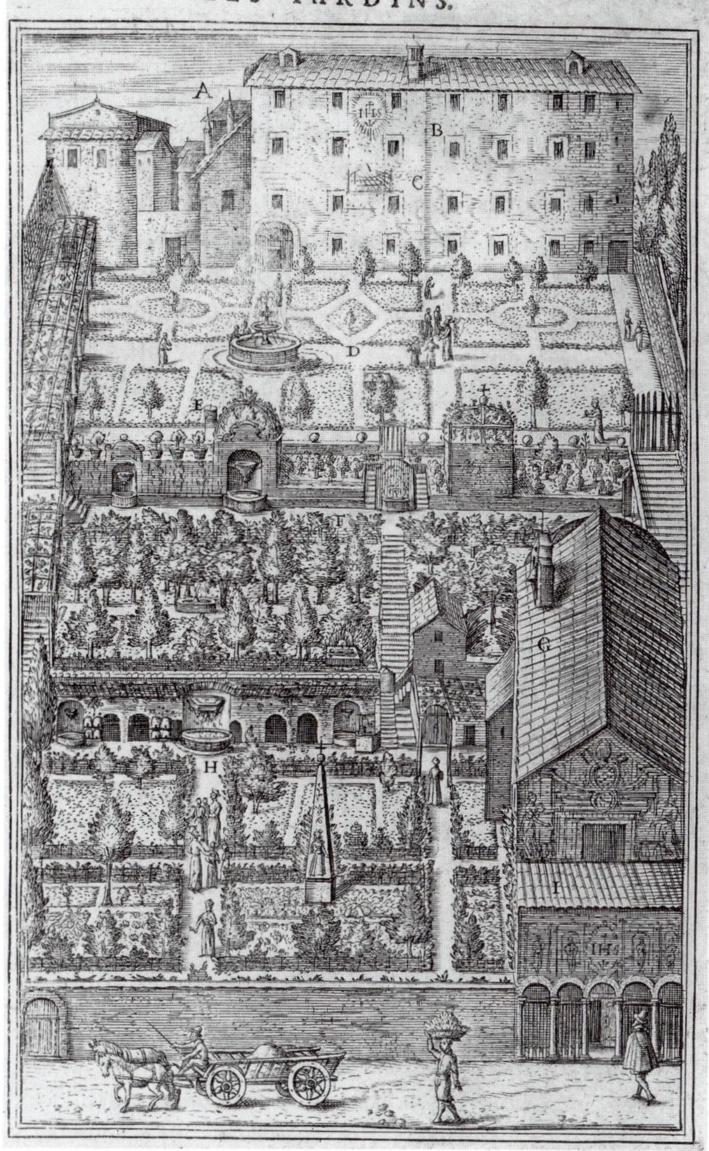

Figure 7.8. Sant'Andrea and San Vitale, from Louis Richeôme, *La peinture spirituelle* (1611). (Photo by permission of the Folger Shakespeare Library)

One may wonder how Isabella came to have such a fortune to bestow. She was the daughter of Guidobaldo II, Duke of Urbino, and had brought a dowry of 40,000 scudi to her marriage to the Neapolitan nobleman Nicolò Bernardino di Sanseverino, Prince of Bisignano. However, her husband's talent for incurring monumental debts was such that at one time he was said to owe a total of 1,700,000 scudi, a state of affairs that finally led to his imprisonment in Naples, where he died in 1606.[38]

The bulk of Isabella's endowment came from the sale of her jewels, a fact which appealed to her contemporaries' sense of decorum, because the original Early Christian Church of San Vitale had been built with funds realized from the sale of the jewels of one Vestina, a Roman matron of the late fourth century. As I have shown elsewhere, it was common for sixteenth-century women in Rome to model their patronage and piety on Early Christian Roman matrons, especially those of the fourth and fifth centuries. Thus Isabella della Rovere was working within a well-recognized tradition of matron as patron in late Cinquecento Rome, one which was noted by the Jesuit writer of the chronicle of the novitiates, who saw the parallel between the first and last matrons of San Vitale as a particular sign of God's providence.[39]

Isabella's patronage of San Vitale was doubtlessly motivated by yet another well-known sixteenth-century tradition: family pride. Her illustrious forebear, Sixtus IV della Rovere, had completely rebuilt the church for the Jubilee Year of 1475. An inscription and his coat of arms still attest to this, and their prominent position over the door of the church tends to obscure Isabella's role as founder of the novitiate. Her own coat of arms (Figure 7.9) can be found on the base of the high altar.[40]

It is often assumed that the Jesuits strictly controlled the iconography of the decorative programs in their churches. To some extent this was true, but in churches where important private patrons were making large monetary commitments, I believe it is a mistake to always treat the patron as a passive receiver of Jesuit instructions.[41]

At San Vitale it seems to me that the decoration can be divided into two categories: the paintings that reflect the ideas and images considered suitable by the Jesuits themselves for novitiate and college churches in the late sixteenth century—that is, scenes of martyrdom—and the paintings that show the influence of the founder and patron, Isabella della Rovere. To the "Jesuit" category belong the now lost façade frescoes, which depicted instruments of torture and martyrdom (Figure 7.8); the interior wall frescoes showing martyrdoms of Early Christian saints (Figure 7.10) which are, however, more poetic and less gruesome than similar scenes at

Figure 7.9. Coat of arms of Isabella della Rovere, San Vitale. (Photo: Cynthia Stollhans).

the Jesuit German College Church of Santo Stefano Rotondo; the transept frescoes by Agostino Ciampelli of the stoning and martyrdom of San Vitale; and the apse paintings, dedicated to the sufferings and triumphs of Saints Protasio, Gervasio, Valeria, and Vitale, with the fresco *Christ on the Road to Calvary* painted above. All these subjects were intended to remind the young men of their roots in the Early Christian tradition and to

Figure 7.10. San Vitale, interior. (Photo: ICCD, Rome, E 21219)

prepare them for the possibility of their own martyrdom in Germany, England, or other Protestant countries.[42]

To the second category of artwork belong two, or perhaps three, of the four altarpieces above the sidewall altars (Figure 7.10). With Isabella's generous endowment of 1598, the renovation of the church moved forward at a rapid pace, and two side altars, those closest to the entrance, were added to the three altars already built. The altarpieces for all four side altars were hung in the spring of 1600; it is thus possible that Isabella paid for all four of them, but she certainly paid for the two over the new altars closest to the portal.[43] These two paintings (Figures 7.11 and 7.12), meant to be viewed as a pair, are dedicated to the glorification of virginity, both female and male, embodied by virgins and confessors.

Virginity was a topic much in vogue in late sixteenth-century Rome, although such a visual homage to the subject was not common to Jesuit paintings in the period, particularly not in the novitiates, where martyrdom was the favored theme. The Catholic Church in general expended a great deal of time and effort espousing this idea, however, partly to defend the concept of clerical celibacy, and partly because of doubts voiced by the Protestants over the virginity of Mary herself. The church hierarchy must have believed there was both a need and a market for works defending virginity, because in the 1560s among the first publications of Paolo Manuzio's newly founded papal press were the major treatises on virginity by Saints Jerome, Augustine, Ambrose, John Chrysostom, Gregory of Nyssa, and Cyprian.[44] Another ever-popular source on the glory of virgins was the *Letters* of Saint Jerome, published by Manuzio in 1565 and again in 1566, and familiar to Romans through countless sermons, especially within the ambience of Philip Neri and the Oratorians at San Girolamo della Carità.[45] Although it has been suggested that the publication of these works on virginity represented the Church's stand on clerical celibacy,[46] these patristic writings originally had been directed largely to women of all types: young virgins, widows, and even wives who lived in a celibate manner. I believe a similar audience was intended in the sixteenth century, particularly in Rome where Early Christian models of female piety were commonly invoked.

The Church Fathers who wrote so compellingly about virginity all shared the belief that it represented the ideal human state, which was almost angelic, because it made possible the spiritual freedom of the soul to adore God: a freedom from the distractions of this world. Furthermore, they all emphasized that married women were in the most precarious

Figure 7.11. Altarpiece, *Confessors*, San Vitale. (Photo: Cynthia Stollhans)

Figure 7.12. Altarpiece, *The Glorification of Virgin Saints*, San Vitale. (Photo: ICCD, Rome 20262)

situation because of their duty to serve their husbands, their natural anxieties about their children, and their predisposition to become ensnared by material goods, which invariably were summed up by fine clothes and jewels. These well-known arguments must have been especially meaningful to Isabella della Rovere, whose duty to her profligate husband had caused her great hardship, whose beloved son, Giovanni Teodoro, had died at a young age, and whose desire to rid herself of her worldly goods was manifested in her gift of jewels to found the new Novitiate of San Vitale. Isabella, like Giovanna d'Aragona, had been closely connected with the Jesuits in Naples during the difficult years of her marriage. Her deep piety was described by the Jesuit writer Luca Pinelli, who dedicated to her a series of meditations on the Blessed Sacrament in 1597,[47] shortly before her endowment of San Vitale.

In the light of this cultural ambience and Isabella's own life, I would suggest that the two altarpieces (Figures 7.11 and 7.12) represent not only her money but her patronage in the fullest sense, because they reveal her own interest in the popular discussion of virginity. In the painting of the confessors (Figure 7.11), all of whom addressed the subject of virginity in some way, we can identify Jerome, Augustine, and Ambrose, the most prolific and best-known writers on the theme. More emphatic is the altarpiece *The Glorification of Virgin Saints* (Figure 7.12), which belongs to a rich literary tradition in late sixteenth-century Rome, including Antonio Gallonio's *Historia deli Sante Vergini Romane* and a work entitled *XII Virgines et Martyres*, published in Rome in 1597 by Paolo Emilio Santoro.[48]

I would further argue that the third altarpiece (Figure 7.13), located on the same sidewall as the previous one, also should be assigned to Isabella's patronage, for it, too, glorifies virginity—to quote Ann Matter, "The Woman who is the All: The Virgin Mary and the Song of Songs."[49] This image of the Immaculate Conception, surrounded by symbols of virginity from the Song of Songs, was becoming increasingly popular in the late sixteenth century; however, this is a subject which must await further development elsewhere.[50]

In conclusion, I would say that although Giovanna d'Aragona and Isabella della Rovere received greater recognition than the Marchesa della Tolfa as patrons of the early Jesuits in their own time, the outcome of the historical process has been about the same for all three women: their munificent patronage has largely been forgotten. In two cases this was facilitated by the fact that their original buildings were replaced by later, grander ones: the new Collegio Romano of Gregory XIII, and Bernini's

Figure 7.13. Altarpiece, *Immaculate Conception*, San Vitale. (Photo: Cynthia Stollhans)

church of Sant'Andrea al Quirinale, built during the reign of Alexander VII. At San Vitale Isabella's presence is still discernible, albeit faintly. A theologian might say that the piety of the three women is enhanced by this lack of recognition of their patronage, but as historians we are obliged to give both aspects equal weight.

Notes

1. Ottavio Panciroli, *Tesori nascoti dell'alma città di Roma*, 2d ed. (Rome: Fabrizio David, 1625), p. 842. The chapel of Santa Maria della Strada, to the left of the high altar, was commissioned by Portia dell'Anguillara Orsini Cesi, and two sisters, Giovanna Caetani Orsini (whose daughter Cornelia married Portia's son, Andrea) and Beatrice Caetani Cesi (whose son, Federico, married Portia's daughter from her first marriage, Olimpia Orsini). Olimpia Orsini was also the patron of the chapel of San Francesco, to the right of the high altar. Salustia Cerrini Crescenzi paid for the chapel of Sant'Andrea (first right), and Bianca Mellini Lomellini commissioned the chapel of the Passion (second right). Settima Delfini and her husband Curzio Vittori were the patrons of the chapel of the Angels (third right). Elisabetta dello Schiavo contributed 430 scudi toward the pulpit, which cost about 650 scudi in all. See Pietro Tacchi-Venturi, *Storia della Compania di Gesù in Italia* (Rome: Dante Alighieri, 1910), vol. 1, p. 605. For another aspect of Jesuits and women, see Ann Carr, *Women Religious and Ignatius of Loyola* (Chicago: Jesuit Community, Loyola University, 1992).

2. The Marchesa was a major patron in late sixteenth-century Rome: she was the benefactress of two hospitals and the patron of four richly decorated chapels in four major churches, including her burial chapel at Santa Maria in Aracoeli. For this chapel see Johanna Heidemann, *The Cinquecento Chapel Decorations in Santa Maria in Aracoeli in Rome* (Amsterdam: Academische Pers, 1982), pp. 111–25.

3. The primary sources for the Collegio Romano are located in the Jesuit Curia Archives, Rome (ARSI), Prov. Rom., vols. 150a, 151, 152. In 150a there is a modern copy of the manuscript entitled *Origine del Collegio Romano e suoi progressi 1551–1743* (hereafter cited as *Origine*). The original manuscript is located in the archives of the Pontifical University Gregoriana, Mss. 142, ff. 147ff. The major secondary sources are: Ernesto Rinaldi, *La fondazione del Collegio Romano* (Arezzo: Cooperativa Tipografia, 1914); Riccardo Villoslada, *Storia del Collegio Romano* (Rome: Universitas Gregoriana, 1954).

4. Tacchi-Venturi *Storia della Compania di Gesù*, vol. 1, part 2, ff. 229ff.

5. Ludwig von Pastor, *Storia dei Papi* (Rome: Desclée, 1963), vol. 6 (Paul IV); Peter A. Quinn, "Ignatius Loyola and Gian Pietro Carafa," *Catholic Historical Review* 67, 3 (1981): 386–400; Carolyn Valone, "Paul IV, Guglielmo della Porta and the Rebuilding of San Silvestro al Quirinale," *Master Drawings* 15, 3 (1977): 243–55.

6. Pompeo Litta, *Le famiglie celebri di Italia* (Milan: Giusti, 1839), 4, plate VI; and F. Casimiro, *Memorie istoriche della Chiesa e Convento di S. Maria in Aracoeli di Roma* (Rome: Bernabò, 1736), p. 201.

7. *Origine*, ff. 15r,v, 16r; Giovanni Martinetti, *Sant'Ignazio* (Rome: Marietti,

1967), p. 21; Jack Wasserman, *Ottavio Mascarino* (Rome: Libreria Internazionale Modernissima, 1966), pp. 79–80.

8. Biblioteca Apostolica Vaticana (BAV), Urb. Lat. 1039, f. 71r,v; Romeo De Maio, *Alfonso Carafa, Cardinale di Napoli 1540–1565* (Vatican City: Biblioteca Apostolica Vaticana, 1961), p. 314.

9. ARSI, Prov. Rom. 126 (insert xviii), f. 40: "perchè non pare l'animo di essa sia firmato in questa o in quella opera pia, se ben ha pensato di certe altre monache." See also *Origine*, ff. 16v, 17r,v.

10. *Origine*, f. 17v.

11. *Origine*, ff. 18r,v, 21r,v; ARSI, Prov. Rom. f. 150a (insert iii), ff. 20–22; Prov. Rom. 126 (insert xii), ff. 84–86; Rinaldi, *La fondazione del Collegio Romano*, pp. 133–36, for a partial transcription of the document of the donation; Villoslada, *Storia del Collegio Romano*, pp. 53–55.

12. ARSI, Prov. Rom. f. 126 (insert xx), ff. 49–50.

13. *Origine*, f. 23r,v.

14. Archivio di Stato, Rome (ASR), Archivio del Arciospedale di Santo Spirito in Sassia, busta 1139 (insert 162), and busta 21, 34ff. Another copy of the will can be found in ASR, Archivio del Collegio dei Notari Capitolini, vol. 464, ff. 410r–416r, plus codicils, 528r–530v, 646r–649r, 654r–657r, 678r–680v, 716r–717v, 756r, 819r–820r, 823r–824r.

15. ASR, Arciospedale di Santo Spirito in Sassia, busta 1139 (insert 162), ff. 8–9; *Origine*, ff. 34r–35v.

16. *Origine*, ff. 36–40; Rinaldi, *La fondazione del Collegio Romano*, pp. 82–98. For the definition of "founder," see ARSI, Prov. Rom. 126 (insert v), ff. 11–14.

17. "La Vecchia sta più ostinata che mai, ma speriamo che ogni cosa riuscirà bene." ARSI, Prov. Rom. 126 (insert xxi), ff. 55–56.

18. Villoslada, *Storia del Collegio Romano*, pp. 146–47.

19. ASR, Arciospedale di Santo Spirito in Sassia, busta 1139 (insert 162), ff. 11v, 12r,v, 13r.

20. ARSI, Prov. Rom. 126 (insert xix), f. 46. For a transcription of the document, see Rinaldi, *La fondazione del Collegio Romano*, pp. 136–37.

21. *Origine*, ff. 49v–50v.

22. *Origine*, ff. 43r–45v.

23. The inscription is as follows:

COLLEGIUM ROMANUM
A SS. Ignatio de Loiola et Franc. Borgia Conditum
A Iulio III Paolo IV Pio IV Pio V PP. MM.
Studiorum Universitatum Iuribus Ornatum
A Gregorio XIII P.M. Census Addito Aedibusque
A Fundam Excitatis Spendidius Instructum Est
A.D. MDLXXXIII Ac Tanti e Nomine Patroni
Nuncupatum Universitas Gregoriana.

24. Thomas M. Lucas, ed., *Saint, Site and Sacred Strategy: Ignatius, Rome and Jesuit Urbanism* (Vatican City: Biblioteca Apostolica Vaticana, 1990), p. 36. In a similar vein, I note that James W. Reites, "Ignatius and Ministry with Women,"

The Way, suppl. 74 (1992): 17–18, cities my research on Marchesa Vittoria della Tolfa, but mistakenly gives my name as Jane Priwer.

25. *Dizionario biografico degli italiani* (Rome: Treccani, 1961), vol. 3:694–96; Litta, *Le famiglie*, vol. 2, plate VII; Amedeo Quondam, *Il Naso di Laura* (Modena: Franco Cosimo Panini, 1991), pp. 131–50.

26. The document of her dowry, dated 11 November 1518, is in the Colonna Archive, Instrumenti diversi, III BB II, no. 12. In the same Archive are two copies of her last will, dated 11 September 1577, which is the date of her death; see Istrumenti diversi, III AA 95, no. 61. I wish to express my thanks to Prince Prospero Colonna for his kind permission to use the Colonna Archive, and to Monsignor Varca, whose assistance in that archive was invaluable. Further confirmation of the death date for Giovanna can be found in ARSI, Prov. Rom. 162, I, ff. 45–46, where on the date of 11 September 1577 it is noted: "morì a hore 16 la Sig.na Donna Giovanna Aragona Duchessa di Tagliacozzo, madre del Marc'Antonio Colonna, vice Re di Sicilia." For the portrait, see Sylvie Beguin, *Les peintures de Raphael au Louvre* (Paris: Éditions de la Réunion des Musées Nationaux, 1984), pp. 54–57; and Elizabeth Cropper, "On Beautiful Women, Parmigianino, Petrarchismo, and the Vernacular Style," *Art Bulletin* 58, 3 (1976): 384.

27. *Dizionario biografico degli italiani*, vol. 3, p. 695. This circle included her sister-in-law, Vittoria da Colonna.

28. *Monumenta Historica Societatis Iesu, Monumenta Ignatiana* (Rome: Matriti, 1906), vol. 1, part 4 (1551–53), pp. 506–11 (letter 3014).

29. For her entry, see BAV, Urb. Lat. 1039, f. 165v; for Ascanio Colonna, see *Dizionario biografico degli italiani*, vol. 27, pp. 271–75.

30. This drawing, and the one in Fig. 7.7, are found in ARSI, Prov. Rom. 167, ff. 4 and 8. I wish to express my thanks to Victor Gramatowski, S.J., of the Jesuit Archives for permission to publish these drawings.

31. For documents pertaining to Giovanna and the founding of Sant'Andrea, see ARSI, Prov. Rom. 162, I, ff. 6–12v, and Prov. Rom. 167, ff. 2–8. Seventeenth-century guide books such as Panciroli, *Tesori Nascosti dell'alma città di Roma*, p. 325, and Filippo De'Rossi, *Ritratto di Roma Moderna* (Rome: Francesco Moneta, 1645), p. 16, also record Giovanna as patron of the church of Sant'Andrea. For a description of the sixteenth-century church, see Louis Richeôme, *La peinture spirituelle* (Lyons: Rigault, 1611), pp. 3–50; and Liliana Barroero, *Guide rionale di Roma, rione I, Monti* (Rome: Fratelli Palombi, 1982), part 4, pp. 102–3. The church had four altars and a painted wooden ceiling. On the main altar was the *Crucifixion of St. Andrew* by Durante Alberti.

32. ARSI, Prov. Rom. 162, I, f. 7v. "Perciò che non havendo voluto il nostro Padre Generale condescendere ad una di lei troppa zelosa, e poco discreta pretentione, che era di fare un corridore dalle stanze sue alla chiesa."

33. For the litigation between the Jesuits and the Capuchin convent, see ARSI Prov. Rom. 163, ff. 244–47. Giovanna founded this first Capuchin convent in Rome, called Santa Chiara al Quirinale (and later Corpus Domini), between 1574–76, placing it under the administration of the Confraternity of the Holy Crucifix at San Marcello. See Vincenzo Forcella, *Iscrizioni delle Chiese . . . di Roma* (Rome: Bencini, 1873), vol. 2, p. 334, and 10 (1877), p. 163, for inscriptions about

her patronage. In August of 1574 or 1575, Giovanna's daughter-in-law, Felice Orsini Colonna, wrote to praise her for this "opera tanto angelica come questa di far un monastero di monache Cappuccine" in the garden on Montecavallo. See Colonna Archive, Letters to and from Giovanna d'Aragona, Coll. II, CA, 3 (insert 3), letter 159. Giovanna provided a carriage to transport four Capuchin nuns from their house in Naples to Rome to open the new convent on 16 April 1576. See Felice da Mareto, *Le Cappuccine nel Mondo* (Parma: Libreria Francescana, 1970), pp. 177–79. The convent was destroyed in 1889. For a description of the church, see Milton Lewine, *The Roman Church Interior 1527–1580* (Ann Arbor, MI: University Microfilms, 1960), pp. 203–7.

34. See Litta, *Le famiglie*, 9, plate VII, for her family. She was the daughter of Guidobaldo II della Rovere, Duke of Urbino, and Vittoria Farnese. Isabella died in 1619.

35. Alessandro Zuccari, *Arte e committenza nella Roma di Caravaggio* (Turin: ERI Editore, 1984), p. 159; and ARSI, Prov. Rom. 163, f. 277v.

36. ARSI, Prov. Rom. 162 I, ff. 166ff. In Prov. Rom. 163, ff. 277–78, there is a list of all the benefactors of Sant'Andrea and San Vitale. Isabella's donation was 98,000 Neapolitan scudi, which equaled 90,000 Roman scudi.

37. ARSI, Prov. Rom. 163, f. 226r,v. When Gian Lorenzo Bernini built the new Sant'Andrea al Quirinale in the seventeenth century, Prince Camillo Pamfili, who gave 28,170 scudi, was named the founder of the new church.

38. Filippo Ugolini, *Storia dei conti e Duchi di Urbino* (Florence: Grazzi-Giannini, 1859), 2:279–80; Litta, *Le famiglie*, 9, plate VI; Giuseppe Coniglio, *Visitatori del Viceregno di Napoli* (Bari: Società di Storia Patria per la Puglia, 1974), pp. 56–57.

39. ARSI, Prov. Rom. 162 I, f. 166v, f. 167r,v. Other writers of the period also commented on the parallel; see, for example, Panciroli, *Tesori nascosti dell'alma città di Roma*, pp. 301–2. The original Church of San Vitale was the last of the Roman Tituli, Titulus Vestinae, and dates from the time of Innocent I (401–17), according to the *Liber Pontificalis*. See R. Vielliard, "Saint-Vital, le dernier en date des titres romains," *Rivista di Archeologia Cristiana* 12 (1935): 103–18. See also Carolyn Valone, "Roman Matrons as Patrons: Varied Views of the Cloister Wall," in *The Crannied Wall: Women, Religion, and the Arts in Early Modern Europe*, ed. Craig Monson (Ann Arbor: University of Michigan Press, 1992), pp. 49–72.

40. For the general history of the church, see Luigi Heutter and Vincenzo Golzio, *San Vitale* (Rome: Mantegazza, 1938), pp. 5–21.

41. For various views on this question, see Howard Hibbard, "Ut Pictura Sermones: The First Painted Decorations of the Gesù," and Francis Haskell, "The Role of the Patrons: Baroque Style Changes," both in *Baroque Art, the Jesuit Contribution*, ed. R. Wittkower and I. Jaffe (New York: Fordham University Press, 1972), pp. 29–49, 51–62; Lucas, *Saint, Site and Sacred Strategy*, pp. 48–49; and Pio Pecchiai, *Il Gesù di Roma* (Rome: Società Grafica Romana, 1952), p. 55.

42. For the question of iconography, see Zuccari, *Arte e Committenza*, pp. 139–70; and L. H. Monssen, "Rex Gloriose Martyrum: A Contribution to Jesuit Iconography," *Art Bulletin* 63, 1 (1981): 130–37.

43. ARSI, Prov. Rom. 162, I, f. 167v; Zuccari, *Arte e Committenza*,

pp. 160–62. The author of these two paintings is uncertain, but generally they are attributed to the Jesuit artist Giovan Battista Fiammeri. See *Restauri della Soprintendenza alle Gallerie e alle Opere d'Arte Medioevale e Moderna per il Lazio* (Rome: DeLuca, 1972), pp. 31–32. However, if Fiammeri's death date, usually given as 1596, is correct he could not have painted these two works.

44. Francesco Barberi, *Paolo Manuzio e la stamperia del popolo romano (1561–1570)* (Rome: Gela Editrice, 1986 rpt. of 1942 ed.), pp. 111–17. See also Gregory Martin, *Roma Sancta (1581)*, ed. G. B. Parks (Rome: Edizioni di Storia e Letteratura, 1969), pp. 135–42.

45. Valone, "Roman Matrons as Patrons," pp. 59–68. On Jerome, see Eugene F. Rice, Jr., *Saint Jerome in the Renaissance* (Baltimore: The Johns Hopkins University Press, 1985).

46. Barberi, *Paolo Manuzio*, p. 117.

47. Luca Pinelli, *Brevi Meditationi del Sanctissimo Sacramento* (Brescia: Marchetti, 1606).

48. Antonio Gallonio, *Historia deli Sante Vergini Romane* (Rome: A. and G. Donangeli, 1591); Paolo Emilio Santoro, *XII Virgines et Martyres* (Rome: Facciotti, 1597). Santoro's volume was dedicated to Clement VIII, who had conferred the church of San Vitale on the Jesuits. For a contemporary description of San Vitale, see Richeôme, *La peinture spirituelle*, pp. 673–790.

49. E. Ann Matter, *The Voice of My Beloved: The Song of Songs in Western Medieval Christianity* (Philadelphia: University of Pennsylvania Press, 1990), p. 151.

50. The Jesuits were also devoted to the virginity of Mary, and the influence of Jesuit writers on this subject should be examined. The fourth altarpiece, *The Agony in the Garden*, is no longer extant.

Anne Jacobson Schutte

8. *Per Speculum in Enigmate*: Failed Saints, Artists, and Self-Construction of the Female Body in Early Modern Italy

> The female body (or the male body) is not merely or primarily an anatomical fact, but rather a *symbolic construction*. Everything we know about the body is embedded in some sort of explicit or implicit discourse.[1]

Thus Gisela Bock succinctly formulated what in the past few years has become a point of departure almost universally adopted by scholars concerned with gender.[2] This premise has enabled us to move beyond the old equation "woman as 'other' = woman as eternal victim," developed most fully by Simone de Beauvoir,[3] which played an essential role in the development of modern feminism but has proved less than fruitful for work in the historically oriented humanistic disciplines. Today we respond to Sherry Ortner's rhetorical question, "Is female to male as nature is to culture?" as she herself did,[4] by saying "yes and no": yes when we try to represent explicit viewpoints in practically all the cultures we study;[5] no when we articulate our comprehension of the present and our plans and hopes for the future.

Recent scholarship has demonstrated unequivocally that no revolutionary breakthrough for women, either in social arrangements or in perceptions, occurred in preindustrial Europe. Italy during the medieval and early modern eras presented no significant exceptions to the stereotype of "woman" generalized in the West until the late eighteenth century and not yet entirely superseded. The constructors par excellence of women—their minds, their place in society, and their bodies as well—were men: the writers and artists who created and disseminated images of women and the holders of authority who enforced the rules governing women's behavior. Even when they did so ostensibly in the interest of women, men's discourse was conducted almost exclusively among and for themselves.

Three examples may help to illustrate this assertion. A first, almost obligatory, case in point is *The Book of the Courtier*, a canonical text that recent scholarship has shown to be much less optimistic and a good deal more complex than it once appeared. Motivated in large part by the desire to salve the psychological wounds of an elite whose power and self-esteem had been seriously eroded by the entry of northern rulers and their armies onto the Italian scene,[6] Baldesar Castiglione created the perfect court lady to complement the courtier—to serve as a mirror in which the male could see his attributes reflected to best advantage. Notwithstanding the author's liberal position on the *querelle de femmes*, the Duchess, Emilia Pia, and the other female characters are not full-fledged participants in the dialogue. On the contrary, their function is instrumental: to listen and occasionally to facilitate by moving the conversation along and keeping it on track.[7]

Analyzing works in a very different genre, gynecological treatises of the fifteenth and sixteenth centuries, Ottavia Niccoli has observed that in most of them,

> the female body strikes us as substantially absent, or better, as merely the support for a network of signs and symbols that refer to realities external to the woman herself, readable and decipherable only by men.[8]

When we turn to the visual realm, we encounter yet another male universe of discourse. As Elizabeth Cropper has demonstrated, many sixteenth-century Italian depictions of women that appear to be portraits were intended not to capture the particular appearance and character of an individual female sitter, but rather to contribute to a philosophical debate about the nature of beauty.[9] Here again, what appears to be the subject is in fact an object referring to something other than herself.

If the cultural artifacts relating to women and the strategies of interpretation at our disposal were limited to negative instances like these, we would be forced back to de Beauvoir's paradigm. In fact, of course, they are not. Some women in late medieval and early modern Italy managed to lay their hands on physical and psychological space, materials, and techniques insufficient for staging a revolution, but adequate for limited exercises in self-determination. They worked to create not only works of literature, art, and music but also themselves.

Integral to fashioning a personal identity is the construction of a physical body. Discourse between the self and others, living and dead, both shapes and is shaped by this cultural project. The process of reciprocal influence is circular but not necessarily vicious, at least not in the strictly logical sense.[10] For some, probably most, women in early modern Italy, however, the existential outcome was less than positive.

The peculiar subset under consideration here comprises three women—Maria Janis, Antonia Pesenti, and Cecilia Ferrazzi—"failed saints" who were tried by the Venetian Inquisition in the 1660s for pretense of sanctity.[11] They are representative of a larger group of Italian and Spanish women, and others living in areas where the enforcers of the rules concerning gender roles were bishops or secular judges rather than inquisitors, who were prosecuted for the same offense.[12] The burden of the Holy Office's case against Janis, Ferrazzi, and Pesenti was conscious, clever fabrication of frequent communications from God the Father, Christ, and the Virgin Mary that, the defendants claimed, assured them of their holy status and endowed them with various means of demonstrating it to others. These means, which inquisitors condemned as feigned stratagems, included visions, raptures, the ability to perform miracles, and (most relevant for our purpose) the capacity to transcend the normal limits of the human body in ways such as bearing the stigmata and living without ordinary food and drink. Satanic influence, if indeed it was involved, played a relatively minor role according to the inquisitorial judges, who saw these women as active collaborators, not passive victims, of the devil, and hence the prime architects of their impious impostures.[13]

To comprehend the attempts by Janis, Presenti, and Ferrazzi to construct holy female bodies, it may be heuristically useful to identify a control group, another set of women involved in the fashioning and exhibition of bodies. The most obvious one would be "genuine" holy women, those who not only gained recognition from their contemporaries but also passed the formal examinations set by the controllers of culture—in this instance, the Congregation of Rites, which oversees processes of canonization.[14] Comparing these two groups, though necessary, would take more space than is available here. Therefore I have selected a different control group: Italian women artists of the sixteenth and seventeenth centuries who painted self-portraits.

Central to the self-portrait, and particularly to the female self-portrait, as Valeria Moretti has made clear,[15] is the mirror. Unlike the brush, the palette, the easel, or the instruments of the musician or writer, the looking glass is an object to which almost every woman has easy, frequent, uncontrolled, and uncontested access. Whether or not she has "a room of her own" and the training and inclination to use it for creative purposes, her mirror is an aid to self-inspection and self-creation.[16] Moretti puts it this way:

> In the mirror we can look at ourselves. We can spy and check on ourselves. Before the mirror we can interrogate ourselves; we can use it to produce more gratifying images. We can play with the mirror. In the mirror we can distort our image, as children often do. With its help we can invent new poses, new masks.[17]

But looking into the mirror, Moretti argues, is more than a solitary, narcissistic pastime. It is a necessary step in making oneself ready to be seen by others as one wishes to be seen.[18] To put the matter in more general terms, the attainment of self-consciousness, or ego formation, involves "a subject which becomes a subject by the act of constructing itself objectively to itself."[19]

For the artist, especially the woman artist, the mirror has additional practical uses. Not only can it be employed for ingenious displays of virtuosity that in certain instances, as Mary D. Garrard has recently argued, convey ironic or even subversive messages about gender.[20] It is technically essential to reproducing oneself accurately on paper or canvas—over and over again, as Sofonisba Anguissola had to do to fulfill numerous requests for self-portraits, which constitute more than one-third of her output.[21] Surely her mirror helped Artemisia Gentileschi to achieve a rather different aim: using herself as a model for Judith, Esther, Susanna, Lucretia, and Mary Magdalen. Some modern scholars have argued that in these compelling images of heroic women's revenge against male aggressors and sullied virtue reattained, Gentileschi reenacted, externalized, and thereby overcame the trauma of being raped by the painter Agostino Tassi, a family friend who had instructed her in perspective.[22]

Did the three Venetian "failed saints" begin their careers by gazing into a looking glass? Ferrazzi and Pesenti, growing up in Venice in artisan households, must have had access to mirrors; Janis, daughter of an unemployed weaver in a mountain village north of Bergamo, perhaps did not. Since our firsthand information about them is largely dependant on their personal testimonies, which differ considerably in the extent to which they touch on early experiences, we must read between the lines and speculate.

Like most defendants before the Holy Office, Janis did not take the initiative in making her voice heard; rather, she responded to questions from the inquisitor, who quite naturally showed less interest in her childhood than in her recent activities. Pesenti, who at first was incapable of providing coherent testimony, focused in subsequent interrogations almost exclusively on the last few months of her life. Ferrazzi, on the other hand, having requested and obtained the unusual privilege of dictating her autobiography to a notary, furnished a detailed, highly self-conscious account beginning in her infancy. In all three cases, however, it is clear that the women were strongly attracted at a relatively early age to the religious life. Janis and Pesenti evinced no interest in marriage, and Ferrazzi explicitly expressed an aversion to it. None spoke with regret of an early addiction to "vanities" like attention to her physical appearance. Therefore it is difficult to believe that they spent hours of their childhood and adolescence in front of a mirror, primping, preening, and dreaming of suitors.[23]

How then did they initially form and subsequently shape images of their bodies? I suggest that they availed themselves of different, nonliteral sorts of mirrors. To some extent, they drew on the information available to them about certified holy female bodies, those of their predecessors in the enterprise of sanctity. But their primary frames of reference were their confessors and other authority figures interested in their spiritual state.

My relegating role models to a subsidiary position requires some explanation. First of all, Janis, Pesenti, and Ferrazzi were lay women. All three desperately wanted to become nuns but were unable to achieve their ambition. Janis's and Pesenti's families were too poor to afford the monastic dowry required to place their daughters in convents. Ferrazzi, after a battle of wills with her father and mother, obtained their consent to enter the religious life, but when they died of the plague in 1630, the plan aborted. Hence these women were deprived of the direct contact with nuns on whom to model their bodies and lives, for the overwhelming majority of nuns by the seventeenth century were shut up behind convent walls in strict enclosure.

Furthermore, unlike most successful holy women of their time, these three were not educated enough to make deliberate, systematic use of books—the lives of saints, instructions on leading a holy life—as mirrors. Pesenti seems to have been totally illiterate.[24] Janis may have learned to read well only after undertaking the enterprise of making herself a holy woman; given the fact that she authenticated the transcripts of her testimony with the sign of the cross, she probably never mastered writing.[25] Although Ferrazzi could sign her name, she was not at home with the printed word.[26] None of them was well equipped to gaze directly at written sources and utilize them fully: that is, to read, reread, and meditate on texts with the aim of fashioning herself in response to the messages she drew from them.[27] Most if not all the information they gleaned about saints and holiness must have come to them secondhand, through listening to others read and preach, as Janis and Ferrazzi acknowledged.[28] In contrast to their more fortunate cloistered contemporaries, they lacked the training and practice necessary to process such information in a disciplined, systematic way.[29]

The three aspiring saints therefore were largely dependent on human mirrors that talked back—above all their spiritual directors, men of the cloth authorized not only to hear their confessions but also to endorse, condemn, or redirect their thoughts and actions.[30] "Mirror, mirror on the wall, who is the fairest one of all?" the Queen in the fairy tale *Snow White* anxiously asked.[31] In response to Janis's, Pesenti's, and Ferrazzi's versions of the same question, their human mirrors provided various answers, which in turn prompted different reactions from the inquirers.

As Fulvio Tomizza has eloquently demonstrated, Maria Janis's mirror responded at first in an ambiguous way that provided his penitent ample opportunity for interpretation, and thus for self-construction of her physical body. In the early 1650s, Janis, a pious woman about twenty years old, left her home in Colzate to follow Don Pietro Morali, a friend of her father, to the nearby village of Zorzone, where he was serving as priest. The attraction between the two, which both perceived as purely spiritual, was obviously something more. Their love remained so deeply sublimated, however, that despite certain witnesses' efforts to insinuate otherwise, it went no further than an occasional pat on the shoulder. Janis, who supported herself by spinning and weaving, was soon enlisted by Morali to conduct classes in Christian doctrine for the children of Zorzone. To prepare her for entry into a convent for poor women which was in the planning stage, the priest taught her to read the Great Office of Latin by rote.

Gradually Janis slipped into holy anorexia.[32] Having developed a psychological and intellectual aversion to ordinary mortals' sustenance, which she referred to as "dirt" and "filth," she came to prefer the spiritually nourishing food and drink available at the altar. She began to experiment, eating less and less and taking communion as frequently as possible. The idea "passed one day through my heart," she testified, of trying to live on communion alone.[33]

When her mentor realized what she was doing, he hesitated. A more erudite and less emotionally involved spiritual director, such as the specialists in "women's problems" who served as confessors to nuns, might well have taken a position and stuck to it.[34] Morali, however, sent Janis mixed signals. First he ordered her to stop her holy fast; next he allowed it to continue under controlled conditions (at least one normal meal a week); then he tried to extricate himself entirely by sending her home to Colzate, where she resumed eating. But finally he reversed himself, allowed her to return to Zorzone, and capitulated, giving her communion at least once a day and sometimes more often. His belief, from this point on unconditional, in what he and Janis called her "privilege" and his confidence that eventually God would allow it to be revealed to the world led him to take her—along with a male chaperon, the devout weaver Pietro Palazzi—on the road to Rome and eventually to Venice. In January 1661, having been spied on while they conducted an improvised private communion ceremony that was sanctioned by their visions but not condoned by ecclesiastical authorities, the woman and the priest were denounced to the Inquisition.

Janis strove to achieve a "body beautiful" pleasing both to God and to Morali. That it pleased God she was assured by the fact that she felt and looked well as long as she followed her self-designed regimen but grew weak and ill when she departed from it. That it came to please Morali as well became evident when he acceded to her wishes, broke rules to satisfy her, and in a reversal of roles became her collaborator, even her disciple. The disappearance of her one physical defect, a goiter, perhaps enhanced their shared belief in her constructed holy body. In any event, their total acceptance of it led them to persist until the very last stage of a long trial in maintaining that never in more than five years had the tiniest morsel of food or drop of drink made its way down her digestive tract. The prosecution, of course, interpreted Janis's and Morali's intransigence as the keystone of a deliberate attempt to deceive. In my view, their stubbornness about what the inquisitor called "the knot of eating"[35] was the very natural consequence of a sincerely held conviction. Because Janis had painted the portrait of her body while gazing into the mirror held by Morali, both had an enormous emotional investment in the image.

If Maria Janis's self-portrait can be likened to a baroque painting, glowing with vivid colors, Antonia Pesenti's more closely resembles a monochrome sketch.[36] Still, there are similarities between them, especially the fact that a prime motivating factor in both cases was love. On the Wednesday of Holy Week in 1668, while visiting a friend who was ill,

Pesenti, who was thirty-four, encountered Francesco Vincenzi, the fifty-seven-year-old rector of a church on the other side of Venice, who had come to bless the sick woman. A few days later she heard Vincenzi preach in her parish church, San Polo. At least in her heart, Cupid's arrow found its mark. She immediately moved across town to Vincenzi's church, Santa Ternita, and joined other pious young women in a "hermitage" adjoining the rectory.

One thing quickly led to another. The Virgin Mary began to communicate with her, commanding that a *Madonna alla greca* (a Byzantine-style image) in the church be installed in a new, more prominent location. Pesenti's raptures in front of the painting, which attracted the devout curiosity of an increasing number of visitors to Santa Ternita, persuaded Vincenzi that God had sent him a living saint, whose virtues and visions he began to publicize. Then, believing that they were following instructions from on high, the two joined themselves in an improvised ceremony of spiritual marriage, complete with a white gown, flowers, and a ring for the bride.[37] As in the case of Janis and Morali, it is virtually certain that their romantic attraction never culminated in sexual union, although Pesenti eventually admitted that she had been tempted by the devil to engage in nocturnal masturbation. Antonia's and Francesco's chaste honeymoon was brief. In mid-June a suspicious canon who said Mass at Santa Ternita reported them to the Holy Office.

Though Pesenti made one passing reference to having fasted assiduously before she met Vincenzi, and he spoke of prompting her flagging appetite with custards he himself prepared, anorexia is not a major motif in the construction of her holy body. Nor did she take as much initiative as Janis in the creation of this new body. Only her very first move—walking out the door of the family home in San Polo, getting into a gondola, and asking to be taken to Santa Ternita, which she did not know how to find by herself—was made on her own initiative. From then on, Vincenzi, who instantly and unquestioningly assumed complete charge of shaping her into a spiritual Galatea, led her by the hand. This is no metaphor: witness after witness, as well as the two defendants, testified to his taking her hand and conducting her between the hermitage, the rectory, and the church. Without activation by a male authority figure, she could hardly move. Vincenzi alone could arouse her from her trances; his commands were the only medicine for paralysis of the legs. When the inquisitor ordered that she return to the family home, she had to be bundled into and out of a gondola and carried upstairs.

Pesenti's tongue was periodically paralyzed, too, both figuratively and literally. Not a single witness testified to having heard her recount her visions; all their information came from the enthusiastic Vincenzi. Consigned to prison, she was incapable of answering the solicitous inquiries of the jailer and his wife but instead threw herself off her cot, began to shake, and proceeded to lick crosses on the floor until an experienced exorcist, the Franciscan friar Candido Brugnoli, restored her power of speech.[38] When she was summoned into the presence of the Holy Office for the second time and told that sobs and nods of the head were not satisfactory responses to the inquisitor's questions, all she could do was stammer "ah, ah, ah, vu, vu." But once the inquisitor loosened it by encouraging her to speak, a coherent, circumstantial account of her adventure flowed out.[39]

Cecilia Ferrazzi's construction of a holy body, a somewhat less "prodigious" one, was even more striking in other respects. She painted the self-portrait of a sick, suffering body with some light touches of abstention from food. Describing herself as "born with grass [or herb] in her mouth," she made it known that she subsisted on very little nourishment.[40] This claim was contested by many witnesses, especially the inmates of the houses she ran for "girls in danger," who described with famished envy their furtive glimpses of delicacies on the plate in her private apartment. In her testimony and autobiography, however, Ferrazzi put greater emphasis on her persistent problems with bladder stones, her fainting fits (raptures in her terms), and her temporary bearing of the stigmata.[41] The significance she attributed to these somatic phenomena was reinforced by the reactions of authority figures, lay "superiors" as well as confessors. Both uncritical acceptance and harsh dismissal of what she told them stimulated her to pursue the project of crafting a holy body.

To a much greater extent than Pesenti or even Janis, Ferrazzi took charge of her enterprise and exercised considerable ingenuity in carrying it out; in other words, she relied less than they on the mirrors of other people. Unsatisfied with what the inquisitor was eliciting from her, she took the initiative of dictating her story as she conceived it, so that a genuine, finished self-portrait—clearly modeled on the lives of female saints—would become part of the trial record.[42] Earlier in her career, furthermore, she generated icons by having portraits of her by the painters Nicolò Renieri and Ermanno Stroiffi retouched to resemble Saint Teresa and the Madonna of the Seven Sorrows. She too improvised a ceremony. When she returned from trips, the girls in her charge were required to process along the bank of the canal where her gondola landed intoning the *Te deum* and a hymn to Saint Cecilia.[43] The intended function of the autobiography, the recycled portraits, and the rite is evident: to project an image of her body as similar, even identical, to those of certified holy women.

We can now return to our control group. Unlike Janis, Pesenti, and Ferrazzi, who, after being condemned to prison by the Inquisition, sank back into obscurity—only in Ferrazzi's case can a post-sentence life course be traced[44]—the women artists of their era flourished. Living in many cases to a ripe old age,[45] they gained increasing fame and the tangible rewards that accompanied it. Their daring projects of self-construction nonetheless raised suspicions of fraud. A major motivation for collectors to acquire their self-portraits, in fact, was to prove to skeptics that the women had really executed them, after which the paintings were sometimes placed in cabinets of curiosities, alongside such marvels as scarabs and two-headed calves.[46] Sooner or later, then, the artists' construction and depiction of a prodigious body, *mulier pictrix*, passed muster.

In conclusion, let me suggest some of the reasons why the women artists succeeded when their spiritual sisters failed. Painters were obviously not subject to a single, definitive judgment by a controlling institution such as the Inquisition. Because they were producing multiple products over a period of time, they were evaluated on numerous occasions by a wide variety of individuals whose opinions were less than completely authoritative. Bearing little resemblance to the holy women's ménages à trois with a priest and God at the altar and in the confessional, artists' studios were crowded, sociable spaces. Women painters' multiple mirrors (mentors, fathers, sisters, pupils, clients), which reflected varied images, were evidently less constricting than the eyes and voice of a single cleric serving as spiritual director to an aspiring saint.[47] Above all, the works created by the artists were "public bodies,"[48] sometimes modeled on but not coterminous with their own bodies. With the partial exception of Ferrazzi, the holy women condemned by the Venetian Inquisition constructed very little or nothing tangible apart from their physical selves. Women artists therefore had an opportunity, almost never enjoyed by the "failed saints," to say, "I am not only this body you see here but also what I make. Look, there it is!"

An Italian version of this essay has appeared previously: "Come costruirsi un corpo di santa," trans. Silvana Seidel Menchi, *Studi storici* 33 (1992):

127–39. The editors of *Studi storici* have graciously consented to the publication of the English original in this volume.

Notes

1. Gisela Bock, "Introduzione: Corpi, donne e storia," in *Il corpo delle donne*, ed. Gisela Bock and Giuliana Nobili (Ancona and Bologna: Transeuropa, 1988), p. 12 (italics in the original). Unless otherwise indicated, translations are mine.

2. For a particularly valuable implementation of this approach, see Margaret R. Miles, *Carnal Knowing: Female Nakedness and Religious Meaning in the Christian West* (Boston: Beacon, 1989; rpt. New York: Vintage, 1991).

3. Simone de Beauvoir, *La deuxième sexe* (Paris: Gallimard, 1949); English ed., *The Second Sex*, trans. H. M. Parshley (New York: Bantam, 1949).

4. Sherry B. Ortner, "Is Female to Male as Nature Is to Culture?" in *Woman, Culture, and Society*, ed. Michelle Zimbalist Rosaldo and Louise Lamphere (Stanford, CA: Stanford University Press, 1974), pp. 67–88.

5. A fascinating exception to this "rule" and the inferiority of women it clearly implies has been brought to light recently by Claudia Lazzaro: "The Visual Language of Gender in Sixteenth-Century Garden Sculpture," in *Refiguring Woman: Perspectives on Gender and the Italian Renaissance*, ed. Marilyn Migiel and Juliana Schiesari (Ithaca, NY: Cornell University Press, 1991), pp. 71–113.

6. Lauro Martines, *Power and Imagination: City-States in Renaissance Italy* (New York: Alfred A. Knopf, 1979), pp. 328–31.

7. See Joan Kelly-Gadol, "Did Women Have a Renaissance?" in *Becoming Visible: Women in European History*, ed. Renate Bridenthal and Claudia Koonz (Boston: Houghton Mifflin, 1977), pp. 137–64; rpt. in ibid., 2d ed., ed. Bridenthal, Koonz, and Susan M. Stuard (Boston: Houghton Mifflin, 1987), pp. 175–204; and rpt. in *Women, History, and Theory: The Essays of Joan Kelly* (Chicago: University of Chicago Press, 1984), pp. 19–50.

8. Ottavia Niccoli, "Il corpo femminile nei trattati del Cinquecento," in Bock and Nobili, *Il corpo delle donne*, p. 26.

9. Elizabeth Cropper, "The Beauty of Women: Problems in the Rhetoric of Renaissance Portraiture," in *Rewriting the Renaissance: The Discourse of Sexual Difference in Early Modern Europe*, ed. Margaret W. Ferguson, Maureen Quilligan, and Nancy J. Vickers (Chicago: University of Chicago Press, 1986), pp. 175–90.

10. For a sensitive treatment of this issue in nineteenth- and twentieth-century literature, see Jenijoy La Belle, *Herself Beheld: The Literature of the Looking Glass* (Ithaca, NY: Cornell University Press, 1988).

11. For the aspiring holy women focused on here, I use the deliberately paradoxical term "failed saints" (my coinage) in preference to the tendentious labels "false saints," "feigned saints," and "pretended holiness" (*false sante*, *finte sante*, *affettata/pretesa/simulata santità*) employed by the Inquisition. On the prob-

lem of what to call these women, see the collection of essays *Finzione e santità tra medioevo ed età moderna*, ed. Gabriella Zarri (Turin: Rosenberg and Sellier, 1991), in particular Zarri, "'Vera' santità, 'simulata' santità: Ipotesi e riscontri," pp. 9–36; Albano Biondi, "L' 'inordinata devozione' nella *Prattica* del Cardinale Scaglia (ca. 1635)," p. 313. Janis, Pesenti, and Ferrazzi stand at the center of my forthcoming book, tentatively entitled *Clipped Wings: Pretense of Sanctity, the Inquisition, and Gender in Seventeenth-Century Venice*. The records of their trials are in Venice, Archivio di Stato, Sant'Uffizio, buste 110 (dossier Pietro Morali and Maria Janis), 112 (dossier Cecilia Ferrazzi), and 115 (dossier Francesco Vincenzi and Antonia Pesenti); since the trial transcripts are for the most part unpaginated, I shall omit further precise references to them. On Janis, see Fulvio Tomizza, *La finzione di Maria* (Milan: Rizzoli, 1981), available in English as *Heavenly Supper: The Story of Maria Janis*, trans. Anne Jacobson Schutte (Chicago: University of Chicago Press, 1991); citations below are to the English edition. On Ferrazzi, see Cecilia Ferrazzi, *Autobiografia di una santa mancata*, ed. Anne Jacobson Schutte (Bergamo: Pierluigi Lubrina, 1990); Schutte, "'Questo non è il ritratto che ho fatto io': Painters, the Inquisition, and the Shape of Sanctity in Seventeenth-Century Venice," in *Florence and Italy: Studies in Honour of Nicolai Rubinstein*, ed. Peter Denley and Caroline Elam (London: Westfield College, 1988), pp. 419–31; Schutte, "Un caso di santità affettata: L'autobiografia di Cecilia Ferrazzi," in Zarri, *Finzione e santità*, pp. 329–42; and Schutte, "Inquisition and Female Autobiography: The Case of Cecilia Ferrazzi" (English version of "Un caso"), in *The Crannied Wall: Women, Religion, and the Arts in Early Modern Europe*, ed. Craig Monson (Ann Arbor: University of Michigan Press, 1992), pp. 105–18.

12. On pretense of sanctity in Italy, see Giuseppe Paladino, "Suor Cristina Rovoles creduta santa e il suo processo," *Archivio storico siciliano*, n.s. 36 (1911): 113–25; Giovanni Romeo, "Una 'simulatrice di santità' a Napoli nel '500: Alfonsina Rispola," *Campania sacra* 8–9 (1977–78): 159–218; Luisa Ciammitti, "Una santa di meno: Storia di Angeli Mellini, cucitrice bolognese (1667–17 . .)," *Quaderni storici* 41 (maggio-agosto 1979): 603–39 (English trans. Margaret A. Gallucci in *Sex and Gender in Historical Perspective: Selections from* Quaderni Storici, ed. Edward Muir and Guido Ruggiero [Baltimore: Johns Hopkins University Press, 1990], pp. 141–76); Marina Romanello, "Il caso di Marta Fiascaris tra affettata santità e rete di solidarietà femminile," in *Ragnatele di rapporti: Patronage e reti di relazione nella storia delle donne*, ed. Lucia Ferrante, Maura Palazzi, and Gianna Pomata (Turin: Rosenberg and Sellier, 1988), pp. 240–52; and the essays in Zarri, *Finzione e santità*. As one reviewer observed, the case of Benedetta Carlini, protagonist of Judith C. Brown's *Immodest Acts: The Life of a Lesbian Nun in Renaissance Italy* (New York: Oxford University Press, 1986), has more to do with pretense of sanctity than with lesbianism. Mary R. O'Neil, review of Brown's *Immodest Acts*, in *Sixteenth Century Journal* 17 (1986): 392. A French "pretender" analogous in some respects to her Italian contemporaries tried for pretense of sanctity is the Visitandine nun Jeanne des Anges, rendered famous by Aldous Huxley in *The Devils of Loudon* (London: Chatto and Windus, 1952). There are two recent Italian editions of her autobiography: *Autobiografia: Il punto di vista dell'indemoniata*, ed. Mino Bergamo (Venice: Marsilio, 1986); and *Storia della mia possessione*, ed. Angelo Mo-

rino (Palermo: Sellerio, 1986). A German instance of the phenomenon was unearthed by Friedrich Roth, "Die Geistliche Betrügerin Anna Laminit von Augsburg (ca. 1480–1518): Ein Augsburger Kulturbild vom Vorabend der Reformation," *Zeitschrift für Kirchengeschichte* n.s. 6, 43.2 (1924): 355–417; on Laminit, see also Lyndal Roper, *The Holy Household: Women and Morals in Reformation Augsburg* (Oxford: Clarendon, 1989), pp. 262–63. Pretense of sanctity on the Iberian peninsula is now being actively investigated. See, for example, Jodi Bilinkoff, "Charisma and Controversy: The Case of María de Sto. Domingo," *Archivo dominicano* 10 (1989): 55–66; and Mary Elizabeth Perry, *Gender and Disorder in Early Modern Seville* (Princeton, NJ: Princeton University Press, 1990), pp. 103–17.

13. On seventeenth-century inquisitors' skepticism about the intervention of the devil, evidenced also in prosecutions for magic and sorcery, see John Tedeschi, "The Organization and Procedures of the Roman Inquisition: A Sketch," in his *The Prosecution of Heresy: Collected Studies on the Inquisition in Early Modern Italy* (Binghamton, NY: Medieval and Renaissance Texts and Studies, 1991), pp. 134–35; Anne Jacobson Schutte, "Donne, Inquisizione e pietà," in *La chiesa di Venezia nel Seicento*, ed. Bruno Bertoli (Venice: Studium Cattolico Veneziano, 1992), pp. 235–51.

14. On criteria for canonization in the post-Tridentine period, see Romeo De Maio, "L'ideale eroico nei processi di canonizzazione della Controriforma," in idem, *Riforme e miti nella Chiesa dell Cinquecento* (Naples: Guida, 1973), pp. 257–78; Peter Burke, "How to Be a Counter-Reformation Saint," in *Religion and Society in Early Modern Europe, 1500–1800*, ed. Kaspar von Greyerz (London: Allen and Unwin, for the German Historical Institute, 1984), pp. 45–55 (rev. version in Burke, *The Historical Anthropology of Early Modern Italy* [Cambridge: Cambridge University Press, 1987], pp. 48–62); and Giuseppe Dalla Torre, "Santità ed economica processuale: L'esperienza giuridica da Urbano VIII a Benedetto XIV," in Zarri, *Finzione e santità*, pp. 231–63.

15. Valeria Moretti, *Le più belle del reale: Pittrici in autoritratto dal Cinquecento all'Ottocento* (Rome: Nuova Editrice Spada, 1983).

16. La Belle, in *Herself Beheld*, comes to a much less positive conclusion about most women's use of the mirror.

17. Moretti, *Le più belle del reale*, p. 16.

18. Moretti, *Le più belle del reale*, p. 19. La Belle, *Herself Beheld*, also rejects the proposition that gazing at oneself in the mirror is always narcissistic; see especially pp. 69–75.

19. Samuel Taylor Coleridge, *Biographia Literaria* (1817), quoted by La Belle, *Herself Beheld*, pp. 47–48, 151.

20. Mary D. Garrard, "Here's Looking at Me: Sofonisba Anguissola and the Problem of the Woman Artists," paper delivered at the Sixteenth Century Studies Conference, Atlanta, 22 October 1992. On the quite different subject of the mirror in male artists' images of women, see Miles, *Carnal Knowing*, pp. 129, 217–18.

21. Moretti, *Le più belle del reale*, pp. 29–30, 38, 43. See also Flavio Caroli, *Sofonisba Anguissola e le sue sorelle* (Milan: Arnoldo Mondadori, 1987).

22. Moretti, *Le più belle del reale*, pp. 52, 109–13. See also Lucia Ferrante, "L'onore ritrovata: Donne nella casa di soccorso di S. Paolo a Bologna (sec.

XVI–XVII)," *Quaderni storici* 53 (agosto 1983): 499–527 (English trans. Margaret A. Gallucci in Muir and Ruggiero, *Sex and Gender in Historical Perspective*, pp. 46–72). The autobiographical element in Gentileschi's "revenge" paintings, an issue hotly debated in current scholarship, is treated in a carefully nuanced and persuasive way in two recent contributions: Mary D. Garrard, *Artemisia Gentileschi: The Image of the Female Hero in Italian Baroque Art* (Princeton, NJ: Princeton University Press, 1989); and Luciano Berti, "Artemisia da Roma tra i fiorentini," in *Artemisia* (catalogue of the exhibition at Casa Buonarroti, Florence, 18 June–14 November 1991), ed. Roberto Contini and Gianni Papi (Rome: Leonardo-De Luca, 1991), pp. 9–30. (In n. 19 of this article Berti supplies a complete transcription of Gentileschi's deposition of 18 March 1612 concerning the rape.)

23. The sole reference to a mirror in these trials comes from a witness who mentioned Janis's having her hair done by a young noblewoman in whose villa she was a guest. Tomizza, *Heavenly Supper*, pp. 114–15.

24. The trial record contains no mention of her reading, and she made a mark in lieu of signing her name.

25. Tomizza, *Heavenly Supper*, pp. 22, 70, 72–73, 76, 89, 96, 132, 137.

26. See Ferrazzi, *Autobiografia*, pp. 103–4. A compelling argument about varieties of literacy, including a review of recent work on the subject, is presented by Barry Reay, "The Context and Meaning of Popular Literacy: Some Evidence from Nineteenth-Century Rural England," *Past & Present* 131 (May 1991): 89–129.

27. For the conceit of the book as a mirror, see a spiritual guidebook published in Barcelona in 1585 that was translated from the Spanish by Florentine Dominicans and issued three times in Italy: Diego Pérez de Valdivia, *Avvertimenti spirituali per tutti quelli che specialmente si sono dedicate al servitio di Dio* (Florence: Filippo Giunti, 1590 and 1592; Venice: Pietro Bertano, 1650). Directed toward Spanish *beatas*, it is especially relevant to the situation of devout laywomen. Pérez states, "Therefore the good servant [*serva*: female] of God should read at the appropriate times, looking at herself in the book as in a mirror, according to what St. James the Apostle says, so that she may first see how little her image conforms to that of true holiness and then seek to remove the blemishes of sin" (1592 ed., pp. 328–29).

28. At the end of her trial, Janis said that the key element in her self-designed body (to be examined below) had been reinforced by what "*I had heard* [or understood] some saints did" ("*havevo inteso* havessero fatto alcuni santi") (emphasis added); Tomizza, *Heavenly Supper*, p. 160. Her co-defendant, don Pietro Morali, testified that she read the lives of the saints; ibid., p. 96; and Archivio vescovile di Bergamo, Ms. 47, *Visitatio Barbadica tomus primus*, f. 91r. Therefore she may well have been exposed via the printed page to accounts of prodigious abstinence from food by such saints as Catherine of Siena. It is significant, however, that she herself did not refer explicitly to reading. For Ferrazzi's listening to others read, see her *Autobiografia*, pp. 45, 47.

29. In this regard they differ significantly from the holy women examined in Caroline Walker Bynum's important study *Holy Feast and Holy Fast: The Religious Significance of Food for Medieval Women* (Berkeley: University of California Press,

1987). Miles's discussion of Hildegard of Bingen is also relevant here; see her *Carnal Knowing*, pp. 99–105, 114–16.

30. On the mirror as an adjunct of patriarchal structures and the male as a mirror, see La Belle, *Herself Beheld*, pp. 26–30. On the spiritual director as an artist designing his penitent, see Gabriella Zarri, "Ginevra Gozzadini dall'Armi, gentildonna bolognese (1520/27–1567)," in *Rinascimento al femminile*, ed. Ottavia Niccoli (Rome and Bari: Laterza, 1991), pp. 130–32.

31. La Belle, *Herself Beheld*, p. 38. Michael Knapton has kindly called my attention to another significant mirror image in the tale of the Ugly Duckling, who gazes into a pond and sees a beautiful swan.

32. Unlike some readers of Rudolph M. Bell's *Holy Anorexia* (Chicago: University of Chicago Press, 1985), I have no problem with the concept of holy anorexia, which Bell carefully distinguishes from modern anorexia nervosa. Because it focuses on elite mystics, Bynum's complementary study, *Holy Feast and Holy Fast*, is less relevant than Bell's for the nonelite women under consideration here. On Janis as an anorexic, see Linda L. Carroll, "Bread of Angels or Bread and Salami? The Rhetoric of Fasting in Fulvio Tomizza's *Heavenly Supper*," paper delivered at the Sixteenth Century Studies Conference meeting, Philadelphia, 19 October 1991.

33. Tomizza, *Heavenly Supper*, pp. 53, 160.

34. On confessors and nuns, see Ottavia Niccoli, "Il confessore e l'inquisitore: A proposito di un manoscritto bolognese del Seicento," in Zarri, *Finzione e santità*, pp. 412–33; Giovanna Paolin, "Confessione e confessori al femminile: Monache e direttori spirituali in ambito veneto tra '600 e '700," in ibid., pp. 366–88; and Paolin, "Inquisizione e confessori nel Friuli del Seicento: Analisi di un rapporto," in *L'Inquisizione romana in Italia nell'età moderna: Archivi, problemi di metodo e nuove ricerche*, ed. Andrea Del Col and Giovanna Paolin, Pubblicazioni degli Archivi di Stato, 19 (Rome: Ufficio centrale per i beni archivistici, 1991), pp. 175–87.

35. Tomizza, *Heavenly Supper*, p. 122.

36. This summary is based on the trial record, cited in n. 11.

37. The wedding band, borrowed from the priest's sister, was an *anello di S. Carlo*, associated with the cult of that archmisogynist and paladin of chastity Saint Charles Borromeo.

38. In this case the Holy Office demonstrated in an especially vivid way its skepticism about the possibility of diabolical possession. After the exorcist, fra Candido Brugnoli, submitted his report on Pesenti, he was ordered by the inquisitor, Agapito Ugoni, never again to perform an exorcism in the diocese of Venice.

39. In none of these trials were the defendants tortured, although the inquisitor employed the threat of "other means" to persuade them to tell the whole truth.

40. *Nata con l'erba in bocca* may signify simply "born lucky," but Ferrazzi's use of the term implies a different meaning—perhaps, as Marisa Milani has suggested to me, an inversion of the pejorative Venetian expression *morir con l'erba in bocca* (to die of hunger through one's own fecklessness), reported by Giuseppe Boerio, *Dizionario del dialetto veneziano*, 2d ed. (Venice: Giovanni Cecchini, 1856),

s.v. *morir*. On Ferrazzi's eating habits, see her *Autobiografia*, pp. 12, 22–24, 47, 54, 78–79, 84, 87, 108.

41. Ferrazzi, *Autobiografia*, pp. 23, 24, 30–32, 45–47, 54–57, 58, 61–67, 71–72, 73–75, 92–93, 108–10.

42. Ferrazzi, *Autobiografia*, 103–6.

43. On these aspects of Ferrazzi's self-presentation, see Schutte, "'Questo non è il ritratto che ho fatto io.'"

44. See Ferrazzi, *Autobiografia*, p. 13.

45. An exception is Elisabetta Sirani, the mystery of whose premature death has been solved by Valeria Moretti, *Il pennello lacrimato: Sulle tracce di Elisabetta Sirani* (Ancona and Bologna: Il Lavoro Editoriale, 1990).

46. Moretti, *Le più belle del reale*, pp. 29–30. On cabinets of curiosities, see the exhibition catalogue *The Age of the Marvelous*, ed. Joy Kenseth (Hanover, NH: Hood Museum of Art, Dartmouth College, 1991), in which two essays are particularly pertinent to my investigation: Joy Kenseth, "'A World of Wonders in One Closet Shut,'" pp. 81–101; and Zirka Zaremba Filipczak, "'A Time Fertile in Miracles': Miraculous Events in and Through Art," pp. 193–211.

47. "Multiple mirrors mean multiple perspectives on the self," which has positive consequences for some women; for others, however, "the multiplication of images is tantamount to fragmentation of identity"; La Belle, *Herself Beheld*, p. 118. The latter outcome characterizes perfectly the conflicting messages Ferrazzi received from multiple mirrors, human and divine: see Ferrazzi, *Autobiografia*, pp. 28, 34–37, 69, 72, 80–83, 91–92, 97–98, 107–8.

48. Moretti, *Le più belle del reale*, p. 86; see also La Belle's final chapter, "A Mirror of One's Own," in *Herself Beheld*, pp. 173–85.

E. Ann Matter

9. The Commentary on the Rule of Clare of Assisi by Maria Domitilla Galluzzi

All the essays in this volume outline ways in which religious life became a vehicle for autonomy and self-expression of Italian women in the medieval and early modern period. But these essays also suggest that this life which in some ways made women's creativity possible nevertheless imposed notable restrictions on women. In fact, the last session of the Council of Trent (1563) confirmed and made official a number of limitations on the mobility of women with spiritual gifts.[1] This was not exactly news, since limitations on the lives of religious women had been growing throughout the later Middle Ages, perhaps in partial response to the remarkable creative accomplishments and religious leadership of women from the thirteenth to the seventeenth centuries.[2] Even though we are still working on the reasons why, it is clear that society at large, the institutional church, individual confessors, and religious women developed in these very centuries a "horizon of expectation" regarding the divinely inspired creative potential of women.[3]

I think the dynamic tension is worth exploring between these increasing restrictions and the well-defined typology of holiness that becomes especially clear in the latter part of this period, the sixteenth and seventeenth centuries. I am particularly interested in two aspects of this phenomenon: the ways in which religious women used their particular context to claim a creative voice for themselves, and the function of this stereotypical piety in the transition from the medieval Church to early modern Roman Catholicism. These are potentially very broad concerns, but I wish to bring them to our attention by means of a detailed examination of one text. Actually, the text is at the *center* of three concentric circles, since I will speak about one particular religious community, one prolific and gifted woman author who flourished within the strict *clausura* of that house, and one treatise which this woman wrote in defense of the way of life she had chosen. The religious community is the monastery of Capuchin nuns of Pavia; the author is Maria Domitilla Galluzzi; the text is her first work, a commentary on the *Regula* of Clare of Assisi.

In 1616, when Maria Domitilla joined the Capuchin nuns in Pavia, she entered a house dedicated to a post-Tridentine strict reform of the already severely cloistered *Regula* attributed to Clare of Assisi. There is some irony in the fact that Clare, one of the original followers of Francis of Assisi, became known as the author of a strictly enclosed, clearly monastic, rule for women. Given this disjunction, it is significant that this rule is not the one by which Clare's community lived for their first forty years, but rather a document written with the significant help of a bishop and a pope, on her deathbed.[4] I think that Clare's *Regula* is a significant moment in the history of monasticism. If it can be said that Clare wrote it, then it is the first rule written especially for monastic women, rather than an adaptation of a monastic rule for men to the particular situation of women, as is the case of the rule of Benedict. Of course, Clare did adapt her *Regula* from the second rule written by Francis for his community, but with striking differences.[5] It is this document that turns the *apostolic* life envisaged by Francis into the strictly enclosed life of a cloistered nun. Rather than going out to preach the conversion of the world, *Clarisse*, the nuns of the order of Clare, stayed behind walls and prayed for it.

The development of religious life for Franciscan women is thus a mirror image of that for Franciscan men. While the friars branched out into congregations of various levels of worldliness, but always living within the world, the Poor Clares, or Clarisse, split into separate congregations by means of progressively stricter reforms of Clare's rule. The *Cappucine* were an order of nuns founded in assiduous observance of the rules of both Clare of Assisi and the Council of Trent. The house of Capuchins in Pavia was a result of the patronage of two noble ladies, Giovanna Mezzabarba Beccaria and Giovanna Veggi Beccaria, who in 1588 took over a defunct monastery of Cistercian nuns known as Santa Franca and invited Capuchin nuns from Milan to begin a new community.[6] Thus Maria Domitilla entered a newly founded house of a newly reformed congregation, but one that lived out an ancient form of religious life, and with the patronage of the important Beccaria family.

Maria Domitilla Galluzzi was well aware of all aspects of this special combination. Her autobiography describes a triumphant entry into religious life in Pavia under the patronage of the Countess of Maino.[7] She was clearly aware of the patronage of the world, yet she used it to shut herself off in an environment that encouraged a decided otherworldly focus.

Maria Domitilla's autobiography tells us that from the time of her birth in 1595 until she entered the community in 1616 she actively sought a life that would allow her to dedicate herself to contemplation and imitation of the passion of Christ.[8] A focus on the redemptive sufferings of Christ, although characteristic of monastic spirituality before the advent of the mendicant orders, was particularly central to the Franciscan ideal. Francis of Assisi was the first of the famous stigmatists. In late sixteenth- and early seventeenth-century Italy, the ideal of a graphic *imitatio Christi* was preached to the faithful in the world by Barnabite priests and Capuchin friars, and acted out in the daily devotions of pious laypeople.[9] Maria Domitilla's parents and her beloved Aunt Domitilla, all practitioners of this spirituality in the world, awakened in the young girl the desire to follow it in its most extreme form.

The text with which I am concerned here, the *Lume sopra la prima Regola di S. Chiara*, is the first of four treatises by Maria Domitilla Galluzzi. Later in her career, she also wrote a book of visions, a book of her life, and a guide to the *Quarant'ore*, the forty-hour devotions on the passion of Christ.[10] All these works glorify devotion to Christ's suffering. None was every printed, but the *Passione*, her book of visions, is extant in at least ten manuscript copies.[11] There is evidence that Maria Domitilla Galluzzi's commentary on the rule of Clare was read outside the community of Capuchins at Pavia, since three copies survive, two in different libraries in Pavia and one in the Biblioteca Trivulziana in Milan.[12] Yet it is not easy to imagine a reading audience outside of the Capuchin order, since the *Lume* is a manifesto for the enclosed, contemplative life of the congregation.

There is a medieval tradition of commentaries on monastic rules, usually clarifying points of observance, and bringing an ideal of religious life into the focus of spiritual concerns of a given time and place. Monastic rules lend themselves to this process, since they are the bare bones of an observance, concerned with hours of sleeping and rising, prayer and work, hierarchy and discipline, but never very expansive about either the society surrounding, or the inner life of, the practitioners. Hildegard of Bingen's *Regulae S. Benedicti Explanatio*, a twelfth-century commentary on parts of the Benedictine Rule, typically adds details such as adaptation to changes in dress (monks in Benedict's age did not wear undergarments, but twelfth-century monks, says Hildegard, ought to do so to shield themselves from the sins of the flesh—28), or a spiritual explanation of some acts advocated by the Rule, such as the washing of the feet of guests (done in imitation of the acts of Jesus at the Last Supper—26).[13] But, while Hildegard's *Explanatio* seems to have been written for a community of men, Maria Domitilla Galluzzi's *Lume* clearly addresses specific problems faced by women in religious life. This is a commentary by a woman on a rule for nuns, written by a woman, for women. Perhaps it is the first such document in the history of Christianity.

It is not a minor detail that Maria Domitilla's commentary is entitled *Lume*, light on, or enlightenment about, the Rule of Clare. The preface dedicates the work to her confessor, Giovanni Battista Capponi, the intended audience (and perhaps the redactor) of her later collection of visionary writings. The preface is very much like the dedicatory letters to her visions because she presents the commentary *as* a vision. She says:

> One night after matins, fifteen days before the Most Blessed Nativity [Christmas], in the third year of my profession, at the age of twenty-three, I found myself in front of the Most Blessed Sacrament [the reserved eucharistic host] in the act of leaving the choir to go to the dormitory with the other mothers and sisters, more than ever lost in the abyss of my nothingness [*più che mai inabissata nel mio niente*]. I found myself overshadowed by great light [*adombrata da gran luce*] in which I ardently enjoyed God the Highest Good with marvelous effect of his immense love, and in His Majesty I understood the way in which the Holy Rule was observed in the time of Holy Mother Clare. . . . Out of obedience I agreed to write down as much as I can, a small part of that light, since I do not have words to express it fully. Nor do I know if, because of my great ignorance, I will know how to form words in proportion to that little that I can explain.[14]

Maria Domitilla uses the ancient language of mystical inversion, the "overshadowing of a great light," to assert that the insights into the Capuchin life offered by this treatise are not simply her thoughts, but the will of God. She is careful to place herself under obedience to Mother Church and Father Theologians, and to disavow any "diabolical tricks" while receiving the illumination. In several places at the beginning of the commentary, Maria Domitilla likens her reception of this divine light on the rule to an experience of Francis of Assisi with regard to the reception of his rule. According to the *Legend of Perugia*,[15] when Francis withdrew to a mountain to write his *Second Rule*, his companions (*ministri*) sent a delegation to tell him that they feared the new rule would be too difficult, and that they therefore did not wish to be bound by it. "You may write a rule for yourself," the messenger concluded, "but not for them." The story continues:

> Blessed Francis turned his face heavenward and, addressing Christ, said: "Lord, did I not tell you that they would not have confidence in you?" The voice of Christ was immediately heard in the air: "Francis, nothing in the rule comes from you; everything in it comes from me. I wish this rule to be observed to the letter, to the letter, to the letter, and without gloss, and without gloss, and without gloss [*ad litteram, ad litteram, ad litteram, et sine glossa, et sine glossa, et sine glossa*]."[16]

Maria Domitilla stresses and elaborates on the point of this story, even as she ignores the spiritual waverings of some of the early Franciscans. She says of Clare and her followers:

> They received this holy rule, which is the true form of the Evangelical life, which they observed perfectly, and knowing the great good which it follows, with perfect charity, they bound us, their daughters and heirs, with a vow, so as to observe as the Lord said, *ad litteram, sine glosa* [sic], without privilege or dispensation, without the interpretation of human knowledge, but simply according to the letter, as did these and their true imitators.[17]

Here we have another irony: the writing of a gloss on a text so that the text may be understood *ad litteram, sine glossa.* For Maria Domitilla's commentary *is* a gloss, a continuous interpretation that works its way through all twelve chapters of Clare's rule, taking units of two or three sentences, and clarifying the meaning behind and the way of strict observance of each part. It is, in fact, quite interesting to see Maria Domitilla employ the traditional form of commentary on sequential pericopes of text, the form of biblical exegesis from the early Middle Ages on, while denying that she is writing commentary at all. But, of course, she can only deny that her gloss is a gloss by claiming that it is *God's* gloss, as divinely inspired as the Franciscan rules themselves.

Years later, Maria Domitilla had a vision of Mary's womb in which she was reassured about the divine inspiration of the *Lume*.[18] Throughout the commentary, she continually reminds the reader that this text is divinely inspired by prefacing her interpretation of each part of the rule with verbs that underline the passivity of her role. Paragraphs begin: *Conobbi* (I knew), *Compresi* or *Intesi* (I understood), *Vidi* (I saw). I have suggested elsewhere that this tactic, common to all Maria Domitilla's works, allows her an authoritative space for her own creative voice.[19]

The *Lume*, as Maria Domitilla's first and most scholarly work, offers us important clues about her sources, her literary context, and the development of her authorial voice. She works through an Italian version of Clare's rule in a systematic way, quoting passages of the text (with very few omissions) and commenting, often extensively, on each quotation. I do not yet know whether this translation of Clare's rule, which was originally written in Latin, is Maria Domitilla's own work. It could well be, since she clearly had enough knowledge of Latin to quote from the Vulgate Bible. She is also capable of paraphrasing passages from the Vulgate Bible in Italian, and of recording God's direct speech in Latin.

On the other hand, although the Latin text of Clare's rule has been critically edited several times in our century, there has been little work on the profusion of the Italian versions of this rule that were evidently used in everyday monastery life. It is also possible, although it is hard to say how, that Maria Domitilla is a step away from the original rule she is claiming to defend. Looking at her text, though, there are a few things we can say. First, she is using a version of the rule that has undergone an initial step of editorial change from the original, that is, the division of the text into twelve chapters. Maria Domitilla seems also to be adjusting the text to a stricter standard than Clare's original. For example, her commentary absolves only the weak from the continual fasting of the Capuchin life, while the original Latin rule extends the privilege also to the young girls in the community and the servants who live outside it (3.10). In another place, she insists on a closed and locked grille separating the nuns from the world even at times when Clare allowed for it to be open, such as during the Office (5.13).

Maria Domitilla's understanding of her religious life is thus uncompromisingly harsh, even harsher than that of Clare of Assisi. Commenting on a passage from chapter 2—"and diligently explain to [a candidate for admission to the community] the way of our life and rule" (2.6)—Maria Domitilla creates a detailed list of the difficulties the life presents for a new member:

> Show her how we dress in vile clothing, always go barefoot, get up in the middle of the night, sleep on hard boards, fast continually, and eat crass, poor, and lenten food, and spend the major part of the day reciting the Divine Office and in long mental prayers, and how all of our recreation, pleasure and happiness is to serve, love, and give pleasure to the beloved Lord, attempting to imitate his holy virtues, to mortify and villify ourselves, to suffer contempt, hunger, thirst, heat, cold, and other inconveniences for his love.[20]

This list of the difficulties of the monastic life is paraphrased by the second set of *Constitutions* written especially for this community, a document of 1648 which Maria Domitilla signed on the last folio.[21] This means that Maria Domitilla's loving detail about the suffering inherent in the life of a *Cappucina* were not just a personal preference, but a reflection of the imagination of the community.

Other details of the *Lume* illuminate small portraits of the intimacy of the ideal community of Franciscan women. For example, in the commentary on the passage in Clare's rule:

> The Abbess should provide them with clothing prudently, according to the needs of each person and place, and seasons and cold climates, as it shall seem expedient to her by necessity.[22]

Maria Domitilla explains how the original community, and perhaps her own, managed to clothe each member appropriately:

> . . . as the somewhat used tunic is lighter than a new one, in times of heat, with much charity and love, if some healthy young woman had this kind of light tunic, and saw an old or weak or sick woman who had a new and heavier one, with permission of the holy mother [the Abbess], she changed it, giving her the light one, and herself taking the heavy one until the heat passed. . . . In this way they overcame their need without detriment to holy poverty. And they did the same thing in cold weather, so that the young, healthy women who had a new tunic helped those who, because of weakness, could not wear more than one tunic in that season, giving these the new habits, and the more robust ones wearing two of the less good ones, so that all overcame their need with great love and charity. And they made these exchanges with such rejoicing and internal and external happiness that I saw that they were well described by the words "Behold how good and how pleasant it is (as I would put it) for sisters to dwell together in unity." [*Ecce quam bonum et quam iocundum habitare (dirò) sorores in unum*] (Psalm 132 [133]:1).[23]

But, while Maria Domitilla is sometimes overtly concerned with such practical points of communal life, her comments on other passages having to do with dress and appearance (a subject she treats in some detail) wax allegorical. For example, she explains Clare's dictum that candidates entering the house should have their hair cut round because of an association between an external round haircut and an internal clinging to *Dio vera rotondità principio* ("God the true round beginning"). The rule says that each nun should receive three tunics, she continues, because they express corporeally the three spiritual ornaments of the soul: purity, obedience, and humility.[24]

Such use of allegory is only one way in which Maria Domitilla Galluzzi's *Lume* seems a very literary document. Even though Maria Domitilla's breathless syntax sometimes defies strict rules of grammar and challenges the translator, her writing is always vivid, full of description and allusion. Moreover, even though all her writings protest that she has little learning, her ability to quote, translate, and comment on the Vulgate Bible is evidence that she has a basic education in ecclesiastical Latin. This should not be surprising, since we know that some seventeenth-century Italian women had more than a little Latin. For example, the Ursuline Isabella Leonardi, a gifted composer from Novara and a contemporary of Maria Domitilla, used phrases from Virgil to describe the battle of a faithful soul.[25]

In comparison to Maria Domitilla's other works, the *Lume sopra la prima Regola di S. Chiara* is her most scholarly treatise. This first book is traditional in more ways than one: it is a conservative defense of a conservative view of women's religious lives. If the author really was an intelligent and educated woman, we might ask ourselves why such a woman would defend such a life. I would like to conclude by returning to the idea with which I opened this essay, that in the seventeenth century (as in other ages in other ways) institutions that made women's creativity possible also imposed notable restrictions on them. The obvious disadvantages of Maria Domitilla's life—enclosure, subservience, poverty, hunger—were compensated for by the advantages of a spiritual tradition—credibility, space, a voice. I would like to suggest that Maria Domitilla Galluzzi actively defended her life as a *Cappucina* because she understood, and was a direct beneficiary of, the reality that the institution of monastic life as she knew it offered patronage for women of her creative talents.

Notes

1. 3 December 1563, "Decree on the Reform of the Friars," especially number 5, which demands strict cloister for religious women. See Hubert Jedin, *Der Abschluss der Trienter Konzils 1562/63, ein Rückblick nach vier Jahrhunderter* (Münster in Westf.: Aschendorff, 1963); and Raymond Creytens, "La riforma dei monasteri femminili," in *Il concilio di Trento e la riforma tridentina* (Rome: Herder, 1963), 1:45–83. I am grateful to Katherine Gill for these references.

2. Gabriella Zarri, *Le sante vive: cultura e religiosità femminile nella prima età moderna* (Turin: Rosenberg and Sellier, 1990).

3. For the concept of a "horizon of expectation," see Hans Robert Jauss, *Toward an Aesthetic of Reception*, trans. Timothy Bahti (Theory and History of Literature, vol. 2) (Minneapolis: University of Minnesota Press, 1982), passim.

4. Clare of Assisi, *Regula*, by Marie-France Becker, Jean-François Godet, Thaddée Matura, Claire d'Assise, Écrits, Sources Chrétiennes 325, (Paris: J. Vrin, 1985), pp. 120–65; English trans. Regis J. Armstrong and Ignatius C. Brady in *Francis and Clare: The Complete Works* (New York: Paulist Press, 1982). See also J.-F. Godet, "The Text of the Rule of St. Clare," *Greyfriars Review* 5 (1991): 21–28; Sr. Chiara Augusta Lainati O.S.C., "La clôture de Sainte Claire et des premières Clarisses," *Laurentianum* 14 (1923): 223–50; and L. Oliger, "*De origine regularum ordinis sanctae Clarae*," *Archivum Franciscanum Historicum* 5 (1912): 181–209, 413–47. I thank Catherine Mooney for these secondary references.

5. For an examination of the relationship between the Second Rule of Francis for his "little brothers" (*fratrum minorum*) and approved by Pope Honorius III in 1223, and the *Regula* attributed to Clare, see M. Carney, "Francis and Clare: A Critical Examination of the Sources," *Laurentianum* 30 (1989): 25–60.

6. For the history of this community, see Maria Grazia Bianchi, "Una 'illuminata' del secolo xvii: Suor Maria Domitilla Galluzzi, Cappucina a Pavia," *Bollettino della Società Pavese di Storia Patria*, n.s. 20–21 (1968–69): 3–69.

7. Milano, Biblioteca Ambrosiana, Ms. G 97, f. 54v. For a list of the extensive manuscripts of Maria Domitilla's autobiographical writings, the *Vita* and the *Passione*, see E. Ann Matter, "The Personal and the Paradigm: The Book of Maria Domitilla Galluzzi," in *The Crannied Wall: Women, Religion, and the Arts in Early Modern Europe*, ed. Craig Monson (Ann Arbor: University of Michigan Press, 1992), p. 100 n. 18. None of Maria Domitilla's writings was ever printed.

8. Matter, "The Personal and the Paradigm," pp. 89–90.

9. See Danilo Zardin, *Confraternite e vita di pietà nelle campagne lombarde tra '500 e '600* (Milan: Nuove Edizioni Duomo, 1981); and Christopher Black, *Italian Confraternities in the Sixteenth Century* (Cambridge: Cambridge University Press, 1989) for this movement of lay piety; and Bianchi, "Una 'illuminata,'" for some books of spiritual direction which Maria Domitilla may have known. More generally, see Matthias a Salò, *Historia Capuccina*, ed. Melchiore da Pobladura (Rome: Institutum Historicum Ordinis Minorum Capuccinorum, 1946); and Orazio M. Premoli, *Storia dei Barnabiti nel Cinquecento* (Rome: Desclée, 1913).

10. The *Vita* is extant in at least six manuscripts, the *Passione* (or book of visions) in ten, the *Quarant'ore* in only one. I have discussed these works in "Interior Maps of an Eternal External: The Spiritual Rhetoric of Maria Domitilla Galluzzi d'Acqui," in *Maps of Flesh and Light: Aspects of the Religious Experience of Medieval Women Mystics*, ed. Ulrike Wiethaus (Syracuse, NY: Syracuse University Press, 1993) pp. 60–73.

11. The *Passione* appears by itself in Pavia, Biblioteca Universitaria, Mss. Aldini 306 and 145; Milan, Biblioteca Trivulziana, Mss. 268 and 490; Acqui Terme, private collection of Dott. Massimo Archetti-Maestri. The copies of the *Passione*

that appear with the Vita are all in Milan's Biblioteca Ambrosiana: Ms. D77, sussidio; Ms. G97, sussidio; Ms. H47, sussidio; Ms. 141, sussidio; Ms. H91, sussidio.

12. *Vero lume del modo d'osservare l'antica regola di Santa Chiara* is found in Pavia, Biblioteca Universitaria, Ms. Aldini 306, *Lume*; Pavia, Biblioteca Civica, Ms. 1, 11; Milan, Biblioteca Trivulziana, Ms. 491.

13. Hildegard of Bingen, *Regulae S. Benedicti Explanatio* PL 197:1053–66, English trans. Hugh Feiss (Toronto: Peregrina Publishing, 1990).

14. "un notte doppo mattutino quindeci giorni inanzi al S[antis]simo Natale l'anno terzo de mia professione d'età d'anni ventitre me trovavo avanti il S[antis]simo Sacramento in atto di partirmi dal choro per andare al dormitorio con l'altre madri e sorelle più che mai inabissata nel mio niente fui in un istante adombrata da gran luce, nella quale vivam[en]te godei Dio sommo bene con mirabili effetti del suo immenso amore et in sua Maestà compresi il modo con che fù osservata la S[an]ta Regola al tempo della Santa Madre Chiara . . . per obedire accenerò nel scrivere che farò una particella di detto lume, poichè non ho parole per esprimerlo à pieno, ne so se per la mia grandis[sim]a ignoranza saprò formare parole proportionate à quel pocho che puotrò esplicare." Pavia, Biblioteca Universitaria, Ms. Aldini 306, *Lume*, ff. 3v–4r.

15. Legend of Perugia, *Scripta Leonis, Rufini et Angeli Sociorum S. Francisci*, ed. and trans. Rosalind B. Brooke (Oxford: Clarendon, 1970).

16. "Tunc beatus Franciscus uertit faciem suam uersus celum et loquebatur sic Christo: 'Domine, nonne bene dixi quod non crederent tibi?' Tunc audita est uox in aëre Christi respondentis: 'Francisce, nichil est in Regula de tuo; sed totum est meum quicquid est ibi; et uolo quod Regula sic obseruetur ad litteram, ad litteram, ad litteram, et sine glossa, et sine glossa, et sine glossa.'" 113, ed. Brooke, pp. 286–87.

17. "essi ricceverono questa santa Regola che è vera forma della vita Evangelica, la quale loro perfettam[en]te osservorono e condescendo il gran bene che heseguia con carità perfetta obligorono noi sue figliuole et heredi con voto, acciò si osservasse come disse el Signore ad litteram sine glosa, senza privilegio ne dispense, senza interpretationi o humana scienza, ma semplicem[en]te secondo la littera come essi et li suoi veri immitatori." Pavia, Biblioteca Universitaria, Ms. Aldini 306, *Lume*, ff. 7r,v.

18. Milano, Biblioteca Ambrosiana, Ms. D77, sussidio ff. 355v–356r.

19. Matter, "The Personal and the Paradigm," and "Internal Maps."

20. "mostrarle come si vestiamo de vili vestimenti, si và sempre scalze, si leva à mezzanotte, si dorme soppra dure tavole, si digiuna continuam[en]te, et il vivere è di cibi grossi, poveri, e quadragesimali, et si spende la mag[ior] parte del tempo in recitare li divini offitii, e longhe orationi mentali, e tutta la nostra recreatione, gusto e contento hà da essere in servir, amare, e dar gusto all'amato Sig[no]re: procurando d'immitare le sue S[an]te virtù, mortificarsi, avilirsi, patir dispreggi, fame, sete, caldo, freddo, et altri incommodi per suo amore." Pavia, Biblioteca Universitaria, Ms. Aldini 306, *Lume*, f. 13v.

21. Pavia, Biblioteca, Universitaria, Ms. Aldini 502, part 2, f. 4r.

22. Clare of Assisi, *Regula*, 2.16, trans. Armstrong and Brady, p. 11.

23. "cioè si come la tonica alquanto usata è più leggera che la nuova con

molta carità, et amore ne tempi di caldo se alcuna giovina sana haveva alcuna tonica in talmodo legera, e vedeva che una vecchia o debole o inferma l'haveva nuova, o più greve con licenza della Santa Madre la cambiava dandogli la leggera, e togliendo lei la greve sino passato il caldo . . . in tal modo erano sovenute nelle loro neccessità senza detrimento della s[an]ta povertà et il simile facevano nel tempo del freddo, cio se le giovine sane havevano toniche nuove ne servivano quelle che per fiachezza non puotevano portar in tal stagione se non una tonica, onde dando a queste le toniche nuove, loro più robuste ne portavano due di quelle meno buone, si che tutte venivano à sovenire alla neccessità loro con gran amore, e carità, e facevano questi cambii con tanto giubilo, et allegrezza interna, et esterna, che vidi benissimo in loro s'estendevano quelle parole. Ecce quam bonum et quam iocundum habitare (dirò) sorores in unum." Pavia, Biblioteca Universitaria, Ms. Aldini 306, *Lume*, f. 21v.

24. "à chi lascia l'habito secolare per servire à Dio le sono concesse tre toniche da religiosa si corporalmente, come spirtualmente, ornando S[uo] D[ivino] M[aestà] tal anima d'una colombina semplicità e purità d'una pronta obedienza, et d'una profonda humilità." Pavia, Biblioteca Universitaria, Ms. Aldini 306—*Lume*, f. 17r. Cf. Clare of Assisi, *Regula*, 2.11.

25. Isabella Leonardi (1620–1704), "Ad arma, o spiritus," *Motetti una, due e tre voci*, Opus 13 [no. 3] (Bologna, 1687), in *Isabella Leonardi: Selected Compositions*, ed. Stewart Carter (Madison, WI: AR Editions, 1988).

Antonio Riccardi

10. The Mystic Humanism of Maria Maddalena de' Pazzi (1566–1607)

The effort to activate and regulate the experimental knowledge of God was the central point and the fulcrum around which Renaissance and early modern mysticism revolved. In that particular historical moment, this kind of experimental perception served as the basic tension in the definition of a complex mystical science, one as open as rationalist science to the questions and needs of a new world.

The works of Michel de Certeau have outlined this "reading" of mysticism and its historical dynamics, its traditions and results. From Certeau's studies, other authors have gone on to trace the profile of an often misunderstood spirituality, doing so from a perspective cognizant of both traditional (historical and theological) and more specialized (philosophical, linguistic, anthropological, and psychoanalytic) heuristic tools. The perspectives opened up by this line of research are far from exhausted; rather, some insights are still in need of follow-up and deepening, while others require further verification in the context of an only partially explored testament of mystical traditions and texts.

A first step in such verification should be carried out in light of the major intellectual currents of the time. Thus it is necessary to establish the deep-rooted connections between humanist culture and contemporary mysticism, including their reciprocal implications and intellectual debts. Such verification is ceaseless; the process activates and includes a series of interwoven relationships between the experiences (religious or secular) of an individual and the entire trajectory of Renaissance thought. We should therefore grant to mystic theology that propositional and theoretical value which it had in historical reality.

The Florentine Carmelite Maria Maddalena de' Pazzi is a key figure

Translated by Robert L. Kendrick.

in Renaissance mystic spirituality.[1] Maria Pacifica del Tovaglia, a colleague of Pazzi in the Florentine female monastery of Santa Maria degli Angeli, begins her *Breve ragguaglio della vita di Maria Maddalena* (I, 64–93) in full accord with hagiographic conventions:

> Sister Maria Maddalena was born in the city of Florence on St. Francesco di Paula's feast day, 2 April 1566. Her father was named Messer Camillo di Geri de Pazzi, and her mother Maddalena Maria, daughter of Messer Lorenzo Buondelmonti. She was baptized Caterina, after her maternal grandmother, but her parents were not happy with this, since it seemed that [her naming] had taken no account of her paternal grandmother. So they began to call her Lucretia after the latter, and this continued. When the little girl was old enough to discover this, she was most unhappy, both because they had wrongly taken her baptismal name from her and because she was greatly devoted to Saint Catherine of Siena. This was not accidental, since the Lord gave her such devotion because He had chosen to make her similar to that glorious saint in many respects, as will be seen in the course of this her biography.[2]

Caterina entered the convent (the Florentine house of San Giovannini de' Cavalieri, subject to the Jesuits) for the first time on 25 February 1574, on the advice of the family's confessor, the Jesuit Pietro Blanca. Her education, interrupted by several returns to her paternal house, ended in 1581. On 14 August 1582, Caterina entered the Carmelite monastery of Santa Maria degli Angeli for a two-week trial period. Here she learned the monastic rule and, in December of the same year, officially confirmed her wish to enter that order. On 30 January 1583, she was clothed in the Carmelite habit, taking the name of Sister Maria Maddelena de' Pazzi. Thus her novitiate year began.

In early March 1584 she fell gravely ill; her condition worsened without apparent cause, and the father confessor of the monastery, Agostino Campi da Pontremoli, decided to have her profess her final vows. After her profession, Pazzi had a forty-day period of extraordinary ecstatic experiences, during which she repeatedly relived the drama of the Passion, receiving Christ's heart (which she exchanged for her own) and the stigmata. When brought to pray before the body of Blessed Maria Bagnesi, kept in the same house, Pazzi was suddenly healed. During late 1584 and 1585, Pazzi experienced intense and frequent ecstacies, among them the session of 17 May 1585, lasting forty hours at a stretch, or the one beginning 8 June, extending over eight days. On 16 June 1585 Pazzi began to undergo a long period of suffering, in which ecstasy was also a determining factor.

This was the test that she herself would call (in the words of Daniel) the "lions' den," lasting some five years. On 20 July, while enraptured, Pazzi declared herself called to the renewal of the Church. In the course of the next few days she dictated a series of letters dealing with the moral decay of the Church and the need to reestablish moral and political order in it.[3]

On 30 September 1589, Pazzi was given the duty of vice-superior to the novices. On 10 June 1590, she was liberated from the "lions' den." Her confessor Agostino Campi died in 1591; he was succeeded by Canon Francesco Benvenuti. In 1592 she was made the sacristan; in 1595 she became the superior of the girl pupils and three years later the superior of the novices. In these years her ecstasies occurred quite regularly; they ended completely in 1604. In that same year the house chapter elected her vice-prioress. In 1605 Vicenzo Puccini, Pazzi's first biographer, became the monastery's confessor.

Pazzi died on 25 May 1607. The process for her beatification began in 1611; Urban VIII proclaimed her Blessed on 8 May 1626. The process for her canonization was opened in 1662, and on 28 April 1669 Clement IX pronounced her a saint.

The ecstatic experiences in Pazzi's life were of great intensity and frequency. From the time of her first ecstasies in 1584 (if we exclude the childhood reports, documented only in the hagiographic tradition), the monastery's confessor Agostino Campi had had Pazzi's "ecstatic words" transcribed. Her sister Carmelites carried out this transcription simply and efficiently: two or three nuns (sometimes four) were simultaneously present for Pazzi's mental raptures, thereby preserving the exact sequence of her sayings. During these sessions, each nun was helped by two others, who were charged with memorizing the ecstatic's words and then repeating them to the amanuensis in the order in which they had been spoken:

> While Sister Maria Maddalena spoke for a while, the nun who had memorized her words dictated them to one of the scribes. While the latter wrote, another nun memorized [Pazzi's] continuing words, then repeating her sayings to another scribe. Thus they went on by threes. . . . The first two who finished writing took their turn again after the third, and so they continued in order, each numbering the section she had written. Thus the first scribe numbered [her section] 1, the second 2, the third 3, and then the first one continued with 4, and so they went on by number.[4]

In Pazzi and in her ecstatic words there breathe the most profound ideals of humanist culture. It is telling that, for Pazzi, the continuous quest for personal humility—both as the condition of attaining union with God and as the affirmation of human activity in the spiritual path toward deification—represents not so much the tenacious and daily pursuit of virtue but rather a primary and undeniable spiritual necessity. With formidable expressive intensity, Pazzi brings these ideals from the late Renaissance to the mystic science of the seventeenth century.

In the course of the Cinquecento (more precisely in the second half of the century), Catholic mysticism expressed the tenacious quest for an authentic spiritual language, one capable of mediating between human and angelic language. This was the search for a strong and truthful opposition to the Babel that had arrived with Protestantism. Within the space it carved for itself, mystical discourse continued to repeat the entire vocabulary of ecclesiastical reform: the wounds, the rifts, and the divisions.

In all its complexity and its internal epistemological valence, the body became the privileged space of mystical discourse. Above all, Renaissance Catholic mysticism sought the definition of an ecclesiastical "body," the basis of a Church renewed. If the Reformation had privileged the centrality of the scriptural corpus (thereby implicitly defining the historical coordinates of the relationship between humans and God), the Catholic reform (first in the so-called pre-Tridentine phase and later in the Council of Trent) continued to point to the sacramental nature of the Eucharist as the primary stabilizing centrality. A strong bond between the church hierarchy and a mystical worldview was instituted, even in the various approaches to reform (Ignatius of Loyola, Carlo Borromeo). This tendency toward individual experiences—private or group, confraternal or congregational (the latter outlining the diffusion of sixteenth- and seventeenth-century mystical trends)—flowed from the need to reestablish order in church structure. In the course of the seventeenth century, it would become suspect, as a certain antimystical reaction grew within the Church itself, culminating in the 1687 condemnation of Quietism.

In addition, Renaissance mysticism established a relationship of meaning between individual bodies (souls) and the complexity of the cosmic body. Since the late fourteenth century, the cosmic body had lost its organic nature, a consequence of, inter alia, the profound changes in the social, political, and cultural fabric. At this point the cosmos became and would remain both the area of the most eager human study and the battleground between the new scientific concepts (based on mechanistic and mathematic interpretations of the universe) on the one hand, and this nascent, mystic "science" on the other. Here, modern rationalism would abandon mysticism's claim to restore the fracture between subject and object. This claim of mysticism presupposed other, wider intentions: that of restoring cosmic multiplicity to the unity of divine order; that of remaking humankind in deification, thus making it a participant in the entire cosmos by means of its undifferentiated union with God; and that of leaving to the Church (the depository of revelation and of the One Truth) the dispersion of heresies.

Finally, a point of great interest, sixteenth-century mysticism restored particular attention to the individual body. The body was the physical locus of a tension between two extremes. On the one hand, it was the bearer of a discourse based in God, simultaneously expressing this discourse. On the other hand, it did not cease to be (as it did for the ascetic and mystical tradition) a potential vehicle for sin. Precisely in this double sense the individual body was the site of an extraordinary event; in it are united existence (in this case a mystic being, fully realized in ecstasy) and annihilation (fall). The manifestation of this extraordinary event was not bound to a primary assumption of non-will; on the contrary, it had its cause and roots in the voluntary adherance to the *exemplum* of a God made human, incarnate in the humility and power of Christ. Certainly, the suppression of all difference between subject and object takes place in mystic union, at the highest point of the path toward deification. The confluence of, and confusion between, God and human comes about in this union; but this union brings both to this nothingness only by virtue of the integral humanity of the individual (both body and spirit), humble in body and reason. The future of the world has its endpoint in the same silence, and so closes the circle of cosmic order. Mystic *annichilatio* is the path which the mystic (a complete person due only to his or her humility) must take in order to become the "tabernacle of God," to use a telling expression of Maria Maddalena de' Pazzi.

At the center of the self, in the depths of the soul, a human being creates a vacuum with his or her willed humility, a vacuum that God fills. This is the path taken by modern mysticism after humanism proclaimed the existence of a complete person, maker of one's own history. The action of divine grace (always marked by the limitless love of Creator for creation) has a decisive role in this *unio mystica*, just as (and perhaps in the same way as) human volition to be a "nothing," a vacuum that welcomes God, determines the union.

In mystical literature, the centrality of the body is not just a thematic and theoretical foundation. It is no accident that the Christology of Renaissance mystics, even more than that of late medieval figures, should be bound to such a markedly humanized vision of Christ. Mystical theology also produces a noteworthy vocabulary of topoi derived from bodiliness: the stomach with the viscera, the heart, blood, eyes, hands, and so on. These various bodily parts, resulting from the fragmentation of the body and placed in a precise physiological hierarchy, repeat the character of the whole from which they derive, each like a microcosm. Furthermore, they represent elements of a dynamic enunciative outline for mystic discourse. Although they may function in the discourse as milestones in an extraordinary narrative that unravels in miraculous deeds, articulated in the act of the *unio mystica*, still the various blazons of the body fill a double linguistic function. On the one hand, they comprise symbolic stories, from which there derive metaphoric products that substantially feed into the theological plot of mystic experience. On the other, they outline the limits of a wide (encyclopedic, in Certeau's words) litany of bodies, or parts thereof, as if preparing the ground for the production of meaning as defined by the primary symbolic function. In reality, an order of priority is never established and each interpenetrating function fulfills the other.

Early modern mysticism distances itself from the conception of the body expressed by medieval mysticism; it makes the body into a focal point, a determinant place for tensions, in which the integralness of humanity (and thus the *unio mystica*) is realized. The distrust of the body (more precisely, of sexuality) found in ascetic monastic mysticism continues to some degree. Even through the era of the Counter-Reformation, this distrust finds certain spectacular definitions; but, tellingly, in the Renaissance the body becomes the theater and the open arena of extraordinary events, the moment of exaltation of the creature as absolute essence and value. When contemporary mystics speak of "anima" as the place of union with God, they mean a nuclearity in which body and spirit penetrate each other, and therefore they speak of a state in which there is expressed the vital act, that with which one receives the action of God.

I will reconstruct the thematic plot and the theologically most relevant results of Pazzi's ecstatic experience, in which the content of humanist culture is also recognizable. Union with God, the fulcrum of mystic experience, is pure movement for Pazzi. The human center, one's internal and spiritual root that also reveals the distinct presence of death, should coincide with the divine center, at the end of a path marked by the constant action of individual will. In this way one moves toward one's natural fulfillment, in which the order of creation is manifest. Obviously, this is not a state of complete passivity and emptiness in the perception of God. Instead, the complete humanity of those who welcome the spirit, of those who receive and understand it, remains as a specific attribute of union. One might say that a human being, who manages to see oneself in the person of Christ as a creature completely (and exemplarily) "assumed" to the grace of God, is the locus of union with God, the place in which paternal divine love manifests itself. In body and in spirit, as a creature simultaneously finite and complete, a person becomes the tabernacle of God.

In Pazzi's theology, anthropocentrism, Trinitarian theocentrism, and Passion Christology usually coincide in a perpetually mobile doctrinal system, guided and supported by sudden visions of the kingdom of heaven. This is a theology and a philosophy that proceed by means of frequently violent accumulation and that clearly reveal a terminal and natural outlet point: the entire order of creation. For Pazzi, God takes possession of the human soul and thereby regulates it, renders it "supercreated," transforms and vivifies it, makes it both active and deeply "reactive," a part of creation yet strikingly unique.[5]

This order can be known by humans through the humanity of the incarnate Christ (epistemologically this is still an intuition of the profound, immersed in the mystery of revelation). Out of love toward creation,[6] Christ makes Himself into soteriological history in the mystery of the eucharist.[7] In Christ, Pazzi recognized cosmic order itself. From Christ's blood, from the painful testimony of love He offered to humans, she understood the entire dynamic of the cosmos: blood and life.[8] Each individual moment of creation had been carried out for the Logos by virtue and foresight of His saving work; that is, each moment had had real existence and completion in the entirety of the divine plan. And if the Word, made incarnate with love and pain, is the place in which human beings are sanctified and the "theater of operations" where union with the internal experience of God takes place, then it follows that creation in all its entirety tends the anthropocentric and humanist basis of Pazzi's theology; this love is extended to the receptive person for personal fulfillment and salvation, and returns to God to the greater glory of God's name. In the glory of its Creator, in the inscrutably sweet basis of the mystic union,[9] the creature is made unique and distinct. But it still participates in the entirety of creation.[10]

For Pazzi, God grows in the welcoming soul, not through substitution or destruction (as occurs in other mystical experience) but rather through transformation. The Real Presence of the Word in history (Christ crucified) *says* that Revelation demands the integral completion of humble humankind: "Thus the Soul, having its eyes on those of Jesus, sees itself in God, and sees God in everything. . . . And so the soul, having its mouth on the mouth of Jesus, tastes and savors the good of all things" (I, 121). Hence the sense of assumption into God "by participation," as well as the sense of "dying to the world" and the wish to become the central place of God's fullness.[11]

The light of grace streams through the soul, making it transparent to the truth and purity of good. The soul, humbled by the memory of the earthly sacrifice of God, opens itself to the light in full grace and in God's gift, welcoming this light in the spirituality of abandonment and in a state of relaxed trust (thus active and faithful). The humility with which one receives God, in both the material body and the spirit, is the way to "self-creation" from divine energy in humanity itself. This energy makes human will capable of receptivity toward God while simultaneously capable of knowing how to accept itself completely within its limits as creature. Humility is thus not a theft or a diminution of the self, but rather a symbiosis of the human and the divine, an act in which the maximum possibility of existence is realized through grace.

In humility in this sense, as human action and a gift of grace, the soul has complete self-awareness as a creature and expresses the complete will of self-realization in its love for God. For Pazzi, the humbling of the soul also expresses itself in prayers and penance (that is, in obedience to the monastic Rule). But the deepest and most authentic state of humility, its radical reality, is achieved only by the inclusion of will and grace. In this way, one recognizes oneself as existing and aware without ruptures, finally whole, beyond the separation of death and sin, tried and tested by temptation. In this regard, a brief marginal note written in the "Colloquio quadragesimo terzo" by one of Pazzi's female monastic amanuenses is telling: "[Pazzi] meant that the Lord vivifies, that is, exalts those who humble themselves" (III, 114).

"This humility is of such value in me, and of such worth to the soul that has it, and of such strength, that it can make a soul regain this purity, even if [the soul] might have lost its virginity; this is a most singular means of being able to regain this purity" (III, 347). Thus humanity is (or again becomes) whole, with a completeness (or virginity) never to be lost again: "Nonetheless, without this virginity the soul cannot possess this purity in itself by means of humility. In Hell there will be many virgins, but humble souls will not be able to go there" (III, 347).

In Pazzi's mystic theology, the concept of virginity is closely linked to the reception of the divine; thus it expresses the perfect state of being "open to God." In this sense, the Virgin Mary is "perpetually virgin," open to receiving God at every moment of her life. Pazzi, so sensitive to Mary's presence, completely understood the meaning of this virtue and the importance of such a state, which has a simple but fitting expression in physical purity.

The annihilation of which Pazzi often speaks, namely the fact that in order to unite itself to God the soul "dies a living death," should be understood (as noted above) as a "humble abandonment" and not as a nullification of being. Being a "nothing" is not the sign of one's own annihilation, but rather the feeling of one's own human consistency, fully receptive toward God. It is the perception (we might say internal perception) of a self that empties itself in order to be filled by God, by that eternal and immutable truth which from this point on holds and encompasses the self.

Nichilo (Pazzi's term) is not nothingness; even less does it have anything to do with sin and death. *Nichilo* is simple being, the humble. Even in ecstasy Pazzi was told: "Just as much your powers grow, so much will grow the knowledge of your non-being" (III, 384). Against nothingness there stands the fullness of sin, which denies the comprehension of mystery, which does not allow truth to manifest itself in evidence. Sin is opaque, making the welcoming of God impossible and separating the soul from purity. In the chapter "On Prayer" in her "Ammaestramenti," Pazzi says: "Go toward God with humility, not bounded by your selves and with great trust in Him, recognizing that you are vile and abject, *nichilo* itself" (VII, 237). The humanity of the Word, its example felt thus centrally, enters into the soul "with all itself, which contains the unity of the Holy Trinity" (IV, 136); it fills the soul completely and exhaustively. The reason

> which makes the Word unite itself to the soul is the humility found in the latter. This humility serves as the magnet which draws God to the soul. There He gives it a being without beginning or end, since He recognizes that the soul's composition has lost its being through humility, knowledge, and annihilation and that the soul sees only its own nonbeing. And God is so pleased by this annihilation that He increases its nonbeing and makes His

dwelling there, because He cannot and does not wish to unite Himself to any soul without this annihilation. (IV, 147–48)

The receptive state of "living death" is the knowledge that "wanting to share in divine purity, it is necessary to be completely naked, without any desire or wish whatsoever, acquiring this purity through wishing, knowing, desiring, and intending absolutely nothing" (II, 436–37). In humility and in God, the soul is "a nothing, a nil" (III, 91). This is the basis of the gnoseological problem, centered more on human capacity than on intellectual activity, and focused on the ability to understand truth internally. The simple soul—humble and obedient to the sacrifice of the Passion—becomes aware of its own emptiness needing to be filled, of its own nothingness. It is aware (or becomes active and pure) of the grace and truth that fill it in the loving union with God. It presumes the knowledge of its own completion, and in this state is made capable of comprehension. God placed "a torch, the knowledge of one's own nothingness and lowliness" (V, 234) in the human soul. For the humble soul, the emptiness of its depths always reveals the sure tension of God's fullness.

Pazzi's humanism is centered around the completed realization of God's work, namely in the completion of creatures' essence in love and in grace. This becomes even more apparent if we consider the soul's thoroughgoing humility (or receptive passivity) in relation to pride, the sin which more than any other in Pazzi's thought reveals humans' refusal of God.

Indeed, if the soul's passive state expresses this sense of deep openness to God and of transparence to the truth, namely the true sense of human nature (as if it were a vacuum to be filled with *kerygma*), then it is because pride, on the contrary, is a closure to light's penetration, a deafness to grace's call, a most serious sin that reveals a state of fullness and vainglory in the self equivalent to a refusal. Pride—the cause of fall, the reason for blindness—has distanced the presumptious human being from God. Pride has ossified human beings, thus making them impermeable to the living water, to Christ's blood shed for them in history. "But this air of pride causes great damage, and so it must be opposed by great diligence and self-examination for a long time, so that the soul is well-based in humility" (III, 29). In the sin of pride we recognize the negation of human essence itself:

Pride is an elevation of the mind above its own being, one might almost say a nonbeing, with the result that we have no being. And this pride is also a desire not to be subject to any other creature. I do not know any soul, any

> mind, any body possessed by this pride, and I will not compare it to anything but a handful of straw good for nothing but making a small fire, quickly extinguished, and when put out it becomes vile for its charredness. Such is pride. (III, 29)

As seen in Pazzi's words, this is the sin which cast Lucifer into Hell (V, 177; VI, 169), which makes reason disappear (I, 169), and which causes humans to lie (the incapacity for truth) to others and to God; it leads to dissipation (including of the love which, in humility, is the reciprocal tie to the good) and to vice. The proud live the deceit of a seeming fullness; full of self, of vain pride, they do not realize the fearful emptiness in which they are trapped. This vacuum (the nothingness which we have already discussed) is the mirror image and the inverse of that emptiness which the encounter with God creates in the human soul. The former is the emptiness of chaos, error, and heresy. Heretics do not understand (truth) because self-love makes them full of error; their being does not become empty and embracing; it distances itself from the example of the Incarnate Word's humility.

* * *

Let us retrace the intellectual journey that leads to the idea of stillness, from the finiteness and anguish of a state of incomplete humanity to the conscious fullness that generates inner peace in an integral person. We have already seen how the completion of human essence, which is equivalent to the original state of being itself before the Fall, is realized again through the union with God by means of His essential humanity. In the mystery of love for creation, human beings can look beyond the world of sin to their own salvation, to their own rejoining with God, "the end of all good, the end of all content, of all joyfulness and all blessedness" (III, 16). In this union humans return to the peace of their origin; they are simple and aware of being "nothings" open to the revelation of truth. Only in the rest found in God do human beings fully achieve the truth of their own beings.

Thus the fullness of human essence is reestablished, because people return to the ideal according to which they have been created: "O happy that soul which is united with You, o Word, and that feeds on and is nourished from You, o Word, and that finds no peace or contentment outside of You, o Word. Only love of You, o Word, can make us peaceful, because we have been created to love and possess You" (II, 342). This takes place not only through the loving participation of grace, but also by the soul's active opening of itself to God. At a moment of great intimacy and nearness, God says to the soul:

> O how happy your being was, my daughter, and how pure it was then! First I say that before your being was in the world, it was glorious in me; it was pleased and content only in the enjoyment of the unitary essence of my idea. This purity then was such that it was almost another Me in its participation. (III, 340)

Humanity, deified in humility and elevated to God in its distancing from the self (this a recognition of the path leading to true self-being) intuits, or becomes certain, that union and peace in God are a recomposition of a previous whole.

This is a very important doctrinal point: creation, redemption, and grace together express the fullness of reciprocal love between God and human beings. And the peace in which they obtain certainty of the divine center which they carry in themselves and which motivates him is nothing but dynamic rest, the consolation and glory of God himself. This is the message from the Creator to His creature. In a passage from the "Eighth Colloquium," in which the idea of "breath" returns as the mode of mystic union, Pazzi says that: "The eternal Father aspired, or willed the welfare of His creatures. We say so-and-so aspires to a certain honor or a certain thing because she desires and seeks that thing with great fervor." In the scribe's reconstruction, Pazzi proceeds:

> It is greater to aspire than to desire; and so this blessed soul [Pazzi] meant that the eternal Father aspired to our well-being, meaning that He sought it burningly, more than can be said. And the Son respired, that is, making his resting place in creation, He made it pleasing to the Father and to Himself, together with the Holy Spirit. To respire means to repose. . . . And the Holy Spirit inspired, or continued to illuminate creatures, so that they might proceed from strength to strength, making themselves more and more pleasing and acceptable to God. (II, 115)

Human beings, desiring their own completion, give themselves over to a dynamic process of self-searching which continually replenishes but never fills them.

In God's peace, in the extraordinary intimacy of revelation and dialogue, humans are remade:

> Come, my little daughter, come my bride, for I will take you into the house of your mother, namely my Divinity; because my Divinity has given birth to

> both your soul and that of all other creatures. Come my dove, my beautiful one, for I will take you into the bedroom of my humanity, in the bed of your mother; and I want you to rest now in this my humanity, in which my Divinity also rests, your genitrix and mother in creation. This is because you are her daughter by obeying and loving her, and also since you delight in continual repose in this Divinity and humanity of mine. (II, 236)

This stillness is the state of fullness which humans achieve in God, in the depths of a mystery which love brings closer and vivifies. It is a fullness flowering also in the depths of the self, in the divine center of anyone who is blessed, in such a person's simple and complete humility. God reposes

> in creatures, not in those ugly and dissimilar from You [God], but rather in those who make themselves capable of receiving Your own pure similitude in themselves by means of the communication of Your gifts. And You repose in those who receive the effect of the Word's blood in themselves, for they are a fitting dwelling place for You. (IV, 53)

Thus Pazzi seems to extend the locus of God's stillness to the entire cosmos:

> And this [God's] throne continues to encompass the whole universe, filling the sky and circling the earth. Just as the sun in the heavens shines its rays on earth, so is this divine Spirit in heaven and earth. In itself it is in the heavens and in all blessed souls; on earth [it is] in all creatures. (IV, 53)

With an image of great allegorical and evocative power, Pazzi watches the soul approach holy stillness, in a by no means passive continuum.

> Also, there is the rare and far-flying eagle, which is love in the soul; this love is not rare, but is possessed only by the rare.—The eagle flies high and by nature does not feed on the rinds of fruit, but rather on the core of such fruit, especially of the citron. Love is as great as God, because God is love. It flies so high that it reaches the Most Holy Trinity's throne, and there it enters the breast of the eternal Father. From the Father's breast it proceeds to the Word's [wounded] side, and from the side to His heart. There it reposes and feeds. In the same way, the soul which has love in itself seeks nourishment only in God and to receive peace from Him. (IV, 236)

In the same vein, Pazzi's allegorical account of virtue continues:

> Another bird keeps flying in this little world, one which rests in certain trees. Making its nest there, it bears its beloved and beautiful young similar to itself,

> feeding them with the blood from its breast. This is the pelican, symbolizing justice in the soul. This justice rests in the other virtues: charity, humility, patience, love, and many others, generating righteousness. It does not eschew mercy, as long as it is just. Then it nourishes its offspring with the blood from its breast. And this is nothing other than the Word's humanity, which nourishes with its words, works, and example, but above all with the spilling of Its most precious blood. (IV, 237)

These last two extracts from a longer section make Pazzi's indebtedness to the mystical tradition clear.[12] In the complex and variously articulated relationship between Pazzi and the history of mystical theology, I would briefly highlight one interesting aspect: the double similarity of her thought to the sixteenth-century Spanish Alumbrados and to medieval Flemish mysticism. One might assert that the Florentine mystic was aware of the latter via the former. The Alumbrados' mysticism derives directly from that of the Rhenish school: in both, the primary intention which brings one to consciousness is one's pure impulse toward God. This impulse grasps the profound unity of the divine without recourse to intermediaries, whether human points of transition (members of the church hierarchy) or discursive constructions of spiritual experience (forms of discourse). One reaches God in His unity, distancing oneself from images and gradual knowledge. In this way, the Alumbrados postulated the total annihilation of created being in the creative essence. This is the surrender to God on the part of the now passive being. Thus humans can grasp the essence of God by means of contemplation, even while still on earth. Furthermore, they can even retain this essence, since the work of grace has freed them and made them profoundly welcoming by bringing them to the perfection of the encounter with God. But it is important to stress another point present with equal emphasis: the soul's path to stillness is to be taken in the active observance of Christ's humanity and in adherence to His suffering, in devotion to His love. In light of the exegesis earlier in this essay, one theme implicit in the text emerges clearly: the dialectic between human consciousness of this incompleteness and the drive to overcome this finitude by the expression of profound essentiality (simple human essence), in order to achieve wholeness.

Christ's humanity, His flesh, activates human perfection and the triumph over death:

> Expiring in the tomb so that Your bride might bury You in herself, and You bury her in Yourself.—You breathe into limbo so that Your bride might

> overcome not only limbo but Hell itself.—You breathe into the Father's breast so that Your bride might repose after its labors in that eternal stillness of the fruition and vision of the Most Holy Trinity's essence. (III, 160)

Only by means of total adherence to Christ's sacrifice do human beings overcome death, reestablishing the circle of original life by grace's intervention. Christ's example speaks to humans about this dynamic: when "Jesus expired on the Cross, his soul flew to the breast of His eternal Father, and rested there just as the Word had done before Its incarnation" (II, 314).

For Pazzi, the Cross is the real sign, the *index*, of the whole life of creatures, of the carnal condition. The Word ("being in the Father's breast, humbled and lowered himself so much for creatures, that He permitted Himself to be led even to the scandalous death on the Cross, with such ignominity"; IV, 202) thus expressed his own participation in the cosmic plan of salvation, a plan he shared with the Father from all eternity. "The mirror that I have to view," said Pazzi, "in that humanized Word has no being other than that very Word nailed to the cross" (VI, 103). She added: "In this mirror we perceive the whole circuit of the heavens, all His [Christ's] ornaments, all His gifts and graces, and finally what else if not His loving side?" (VI, 104). The whole cosmos seems enclosed within the side of Christ crucified; His love and suffering are the basis for the *cosmic* Soul, the human who receives and *becomes*.[13] As we have noted, Christ on the cross "makes Himself the source of water and blood to purify us" (II, 285); thus He is very near to the creature in pain, and shares also the work of justice and mercy.[14]

One of her monastic amanuenses recounted that Pazzi

> understood that God's interior action makes work perfect, and the soul makes itself capable of this action with the question that it asks of God. Thus she [Pazzi] asked to enter into the breast of her own humanity's genitrix, repeating these words in Latin five times: "Absconde me in ubere genitricis humanitatis tue, et in capite essentie tue." Then she put all her feelings and powers into the feelings and powers of Jesus' body, with such beautiful order and method that it was marvelous to hear it. (II, 332–33)

Yet another central element of the mystical tradition, in this case the "Absconde me" theme as the fulcrum of the unifying relationship with God, is here reinterpreted by Pazzi in the sense of an acute dramatic tension, that of the Passion, the torture instruments, and the wounds of Christ.[15] "Jesus-Love has made His body into a ladder" so that the soul might "enter into His five wounds which He made like five shelters so that [the soul] could flee and hide in them when persecuted by its enemies; there it can repose when tired of the battles and labors of this miserable life" (II, 127).[16] Humble souls, transformed, rest "in the bed of Jesus' humanity," with "Jesus crucified in the mind's eyes" (II, 238). In the sacrifice of His humanity, with the Passion and death on the Cross, the Word has told the humble that the way of truth (hence of salvation) traverses suffering, the test of temptation, and that their will must continually immerse itself in His flesh.[17]

Stillness is the complete realization of the kingdom of God on earth, that is, in human bodies, in that humanized essence assumed by the Word out of grace and love.[18] Furthermore, the state of stillness is the moment in which the Holy Spirit's word, truth, and action resound in humanity. Humanity in stillness is the complete and humble essence, the actively spiritual being.[19]

Pazzi's mysticism certainly does not present the degree of systematic elaboration to be found in the works of Teresa of Avila or John of the Cross, if only because it remains within the orbit of Carmelite spirituality. Her thought, strongly based in the perception of Christ's humanity and of the pure humanity (or humility) of those who receive it, is expressed in a circular form. Both the doctrinal concepts and the efflorescence of images that support and complete them revolve around this perception. This should not be taken to mean that Pazzi's doctrine does not directly refer to a well-known theological reflection. Indeed, it clearly follows the path of those authors who most influenced her: Paul and Augustine, Bernard of Clairvaux, Thomas Aquinas, Catherine of Siena, and the Rhineland mystics of the *Istituzioni*.[20] If it is fruitless to seek a systematic linear construction in Pazzi's thought, it is nevertheless necessary to delimit the outlines of an articulated philosophy therein, even though certain passages, certain images must inevitably remain obscure and impenetrable.[21] Indeed, this activity would also help shed light on the history of Seicento spirituality.

It is true that Pazzi, like other ecstatics, completely follows the impulses of the *spirit* revealed to her from her innermost depths, transforming her. The spirit forcibly infuses her and gives her voice, words, truth. In the reading of her ecstasies, the doctrinal formulations can be gathered, even if they are difficult to understand. They can be grouped synoptically, without omission, according to nonlinear logic.

For Pazzi, this kind of analysis of doctrinal content is almost inevitable.

This is primarily because Pazzi's thought is not suited to a complete reconstruction of what she experienced with great visionary and symbolic power during her ecstatic raptures. In addition, the accounts of her ecstasies as transmitted by her scribes are not consistent among themselves. At some points, the saint's words are interlaced with the notes of a nun amanuensis working on the collation and redaction of the definitive text. At other points, they are fragmentary and display lacunae in direct intelligibility, because Pazzi spoke too quickly or *sotto voce*.[22]

Thus it is inevitable that her mysticism—especially the most original points, such as her Trinitarianism; her definition of the bond between human beings, Christ's humanity, and the Virgin; her concept of personal deification; and her idea of rest in pure love and humility—should seem to lack internal order. But the point is that the kernel of Pazzi's mystic experience is to be found precisely in the accumulation of images and thoughts in which the production of the whole person becomes the meaning of the abjuring of the nonvital (the world). This goes so far as complete self-abandonment to the flux of life (*annichilimento*) and deification. This is the hermeneutic key that permits an organic reading of Pazzi's work, one in which the antinomies are only apparent. In Pazzi, the dualities of growth and renunciation, attachment and distance, spirit and nature articulate the entire plan of her thought, not only its development; that is, they define the manner in which, time and again, the thematic content and imagery prove invariant, then suddenly transform themselves into new content and new imagery.

Pazzi's thought is thus a dynamic philosophy, always transcending itself by exigency. This same procedure had characterized the highest mysticism of the Middle Ages;[23] it is radical transformation in God. But for Pazzi it has its center and original consistency in the original and dramatic affirmation of individual humanity, of human essence as a vehicle for transformation, and even as the meeting place for the binary terms of the union between God and human beings.

Pazzi's thought displays a unitary basis from which a theological thematic arises according to the path of personal ecstatic development, in a development with internal dynamics and necessities: the unity of the "mysterium Christi," given by the Word and by the Incarnate Word's humanity. The knowledge of the Word, human certainty of this passionate humanity that is both close and simultaneously salvational, becomes the fulcrum of the symbolic and synthetic capability of Pazzi's thought.[24]

Notes

1. All references to the works of Pazzi are to the collected edition, Maria Maddalena de' Pazzi, *Tutte le opere dai manoscritti originali*, 7 vols. (Florence: Nardini, 1960–66): vol. 1, *I quaranta giorni*, ed. E. Ancilli (1960); vols. 2–3, *I colloqui*, parts 1–2, ed. C. Catena (1961, 1963); vol. 4, *Revelazioni ed intelligenze*, ed. P. Visantin (1964); vols. 5–6, *Probazione*, parts 1–2, ed. G. Agresti (1965); vol. 7, *Renovazione della chiesa*, ed. F. Valenzia (1966). Hereafter references are to volume and page numbers only.

2. "Nacque Suor Maria Maddalena nella Città di Firenze il giorno di San Francesco di Paula Addì 2 d'Aprile 1566. Suo Padre si domandò Messer Camillo di Geri de Pazzi; e suo Madre Maddalena Maria di Messer Lorenzo Buondelmonti. Hebbe nome alla Fonte Catherina per la Madre di sua Madre, ma non sendo contenti e'Parenti, parendogli no' havessi fatto conto della Suocera, la cominciorno a charmar' Lucretia per la detta, e così si sequitò sempre; il che, scontenta, sì perché haveva per male gli fussi stato levato il nome che haveva havuto alla Fonte, si ancora perché portava gran devotione a Santa Caterina da Siena; e non era questo a caso, ma Iddio gli dava tal' devotione havendosi eletta questa creaturina per farla simile a detta gloriosa Santa in di molte cose, come si vedrà nel sequito della Vita sua." Indeed, Pazzi's life is not terribly different, at least in its fundamentals, from that of other early modern female mystics. A fully detailed reconstruction, especially for the period after 1400, can be found in S. Groppi, *L'archivio Saminiati-Pazzi* (Milan: EGEA, 1990).

3. These letters were addressed to Sixtus IV (letter of 27 July), the archbishop of Florence (30 July), the College of Cardinals (3 August), the superiors of various religious orders (Dominicans, Jesuits, Minims of Saint Francis of Paola), and Saint Catherine de Ricci (5 and 10 August). Cf. Pazzi, *La rinnovazione della Chiesa: Lettere dettate in estasi* (Rome: Nardini, 1986).

4. "Come Sr. Maria Maddalena haveva proferito un periodo, quella monaca che l'haveva tenuto a mente lo dettava a una di quelle che scrivevano et mentre quella scriveva un'altra teneva a mente quello che seguitava di dire et lo dettava et ricordava a un'altra di quelle che scrivevano; et così seguitavono le terze. . . . Le due prime finito di crivere ripigliavano dopo le terze et così seguitavono per ordine et ciascuna faceva il numero al periodo che haveva scritto, cioé: la prima il numero uno, la seconda il numero due, la terza il numero tre et poi ripigliava la prima il numero quattro et così seguitavono di uno in uno per ordine") (testimony of a nun taken from the proceedings of the canonization process, cited in E. Ancilli's introduction to Pazzi's works; I, 48). Despite this systematic effort, some of Pazzi's raptures have been lost, due to the frequency and unpredictability of her trances or to the difficulty of understanding her words, spoken too softly or quickly.

5. According to M. Adriani (*Italia Mistica: Profilo storico della spiritualità italiana* [Rome: Acura dell' Ente per la Diffusione e l'Educazione Storica, 1968], pp. 289–316), the profound sense of natural cosmic vitality—one found in much of the Italian Cinquecento, in the varying expression of figures from Gerolamo

Cardano to Della Porta, from Catherine de Ricci to Battista Vernazza—would support the idea of an analogy between Pazzi and Giordano Bruno. If it is permissible to emphasize a theme common to both, it would be the centrality of the miracle that God carries out in human beings, who have been placed in the cosmos as witness and praise to Him. Of course, it must also be remembered that Thomism (in which Bruno had been trained during his years at San Domenico Maggiore in Naples; cf. M. Ciliberto, *La ruota del tempo* [Rome: 1986], pp. 86–88) had been transmitted to Pazzi, even if in a diluted form, by her confessors Campi (to 1591) and Benvenuti (to 1605), as well as by her reading of the Spanish Dominican Luis de Granada.

6. The reception of the eucharist, the union with the Real Body of Christ, was very important to Pazzi from the time of her entrance into the monastery S. Giovannino de' Cavalieri onward. It was precisely at S. Giovannino (which she had entered in 1574, remaining until 1581 under the supervision of her maternal aunt Suor Lessandra Buondelmonti) that she received the extraordinary privilege of taking Communion daily. On the importance of the Eucharist in Pazzi's ecstasies, cf. I, 230 ("through the Holy Sacrament" she found herself "suddenly" united with God, "separated from all things"); II, 99 (mystic union, when the soul is "communicated with the Eucharist with which it is united, comes to contain in itself the perfection of this love"); II, 79 (the sacrament is the visible historical place of God's self-lowering for the salvation of humans: "And covering His own greatness, His own divinity and all that is such a small matter in His light, [God] has made such a small and incapable creature able to receive that which fills the universe, namely God Himself, eternal, immense, incomprehensible, and infinite. This He did out of His great desire to rest in such a creature"; "Et coprendo esso la sua grandezza, la sua Divinità e tutto quello che è sotto l'ombra di quella sì piccola cosa, ha fatto che la creatura tanto piccola e incapace, ha potuto ricevere in Sé quelle che empje il' tutto, che è lui stesso, Dio, eterno, immenso, incomprehensibile e infinito; e questo l'ha fatto per il desiderio grande che ha di riposarsi in essa creatura"); II, 391 ("And thus as the sun is in Heaven and Earth, so You, o Word, are in heaven at the right hand of the Father and on earth in the species of the Sacrament"; "Et sì come il' sole è in cielo e in terra, così tu, Verbo, sei in cielo alla destra del' Padre, e in terra nella spetie del' Sacramento"); and II, 325; III, 147; III, 204; III, 236 (in this passage, as in others, Pazzi awakened from her mystic rapture when the father confessor arrived with the host for the nuns' communion); III, 314; III, 315 (in which she shows her fear that the Sacrament would become a ritual habit); V, 3 (in which she says that the second of the three gifts granted her "from the time she was in her mother's womb" was a "loving and continual desire to unite herself with Him [God] in the Sacrament"; "sino che stava nel' ventre di suo madre . . . amoroso e continuo desiderio di unirsi con lui nel' S.mo Sacramento").

7. See III, 402: "O crazy Love, o eternal Word, o infinite Wisdom, o highest Goodness, what has the creature that You love so much done? You have made it in Your own image and likeness so that it might be equal to You. No, not equal, but it participates in You, the eternal Truth, infinite Love, eternal Word. What have you done for this creature, and what do You wish from it if not love?—Who

is this creature that You love it so much? What do You give him? What do You want from him?—You love him like yourself, You give him Yourself, you who are everything. Outside of You there is nothing" ("O pazzo Amore, o eterno Verbo, a Sapientia infitia, o Bontà somma, che t'ha fatto la creatura che tanto l'ami? L'hai creata all'immagine e similitudine tua per farla equale a te. Non equale, no, ma partecipe di te che sei Verità infallibile, Charità infinita, eterno Verbo. Che hai fatto a questa creatura, e che ricerchi da lei se non amore?—Che è questa creatura che tanto l'ami? Che gli dai? Che vuoi da lei?—L'ami come te stesso, gli dai te stesso che sei ogni cosa. Et fuor di te non è nulla").

8. In Pazzi's mystic theology the symbolism of blood is articulated and central. Through blood she expresses primarily a dramatic complex of Christ's mystery: the word of the Logos, His acts and death on the Cross, His prayer to His Father. The most striking fact is that Christ's blood, in which the saving mediation between God and humans is expressed, tends to equal Christ Himself. It is worthwhile to cite a passage from the *Revelatione* in which Pazzi clarifies the complex relationship between salvation and "Trinitarian wisdom": "The Divine Word and humanity suffers greatly [from the disdain that some people have for Divine mercy] (if indeed they can feel suffering) because they see that even though God the Father grants [mercy] to all those who want it and are prepared to receive it, still the desire of the divine Word and humanity is not satisfied, namely the desire to extend this mercy to all humankind. And so both continually think what they can do to please the Father and predispose such people to receive mercy. But Divinity, looking at itself, finds itself so large that there is nothing to match it. Similarly, humanity looking at itself finds itself like a worm, equally with nothing to match it. So both find themselves alone, and decide to select something found in both of them as a companion. And this is blood, which issues from both divinity and humanity; from divinity, because Divine love has moved humanity to spill [this blood], and it is this humanity which has spilled it. So all three in unison go to the Father to present this petition" ("esso Verbo divino e humanità n'hanno gran dolore [se però dolore può essere in loro] perché veggono che se bene il' Padre gliene concede per tutti quelli che la vogliono e sono disposti a ricerverla, non si adempisce il' desiderio di esso verbo divino e humanità che è di conferire essa misericordia a tutte le creature. Et però la divinità, risguardando in se stesssa, vedesi esser tanto grande che non trova alcuna cosa simile a lei con chi si possa accompagnare. Et il' simile l'humanità risguardando se stessa si vede esser un verme, però ancor lei non trova con chi si accompagnare, tanto che tutt'a due si trovon soli, però si risolvon di torre per compagnio una cosa che sia proceduta dall'uno e dall'altro. Et questo è il' Sangue, che è proceduto dall divinità e humanità. Dalla divinità, perché lei è stata quella che con l'amore ha mosso l'humanità a spargerlo, e essa humanità è quella che l'ha sparso; e tutt'a tre d'accordo se ne vanno al' Padre a fare questa petitione"; IV, 158). In Pazzi, as in the entire Judeo-Christian tradition, Christ's blood (His essential humanity) also expresses the real epistemological possibility of human beings toward the mystery of Divine mercy. Blood is the reality of consciousness and salvation. In the beginning of this passage, humans find their own peace and also the truth of the cosmos in blood: "The active Father and the dead Word [are together] in the breast of the Father.

The Holy Spirit [is] separate and always united.—This great Father works in the circuit of the heavens and in the abyss of earth. . . . The manifestation of His work is carried out not by the Father or the Son or the Holy Spirit, but by blood, which issues forth from the viscera of the Incarnate Word," infusing, raising, and inebriating man ("L'operante Padre e il' morto Verbo, nel' seno di esso Padre. Il' separato e sempre unito Spirito Santo.—Opera questo gran Padre nel' circuito del' cioelo e nell'abisso della terra. . . . La manifestatzione dell'opera non la fa né il' Padre né il Verbo né lo Spirito Santo, ma il' Sangue, quale uscendo dalle viscere del' Verbo incarnato"; IV, 149–50). This also includes the relationship between silence and blood, expressed at various points in Pazzi's ecstacies: "Anyone wanting to taste [the sweetness of the Passion] should approach this blood; there to find all repose and consolation" ("Chio la vuol gustare accostisi pure a questo Sangue, che quivi troverrà ogni riposo e consolatione"; III, 90; see also III, 218). The list could be much longer if we consider less direct symbolic relationships, still related to blood, which feed into the symbolic polyvalence: Christ's side and wounds, the fountain, the sea and river, milk.

9. "O sweet union, in which the soul becomes another You!—Yes, if union makes two things into one, there is no difference because one thing is transformed together with the other, even though each retain its essence.—What does union do? It makes the whole soul and body assumed into you, o Word, all in Your death" ("O che dulce unione, dove l'anima diventa un altro te!—Sì, che se unione fa di dua cose una cosa stessa, non c'è differentia perché si transforma una cosa con l'altra, se ben ciscuna rimane nel' suo essere.—Unione che fa? Rende tutta l'anima e il' corpo assorta in te, Verbo, et in tutto a te stesso, come morto"; III, 187). The interrelatedness and experiential nature of Pazzi's central theological concepts are evident from this passage.

10. The purpose of humanity and creation is the glory of God: "Everything which God has made with such marvelous order, has all been done for the creature, whom God has made for Himself, and in whom God would rest. Nor does He want us to find repose and rest in anything other than Him Himself; because He has made everything and everything is contained in Him. The soul that has and possesses Him thus finds and possesses everything. I also saw that the creature has been made by God in this way: when one is united to God, one gives God rest in one's heart. We have been arranged for God to rest in us, but even more has God been arranged for us. Even though God has no need of humans, He has still deigned to take His rest in humanity, so that we might enjoy and delight in Him for eternity, and be perfectly able to see Him, to enjoy Him face to face, together with the holy angels and all Paradise" ("tutto quello che esso ha fatto e creato con' detto mirabile ordine, tutto l'ha fatto per la creatura, et essa creatura ha fatto solo per sé, e vuole riposarsi in lei, né vuole che essa si riposi e quieti in altro salvo che in lui solo, però che havendo fatto ogni cosa, ogni cosa si contiene in lui. Et l'Anima havendo, e possedendo esso, viene in esso a trovare, e possedere ogni cosa. Vedevo ancora che la creatura, è ordinata per Dio in questo modo: che sendo essa unita, a' Dio, viene a dare riposo a Dio nel suo cuore e però essa, è ordinata per Dio, perché esso Dio si vuole potere riposare in Lei, ma maggiormente Dio, è ordinato per lei, poiché egli non havendo alcuno bisogno di lei, si degna volere in

essa fare il suo riposo, perché lei lo possa poi fruire a godere in eterno, e esserne capace perfettamente per sempre, et vederlo, e goderlo affaccia affaccia, insieme, con li santi Angeli, e tutto il Paradiso"; I, 223–24). Cf. VI, 63; III, 180–81; III, 192; 160–61.

11. In Pazzi's thought, pain (along with love) is a motif that connotes spiritual evolution and internal growth. Pain (like love, in an ineluctable reciprocity) shows the path that humans must follow in order to follow the complete meaning of creation. This exaltation of pain (which often evokes intense literary expression in Pazzi) should be read and understood together with the "excess of love" that unites God to human beings, just as death should be understood as a vivifying act. This active (rather than dialectical) tension, which enters and transfigures humans, provides an analogue to Christ's Passion.

12. Pazzi certainly knew the mysticism of the Alumbrados. In the *Breve ragguaglio della vita della Santa Madre fatto dalla Madre Suor Maria Pacifica del Tovaglia*, (Pazzi, *Tutte le Opere*, vol. 1) we read that Maria Maddalena "did not acquire the enlightenment and cognition of the divine by reading unusual books; rather she read the Gospels and certain other pious books like the meditations of Luis de Granada, Fr. Gaspar Loarte" ("il lume e la Cognitione che haveva di Dio non l'acquistò in leggere libri curiosi, per ché leggeva il libro de' Vangeli e certi altri libretti devoti come la meditatione del Granata, il P. Guaspar Loarte" (p. 75). She had received these works from her father confessors, the Jesuits Andrea Rossi and Pietro Blanca, even before entering the monastery.

It is interesting that the archive of Pazzi's monastery had two copies of Loarte's *Instrutione et avertimenti per meditare la passione di Cristo nostro, con alcune meditazioni intorno ad esse*, one a 1571 edition and one from 1572. This latter is bound with two other works: *De l'obligo ch'havemo di servire N.S. per li benefici ricevuti, cavato dall Guida de'Peccatori del R.P. fra Luigi di Granata* (Macerata, 1577), and *Meditatione per incamminar uno a far oratione mentale, cavata dal libro del conforto degli afflitti del R.P. Gaspar Loarte* (Macerata, 1577). It is likely that *De l'obligo* is identical to Granada's widely diffused *Meditazioni molto devote sopra alcuni passi e misteri della vita del nostro Salvatore, et particolarmente della sua santa Natività, per sino alla sua gloriosa Ascensione*, one of the most important texts of Alumbrado spirituality (Venice, 1576). Pazzi also knew two anthologies of Granada's writings: *Della introduzione al simbolo della fede* (4 parts; Venice, 1587), and *Pie e devote orationi raccolte da diversi santi dottori per il R.P. Luigi da Granata et sparse in diversi luoghi delle sue opere* (Venice, 1574). Besides these works, another miscellany strongly influenced her thought: the *Institutiones* attributed to Johannes Tauler, probably written by Peter Canisius (see J. Orcibal, *Jean de la Croix et les mystiques réhno-flamands* [Paris: Gallimard 1966], pp. 119ff.). The influence of Granada's thought, and indirectly that of the Rhineland mystic Harpius (for instance, the theme of the harm that can affect humans because of their pleasure in sensory consolation), on Pazzi is certain. In particular, it is possible that Pazzi, brought up on these texts, might have absorbed Granada's personal elaboration of the means for mental prayer, this latter based primarily on nondiscursive forms.

It is thus documented that Pazzi had direct knowledge of Spanish mysticism. The idea that she also might have had access to Rhenish mysticism (via the *illu-*

minati) would help clarify, at least in part, the internal development of her thought. Still, the most striking and central points of her theology—for instance, the experiences gained among the "turns" of the active and dramatic state of silence which humans reach through humility and annihilation—should be considered the result of a concatenation of influences. The intense and emotional devotion to Christ's Passion, in the tradition of Catherine of Siena, is the basis for her fundamental ideas, deriving on one hand from Flemish mysticism and on the other from the flowering of Florentine humanism.

13. In the twentieth century, these ideas would be taken up by Pierre Teilhard de Chardin. For him, original sin is that aspect of the human condition which dictates a necessary passage through destruction, so that the completion and integrity of being may be attained. The acceptance of the daily "cross" thus expresses total obedience to this dynamic. See Teilhard de Chardin, *Chute, rédemption et géocentrie*, in *Oeuvres*, vol. 10 (Paris: 1969), pp. 49–57; and idem, *Réflexions sur le peché originel*, in ibid., pp. 221ff.

14. "Justice" here does not mean the recognition of a state, but rather the creation of its own possibility for being. Thus this is a case not of declarative, but rather of constituative, justice.

15. Once again humble devotion to the Passion, with all its physical details, leads "naturally" to silence. Unlike other writers, Pazzi does not exalt suffering in itself, but rather the *result* of the bloody passage through death to the fullness of life.

16. Cf. also II, 97; II, 238: "You are the house where Divinity rests, and Your wounds are the rooms" ("Tu sei quella casa dove si riposa la Divinità, e le piaghe son le camere"; II, 411); "Nor is the place [on Christ's head crowned by thorns] missing where these souls can perch and rest at ease, the spaces between the thorns. Part of these thorns went to heaven as the ornament, glory, and happiness of the blessed souls placed on them" ("Né ci mancò il' luogo dove esse anime si potessino posare e stare al lor bello agio, che erano quelli spatij che sono tra l'una spina e l'altra; et parte ancora di esse spine andassino verse il' ciolo per ornamento, gloria e contento di quelle anime beate che quivi havevono a esser collocate"; III, 77); III, 186. For Christ's side, see I, 209: "And I put all your predetermined brides in your Divine side, in your heart, for this is the place where they will make their nest, and the cell where they will rest and take all comfort" ("Et le tua spose praeelette tutte le metto hora nel' tuo divin Costato, dal' tuo cuore, che questo è il luogo dove esse hanno a fare il' nido, a la cella dove si hanno a riposare e pigliare ogni conforto"; III, 100–101).

17. "And just as the will is in the heart, so obedience is acquired from Jesus' side where His heart is" ("Et così come nel' cuore sta la volontà, così l'obbedientia s'acquista dal' Costato di Jesu dove sta il' Cuore"; II, 239).

18. Repose occurred in Pazzi's ecstacies in reference to daily reality (along with the drama of the Passion). For instance, God the Father directed these words to the soul: "My daughter, do you know how I operate in a pure soul? Just like a great lord at war, who, attacked by his enemies, retires to his fortress where he can rest without fear of attack, and delight in his pleasures. In the same way I use this pure soul like a fortress, furnished with all provisions. I retire to this soul, resting

there, when I am offended by worldly things and attacked by sinners with their sins. I delight in [this soul's] pure desires and in those fiery darts of love when I face all those arrows and arquebusses of sins sent by my enemies. And when I am attacked by evil ones, I retire to these pure souls, and please myself in them" ("Figliuolina mia, sai come io fo' in un'anima pura? Propriamente come un gran signore, che havendo guerra, e sendo perseguitato da alcuno, si ritira in qual'che suo fortezza dove si sta senza paura di essere offeso, e si gode delle suo delitie. Così io mi servo di questa anima pura come di una mia fortezza, fornita di tutte le vettovaglie, nella quale quando sono offeso da' mondani e perseguitato da i peccatori con i lor peccati, mi ritiro faccendo in essa il' mio riposo, dilettandomi nelli sua puri desiderij, et di quelli affocati dardi di amore, all'incontro di tante saette e archibusate di peccati che mi son mandate dalli mia nimici. E quando sono cacciato da cattivi, me ne vò in queste anime pure, e in esse mi compiaccio"; II, 126). Cf. also IV, 184–85.

19. "The remainder of work is to rest totally dead in God, so that God may work in [the soul] and it in God. Thus in a certain way the soul at work is not even conscious of working" ("Il restar d'hoperare è il' rilassarsi tutta morta in Dio, a tale che esso Dio operi in lei e lei in Dio, e così in un certo modo essa, operando, non si avvede di operare"; IV, 185).

20. This has been pointed out by the Augustinian historian Salvatore Thor-Salviat in *Secrets of a Seraph: The Spiritual Doctrine of St. Mary Magdalene de' Pazzi* (Downers Grove, IL: Carmelite Third Order Press, 1961). Thor-Salviat also raised, somewhat obscurely, the possibility of the influence of Ficinian humanism on Pazzi's spirituality via Augustinian Platonism. He says that Augustinian doctrine, largely colored by Platonism, was by no means unknown in the Florence of Cosimo il Vecchio; the humanist Marsilio Ficino and his Accademia di Careggi had revived Platonic thought, and had attempted to Christianize (as far as possible) the speculations of the author of the *Phaedrus* by using the resources of Augustinian philosophy and theology. In Pazzi's doctrine there is this individual aspect (for instance, the idea of humanity as the complete microcosm of the cosmos, as the image of God eternally present in the Divine idea, of which the Word was the personal and perfect expression) which simultaneously recalls Plato and his interpretation in Augustine.

21. See E. Ancilli, *S. Maria Maddalena de Pazzi Tutte le Opere*, vol. I, pp. 71ff.: "Certain pages will remain impenetrable even to the most diligent scholar," since the transcriptions of her ecstacies contain "mysterious words, even more mysterious images, apocalyptic symbols, meaningless formulations, descriptions of Trinitarian life which escape any possible analysis."

22. For details on the transcriptions of the ecstacies, see *Summarium actionum, virtutum et miraculorum servae dei Mariae Magdalenae de Pazzis Ordinis Carmelitarum ex processu remissoriale desumptorum*, ed. L. Saggi (Rome: Institution Carmelitanum 1965).

23. See G. M. Bertin, *I mistici medievali* (Milan: 1944), p. 127.

24. Of course this does not mean that the entire historical trajectory of the "theologia Verbis" is present in Pazzi's thought. This has been accurately demonstrated (with numerous textual citations) by B. Secondin, *Santa Maria Maddalena*

de' Pazzi: Esperienza e dottrina (Rome: Institutum Carmelitanum 1974), pp. 259–329. Here I would only emphasize that Pazzi's Christology is expressed with an originality derived from her openness to the culture of her time. Concerning the centrality of the mediation of Christ-Man in Pazzi's theological discourse, Secondin has pointed out that the Florentine mystic "is certainly a daughter of her time, an epigone of numerous trends and ideas which are connected to the *devotio moderna* and the Rhenish mystics." Furthermore, "the most direct influence (outside of female psychology and the Carmelite tradition) on Pazzi was provided by Laorte's meditations and the Franciscan tradition summarized in the *Meditationes vitae Christi*" (p. 285).

Gabriella Zarri

11. Ursula and Catherine: The Marriage of Virgins in the Sixteenth Century

In 1566, more than twenty-five years after the death of Angela Merici, Father Francesco Landini sketched the first profile of this saintly woman's life and miracles. Merici (1470/75–1540) founded the Company of Saint Ursula, from which several groups bearing the name Ursuline branched off: "virgins in the house" living in their family homes; congregations of sisters taking simple vows; and a cloistered branch that spread from France to Canada, where it became the first female missionary organization.[1] Transformed with great rapidity, the Company stimulated the foundation of still other female religious groups in diverse historical settings. Merici's innovative and flexible model inspired both the French *dévotes*, recently examined by Elizabeth Rapley,[2] and the Englishwoman Mary Ward's company, stillborn in its first incarnation as "Jesuitesses," which was reconstituted in the early eighteenth century as the Institute of the Blessed Virgin Mary.[3]

Numerous *vitae* of Angela Merici and abundant documentary sources, some of them published, provide the opportunity to locate her foundation in a context broader than that employed in current historical writing. The two most recent and most fully documented biographies, although at odds with each other, both posit the traditional conflict between Catholic and Protestant Reformations.[4] With the abatement of ideological pressures and the growing consensus among scholars on a new periodization of the age of religious reforms,[5] however, the time has come to move beyond anachronistic historiographical polemic and reinterpret the company founded by Angela Merici as a highly significant phenomenon in the history of gender.

Translated by Anne Jacobson Schutte.

Between Heaven and Earth

According to hagiographers, the vision that launched the Company of Saint Ursula in 1536 is emblematic of the new historical interpretation I intend to propose. Here is the story in Father Landini's succinct but fundamental version:

> The founder of this holy Company was a certain Angela, [angelic] in both name and life, a little peasant girl by blood but of noble and renowned sanctity. . . . And while her other companions gleaning in the field paused for refreshment, she launched into prayer, and once her spirit was elevated, she saw the sky open. A marvelous procession of angels and young virgins came forth, two by two, the angels playing various kinds of instruments and the virgins singing. . . . Once the procession had passed, there came a virgin, her sister . . . recently gone to paradise, who . . . predicted that God intended to make use of her, and that she would found a company of virgins that would grow, and similar things.[6]

In this account, the chief characteristic of the Company is virginity associated with the angelic life, which connotes the condition of primeval innocence in the garden of Eden and the privileged route for reaching paradise. Virgins and angels form couples uniting heaven and earth. Although the track on which this procession moves is not specified, there is a clear allusion to Jacob's ladder, an image widely diffused in ascetic and mystical literature of the Middle Ages, which would be employed in Merician iconography to represent Angela's prophetic vision. Also noteworthy in Landini's account is an element extraneous to the prodigious event, Angela's humble social origin. Landini juxtaposes the peasant status of the Company's founder with the royal status of the saints whose exemplary lives inspired her: Ursula and Catherine of Alexandria.

Anthropologists like Anton Blok who have studied virginity in Mediterranean Europe—a status characterized by a sharp distinction between men and women—have identified in virginity a liminal condition that can mediate between masculine and feminine, between social classes, and, in the religious sphere, between human and divine.[7] Whether imposed or chosen, this type of virginity centers on an interiorized value, physical integrity or chastity, that prompted a new formulation of the cultural relationship between body and spirit. Linked to this construct are changes in the realm of moral theology and prescriptive interventions in matters of sexuality.[8]

To establish the historical validity of the interpretive model just sketched out, I shall examine one particularly significant case, the Company of Saint Ursula. Its liminality, not restricted to the type of mediation between heaven and earth represented in her vision, includes mediation between female states of life (virgins, married women, widows), between social classes, and between processes of cultural transformation. Limited space permits me to outline only a few of these issues.[9] Nonetheless, Landini's account of Angela's vision will serve to synthesize by way of example the historical development that I wish to emphasize: the progressive transformation of Jacob's ladder—previously interpreted by Saint Bernard as a ladder of humility necessary for monks to attain the contemplative state and often depicted as a ladder of virtue[10]—into a procession of virgins uniting earth to heaven that associates contemplation with activity in society and in the Church.

In a cultural context closer in time to Angela Merici, we find two images of Jacob's ladder. The first, contained in Pietro de' Natali's widely diffused *Catalogus sanctorum*, depicts the descent of angels from heaven to earth.[11] The second, found in a work of piety printed by commission of the abbess of the Brescian convent of Santa Giulia in 1527, represents the contemplative life as a ladder, the top of which has been reached by young women without the attributes that would indicate their membership in a religious order (Figure 11.1).[12]

Merici's vision as described in Landini's testimony of 1566 associates the angels of Jacob's dream with the virgins who ascend rung by rung to heaven, where the crown earned by those who have struggled (2 Tim 2:5) awaits them. From its inception, the Merician hagiographic tradition assigned central importance to Angela's vision as a miraculous event justifying the foundation of her Company. Not until the late seventeenth century, however, did the dream enter into the institute's iconographical repertoire when it was incorporated in paintings in the Brescian Church of Saint Ursula, to which the new Oratory of the Virgins was annexed.[13] Only in the eighteenth century was the image of the ladder employed to symbolize the original character of the institute. It appears in an engraving made on the occasion of Merici's beatification, proclaimed in 1768 (Figure 11.2),[14] and in the portrait included as the frontispiece to the *Vita* printed ten years later (Figure 11.1).[15] In these representations the vision is cast as a procession of crowned virgins in pairs climbing a ladder leading to heaven. Over the course of a century, then, the Company codified and transformed symbols which at the time of its establishment had different meanings.

Figure 11.1. G. Lombardi, *Vita della B. Angela Merici, fondatrice della Compagnia di Sant'Orsola*. Venice, 1778. (Reprinted by permission of Biblioteca Queriniana, Brescia)

Figure 11.2. Engraving from a page of the anonymous *Mater Angela Merici, fundatrix ordinis Societ. S. Ursulae* (1768). (Reprinted by permission of Unione Romana Orsoline)

Pilgrimage and Mission

Until now, all historical treatments of the Company of Saint Ursula have drawn exclusively on written sources: hagiographical testimonies, material assembled at various stages to promote Angela Merici's canonization, and scanty surviving documentation of other kinds. I propose instead to interpret this institution's significance through symbolic interpretations contained in paintings and prints that can be connected directly to the Brescian environment, the ritual of entrance into the Company, and a few visions. I shall emphasize the character of the Company in the period of its foundation, with only a few forward glances at its transformation in the post-Tridentine era.

Important theoretical works on the functions of symbolic elements in history and numerous studies of the connections between images and visions obviate the need to justify my approach.[16] The significance of this institution's origin is not restricted to the religious and social history of the early modern era. We should keep in mind, however, that the young women who joined the Company of Saint Ursula came from a group at the lower end of the social scale and that most were illiterate. For them, altarpieces, woodcuts in lives of saints and devotional books, images painted on the walls of the oratory in which they gathered to pray, and the rule of the Company read aloud by a literate person[17] impressed on their memory and helped them to internalize the experience of life which they had chosen to lead.

Further removed, perhaps, from the learning process of Angela Merici's earliest followers, but culturally relevant to the noble families who promoted the institution, were the images and moral mottos transmitted in the woodcuts, engravings, and emblems that flooded the market from the 1530s on.[18] As a primer of symbolic language, these printed figurative materials, whether or not they included a textual component, often superimposed ethical significances destined in time to obscure the theological messages of religious images by translating them into moralism and devotionalism. To the figurative material directly related to the Company of Saint Ursula, therefore, we may legitimately add, where appropriate, the products of that new cultural medium which in the course of the sixteenth century codified a bipolar female image—"angel or devil," as Sara Matthews Grieco has termed it.[19]

During the middle decades of the Cinquecento, however, those in religious circles close to the Company of Saint Ursula read this image in a decidedly unilateral way: they saw only the angel. In this respect the iconography of Angela Merici is absolutely univocal. Representations of the foundress were based on an illustrious prototype: the funeral mask painted by a Brescian artist who viewed Merici on her deathbed. Alessandro Bonvicino, called Moretto, belonged to the group of devotees who clustered around the holy woman, and his daughter joined the Company. Thus his work was intimately linked to the religious experience of the group.[20] Engraved copies of Moretto's image inspired a painting attributed to Bartolomeo Cesi.[21] A portrait of Merici painted during her lifetime by Girolamo Romanino, however, had no such impact because it remained in private hands.[22]

The standard image of Angela Merici shows an elderly woman in the habit of a Franciscan tertiary, either carrying a pilgrim's staff or in the act of receiving a banner emblazoned with the cross which is consigned to her by Saint Ursula. Both iconographical attributes of Angela, the staff and the banner,[23] refer to central features of the foundress's life and of the company's symbolic significance. Hence they enable us to identify the imprint of the cultural context in which the institute was planned and founded: the missionary impulse set off in Europe by the discovery of the New World.

In sixteenth-century figurative parlance, the pilgrim's staff, traditionally a sign of protection, acquired an additional connotation: safeguarding the body. This is clearly evident in an engraving attributed to Mercure Jollat that illustrates the emblem *Custodiendas virgines* in the edition of Andrea Alciato's emblem book published in Paris in 1536. This image—in which the virginal Pallas Athena of Alciato's caption is transformed into a tertiary, clutching the banner like a lance, who is accompanied by a dragon to protect her virtue—exemplifies the conception, widely diffused in late medieval culture, of the religious habit and membership in a monastic order as the best safeguards of virginity. In the edition of Alciato's text issued in Lyon in 1548, on the other hand, the illustration of the same motto stresses the woman's responsibility for protecting her own body.[24] In this engraving, attributed to Pierre Eskirsh, Pallas in armor, brandishing her lance like a virgin warrior, stands over a watch-dragon, a faithful companion accompanying the victor in her triumph.

Emblems long associated with the protection of virginity, the pilgrim's staff and the warrior's lance as depicted in the sixteenth century suggest women's increasing responsibility for custody of their own bodies. Supplementing rather than contradicting Alciato's ethical message, their religious significance highlights the innovative function of the Company of Saint Ursula. Merici's foundation sought to address the social problem of protecting female honor in two ways: by equipping women through literacy and moral instruction to control their bodies;[25] and by assigning them a mission in the church linked with the myth of *renovatio*, which played such an important part in the religious aspirations and experiences of many spiritual groups in sixteenth-century Europe.

In the Franciscan tradition, missionary activity, defined as "going to the infidels" (*ire ad infideles*), began as pilgrimage.[26] During the fifteenth century the movement of the Observance took as the symbol of its preaching activity the standard with a cross, an emblem associated particularly with Giacomo della Marca.[27] Pilgrimage to Rome or to the Holy Land—which had featured prominently in the spiritual careers of such medieval women as Margaret of Cortona, Birgitta of Sweden, and Catherine of Siena—continued in the early sixteenth century to be the most typical form of female participation in the mission of renewing the Church.[28] Angela Merici, who set off as a pilgrim to the Holy Land in 1524 and to Rome in the following year, was following in the footsteps of Saint Francis and the courageous martyr Ursula.

A Breton princess who lived in the fourth century, Ursula, having converted her future husband to Christianity, asked his permission to make a pilgrimage to Rome before their wedding in the company of eleven thousand virgins. Along with her companions, her fiancé, Pope Cyriac (who according to the legend had resigned his office to follow the virgins), and many bishops, she was martyred on the way back at Cologne, which the party had reached by ship via the rivers in Germanic territory. Their collective sacrifice at the hands of Huns besieging the city brought about the liberation of Cologne. The earliest version of this martyr's legend, composed in the tenth century, was subsequently enhanced by borrowings from the *Revelations* of Elisabeth of Schönau. Popularized most notably in Jacopo da Voragine's redaction, it acquired additional elements from the legend of Saint Wilhelmina.[29]

In the Middle Ages, the cult of Saint Ursula spread widely throughout Europe. On account of Ursula's power of intercession on behalf of Cologne, she first gained popularity in the Holy Roman Empire. There the martyr was represented in two main ways: as the Mother of Mercy gathering under her mantle women, high prelates, or members of confraternities; and as a ship's captain who, after being killed, guides the vessel to salvation.[30] German bishops, abbots, and kings enrolled in confraternities dedicated to Saint Ursula's Ship, in which other iconographical motifs were introduced to convey a more complex message. The mystical winepress and the fountain of life served to represent the spiritual benefits of participation in the Mass and the eucharist and the mediatory powers of the Virgin Mary man and the martyr Saint Ursula.[31] On her pilgrimage to Rome and the Holy Land, Ursula fulfilled her mission to the infidels by converting her fiancé and her cortege of virgins in the role of a ship's captain whom all obey. As Jacopo da Voragine put it, "virgins from many kingdoms followed her orders. . . . When supplies sufficient to last three years were put on board, the queen revealed her plans to her troops and swore all of them into the 'new militia.'"[32]

In Italy as early as the fourteenth century, particularly in the Veneto, churches and confraternities dedicated to Ursula and paintings commemorating her proliferated. A famous example in the Venetian Republic, which annexed the city of Brescia in 1426, is the fourteenth-century Saint Ursula cycle by Tomaso da Modena in Treviso.[33] In the mid-fifteenth century Vittore Carpaccio painted the splendid canvases now in the Accademia for the Venetian *Scuola* of Saint Ursula, which had been founded in July 1300 under the inspiration of the Dominicans of Saints Giovanni and Paolo.[34] Carpaccio's masterpieces are too well known and exhaustively studied to require extended discussion here. It is worth noting, however, that recent scholarship stresses his capacity to incorporate those spurious elements of Ursula's legend, the borrowings from the legend of Saint Wilhelmina, most conducive to linking Ursula's story with the myth of Venice. Carpaccio, furthermore, was attentive to the gestural repertoire of pantomime and theatrical presentation and to the thematic condensation of *sacre rappresentazioni*, which he translated into more elevated pictorial language.[35]

The *Golden Legend*, the legends of holy virgins, theatrical representations, paintings, oral accounts by members of confraternities: these must have been the means by which Angela Merici came to know the life of Saint Ursula.

The Militia of Christ

In late fifteenth-century Italy, the cult of Saint Ursula and the eleven thousand virgins began to focus various religious tensions and to incorporate women's desires for active involvement in missions and ecclesiastical reform. The Christian militia is represented first of all by such holy woman warriors as the Maid of Orleans. Her story was included in Giovanni Sabadino degli Arienti's *Gynevera de le clare donne*, a collection of lives of illustrious women of the fifteenth century which circulated widely in manuscript.[36] It was disseminated in print in Jacopo Filippo Foresti's *De claris selectisque mulieribus*.[37] The latter work, published in Latin with numerous female portraits illustrating the merits of mythical heroines of antiquity and contemporary women, presents a gallery of exemplary females, leaders in society and the Church. Among them are Joan of Arc, depicted as a young Diana in armor with bow and quiver who leads armies to victory, and Bona di Valtellina, the legendary prototype of heroines in contemporary chivalric literature.[38] Foresti exalts the military valor not only of woman warriors but also of those who played a role in guiding the Church—from Pope Joan, portrayed with the triple tiara, to Birgitta, who admonishes the pope to remember the poverty of the primitive church.[39] Ursula, depicted as the Mother of Mercy covering her virgin companions with her mantle and raising a banner in triumph (Figure 11.3), is one of many female figures, among them Catherine of Siena, who struggled val-

Figure 11.3. Saint Ursula, f. CXXV, from Jacobus Philippus Bergomensis, *De claris selectisque mulieribus* (Ferrara: Lorenzo Rossi di Valenza, 1497). (Reprinted by permission of Biblioteca del Archiginnasio, Bologna)

iantly against the world, the flesh, and the devil in order to win the triple halo-crown of virginity, martyrdom, and teaching authority.[40]

The standard, a processional and military ensign, is also an eschatological symbol, for it recalls the risen Christ standing near the empty sepulcher with a banner bearing His cross. Such a banner is a standard feature in the iconography of Saint Ursula, though the number of them varies: one when the saint's leadership role is emphasized (as in the image from Foresti's book), two when the reference is to spiritual combat—the virgin's struggle against the flesh, the martyr's triumph over the world, the victory of orthodox doctrine over heresy. This usage conforms to the treatment in spiritual literature, codified in scholastic treatises of the thirteenth century, of meritorious actions that justify awarding of the halo-crown. According to Alexander of Hales, for instance, the triple halo-crown has what might be termed an anthropological function, for it represents the prizes of a battle waged by the three parts of the self (mind, soul, spirit) against, respectively, the world (martyrdom), the flesh (virginity), and the devil (preaching).

References to Alexander of Hales's teaching may be found in the cultural milieu surrounding the foundress of the Company of Saint Ursula. The inscription on the arch over Merici's tomb attests to her having waged a victorious battle meriting the triple crown of martyrdom, virginity, and preaching. Particularly noteworthy, at a moment preceding by only two years the founding of the Roman Inquisition and the opening of the papal offensive against the *spirituali*, is the emphasis of the inscription on female teaching:

> Proposito Martyr, virgo actibus, ore magistra
> Sic tribus aureolis Angela dives ovas
> Angela nuper eras morum vitaque magistra
> Nunc patriae tutrix praesidiumque veni.[41]

In most representations there are two banners. A prime Venetian example from the late fifteenth century that may well have influenced Merici is Antonio Vivarini's "Ursula and Her Companions" (Figure 11.4), originally in the Brescian monastery of San Michele in Uliveto.[42] This painting was undoubtedly the prototype for Moretto's works, which as we have seen were intimately linked with the founding and spread of Merici's Company.

Before examining other paintings connected with the institution that took Saint Ursula's name, we should recall that the image of two banners

Figure 11.4. Antonio Vivarini, *Ursula and Her Companions*, Brescia. Fifteenth century. (Photo: Fantini)

as standards of military contingents were featured in visions about reform of the Church and missions to convert infidels. Among the best known of these is Ignatius Loyola's meditation on the two banners rallying the armies of Christ and Lucifer: Christ stations himself in the field of Jerusalem.[43] Caterina da Racconigi's vision of 1525 as reported by one of her most illustrious hagiographers, Count Giovanfrancesco Pico della Mirandola, is practically identical.[44] Both visions, the possible connections between which should be investigated, present faith as a battle ending in universal conversion. In sixteenth-century collections of saints' lives, too, the martyrdom of Ursula is depicted as a battle on land.[45] The image of Saint Ursula's ship, however, is seldom found in Italian art.

The Company of Saint Ursula as "Church"

During the period in which Angela Merici lived and worked, renewal of the Church and conversion of the Turks, foretold in presages and prophecies, came to preoccupy various pious groups operating in restricted elite circles that sought to realize the ideals of the primitive Church. Intensive research on these groups has usually focused on attempting to identify the theological matrix of their ideas and their links with transalpine reformers. The urge to classify that so often distorts scholarly efforts has resulted in a misleading reconstruction after the fact of "true" and "false" churches. Still, Merici's Company and similar spiritual groups founded in this period did in fact organize themselves as potential "churches" modeled on the primitive Church, in open conflict with existing ecclesiastical institutions and in the expectation of millenarian renewal.

The Company of Saint Ursula had a precise institutional profile and purpose. Editions of its Rule and accounts of its establishment characterized it as a female company with the potential to become a congregation, a religious order. In the beginning, however, it was, like Saint Ursula's ship, a "church" open to everyone. This conception is clearly enunciated in the prologue of the earliest manuscript of the Rule that has come down to us, the Trivulzian Codex redacted between 1545 and 1546. After having stated that the Rule had been composed in consultation with many wise persons, "especially the most senior and expert virgins of the Company," the author of the Prologue affirms that the spiritual norms laid out in the Rule should be observed principally by the young women enrolled in the confraternity. Other followers and adherents, however, are not excluded. "The more numerous they are, the happier they will be and the more Jesus Christ Our Lord will be among us and manifest His virtue and power."[46]

Explicit allusion to the verse "For where two or three are gathered in my name, I am there among them" (Matt. 28:20) makes clear the ideological context in which the Company arose. Its orientation is confirmed by additional ways of identifying its inspiration and purpose of recreating the Church of the Apostles: the association between virginity and martyrdom expressed in the choice of Ursula as patron saint and the patterning of "Christ's following" on the Roman matrons who followed the Apostles. This ideological program, set forth via the scriptural passages cited in the Rule and in the writings of Angela Merici's chancellor, Gabriele Cozzano,[47] also finds symbolic expression in the Company's iconography and rituals. A good example is the depiction of the "New Company" dated 1540, which shows Angela and some of her companions gathered in Christ's name, which is included on the sides in the monogram devised by Saint Bernardino of Siena (Figure 11.5).[48] On the upper plane is a crown, which by this time, as we shall see, was an important symbolic referent of the Company of Saint Ursula. The semicircular deployment of the virgins makes clear the identification of the congregation as a monastic order ruled by a superior and as an ecclesiastical assembly gathered around Saint Peter's chair.[49] The book held by each of the women has a double significance. On the one hand, it reinforces the character of Merici's congregation as a "New Company" in which sisters' obligations included monthly reading of the Rule. On the other hand, following an iconographical pattern in place by the thirteenth century, it alludes to the Scriptures, which convoke the Church.[50]

In the Company's early years, Ursuline virgins met in an oratory set up in the house of Isabetta Prato in Piazza del Duomo. Merici's teachings were conveyed not only by the Rule but also by the paintings that from 1533 on adorned the walls of the oratory, since destroyed. Through Bernardino Faino's description of these paintings, contained in a manuscript of the late seventeenth century in the Biblioteca Queriniana of Brescia, we know their subjects.

Behind the altar of the chapel was a fresco representing the crucified Christ surrounded by angels and saints. Depicted on the side walls were the mysteries of the Rosary and images of virgins and martyrs. Among them were Ursula on a ship with a banner in her hand; and Afra, a

Figure 11.5. Anonymous Lombard painter, *La Nova Compagnia* (1540), Brescia, Civici Musei. (Photo: Rapuzzi)

Brescian martyr whose relics were preserved in the church of the Lateran Canons bearing her name, where Merici would spend the last years of her life. A painting of the Roman widow Paula and her daughter Eustochium, to whom Saint Jerome directed several of his writings, linked the Ursuline with the female followers of the Apostles and Fathers of the primitive church.[51] These and other paintings were copied at the end of the seventeenth century in the Church of Saint Ursula, which adjoined a new oratory where young Brescian women belonging to the Company met.[52] The link between widows as patrons and virgins as members of the Congregation, of course, is one of the most distinctive characteristics of the Company—not only of its ideological matrix but also of its institutional structure. The assignment of four "female colonels" (*colonelle*) to guide young members accentuated the Company of Saint Ursula's militant character.[53]

Further evidence of the Company's aim to found a renewed "church" based on the model of the primitive Church and the Scriptures and devoted to moral and religious education is provided by the enthusiastic reaction of a well-known Erasmian of Brescia, Vincenzo Maggi. In his treatise on female excellence published in 1545, after having noted that women's wearing "military" dress foreshadowed a reversal of roles, he states through the mouth of a widow that in Brescia, men "let themselves be governed by women." Maggi adds that female members of religious orders, much more observant than friars, have come close to the model of virgins in the primitive Church:

> I know of no convent in which there are not many women who remind me of Eustochium, Marcella, and Blesilla. I am acquainted with an infinite number about whom, when I talk with them, I say to myself, "That's what the glorious Melania must have been like. The most devout Asella and the Roman matron Paula, I believe, must have been just as modest and holy."[54]

Jumping from Maggi's testimony to the conclusion that Angela Merici's cultural ambience was "Erasmian" would be unwise. We should not, however, discount the reformist impulse permeating the writings of her amanuensis Gabriele Cozzano and the militant character of this new form of religious life, which is not far removed from the spirituality of the *Enchiridion militis christiani*, first translated into Italian and printed in Brescia in 1531.[55] Nor should we forget that the Company's emphasis on education parallels the foundation by Brescian Erasmians of colleges for the instruction of boys.[56] A strong commitment to education, furthermore, marks

Merici's *Testamento* and the *Ricordi* addressed to her associates, the *colonelle di quartiere*. That religious inspiration takes second place to pedagogy in these texts justifies including the Company of Saint Ursula among the institutions that aimed both to safeguard female honor and to educate women of all social classes.

Yet another iconographical attestation to the churchlike character of the company, rooted in the cults of local martyrs and in the conception of the confraternity as Saint Ursula's ship, is provided by the woodcuts adorning the first edition of the Rule, printed in semi-Gothic type by Damiano Turlino at an unspecified time between 1546 and 1569 (Figure 11.6). The woodcuts include images associated with Saint Ursula's ship: the instruments of the Passion and the eucharist, those symbols of flesh and food that Caroline Bynum has taught us to consider distinctively feminine.[57] Alongside the two central figures, the Brescian martyrs Faustino and Giovita, stand the patronesses of the Company: Ursula, dressed as the Mother of Mercy, and Catherine of Alexandria (Figures 11.7 and 11.8). The illustration of the risen Christ holding a banner bearing His Cross further emphasizes the eschatological value of Ursula's and the members of the company's virginity (Figure 11.9).

This iconography is supported by written texts, notably a passage from the Capuchin Mattia Bellintani de Salò's unpublished life of Angela. Commissioned in the last quarter of the sixteenth century by the superior of the Brescian Ursulines to write Merici's biography, the friar encapsulated the significance of the Company in his equating of virginity with martyrdom. Angela herself made the same linkage by electing to lead a life of prayer in the church of Sant'Afra. According to Bellintani, it appeared "that by divine revelation she came there to live, so that in the place of martyrdom, the spot watered by the precious blood of Christ's holy friends, this new virginal state and institution of our times would germinate and sprout."[58]

The Marriage of Virgins

In the preface to his biography of Angela Merici, Bellintani sums up in a single phrase the achievement of the Brescian woman: having planted the fruitful tree "of the new manner of marrying Christ."[59] Catherine of Alexandria was chosen as a patron of the Company not only because she was a virgin and a martyr but also because she was the prototypical "bride of

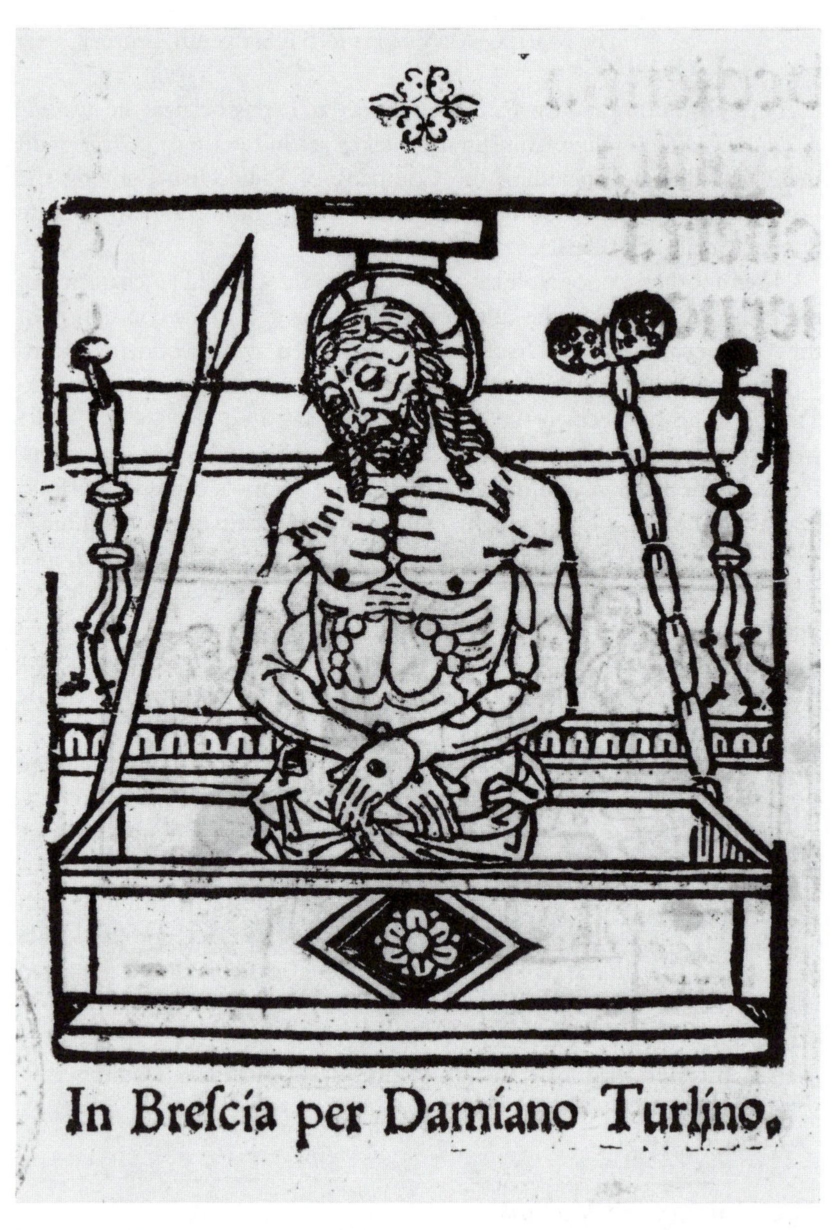

Figure 11.6. Frontispiece, *Regola della Nova Compagnia di santa Orsola di Brescia: per si quale si vede come si habbiano a governar le vergini di detta compagnia accioche vivendo christianamente possino doppo la lor morte fruir i beni di vita eterna* (The Rule of the Congregation of Saint Ursula of Brescia: by means of which it is seen how the virgins may govern the same congregation so that living in a Christian manner they may, after their deaths, enjoy the fruits of eternal life). Brescia: Damiano Turlino, n.d. (Reprinted by permission of Biblioteca Queriniana, Brescia)

Figure 11.7. The Last Supper with Saints Faustino and Giovita, from *Regola della Nova Compagnia di santa Orsola di Brescia*. (Reprinted by permission of Biblioteca Queriniana, Brescia)

Figure 11.8. The Deposition of Christ, with Saints Ursula and Catherine, from *Regola della Nova Compagnia di santa Orsola di Brescia*. (Reprinted by permission of Biblioteca Queriniana, Brescia)

Figure 11.9. Christ rises from the dead, from *Regola della Nova Compagnia di santa Orsola di Brescia*. (Reprinted by permission of Biblioteca Queriniana, Brescia)

Christ." Ursula's and Catherine's joint patronage of the Brescian confraternity is evident in Girolamo Romanino's well-known painting of Catherine's mystical marriage (Figure 11.10). Romanino's painting, privately commissioned around 1535 and held for centuries in the Maffei collection in Brescia before being acquired by the Brooks Memorial Gallery in Memphis, has a clearly celebratory purpose. Witnesses to the mystical marriage, Baby Jesus' placing a ring on Catherine's finger, are Angela Merici in the habit of a Franciscan tertiary and Saint Ursula with her banner. Outside the scene on the left, one can see Saint Lawrence, modeled perhaps on Lorenzo Muzio, vicar general of the diocese of Brescia, who had approved the foundation of the Company of Saint Ursula in April 1536.[60]

Catherine's co-patronage of the Company is attested to also by the fact that from its inception, virgins made their solemn entrance on 25 November, the Alexandrian martyr's feast day. As in every confraternity, the first step in joining the Company was placing one's name in its book, an act reserved to virgins who had "a firm intention to serve God in this sort of life."[61] Notwithstanding its previously mentioned status as a "church" similar to confraternities, whose privileges were shared by all members, the Company of Saint Ursula was specifically designed as an institution for young women destined to celibacy. Unlike nuns, they did not take a vow of virginity, but they promised not to marry. The strong spiritual thrust of the original group (for which the works of Angela's confessor, the Lateran Canon Serafino Torresini da Bologna, provide additional evidence), the promise of celibacy, and the practice of prayer in common ensured that the Ursulines' life would not be far removed from the monastic state. Over time, the resemblance became closer as the entrance ceremony was assimilated into the ritual of religious profession.

In painting the mystical marriage, Romanino did not depart from the traditional iconography employed for this subject. He made explicit reference to the Company, however, by including the figures of Saint Ursula carrying her banner and Angela Merici, foundress of the institution. It should be noted that Catherine has no crown, symbol of royalty and martyrdom, on her head. Instead, she has abandoned it on the ground (Figure 11.11) as a sign of humility, just like King David in prayer portrayed in many illuminated liturgical texts of the period.[62] As I shall show, the location of Catherine's crown, on her head or on the ground, acquired concrete importance in the Company of Saint Ursula's system of symbolic references.

We have seen that during the early years, joining the Company

Figure 11.10. Girolamo Romanino, *The Mystical Marriage of Saint Catherine of Alexandria*, c. 1535. Memphis, Brooks Memorial Gallery. (Photo: Carolyn Valone)

Figure 11.11. Detail from Girolamo Romanino, *The Mystical Marriage of Saint Catherine of Alexandria*, Figure 11.10.

necessitated inscription in its book, a register similar to the *matricola* of a confraternity in which a notary wrote the name of each new member. The Company of Saint Ursula, however, was not exactly a confraternity. It occupied a liminal position: between old and new institutions (the "New Company"), and between personal and social status. Here this position can only be described briefly. At the time of its establishment, the Company of Saint Ursula's organizational structure reflected the patronage system characteristic of contemporaneous charitable institutions both public and private. The sole full-fledged members of the Company were young virgins (personal status), at the beginning poor ones (social status); noble widows, "mothers of mercy" from the outside world who served as governesses of the institution, belonged to it only as affiliates.[63] During the Company's early decades, distinctions between widows and virgins, noblewomen and girls of artisan or even servant origin, were marked. Later on this situation changed. In different political, religious, and cultural circumstances the Company of Saint Ursula came to play a role in articulating a set of alternatives for young women that was no longer binary—*aut mas aut murus*, either a man or the convent—but included a "third praiseworthy status in the Church": that of *dimessa*.[64]

The complex problem of the social and cultural changes contributing to this shift cannot be fully addressed here. Suffice it to say that in the post-Tridentine period, the Church's cultural strategy, tending toward centralization of institutions and systems of communication, led to the focusing of religious life on the parish, which took over from religious orders and confraternities the responsibility for cure of souls.[65] Once the teaching of Christian doctrine, which emphasized the incorporation of the marriage bond and the family into the sphere of the sacred, had become the Church's primary objective, Ursulines, virgins but above all "brides of Christ," were elevated in recognition of the sacrality of the family. The presence of a young unmarried woman in a domestic aggregate was no longer a dishonor; rather, it signaled that family's holiness. This transmutation had dramatic social and cultural consequences. Fathers' and brothers' financial incentive to avoid paying dowries induced patricians and merchants to accept the Church's strategy. Patrician and bourgeois families containing Ursuline brides of Christ acquired holiness. On the symbolic level, the presence of a "nun in the house" transmitted to the middle orders of society the aristocratic tradition of the "saint" in the noble family or at the prince's court.[66] Those who could not boast of a domestic saint could sacralize the hearth with a bride of Christ—not the same thing as a "virgin," whose main significance was that of sacrificial victim.

Since the means by which the *dimessa* was transformed into the bride of Christ remain for the most part to be explored, I shall confine myself to symbolic evidence of the shift. The *Ordine* for acceptance of virgins into the Company of Saint Ursula published by Damiano Turlino constitutes proof that between the mid-1540s and the late 1560s, the Company was transformed from a confraternity into something resembling a religious order.[67] The ceremony of enrollment in the Company became the first step on a route similar to that of religious profession. Inscription of the virgins was followed after a few years by their acceptance by the chapter (full-fledged sisters), and finally by their definitive incorporation into the group via a ritual very much like that of monastic consecration.

At the center of this ritual, celebrated on the martyr Saint Catherine's feast day, stood the crowning of the *accettate* (novices), who thus became *stabilite*—that is, permanent members of the Company and perpetual virgins. Ursulines were not veiled or given rings, as in the ceremony in which monastic vows were professed. Nonetheless, their crowning is a significant element connecting the two statuses. During the Ursuline "stabilization" ceremony, candles were blessed and distributed to commemorate the vigilance of the "prudent virgins" in the Gospel. The cords with which Ursulines belted their habits, a distinctive feature of the *dimessa*'s garb, were also blessed. Then the priest placed crowns on the virgins' heads, saying, "Take this sign of Christ on your head, so that you may become His wife"—a formula echoing the papal ritual for consecrating virgins in use in the fifteenth century.[68]

The ritual in which the virgins of the Company were crowned has obvious symbolic significance. Although it does not constitute a juridical recognition of their religious status, it clearly designates *dimesse* as perpetual helpmeets of Christ, tied to him by a definitive bond that recalls the position of wives who have celebrated the rite of marriage. In contrast, the formula of profession for Benedictine nuns of the Cassinese Congregation printed in Milan in 1607, in accordance with the reformed pontifical ritual promulgated by Clement VIII in 1595, employed the term "bride" rather than "wife,"[69] echoing the bridal imagery of the Song of Songs.

The symbolism of crowns, of course, is multivalent, and the questions inherent in nuptial coronation are complex. From the point of view of ritual, it should be recalled that despite Tertullian's attempt to eliminate from Christian marriage the coronation of brides practiced in pagan ceremonies, the use of crowns persisted in late antiquity. Although nuptial crowning, an element in Byzantine ceremonial, was not included in the Roman Catholic marriage rite, it made its way into the ceremony of religious profession. Coronation of professing nuns, found in the tenth-century pontifical of Mainz and incorporated in the following century into the Roman pontifical, remained in use until the nineteenth century.[70] Between the tenth and the twelfth century, however, much changed. Not only did papal theology draw on the image of coronation to reinforce the popes' sovereign power; the placing of the crown was noticeable by its absence in the ritual of marriage, a status that was no longer considered sacred. Paralleling the extension of a mystical interpretation of the Song of Songs in monastic theology, recently elucidated by Ann Matter,[71] the status of bride underwent an inversion. In the liturgy the nuptial condition was restricted to consecrated virgins. Mystical marriage, which hitherto had signified the union of Christ with the Church and God with the soul—that is, the union of abstract or collective entities—became a personal union. Now, the only real brides were those women who embraced a particular status, that of nuns.

In the early sixteenth century the term "bride" permeated monastic parlance. A woman who was professed as a nun was solemnly crowned in public, whereas a woman entered marriage via a semiclandestine transaction. Only in the latter part of that century, in part to fulfill the political aspirations of the new "modern" state, was the sacramental character of matrimony reaffirmed.[72] Post-Tridentine marriage—in which an arrangement of primarily private character was given public resonance by being celebrated in a consecrated building before a priest—and the sanctification of the domestic sphere through the presence of a bride of Christ were two different means of conferring holiness on the institution of the family.

It is no coincidence that the Ursuline coronation ritual gained official recognition during or just after the Council of Trent. The iconography of Merici's institution, however, demonstrates that the rite was in use well before the conclusion of the Council. According to art historians, two paintings by Moretto of Ursula and her companions in Brescia (Figures 11.12 and 11.13), one in the Dominican church of San Clemente and the other in the convent church of Sant'Agostino, date from the 1550s. As Valerio Guazzoni has observed, reference to the Company is proven by the brooch in the form of an angel pinned at the neck of the Breton martyr's dress.[73] These two images are almost identical, the only significance difference being the transformation of the virgin on the left in the second painting into a crowned Saint Catherine—that is, a "stabilized" Ursuline.

Throughout the later Middle Ages, the mystical marriage of Saint Catherine and the ritual coronation of nuns had conveyed an interpretation of bridal status as an attribute of virgins. The hypothesis that the martyr Catherine in Moretto's second painting represents one of Merici's followers is confirmed by a work executed a few years later. There is no doubt that Luca Longhi da Forlì's *Mystical Marriage of Saint Catherine of Alexandria* (Figure 11.14), signed and dated 1555, is closely connected with

Figure 11.12. Alessandro Bonvicino (Moretto), *Saint Ursula and Her Companions*, c. 1550, Brescia, church of San Clemente. (Photo: Fantini)

Figure 11.13. Alessandro Bonvicino (Moretto), *Saint Ursula and Her Companions*, c. 1550, Brescia, church of Sant'Agostino (now Milan, Castello sforzesco). (Photo: Fantini)

Figure 11.14. Luca Longhi da Forlì, *The Mystical Marriage of Saint Catherine of Alexandria*, 1550. Forlì, Pinacoteca. (Photo: Guerra)

the Company of Saint Ursula.[74] Both the iconography and the destination of this painting, mentioned by Giorgio Vasari, reveal its Brescian inspiration. On the left side, Saint Catherine is espoused with the placement on her finger of a ring, the customary image of the mystical marriage; but she is also crowned by an angel and followed by virgins, who are differentiated from the traditional followers of Ursula by their white head coverings, characteristic of the habit worn by *dimesse*. The fact that Longhi's depiction of Ursuline virgins was painted for the Church of the Buon Gesù in Ravenna solidifies the link with Brescia. The vicar general of Brescia who approved the constitutions of the Company came from Ravenna; the Lateran Canons of Sant'Afra were headquartered in that city; and in Ravenna in the second decade of the sixteenth century, the Blessed Margherita and Gentile da Russi founded a company similar to Angela Merici's. This company gave rise to a congregation of clerks regular taking the name Buon Gesù, which built the church where Longhi's painting was hung.[75]

The Third State

In its original Rule, Merici's Company of Saint Ursula took the form of a female confraternity that governed itself through a system of patronage. Subsequent changes in governance assigned a greater role to diocesan authorities, and finally the Company was placed directly under the bishop. For this reason the companies of Ursulines founded in the post-Tridentine period, while modeled on the Brescian original, had their own Rules and a distinctively civic character.[76] By this time, the Company of Saint Ursula had already assumed a configuration and purpose different from that of the Merician foundation. Above all, although the Company had not been officially recognized as a religious order (a status that could not have been attained without solemn vows and the obligation of enclosure), its members had achieved legitimation as a third state within the Church: some dedicated themselves to contemplation, others to action, and still others to a "mixed life."

In the letter prefacing the Rule of 1587 with which Bishop Giovanni Leoni founded the Company of Saint Ursula in the diocese of Ferrara, the author of the preface defended the institution against those who considered it impossible for women to maintain chastity in the world and unwise for them to live in their fathers' houses, where moral dangers lurked. Asserting that this institution gave new life to an ancient tradition in the church, he lauded the idea of an honorable "third state," in which young women could serve God as virgins in their own homes.[77] Agostino Valier, who wrote the first treatise on the status of Ursulines and *dimesse*, also approved their mode of life, only slightly inferior in perfection to that of nuns:

> I want you to consider that among the four praiseworthy statuses of women, yours is the second perfect grade, for in God's Church some are married women, some widows, some virgins; and among the virgins some have taken vows and are enclosed in convents, while others live outside in their own houses.[78]

Social consequences stemming from acceptance of the third state are made clear in the information provided by the Rules of companies founded in various cities about recruitment of Ursulines, particularly in the chapters concerning acceptance of virgins. These texts show that most young women who entered these companies were of modest social extraction. Many of the Rules specified that the institutions were designed especially for those who could not afford the dowries necessary for entering convents.

No doubt one incentive for poor girls to enter such a company was the hope of receiving protection and financial support. By the last quarter of the sixteenth century, however, a change is evident: even young noblewomen were becoming Ursulines. This trend, reflecting both the Church's recognition of the "third state" and society's acceptance of "virgins in the house," was accentuated by a restriction of access to convents through caps on membership and increased monastic dowries, as well as by the crisis of traditional third orders for women. A significant attestation to social acceptance of "virgins in the house" is the recognition of the nobility of this state expressed by Onofrio Zarrabini, one of the best-known writers on nobility and honor in the second half of the sixteenth century. After arguing that true nobility consists in the possibility that men and women of low estate can render their families famous through their virtuous actions, Zarrabini exhorted virgins to be vigilant, praising especially those "who live in their own houses": "Blessed are you, then, who persevere in such a noble state amidst the uproar of the world. . . . Your room is heaven, your world is divine contemplation, and your spouse is Christ."[79]

Expansion upward, toward the elite, of the Ursulines' social base obviously restricted access by girls in humble circumstances or on the verge of poverty, as we can see, for example, in the Rule of the Bolognese institute founded in 1608.[80] As noted earlier, increasing selectivity in admission to convents swelled Ursuline "vocations," bringing into this status of life a considerable proportion of women destined to remain unmarried. The full acceptance they gained from the Church and the religious and social purposes they were recognized as serving brought about yet another change in mentality: a decreasing preoccupation about young women "in danger."

Virginity had long been considered a possession threatened on the outside by rape and prostitution and on the inside, within the home, by incest. By the end of the sixteenth century, anxiety about protecting young women bereft of male and familial supervision had diminished. The new marital status of *dimesse*, "virgins in the house," circumscribed the liminal condition of unmarried women by bringing them under ecclesiastical tutelage. Authorized to remain virgins because they were brides of Christ, Ursulines could dedicate themselves to the service of Church and family, by which they were recognized as "coadjutors." In the family—rather than against it, like the female "saints" of the Middle Ages, who were constrained to leave their homes or await the death of family members before dedicating themselves to the religious life[81]—the brides of Christ pursued their project of holiness at home, adapting themselves willingly or unwillingly to collaborating in the education of other people's children. Thus they were prototypes of the maiden aunt, so much a part of the Italian bourgeois family until the middle of the twentieth century.

An Italian version of this essay will appear in *Rivista di storia e letteratura religiosa*. I wish to express my appreciation to those who offered helpful suggestions during discussions at the conference and after reading the manuscript, particularly Thomas Connolly, Robert Kendrick, Deanna Lenzi, Sara Matthews Grieco, Giuliana Nobili, Adriano Prosperi, Pierangelo Schiera, Anne Jacobson Schutte, and Carolyn Valone. I am particularly grateful to Anne Jacobson Schutte for preparing the English translation.

Notes

1. In addition to the monographs cited below, see my brief biographical article on Angela Merici (with iconography different from that included here) in *Histoire des saints et de la sainteté chrétienne*, vol. 7, *Une Église éclatée*, under the direction of André Vauchez (Paris: Hachette, 1986), pp. 67–76.

2. Elizabeth Rapley, *The Dévotes: Women and Church in Seventeenth-Century France* (Kingston, Ontario: McGill-Queens University Press, 1990).

3. Josef Grisar, S.J., *Maria Wards Institut vor Römischen Kongregationen (1616–1630)* (Rome: Pontificia Università Gregoriana, 1966).

4. Thérèse Ledòchowska, *Angèle Merici et la Compagnie de Ste. Ursule à la lumière des documents* (Rome and Milan: Ancora, 1968; and Luciana Mariani, Elisa Tarolli, and Marie Seynaeve, *Angela Merici: Contributo per una biografia* (Milan: Marietti, 1986).

5. *Strutture ecclesiastiche in Italia e Germania prima della Riforma*, ed. Peter Johanek and Paolo Prodi (Bologna: Il Mulino, 1983), John W. O'Malley, "Was Ignatius Loyola a Church Reformer? How to Look at Early Modern Catholicism," *Catholic Historical Review* 77 (1991): 177–93.

6. "La fondatione di questa santa Compagnia fu una certa Angela, et di nome et di vita, contadinella di sangue, ma di santità nobile e famosa . . . et mentre che nel campo l'altre sue compagne mietitore andavano a merenda, lei si slontanava all'oratione; et una volta elevata in spirito, parevagli aprirsi il cielo et uscir una processione meravigliosa d'angeli e di verginelle, scambievolmente a duoi a duoi, gli angeli in varie sorte di stromenti sonavano et le verginelle cantavano. . . . Et passando oltre la processione arrivò una vergine sua sorella . . . la qual poco avanti era andata al paradiso, la quale . . . le predisse che Dio si voleva servir di lei, et che essa havrebbe fatta una Compagnia di Vergini, la qual si doveva dilatar, e simili cose." Letter printed in the *Regola della Compagnia di santa Orsola . . .* (Milan: Pacifico Ponte, 1569), pp. 27–32; reproduced in Mariani et al., *Angela Merici*, p. 531.

7. Anton Blok, "Notes on the Concept of Virginity in Mediterranean Societies," in *Women and Men in Spiritual Culture, XIV–XVII Centuries: A Meeting of North and South*, ed. Elisja Schulte van Kessel (The Hague: Netherlands Government Publishing House, 1986), pp. 27–33.

8. See the articles in *Quaderni storici* 75 (1990), an issue devoted to the theme of virginity, especially the introduction by Lucetta Scaraffia, pp. 701–14.

9. On the institutional structure and the post-Tridentine evolution of the Company of Saint Ursula, see the two biographies of Merici cited in n. 4. On the social considerations linked to the Church's approval of the Company, see the section on "The Third State" below.

10. See Adolf Katzenellenbogen, *Allegories of the Virtues and Vices in Medieval Art: From Early Christian Times to the Thirteenth Century* (Toronto: University of Toronto Press, in association with Medieval Academy of America, 1982).

11. Petrus de Natalibus, *Catalogus sanctorum et gestorum eorum ex diversis voluminibus collectus* (Lyon: Jacques Saccon, 1514), f. xlvii. The depiction of Jacob with his eyes open expresses the significance of the vision. Dreams are the way in which the Bible indicates a connection between humans and God that occurs via revelation. In the Middle Ages the distinction between dream and vision was not yet well defined. The recipient of a vision might be depicted with eyes closed (emphasizing the passive aspect of dreaming) or with eyes open (expressing active participation in the vision). See Jean Claude Schmitt, "Bildhaftes Denken," in *Träume im Mittelalter: Ikonologische Studien*, ed. Agostino Paravicini Bagliani and Giorgio Stabile (Stuttgart: Belser, 1989), pp. 9–40.

12. Antonio Meli da Crema, *Libro di vita contemplativa: Lectione, meditatione, oratione, contemplatione: Scala dil Paradiso* (Brescia: Giovanni Antonio Morandi da Gandino, 1527), p. 53.

13. A description of the paintings in the church and oratory of Saint Ursula and in the parish church of Desenzano is included in the material assembled in the eighteenth century to prepare the case for Merici's canonization. Of the twenty-two paintings in the church, executed in 1670–71, sixteen depict Angela. The notary Angelo Facconi's description of the painting representing her vision may be found in Mariani et al., *Angela Marici*, p. 623.

14. Anonymous engraving with the inscription "Mater Angela Merici . . . Fundatrix Ordinis Societ. S. Ursulae" (1768). In five frames the engraving illustrates the educational function of the Company and the miracles of the blessed foundress. It contains all the symbolic elements connected with the Company from the time of its foundation: below, the winged angel representing Merici; above, Ursula and a Franciscan preacher with banners; on the left, the ship bearing Ursula and her companions on their pilgrimage to Rome; on the right, the ladder of her vision climbed by virgins with crowns and palm fronds. I thank Luciana Mariani for having given me the engraving and permission to reproduce it.

15. G. Lombardi, *Vita della B. Angela Merici, fondatrice della Compagnia di Sant'Orsola* (Venice, 1778), frontispiece.

16. Two examples of recent scholarship are Robert Darnton, "The Symbolic Element in History," *Journal of Modern History* 58 (1986): 218–43; and Jeffrey F. Hamburger, "The Visual and the Visionary: The Image in Late Medieval Monastic Devotions," *Viator* 20 (1989): 161–203 (with extensive bibliographical citations).

17. On the origin of the Company and the social status of its earliest members, see Mariani et al., *Angela Merici*. On oral reading of the Rule, see Figure 11.5. Evidence of the first adherents' illiteracy is provided in the will dated 15 September 1558 of a noblewoman, Ginevra Luzzaga. She bequeathed a sum to the Brescian convent of Sant'Afra, where Angela Merici was buried, to endow perpetual reading by a priest of "the Rule of the women belonging to the Company of Saint Ursula." Archivio di Stato di Milano, *Fondo di Religione, Brescia S. Affra alias S. Salvatore*, no. 3353, *Thesoro spirituale e temporale della chiesa e monastero di S. Affra di Brescia*, f. 27.

18. See the bibliography in *Emblemata: Handbuch zur Sinnbildkunst des XVI, und XVII, Jahrhunderts*, ed. Arthur Henkel and Albrecht Schöne (Stuttgart: J. B. Metzler, 1976).

19. Sara F. Matthews Grieco, *Ange ou diablesse: La représentation de la femme au XVIe siècle* (Paris: Flammarion, 1991).

20. A reproduction of this portrait may be found in *Alessandro Bonvicino: Il Moretto*, ed. Valerio Guazzoni (catalogue of the exhibition held in the convent of S. Giulia, Brescia, 18 June–20 November 1988) (Bologna: Nuova Alfa, 1988), pp. 127–28. On Moretto and Brescian painting in the sixteenth century, see also Valerio Guazzoni, *Moretto: Il tema sacro* (Brescia: Grafo, 1981); and Guazzoni, "Temi religiosi e contenuti devozionali," in *Pittura del Cinquecento a Brescia*, ed. Mina Gregori et al. (Milan: Cassa di Risparmio delle Province Lombarde, 1986), pp. 19–201.

21. This painting is reproduced in my article on Angela Merici cited in n. 1.

22. Girolamo Romanino, *The Mystical Marriage of St. Catherine* (Figure 11.10), detail. I am very grateful to Carolyn Valone for obtaining excellent reproductions of this painting, on which see also n. 60.

23. Merici is portrayed with the staff in Giovanni Rolli's engraving, which serves as a frontispiece to the Rule of the Company printed in Bologna in 1672. She appears with the banner in an engraved sheet printed in 1768. Many paintings in the Brescian Church of Saint Ursula built in the seventeenth century show Angela with these attributes.

24. Reproduced in Matthews Grieco, *Ange ou diablesse*, pp. 111–13. Alciato's motto reads: "Vera haec effigies innuptae est Palladis, eius / Hic Draco, qui dominae constitit ante pedes / Cur divae comes hoc animal? Custodia rerum / Huic data, sic lucos sacraque templo colit. / Innuptas opus est cura asservare puellas / pervigili, laqueos undique tendit amor." Andrea Alciato, *Emblemata* (Lyon: Guillaume Rouillé, 1548), p. 25.

25. In the Company of Saint Ursula, "virgin colonels" (*vergini colonelle*) were assigned the task of protecting virginity. In her *Arricordi* Merici left them this message: "You will exert yourselves, each of you, to be faithful to and solicitous about the brides whom you are commissioned to protect, and to stand guard over them, like most vigilant shepherds and good ministers" ("Ve sforzareti, ognuno dal canto sua, a esser fidele e sollecite circa le sua sponse che vi sono state commesse da custodirli, et star sopra la lor guardia, a fozza di vigilantissime pastore et bone ministre"). Mariani et al., *Angela Merici*, p. 507.

26. See Adriano Prosperi, "L'Europa cristiana e il mondo: Alle origini dell'idea di missione," *Dimensioni e problemi della ricerca storica* 2 (1991): 189–220.

27. *Predicazione francescana e società veneta nel Quattrocento: Committenza, ascolto, ricezione*, Atti del II Convegno internazionale di studi francescani (Padova, 26-27-28 marzo 1987), *Le Venezie francescane*, n.s. 6 (1989): 31–60.

28. For the Middle Ages, see Anna Benvenuti Papi, *"Il castro poenitentiae": Santità e società femminile nell'Italia medievale* (Rome: Herder, 1990); for the early modern period, see my brief essay, "Foemina viatrix: Forme della partecipazione femminile alla 'missione' fra Cinque e Seicento," forthcoming.

29. See Guy de Tervarent, *La légende de Sainte Ursule dans la littérature et l'art du Moyen-Âge*, vol. 1 (Paris: Les Éditions G. Van Oest, 1939).

30. See *Die H. Ursula und ihre Elftausend Jungfraunen*, catalogue of the exhibition at the Wallraf-Richartz Museum, Cologne (6 July–3 September 1978), ed. Frank Günter Zehnder (Cologne: Wallraf-Richartz Museum, 1978); Frank Günter Zehnder, *Sankt Ursula: Legende, Verehrung, Bildervelt* (Cologne: Wienand Verlag, 1985).

31. Zehnder, *Sankt Ursula*, pp. 138–45. These images of Saint Ursula are reproduced in Zehnder, *Die H. Ursula*, pp. 64–65. On French treatments of the mystical winepress, see Emile Mâle, *L'art religieux de la fin du Moyen Âge en France: étude sur l'iconographie du Moyen Âge et sur ses sources d'inspiration* (Paris: A. Colin, 1908), pp. 98–122.

32. "Al cui consiglio si raunavano le Vergine da diversi regni. . . . Aparechiate le victuaglie per tre anni, revela la regina a commilitoni i suoi secreti et

coniurano tutti nella 'nova militia.'" Jacopo da Voragine, *Leggende et historie de santi*, trans. Nicolò Malerbi (Venice: Nicolas Jenson, 1475), p. 238.

33. *Tomaso da Modena*, ed. Luigi Menegazzi, exhibition catalogue (Treviso: S. Caterina dei Servi di Maria, 1979), pp. 140–56. See also R. Gibby, *L'occhio di Tomaso: Sulla formazione di Tomaso da Modena* (Treviso: 1981). See also *Il ritorno di Orsola*, catalogue of the exhibition.

34. Ludovico Zorzi, *Carpaccio e la rappresentazione di sant'Orsola* (Turin: Giulio Einaudi, 1988).

35. Françoise Bordon, "La peinture narrative de Carpaccio dans le cycle de s.te Ursule," *Memorie dell'Istituto veneto di scienze, lettere ed arti, Classe di scienze morali, lettere ed arti* 36, no. 4 (1985); Patricia Fortini Brown, *Venetian Narrative Painting in the Age of Carpaccio* (New Haven, CT: Yale University Press, 1988).

36. Giovanni Sabadino degli Arienti, *Gynevera de le clare donne*, ed. Corrado Ricci and Alberto Bacchi Della Lega (Scelta di curiosità letterarie inedite o rare dal secolo XIII al XIX, dispensa CCXXIII) (Bologna: Commissione per i testi di lingua, 1969), pp. 100–114. The tale "De Janna Polcella gaya de Franza" was told to the author by a Bolognese merchant, who had heard it in France from old soldiers of the king.

37. Jacopo Filippo Foresti da Bergamo, *De claris selectisque mulieribus* (Ferrara: Lorenzo Rossi di Valenza, 1487).

38. Foresti, *De claris selectisque mulieribus* f. CLVII. For Joan's story, Foresti drew from the same source as Arienti. This woodcut appears to be the first printed image of Joan in military dress carrying a bow. In French miniatures of this period she is depicted in woman's garb with a lance or a sword; see Zarri, in *Histoire des saints*, pp. 170–77.

39. Foresti, *De claris selectisque mulieribus*, f. CXLIV.

40. Foresti, *De claris selectisque mulieribus*, f. CXXXIX. On the triple halo-crown, see Antonio Volpato, "Il tema agiografico della triplice aureola nei secoli XIII–XIV," in *Culto dei santi, istituzioni e classi sociali in età preindustriale*, ed. Sofia Boesch-Gajano and Lucia Sebastiani (L'Aquila and Rome: Japadre, 1984), pp. 510–25; and Antonio Volpato, "'Corona aurea' e 'corona aureola': Ordini e meriti nella ecclesiologia medievale," *Bullettino dell'Istituto storico italiano per il medioevo e Archivio muratoriano* 91 (1984): 115–82. Catherine of Siena is shown with the triple crown in the frontispiece of her *Epistole* (Venice: Aldo Manuzio, 1500); see Henri Dominique Saffrey, "Les images populaires de saints dominicains à Venise au XVe siècle et l'édition par Alde Manuce des 'Epistoles' de sainte Catherine de Sienne," *Italia medioevale e umanistica* 25 (1982): 241–99; E. Halland and H. Uhr, "*Aureola super Aureum*: Crowns and Symbols of Special Distinction for Saints in Late Gothic and Renaissance Iconography," *Art Bulletin* 67 (1985): 567–630. On the proliferation in Italy of female mystics who imitated Catherine's model of life, see Gabriella Zarri, *Le sante vive: Profezie di corte e devozione femminile tra '400 e '500* (Turin: Rosenberg & Sellier, 1990).

41. By intention a martyr, by actions a virgin, by more a teacher,
Thus, rich Angela, you rejoice in triple gold
Recently you were Angela, in ways and life a teacher
Now, as a tutor, you come to the homeland and fortress.

The author of this verse was the Regular Lateran Canon Valeriano da Bergamo. Mariani et al., *Angela Merici*, p. 587.

42. This monastery belonged to the Canons of San Giorgio in Alga, who disseminated the ideals of the *Devotio moderna* and the spirituality of Saint Lorenzo Giustiniani. See Guazzoni, "Temi religiosi," p. 20.

43. *Monumenta Ignatiana, series secunda: Exercitia spiritualis S. Ignatii de Loyola et eorum Directoria*, ed. José Calveras and Candido de Dalmases, Monumenta Historica Societatis Iesu, 100 (Rome: Institutum Historicum Societatis Iesu), 1: 676 (Italian version [1555] of the 1st ed. of the *Exercitia*). See also Prosperi, "L'Europa cristiana," p. 212.

44. "And then she saw two great armies, one of which had as its standard a red and white banner on which was painted the Virgin Mother with her Son in her arms, and above it an unadorned cross. The other army had a black banner on which was painted a horrible face." ("Vidde già due grand'Esserciti, uno de i quali havea per insegna un stendardo bianco e rosso nel qual era dipinta la vergine Madre con il Figlio nelle braccia, di sopra eravi una croce senza altra pittura. L'altro Essercito havea un stendardo negro, nel quale v'era dipinta un horenda faccia.") Despite suffering great losses, the first army won the ensuing battle. A few months after having received this vision, the holy woman came to understand its significance. "Led onto a plain, she saw a pavilion on which was written the name of Jesus. Above it was a figure of God holding the world in His hand. . . . On the right were an altar was set up to celebrate [communion] and a huge army. On the left side there was another enormous army, whose very handsome general was dressed in golden vestments." ("Condotta in una pianura, vidde un Padiglione nel quale eravi questo nome Giesù. Di sopra eravi una figura d'Iddio qual teneva il Mondo in mano. . . . Alla parte destra eravi apparecchiato un Altare per celebrare con un grandissimo Essercito; Era dalla part manca un'altra copiossisimo Essercito il cui capo era bellissimo di corpo con vestimenti d'oro.") Then she was carried onto a field where she witnessed a fierce battle between the Christian and Turkish armies, which the Christians won. The general on the left, the Turk, was led among the Christian commanders, "one of whom had three crowns on his head; he was taken to the altar, and there, kneeling with many of his warriors, he was baptized" ("Uno haveva tre corone in capo; fu condotto all'altare et ivi inginocchatosi con molti dei suo guerrieri fu battezzato"). Giovanfrancesco Pico della Mirandola and Pietro Martire Morelli, *Compendio delle cose mirabili della venerabil serva di Dio Catterina da Raconisi Vergine integerrima del sacro ordine della Penitenza di S. Domenico distinto in Dieci libri* (Bologna: n.p., 1680), p. 92.

45. *Legendario de sancti vulgare historiado novamente revisto et con summa diligentia castigato trad. dal Manerbi Venet.* (Venice: Agostino Zanni da Portese, 29 April 1516), f. CLXXI; Jacopo da Voragine, *Legendario delle vite de santi . . . Tradotto per il R.D. Nicoló Manerbio, Nuovamente ridotto a miglior lingua, riformato, purgato . . . di vaghe figure ornato* (Venice: Domenico and Giovan Battista Guerra, 1586).

46. "et massimamente delle più attempate et experte Vergini della Compagnia"; "che, quando più saranno tanto mazzor allegreza se pigliarà, et maggiormente Giesù Christo signor nostro sarà in mezzo di noi, et più se ne manifestarà la di lui virtù et possanza." Mariani et al., *Angela Merici*, p. 434. The explicit state-

ment that the Rule was composed in consultation with senior members of the Company, though confirming Merici's contribution to the drafting of founding charters, excludes attributing them solely to her.

47. Cozzano's writings may be found in ibid., pp. 566–82.

48. According to Cozzano, Angela Merici called the new congregation "not her Company, but Jesus Christ's" ("Compagnia non sua, ma di Iesu Christo"), which confirms an inspiration analogous to that of the new clerks regular of the Society of Jesus. Ibid., p. 559.

49. A woodcut entitled *Concerning the Rule of the Abbess* is included in *Prologo de l'Ordine del vivere ne li monasteri de monache et temporale et spirituale*, an illustrated rule for women published as the appendix to Saint Jerome, *Vita e epistole colla Regola del vivere nei monasteri di monache volgarizzate da frate Matteo da Ferrara Gesuoto* (Ferrara: Lorenzo de Rossi da Valenza, 12 October 1497), reproduced in Suor Lucia Pioppi, *Diario (1541–1612)*, ed. Rolando Bussi (Modena: Panini, 1982). The image of the church of Antioch is in Petrus de Natalibus, *Catalogus sanctorum, vitas, passiones et miracula commodissime annectens ex variis voluminibus selectis* (Lyon: Gilles and Jacques Huguetan, 1542), chap. CXL.

50. Piotr Skubiszewski, "Ecclesia, Christianitas, Regnum et Sacerdotium dans l'art des Xe–XIe siècles: Idées et structures des images," *Cahiers de civilisation médievale* 28 (1985): 133–79.

51. Brescia, Biblioteca Queriniana, Ms. K.VI.1: *Descrittione dell'oratorio nel quale la Beata Madre Angela dette principio alla Compagnia di S. Orsola*, ff. 102–4.

52. See the description in Mariani et al., *Angela Merici*, pp. 621–26.

53. A political and institutional profile of Brescia in Merici's day is provided by Cesare Pasero, "Il dominio veneto fino all'incendio della Loggia (1426–1575)," in *Storia di Brescia*; II: *La dominazione veneta, 1426–1575* (Rome: Treccani, 1963), vol. 2, pp. 1–393.

54. "Non veggio io Monastero alcuno di Femine dove molte non sieno che mi rappresentino hor Eustochio, hor Marcella et hor Blesilla, ne conosco io infinite con le quale parlando dico fram me stesso, tal esser dovea la gloria Melania, così modesta et santa crederò fusse la devotissima Asella o la Romana Paola." Vincenzo Maggi, *Un brieve trattato dell'Eccellentia delle Donne composto dal prestantissimo Philosopho (il Maggio) et di latina lingua in italiano tradotto* (Brescia: Damiano Turlino, 1545), p. 39v.

55. See Silvana Seidel Menchi, *Erasmo in Italia, 1520–1580* (Turin: Bollati Boringhieri, 1987), p. 388.

56. See Susanna Peyronel Rambaldi, "Educazione evangelica e catechistica: Da Erasmo al gesuita Antonio Possevino," in *Ragione e "civiltas": Figure del vivere associato nella cultura del '500 europeo*, ed. Jean Claude Margolin, Davide Bigalli, Alberto Tenenti, Alfonso Ingegno, and Cesare Vasoli (Milan: Franco Angeli, 1986), pp. 73–92.

57. *Regola della Nova Compagnia di santa Orsola di Brescia: per la quale si vede come si habbiano a governar le vergini di detta compagnia accioche vivendo christianamente possino doppo la lor morte fruir i beni di vita eterna* (Brescia: Damiano Turlino, n.d.); Caroline Walker Bynum, *Holy Feast and Holy Fast: The Religious Significance of Food to Medieval Women* (Berkeley: University of California Press, 1987).

58. "Per divina rivelatione fosse venuta ad abitare acioche nel luogo del mar-

tirio et nel terreno irrigato del pretioso sangue di santi amici di Christo nacesse et germogliasse il nuovo stato et instituto verginale di questi nostri tempi." Mattia Bellintani da Salò, *Vita della B. Angela da Desenzano*, chap. 22, p. 16. A partial edition of this life is in Matthias a Salò, *Historia Capuccina*, ed. Melchiorre da Pobladura (Rome: Institutum Historicum Ordinis Minorum Capuccinorum, 1946), pp. 77–113.

59. Bellintani, *Vita*, Preface.

60. *Mostra di Girolamo Romanino*, exhibition catalogue, ed. Gaetano Panazza (Brescia: Comitato della mostra di Girolamo Romanino, 1965), pp. 116–17.

61. "ferma intentione di servir a Dio in tal sorte di vita," *Regola della Nova Compagnia*, chap. 2.

62. See Thomas H. Connolly, "The Cult and Iconography of St. Cecilia before Raphael," in *Indagini per un dipinto: La Santa Cecilia di Raffaello*, intro. Andrea Emiliani (Bologna: Alfa, 1983), pp. 119–39.

63. On the institutional structure of the Company and the social origin of its first members, see Mariani et al., *Angela Merici*, pp. 221–56.

64. Agostino Valier, bishop of Verona (d. 1606), is credited with coining the term *dimesse* for virgins belonging to the Company of Saint Ursula, but the same name was used for an analogous company founded in Vicenza by the Franciscan Antonio Pagani in 1584 that spread throughout Venetian territory. The term, referring to the modest garb worn by virgins, even noble ones who renounced the pomp deemed appropriate to laywomen of their social class, thus became synonymous with a status of life. The definition of the "third status" ("terzo stato laudabile nella Chiesa") comes from the prefatory letter "to the Christian reader" in the *Regole della Compagnia delle Vergini di Santa Orsola, stampate per ordine del molto Ill. e R.mo Mons. Paolo Leone Vescovo di Ferrara* (Ferrara: Vittore Baldini, 1587), p. 8.

65. On the reorganization of the post-Tridentine Church, see above all John Bossy, *Christianity in the West, 1400–1700* (Oxford: Oxford University Press, 1985).

66. See André Vauchez, *La Sainteté en Occident aux derniers siècles du Moyen Âge, d'après les procès de canonisation et les documents hagiographiques* (Rome: École Française de Rome; Paris: Diffusion de Boccard, 1981); and Gabriella Zarri, "Prophètes de court dans l'Italie de la Renaissance," *Mélanges de l'École Française de Rome: Moyen Âge, Temps Modernos* 102 (1990): 649–75.

67. *Ordine, et Ceremonie che si fanno con le Vergini che vogliono entrar nella Compagnia di S. Orsola di Brescia* (Brescia: Damiano Turlino, n.d.). (The typeface of this book is the same as that employed by Turlino for the first edition of the Ursuline *Regola*.) I have consulted the exemplar held by the Biblioteca Apostolica Vaticana. On the problem of the company's juridical status, see Angela Faller, *Consecrazione e legame giuridico nella Compagnia di S. Orsola: Studio storico giuridico* (Brescia: Queriniana, 1975).

68. "Accipe signum Christi in capite tuo, ut uxor eius efficiaris," *Ordine et Ceremonie*, p. 8v. The papal ritual approved by Innocent VII, first printed in 1458, extended to the entire Church the rite of consecrating virgins put in use by Guillaume Durant at the end of the thirteenth century. Its wording—"wife" (*uxor*), rather than "bride" (*sponsa*)—assimilates the rite of religious profession to the mat-

rimonial bond. The reformed *Pontificale Romano* promulgated by Clement VIII in 1595, however, dropped the term *uxor* and returned to the formula of consecration adopted by the Roman Curia in the thirteenth century, in which the symbolism of the crown had an explicit eschatological meaning. See René Metz, "La couronne et l'anneau dans le consécration des Vierges: Origine et évolution des deux rites dans la liturgie latine," in his *La femme et l'enfant dans le droit canonique médieval* (London: Variorum Reprints, 1985).

69. *Ordo admittendi Virgines ad monasterii ingressum habitumque regularem suscipiendi Ritus item servendus ad professionis missionem secundum morem Congregationis Cassinensis* (Milan: Heirs of Pacifico Ponte and Giovanni Battista Piccaleo, 1607), p. 23.

70. See Korbinian Ritzer, *Formen, Riten, und religioses Brauchtum der Eheschliessung in den christlichen Kirchen des ersten Jahrtausends* (Münster, Westf.: Aschendorff, 1981); René Metz, *Les consécrations des Vierges dans l'Église romaine* (Paris: Presses Universitaires de France, 1954); and C. Ramais, *La consegracion de la mujer en las liturgias occidentales* (Rome: LEF, 1990).

71. E. Ann Matter, *The Voice of My Beloved: The Song of Songs in Western Medieval Christianity* (Philadelphia: University of Pennsylvania Press, 1990).

72. See, for example, Jean Gaudemet, *Le mariage en Occident: les moeurs et le droit* (Paris: Éditions du Cerf, 1987).

73. Guazzoni, *Alessandro Bonvicino, Il Moretto*, pp. 196–97, 162–63; Pier Virgilio Begni Redona, *Alessandro Bonvicino: Il Moretto da Brescia* (Brescia: La Scuola, 1988), pp. 432–35.

75. *Luca Longhi e la pittura su tavola in Romagna nel '500*, ed. Jadranka Bettini (Bologna: Alfa, 1982), pp. 48–51.

75. On the religious ambience of Ravenna in Margherita's and Gentile's day, see Zarri, *Le sante vive*, pp. 98–99, and the bibliography cited there. The rule of their company was published in the Regular Lateran Canon Serafino da Fermo's *Opere spirituali* (Vicenza: Presso gli heredi di Perin Libraro, 1596), which directly connect Merici's circle with religious groups in Emilia (Ravenna and Bologna) and with the Barnabites. The text is translated into Latin in the *Acta Sanctorum* (28 January), section on Margherita and Gentile da Ravenna.

76. The Brescian institution spread rapidly into the Veneto, Lombardy, and Emilia. On expansion into Milanese territory, see Gualberto Vigotti, *San Carlo Borromeo e la Compagnia di Sant'Orsola* (Milan: Polo, 1972); on Novara and environs, see Thomas Deutscher, "Carlo Bascapé e la riforma delle monache di Novara," in *Da Carlo Borromeo a Carlo Bascapé: La pastorale di Carlo Borromeo e il Sacro Monte di Arona* (Novara: Marietti, 1985), pp. 299–315.

77. The letter is entitled "A brief compendium of the institution and status of these virgins, which will serve not only to disabuse those who are mistaken but also to instruct the ignorant and to confirm and inspire those who have entered" ("Breve compendio della institutione e dello stato di queste Vergini che servirà e per sgannare chi è ingannato, e per ammaestrar chi non sa e per confirmare et inanimare quelle che sono entrate"). Having proved that the status of virgins in their own homes dated back to the earliest tradition of the Church and had enjoyed

such immediate success in society "that at any one time one could find as many as twenty thousand virgins in a single city" ("che si sono ritrovate in un medesimo tempo sino ventimila Vergini in una sola città"), the author demonstrated the social utility of the institution. *Regole della Compagnia delle Vergini di Santa Orsola*, pp. 8–9.

78. Agostino Valiero, *Modo di vivere proposto alle Vergini che si chiamano Dimesse, overo che vivono nelle lor case con voto o proposito di perpetua castità, novella impressione accuratissima* (Padua: Giuseppe Comino, 1744), p. 5.

79. "che vivono nelle loro case. . . . Beate voi dunque mentre perseverete in così nobile stato nei strepiti del mondo. . . . La stanza vostra è il cielo, il vostro mondo è la divina contemplation e il vostro sposo è Christo." Onofrio Zarrabini, *Dello stato verginale maritale et vedovile libri tre* (Venice: Francesco de' Franceschi Senese, 1586), p. 19. On Zarrabini, see Claudio Donato, *L'idea di nobiltà in Italia: Secoli XIV–XVIII* (Rome and Bari: Laterza, 1988), pp. 221, 243.

80. The first chapter of this rule, "Of the condition of those who should be received in the Company," prescribes that an accepted applicant "have an inheritance to support her, or be capable of earning her keep through her own industry or have someone willing to help her for the sake of charity, or [be able to sustain herself] in some other way at the Congregation's discretion" ("habbi patrimonio da sostenarsi, o sia atta con la propria industria guadagnarsi il vivere, o habbi, chi per carità la vogli aiutare, o in altro modo a giudicio della Congregatione"). *Regole della Compagnia di S. Orsola eretta in Bologna da Mons. Illustriss. e Reverendiss. Alfonso Paleotti Arcivescovo di detta Città* (Bologna: Vittorio Benacci, 1608), p. 18.

81. See, for example, Lucetta Scaraffia, *La santa degli impossibili: Vicende e significato della devozione a santa Rita* (Turin: Rosenberg & Sellier, 1990).

Part III

Women's Artistic Expression: Sixteenth and Seventeenth Centuries

Elissa B. Weaver

12. Suor Maria Clemente Ruoti, Playwright and Academician

> A virginella rinchiusa fra quattro mura la via del Parnaso . . . è non pur malagevole, ma quasi incognita. Le Muse par che aborriscano cotanta semplicità.
>
> —Maria Clemente Ruoti, *Giacob patriarca*

Convent playwrights have been little known to the secular world. In Italy their plays were intended for convent performance before an audience of convent women and their lay female relatives, and even the attendance of the latter was not always welcomed by convent authorities. Only rarely, it seems, did the talent of a convent writer come to the attention of a larger public. Beatrice del Sera in the 1550s expressed surprise that her work was known beyond the confines of her convent in Prato, noting that she had written her play, the *Amor di virtú*, "without thinking that it would ever be noticed by learned men" ("senza pensare che mai dai dotti dovessi esser vista").[1] The plays of a few nuns, Raffaella de' Sernigi, Cherubina Venturelli, and Maria Clemente Ruoti, were published, Sernigi's in the late sixteenth, the others in the seventeenth century.[2] In the case of Maria Clemente Ruoti we have two plays, the second written twenty years after the first; they represent very different moments of her life and art and document, I will argue, her shift from writing for an all-female convent audience to writing for an audience that would also include Florence's literati—laypeople and clerics alike. These and other convent playwrights whose work has survived help us today to imagine the richness of convent culture in the early modern period.

* * *

Maria Clemente Ruoti was born Ottavia, the daughter of Prospero Ruoti, in 1609 or 1610, in the Mugello, just northeast of Florence; she died in 1690 in her convent, the Franciscan house of San Girolamo and San Francisco, also called San Giorgio because of its location on the Costa di San Giorgio in Florence.[3] She wrote plays for convent production: the *Giacob patriarca* (*Jacob, the Patriarch*), a five-act play in hendecasyllabic verse published in Pisa "per Francesco delle Dote" in 1637, and the *Natal di Cristo* (*Birth of Christ*), a three-act play, primarily in prose but with some verse passages, known only in an autograph manuscript in the Riccardiana Library in Florence, though that manuscript contains a publishing privilege, dated 1657.[4] It is likely that in the twenty-year period that separates the two texts Maria Clemente wrote other plays as well that are now lost.

In passages prefixed to both plays the author presents herself as a writer who strives to perfect her art though she works under difficult constraints, the circumstances of convent life. The *Giacob* is dedicated to the Grand Duchess of Tuscany, Vittoria della Rovere, wife of Ferdinando II de' Medici, who attended the convent production of the play.[5] The dedication begins with a customary disclaimer, the author's avowal of her inadequacy, which, however, she attributes largely to her condition: she is an enclosed nun and unable, therefore, to familiarize herself sufficiently with secular literature, either through reading or erudite discussion:

> The road to Parnassus, serenissima Grand Duchess, for a virgin enclosed within four walls, is not only difficult but almost uncharted. The muses, it seems, abhor such simplicity. Poetic illumination is extinguished in the ashes of this habit. The harmony of verse can little be heard by the ear that is bound by a thick wimple. The rules for writing and for versification are incompatible with those of obedience and submission, since the former require diverse and frequent reading and almost constant discussion, and the latter allow few books of only certain limited kinds, while the conversation of literati, seen as adverse to our profession, is prohibited. Therefore, it will not come as a surprise if my little work does not present those attributes that are desirable in a dramatic composition.[6]

Similarly, the address to the reader ("Al cortese lettore") that opens the manuscript prepared for publication of her *Natal di Cristo* discusses the play's infractions of certain rules of the genre and its failure to comply fully with the Aristotelian requirement of verisimilitude ("Men in those times broke the laws of God; surely I can take some liberties with the laws of men").[7] The author justifies her use of fantastic characters, allegories that speak and participate in the action, and she defends the entrance of characters on stage in an order that contradicts current theatrical practice, that is, characters of lesser importance entering and speaking before the protagonists of the action.[8] She appeals to poetic license and her own inadequacy, which she again attributes, at least in part, to her situation:

> I know of no world but the close quarters within these four walls where I enclosed myself when I was nine years old; I have no experience with [theatrical] machines, nor ability to put them into practice, for which reasons I have thought it better to adapt my poetry to my own means rather than the purse of others to my inventions as poets do.[9]

For all her protests to the contrary, Maria Clemente Ruoti demonstrates considerable knowledge of the contemporary theory and practice of dramatic art both in her metatextual statements, such as those just cited, and in her plays themselves. Her knowledge of theater is too extensive to depend solely on the internal convent tradition but must also derive from contacts she had with members of Florence's literary establishment. It is clear that her work came to the attention of a group of literary figures associated with the Academy of the Apatisti. At least one, but perhaps more of her plays were published, and in 1649 she was made a member of the Academy.[10]

The Florentine Academy of the Apatisti was founded in the 1630s by Agostino Coltellini. The name Apatisti was to designate persons "dispassionate" in the sense that they did not allow themselves to be ruled by their passions, but rather by reason, and the Academy was supposedly formed in reaction to the pedantic societies of the time. Its interests were civic and religious, and its chosen patrons were the Virgin of the Immaculate Conception, Saint Mary of Egypt, Saint Augustine, and Saint Filippo Neri.[11] The grand dukes belonged, together with prominent laymen, Italians, and numerous foreigners (in 1638 "Giovanni Milton," in 1746 "Monsieur de Voltaire"), and there were many prelates in their ranks. Maria Clemente Ruoti, included in the 1649 membership list, was the only nun and indeed the first female member, if Anton Francesco Gori's eighteenth-century account is correct.[12] Later it seems four more women were admitted and at least one, the Pisan Selvaggia Borghini, is listed among those members who in the years following 1695 had often addressed the society.[13]

It is unlikely that Maria Clemente Ruoti ever attended any meetings; she herself says in the address to the reader that introduces the *Natal di Cristo* that she had, from the age of nine, been confined within the four walls of her convent. Her nomination was probably honorary, as must have been the nominations of many of the illustrious foreigners.[14] The honor obviously meant that Ruoti's writing had come to the attention of members of the Academy. Coltellini himself was the author of *Il figliuol prodigo* (*The Prodigal Son*), a spiritual comedy, that is, the same theatrical genre cultivated by Maria Clemente Ruoti.[15] It is clear, too, that with its large membership of prelates the Academy sponsored religious theater and religious literature in general. The devotion to Saint Filippo Neri was very likely more than civic pride and reflected a common appreciation of musical and theatrical forms of religious devotion not unlike those of the Oratorians. This would explain the interest in Maria Clemente Ruoti. The abbot Anton Maria Salvini was an active member whose academic discourses were published in three volumes beginning in 1695, and his library (sold to the Riccardi family by his heirs in the eighteenth century) contained a large collection of sixteenth- and seventeenth-century Tuscan spiritual comedies, *sacre rappresentazioni, laudi*, and other devotional literature of monastic provenance, and probably included Maria Clemente Ruoti's manuscript of the *Natal di Cristo*.[16] Finally, the Academy may have had a hand in the publication of Ruoti's *Giacob patriarca*, since two years earlier, in 1635, the same publisher, Francesco delle Dote, published a comedy, *Le tre sirocchie cicalate* (*The Three Sisters Burlesqued*), written by Benedetto Buommattei (the Apatista Boemonte Buttidente).

The first of suor Maria Clemente's extant plays, the *Giacob patriarca*, is introduced by a poem and a passage in Latin prose in praise of the author's exceptional talent and unusual circumstance. The poem—seven quatrains that compare and contrast the convent playwright with the muses—is the work of Carlo Ruberto Dati, a member of the Academy and its first secretary.[17] Translated and paraphrased, it reads: while the virgin muses sing on the slopes of Parnassus, the eternal laurel in their hair, adorned with jewels, their rich and beautiful dresses girded by a band of gold, this virgin (that is, Maria Clemente) is enclosed by consecrated walls within which chaste desire has imprisoned her, and God has given her cropped hair a high and pure crown of white veils. She wears, and not without pain, a dress of rough cloth, a belt of crude rope. The muses sing of vain love, she instead of divine ardor, and rather than the transient laurels of the muses she will earn a place in the chorus of the blessed to sing eternally in praise of God.[18] Niccolò Buonaiuti, another member of the Academy, addresses her in a Latin tribute published with her play, proclaiming the old cliché that she surpassed the others of her sex, exceeded a woman's capacities ("Mariae Clementi Rotae, quae licet foemina, foemineum tamen ingenium supergressa").[19] Although the form is that of a tired convention, the public attention and praise for a convent playwright is unique, and, judging from the two known plays, it is clear that Maria Clemente was an accomplished playwright and that the praise is well deserved.

Convent spiritual comedies and tragedies took their subject matter from the *sacre rappresentazioni*; they staged scenes from the Old and the New Testament, saints' lives, and moral allegories. The plays were justified by church authorities as part of the education of the nuns as well as their recreation.[20] Maria Clemente Ruoti based her first play, the *Giacob patriarca*, on the biblical story of the return of Jacob and his family to Canaan from Mesopotamia, the homeland of his wives Leah and Rachel (Gen. 31: 17–34: 31). The conflicts with Laban and Esau constitute the plot that gives structure to the whole, while two love stories provide subplot interest. The story of the rape of Dinah, Jacob's daughter, is given a happy matrimonial ending, dramatically different from the biblical tale of deceit, revenge, and slaughter, and the love of Jacob's son Reuben for a Mesopotamian shepherdess, Norminda, would seem to be entirely invented. This play enjoyed the approval of the convent's superiors (the frontispiece states, "Con licenza de' Superiori"), so there was apparently no objection to this alteration of the biblical account. Like the story in Genesis, the play stresses faith in God, obedience, God's justice, and the destiny of Jacob's descendants. A strong misogynistic message is conveyed through the recurrent disobedience and foolishness of the women and the jealousy of Leah, for which women are shown to need the guidance of men. The point is obviously intended for the benefit of the nuns, and the play, while entertaining them, means to teach them to overcome their "feminine" nature.

At the same time there is a leitmotif of complaint by the women for the subjection. Such a conflict of ideologies is typical of plays written by convent women. The nuns, on the one hand, from their devotional literature and from the hierarchical structure of society and the Church, learned that their place and the place of women in general was a subordinate one; they learned that their sex was weak. On the other hand, Renaissance humanism and Christianity taught that human beings occupied a special position among God's creations, a position that allowed them to rise or fall according to their own merits; the position of women in God's scheme, their merits and defects, and their education were subjects widely debated throughout the sixteenth century.[21] This context, together with the restrictions and suffering that life "imprisonment" in an enclosed convent imposed (the nuns often referred to it as "imprisonment"), encouraged the complaint of convent women, and convent plays written by the nuns themselves provided a vehicle for the expression of the nuns' concerns.[22] In Maria Clemente's *Giacob* (1.2), Lebano says to Leah and Rachel:

> Daughters . . .
> A wife must follow her husband.
> God bless and accompany you.
> Never forget that woman
> must be subject to man, and mustn't want
> to disagree with and oppose everything. (1.2, p. 4)[23]

And this is not presented as only a man's view. It is borne out by the poor judgment and irresponsible behavior of the women in the play: Leah is jealous, speaks ill of Rachel, and nags her husband. Leah's daughter Dinah gets into the trouble she does because of her curiosity. Wanting to visit the city of Salem, to see new places, do new things, she goes off by herself and is consequently (according to the logic of the story) raped by the son of the ruler of the city. He had disguised himself as a woman and tricked her.[24] She is blamed for her predicament, which creates serious political problems. Norminda—a character who is invented, not part of the biblical account—dresses as a man to be near Jacob's son Reuben. Her cross-dressing is severely criticized: it is strictly forbidden in Deuteronomy ("The woman shall not wear that which pertaineth unto a man, neither shall a man put on a woman's garment: for all that do so are abomination unto the Lord thy God," 22: 5). Dressed as a man and far from home, she risks her virtue and her life. The emphasis given to this issue in the play no doubt also had a special resonance for the convent audience, since religious authorities constantly forbade the nuns to wear men's clothing as costumes in their theatrical productions—a prohibition, however, that the nuns seem generally to have ignored.[25] Norminda ends up in a forest exposed to wild beasts and is saved by Reuben, the man she loves. He first refuses to marry such a frivolous woman ("femmina vana e vagabonda," 4.9, p. 66) but later, when informed that she has saved his father, he changes his mind. The women are weak, jealous, dangerously curious, and reckless with their honor, or they act otherwise imprudently, justifying their subservience even as they suffer from and lament it. Leah, for example, tells her servant:

> . . . Oh cruel fate
> that makes us subject to man before birth,
> turns us over to him in slavery. (4.6, p. 63)[26]

Norminda complains of the double standard:

> A man is permitted to do as he likes;
> everything is forbidden to us.
> Sichem tricked Dinah and carried her off.
> No one blames him; it's only Dinah who
> was wrong. What is called a vice in us
> in them is seen as great virtue. (4.9, p. 67)[27]

The playwright is clearly cognizant of these conflicting presentations of women, that is, that they are frail sinners in need of the rule of men, and that, at the same time, they are unjustly treated and judged by the world. She attempts to explain, blaming it all on Eve: "The sin of our first mother caused / you to be subject to the rule of men, and justly so" ("Sí mertò il fallo della prima madre / di farvi all'huòm suggette, e fu giustizia," 4.9, p. 67). Finally, it is significant that the failings and suffering of women are of primary interest; unlike the biblical account of the story, the female characters in the play, both the righteous and the wayward, dominate the action, so that the play might more rightly be entitled "Jacob's Women." This is a play written by a woman for women, with a clear didactic purpose: to teach women to recognize and overcome their weaknesses and to learn how to live together in harmony. The publication of the play would seem unplanned, since its implied audience is clearly that of a community of women.

* * *

Twenty years after the publication of her *Giacob patriarca*, Maria Clemente Ruoti wrote the *Natal di Cristo* for performance during Christmas festivities. The play belongs to a hybrid tradition that combines the story of the birth of Christ and the legend of Emperor Augustus's (Caius Octavius) vision of the Nativity. According to Alessandro D'Ancona, the earliest known Italian play of this variety, called *Aracoeli* plays, is the *Rappresentazione d'Ottaviano*, dated 1465.[28] And among the plays written for convent production in the sixteenth century there is a *Commedia di Ottaviano imperadore*, written by a Dominican, Fra Andrea di Chimenti.[29] Characteristic of this hybrid tradition is the presence of Sibyls, whose function is to reveal sacred truths and specifically to show the emperor a vision of the Nativity—a development of the medieval interpretation of Virgil's Fourth Eclogue, the reading of it as an announcement of the birth of Christ.[30]

This play, as was typical of spiritual comedy in the seventeenth century, has multiple plots; the *Giacob patriarca*, in contrast, had a variety of episodes, but all clearly subordinated to the main action. In the Nativity play the first story introduced is that of a lecherous and hypocritical Pharisee and his chaste, widowed sister-in-law, Naomi. She would marry him, and he, of course, should marry her according to Jewish law, but he would prefer to have her illicitly. Two virtues, Charity and Truth, disguised as beautiful women called Bella Fiamma and Celia, together with Albunea, the Tibertine Sibyl, try to reform the evil man and his cohorts, but, failing at that, they have the Pharisee swallowed up by the earth and save the good woman from unjust punishment. Parallel to this story is a humorous subplot concerning a shepherd who mispronounces, misunderstands, and uses malapropisms. An allegorical character named Error attempts unsuccessfully to seduce him. Like the good widow Naomi, when he resists he is falsely accused and imprisoned, but finally vindicated and freed. Meanwhile, Joseph and Mary find shelter for the night and Christ is born. The plots come together at the end, for the efforts of the Virtues and the Sibyl are not in vain, and other Pharisees, like Emperor Octavian in the *Aracoeli* tradition, together with shepherds are allowed to witness and participate in the adoration of the Christ child. The shepherd with speech difficulties is miraculously cured by the vision, one of the converted Pharisees marries the good widow, and the play ends in celebration.

The complicated plots are woven together in alternation and embellished with music. There is a scene in Act 3 entirely in verse and to be sung in *recitative*. It is scene 5, in which two Pharisees, Giustiniano and Massimo, play cards, a game called *giulé*, with the two virtues disguised as beautiful ladies, Bella Fiamma (Charity) and Celia (Truth); the sibyl, Albunea, a friend of the celestial ladies, watches and comments on the game.[31] The Pharisees, of course, are the villains; they try to cheat but are caught by the women and then lose to them (their three jacks are taken by three queens). There is at least one literary precedent for this game of *giulé* in *Le Mascherate* (2.5), a Carnival play written by Michelangelo Buonarroti the younger in the 1620s or 1603s—a play, or at least a topos, with which Maria Clemente is obviously familiar.[32] Music is used variously throughout the *Natal di Cristo*: a *moresca a sei*, a lively mimed dance that seems to represent a battle (f. 20v); songs for three voices and choirs; angels singing in concert (f. 23r); instrumental pieces (for *flauti*, *pive*, and *nacchere*: flutes, shawms, and nachers, f. 40r); and double choirs. The music builds in a crescendo, culminating in a grand finale sung by two alternating choirs of angels and shepherds in adoration of the Virgin and Child.

The *Natal di Cristo* is a play that must have required complicated staging, a problem alluded to by the author in her introductory letter addressed to "the kind reader," where she writes that "almost all the difficulty is in the staging and not in the writing" and she adds that she, nevertheless, must both write and stage her play.[33] Clearly convent audiences wanted the same sort of entertainment that secular audiences enjoyed, and their in-house playwrights, like Maria Clemente Ruoti, sought to provide them with comparable productions: complicated plots with intrigues, danger, love interest, elaborate sets, and music.

The *Natal di Cristo* differs in many ways from the *Giacob patriarca*, Maria Clemente's earlier play. It was more of a "spectacle" than the biblical play, and despite the author's protestations to the contrary, it must have required some machinery to produce the elaborate stage effects envisioned in the text. But more importantly, if less obviously, it proposes a very different view of women.

In this play all the women are strong, all righteous, and their efforts meet with success, quite a different case from that of the earlier play. Instead of teaching women subservience and humility by exposing their inherent weaknesses, this play shows that women can be strong and virtuous, the agents of God's will on earth. This positive message (and the elaborate music) may depend somewhat on the occasion of the convent performance, the Christmas festivities, while perhaps the earlier, decidedly misogynistic play (with brief choruses, *cori*, as *intermezzi*) was written for Carnival and taught self-examination and repentance in keeping with the coming Lenten season. But there is also another important difference in the contexts of the two plays. It would seem that the earlier play was written with only a convent performance, a convent audience in mind, and that the idea of publishing it came later when the play was brought to the attention of certain laymen, perhaps members of the Apatisti. The later play, on the other hand, as its opening address to the reader and the publishing privilege penned on its last page attest, was written with a view to publication and, therefore, probably with a broader audience in mind from the very beginning. The play's portrayal of a more positive view of women and of their active role in salvation gives convent women examples to emulate and encouragement in the exercise of their vocations, and it also valorizes the virtues of women and the roles that women can play in society, even women who, like Celia and Bella Fiamma, personifications of virtue, belong to another realm. In this play, it seems, Maria Clemente Ruoti has seen herself in an expanded role, that of convent playwright to be sure, but also as spokesperson to the world for her convent sisters and her sex.

* * *

Maria Clemente Ruoti's theatrical activity points to the close connection between convent life and the life of the city, and it also documents the high level of Italian convent culture.[34] There is no longer any question regarding the vernacular literacy of the regular nuns by the seventeenth century, and this can be said for the most part of the sixteenth century as well. The convent recorders in San Girolamo often intercalated stories among the entries of daily expenses—accounts of the plague years, of a fire in the house, even of a dispute over terminology, and ultimately over money, with the grand duke[35]—and this narrative practice, like that of writing plays, was common in other convents as well. The examples of Ruoti and other literate and literary nuns are evidence of the importance of convents for the intellectual development of women. The religious life model of women's creativity imposed notable restrictions, but it also offered advantages unknown to secular women, in this case, a convent literary tradition, women writers and actresses, an informed, demanding audience, and the encouragement, even the obligation to participate in convent theatrical events. Maria Clemente Ruoti struggled with the limitations of the convent stage, regretted that as a nun she lacked experience and resources, yet her particular expertise and her career would have been inconceivable outside the convent setting.

The nuns were not unaware or unappreciative of their advantages. A contemporary of Maria Clemente Ruoti, Clemenza Ninci, a Benedictine playwright at the convent of San Michele in Prato, wrote a play entitled *The Marriage of Hyparchia, Lady Philosopher* (*Lo sposalitio d'Ipparchia filosofa*), whose central issue is whether a woman should marry or study.[36] The protagonist, Hyparchia, a noblewoman, prefers study to marriage and, when pressed by her family, resolves the dilemma by agreeing to marry her teacher so she will have both options. As the subject of this play suggests, convent women were aware of the advantages convent life offered them, whether they had entered religious life willingly or not (the latter in this period was most often the case) and even when they regretted the option they were denied. Maria Clemente's family was not wealthy. They had difficulty paying the 700 scudi they owed for her dowry and that of her sister Margherita, Sister Vittoria Felice; they paid it in installments over a period of years. Neither sister was ever prioress of the convent, an office reserved perhaps for women of more important families. Maria Clemente was once *vicaria*, however, and her talents earned her a place of prominence in the convent's cultural life, as well as notice and approval from the secular world.

Maria Clemente never left the confines of her cloister, and her contacts with the world were always strictly controlled; nevertheless, she knew a surprising amount about theater, secular as well as religious, and she was a practiced, thoughtful, and gifted playwright. Her talents gave her a voice and gained her recognition beyond the confining walls of San Girolamo and led her to be the first woman elected to an academy that included or would include among its members Emanuele Tesauro, Antonio Magliabechi, Gian Andrea Moniglia, John Milton, and Voltaire. It may have been because of Maria Clemente's renown in the city that in 1679 the most prominent contemporary Florentine playwright, Gian Andrea Moniglia, whose play *Il Podestà di Colognole* opened in 1657 the Teatro della Pergola, sent his daughter to the convent of San Girolamo: she took the name Sister Vittoria Felice, the name that had been that of Maria Clemente's sister who died in 1671.[37] I must disagree with Niccolò Buonaiuti, who claimed that Maria Clemente Ruoti had "exceeded a woman's capacities," that is, was a phenomenon of a special sort that need not change one's view of women in general, and I submit that her case is an indication that there were many talented convent women whose voices were not heard beyond the convent walls but whose intellectual and artistic efforts made life interesting within those walls for themselves and for their sisters.

Notes

1. All translations in this paper are mine. Beatrice del Sera, a Florentine woman, was a Dominican nun at San Niccolò in Prato. Her play, the *Amor di virtú*, has survived in a partially autograph manuscript in the Riccardiana Library (cod. Ricc. 2932). The passage cited can be found in the modern edition: Beatrice del Sera, *Amor di virtú*, ed. Elissa Weaver (Ravenna: Longo, 1990), p. 267.

2. Raffaella de' Sernigi was a nun in the convent of Santa Maria della Disciplina just outside of Florence. Her play, *La rappresentatione di Moise quando Idio gli dette le leggie in sul monte Synai*, was published twice in Florence, the first time

without a date, but c. 1550 or 1560 "a istantia di Giuseppe di Pietro da Treviso," and in a 2d ed. "nuovamente stampata" (Florence: n.p., 1578). Cherubina Venturelli (or Venturella), a nun in the convent of Santa Caterina in Amelia, wrote the *Rappresentazione di Santa Cecilia Vergine et martire*, which was published more than once. I have seen the 1640 edition, published in Macerata by Agostino Grisei and the Biblioteca Casanatense has a 1668 edition, published in Rome. Leone Allacci in his *Drammaturgia* (Venice: Giambattista Pasquali, 1755, rev. and enl. ed.; 1st ed. Rome: Mascardi, 1666; modern rpt. Turin: Bottega d'Erasmo, 1966) gives notice of earlier editions published in Macerata in 1612 and 1631 and a later one in 1685. Maria Clemente Ruoti published at least one play, the *Giacob patriarca* (Pisa: Francesco delle Dote, 1637); this play is mentioned by Leone Allacci and by Giulio Negri, *Istoria degli scrittori fiorentini* (Ferrara: Bernardino Pomatelli, 1722; rpt. Bologna: Forni, 1973). There is a copy in the National Library in Florence. The *Natal di Cristo* received a publishing privilege, but there is no evidence that it actually went to press.

3. This biographical information has been largely gathered from convent documents: Florence, Archivio di Stato (hereafter cited as ASF), *Corporazioni religiose soppresse dal governo francese* 96 (San Girolamo e San Francesco sulla Costa di San Giorgio), filze 17 f. 47r, 29 f. 74v, 35 f. 30r, and 171 n. 22. References to her and to her family are also found in the *Poligrafo Gargani* n. 1760 in the Florentine National Library (BNF).

4. The Riccardiana manuscript of the *Natal di Cristo*, Riccardiana MS. 2783, vol. 7, contains a publishing privilege, dated 1657, requested by Maria Clemente Ruoti and granted by two Franciscan friars, her superiors Fra Gio. Batt. dal Borgo alla Collina and Fra Biagio di Fiorenza, and the provincial minister fra Benigno Bruni. A note therein reads as follows: "The Nativity . . . is so filled with devotion and erudition that we judge it to merit publication to encourage piety and learning" ("Il Natale . . . è cosí colmo di devotione e d'eruditione che per svegliar gl'affetti e l'ingegni, meritevole di pubblica luce la giudichiamo noi" (f. 42v). I have been unable to find a published version.

5. The dedication is on unnumbered pp. 2r–3r. Two of the play's choruses end with an allusion to the grand duchess: "Gli darà d'ogn'impresa alta vittoria," last line, Second Chorus, and "Nel fervor dell'offesa è vera gloria / e lodata VITTORIA," Fifth Chorus. It was not unusual for the grand duchesses to attend convent performances. Raffaello Rocchi in his edition of Giovan Maria Cecchi's *Drammi spirituali* (Florence: Le Monnier, 1895), 1: xxvii, notes the presence of Giovanna D' Austria at a performance of *La morte del re Acab* in the convent of the Benedictine nuns of the Spirito Santo sulla Costa di S. Giorgio in 1575. The Riccardiana Library manuscript of this play, 2818, vol. 7, twice (in its prologue and envoy) addressed the "Regina" in the audience.

6. "A virginella rinchiusa fra quattro mura la via del Parnaso, serenissima gran duchessa, è non pur malagevole, ma quasi incognita. Le Muse par che aborriscano cotanta semplicità. Ogni lume poetico nelle ceneri di quest'abito resta offuscato. L'armonia del verso da orecchio fasciato di grosse bende mal può distinguersi. Le regole del dire e del poetare, con quelle dell'ubbidire e del sopportare non si confanno: perché quelle ricercan lezione varia, e frequente, e conferenza

quasi continua, e queste pochi libri concedono, e limitati; e le conversazioni de' letterati, come alla nostra professione troppo contrarie, ci proibiscono. Onde non sarà maraviglia se questa mia operetta non sarà dotata di quelle parti, che si ricercano a drammatico componimento" (nn. 2r, v).

7. "Trasgredivano allora gli uomini alle divine leggi, potrò ben io pigliarmi alcuna licenza con quelle degli uomini" (f. 1v).

8. Leone de' Sommi (Yehuda Sommi di Portaleone), playwright and theatrical director active at the Gonzaga court and in a Jewish theatrical company in Mantova during the second half of the sixteenth century, author of plays in Hebrew and in Italian and of *Quattro dialoghi in materia di rappresentazioni sceniche* (1556), mentions that dieties are not admissible in comedy. He thinks, however, that they should be permitted instead in satires, eclogues, and modern pastoral drama, and he adds that it seems to be legitimate in tragedy as well since Moses had the diety speak in his "tragedy of Job"; see the edition of the *Quattro Dialoghi* edited by Ferruccio Marotti (Milan: Edizioni Il Polifilo, 1968), in the "Dialogo secondo," pp. 35–36. In regard to the supposed practice of having the principal characters enter and speak before minor characters, I have found no reference other than this one; it was not so in classical drama, and a cursory examination of sixteenth- and seventeenth-century texts would indicate that secondary characters, servants for example, are often the first to speak.

9. "non ho cognitione d'altro mondo che dell'angustia di queste quattro mura, ove mi racchiusi di mia età d'anni nove, non ho esperienza di macchine, né facoltà di poterle mettere in pratica a talche mi è convenuto adattar la poesia al proprio potere e non la borsa altrui alle mie invenzioni come fanno i poeti" (cod. Ricc. 2783, vol. 7, f. 1v).

10. Anton Francesco Gori, *Memorie dell'Accademia degli Apatisti*, manuscript A. 36 of the Marucelliana Library, Florence, f. 58r, lists among those admitted to the Academy during the period 1649–50 "suor M. Clemente Ruoti, mon. in S. Girol. di S. Giorgio"; she was the first female member of the Academy, it seems. This manuscript has been partially published by Alessandro Lazzeri in his *Intellettuali e consenso nella Toscana del Seicento: l'Accademia degli Apatisti* (Milan: Dott. A. Giuffré Editore, 1983), pp. 57–121; "suor M. Clemente Ruoti" on p. 82. The *Poligrafo Gargani* n. 1760 puts the date at 1649, citing as his source notes written by a famous member of the Academy, the abbot Anton Maria Salvini (1653–1729). On the Academy of the Apatisti, see also Edoardo Benvenuti, *Agostino Coltellini e l'Accademia degli Apatisti a Firenze nel secolo XVII* (Pistoia: Officina Tipigrafica Cooperativa, 1910); Eric Cochrane, *Tradition and Enlightenment in the Tuscan Academies 1690–1800* (Chicago: University of Chicago Press, 1961), p. 4 and passim; Cochrane, *Florence in the Forgotten Centuries, 1527–1800* (Chicago: University of Chicago Press, 1973), pp. 204, 327, and passim; Michele Maylender, *Storia delle Accademie d'Italia*, vol. 1 (Bologna: L. Cappelli, 1926), pp. 204, 327, and passim; and Giovanni Prezziner, *Storia del pubblico studio e delle società scientifiche e letterarie di Firenze*, vol. 2 (Florence: Carli in Borgo SS. Apostoli, 1810), pp. 80–82, 120–23, 142–45, 168–69, 218–19.

11. Gori, *Memorie dell'Accademia*. Members, at least during the association's early years, took anagrammatic academic names (for example, Agostino Coltellini

called himself Ostilio Contalgeni). After an unsure beginning in the 1630s the academy was reformed in 1649 and flourished until 1783 when Grand Duke Pietro Leopoldo made both the Apatista and the Crusca academies part of the Florentine Academy. The records of the Apatisti have been lost; only some late seventeenth-early eighteenth-century academic discourses and other works produced by members survive. A memoir, dated 31 January 1744 and written by Anton Francesco Gori (Tonfino Gotescari), records academy activities and members and is the most complete document we have regarding the society.

12. Gori, *Memorie dell'Accademia*.

13. Gori, *Memorie dell'Accademia*, f. 74r (not included in Lazzeri's transcription).

14. "non ho cognitione d'altro mondo che dell'angustia di queste quattro mura, ove mi racchiusi di mia età d'anni nove" ("I know no world beyond the narrow confines of these four walls, where I enclosed myself when I was nine years old"; cod. Ricc. 2783, vol. 7, f. 1v). Lazzeri (*Intellettuali e consenso*, p. 54) notes that reports on the activities of the Apatisti show that only a certain core group of intellectuals actually participated in the regular activities of the academy and that others—he gives the example of high-ranking prelates and foreign princes—were purely honorary members.

15. Autograph manuscript, BNF cod. Magliabechiano VII.147.

16. The documents regarding the sale, letters, inventories, and so on are contained in cod. Ricc. 3481. The inventory of the library of Anton Maria Salvini (1653–1729) indicates a number of sacred comedies, the *Coronazione di Salomone*, a *Saul perseguitato*, Cecchi's *Morte di Acab*, the *Tragedia di Eleazzaro Ebreo*, various *sacre rappresentazioni*, *laudi spirituali*, and many other plays listed without title, as, for example, "another similar tragedy" ("altra simile tragedia") or "an anonymous early comedy in tercets" ("commedia antica in terza rima d'anonimo"). The *Tragedia di Eleazzaro Ebreo* was written for convent performance by a nun in the Dominican house of San Vincenzo in Prato (see my Introduction to Beatrice del Sera's *Amor di virtú*, p. 32).

17. Lazzeri, *Intellettuali e consenso*, p. 20.

18. *Giacob patriarca* (Pisa: Francesco delle Dote, 1637), nn. 4r,v. The poem, consisting of seven quatrains of hendecasyllables rhymed ABAB, begins, "Erme piagge sonar fan de i lor canti."

19. *Giacob patriarca* nn. 5r. Niccolò Buonaiuti and Carlo Ruberto Dati are on the list of members inducted in 1635 (Lazzeri, *Intellettuali e consenso*, pp. 69–70).

20. See Elissa Weaver, "Spasso spirituale, ovvero il gioco delle monache," in *Passare il tempo: La letteratura del gioco e dell'intrattenimento dall XII al XVI secolo*, Proceedings of the Conference held in Pienza, September 10–14, 1991 (Rome: Salerno Editrice, 1993), pp. 351–71.

21. See Pamela J. Benson, *The Invention of Renaissance Woman: The Challenge of Female Independence in the Literature and Thought of Italy and England* (University Park: Pennsylvania State University Press, 1992); and Constance Jordan, *Renaissance Feminism: Literary Texts and Political Models* (Ithaca, NY: Cornell University Press, 1990).

22. See Gabriella Zarri on the "incarceration" of nuns, "Monasteri femminili e città (secoli XV–XVII)," in *Storia d'Italia: Annali 9: La Chiesa e il potere politico dal Medioevo all'età contemporanea*, ed. Giorgio Chittolini and Giovanni Miccoli (Turin: Einaudi, 1986), pp. 403, 412, 414. On p. 414 Zarri cites Cardinal Alessandro de' Medici in his *Trattato sopra il governo de' monasteri* (1601), Vat. lat. 10444, f. 347v:

"Poiché l'hanno messe in carcere senza vero e libero loro consenso, vorrebbero ristorare con procurare loro libertà e licenze senza pensare alla salute dell'anima" ("Since they put them in prison without their true and free consent, they would compensate by obtaining for them freedoms and permissions without thinking of what is good for their souls"). In the same treatise (on f. 341v) the cardinal writes that the nuns protest using words like "Noi siamo abandonate da ognuno e siamo in carcere e ci stiamo volentieri se ci volete serrar piú ce ne contentiamo, ma dateci da vivere perché se ci serrate et non ci provedete nascerà qualche disordine" ("We have been abandoned by everyone, and we are in prison and we accept this willingly; if you want to lock us up more tightly we won't complain, but give us what we need, because if you lock us up and don't provide for us there will be trouble").

23.

Figlie . . .
La moglie dee seguire il suo marito.
Iddio vi benedica e vi accompagni.
Non v'esca mai di mente che la donna
all'huom dee star suggetta, e non volere
di tutto contrastare e a tutto opporre.

24. "Sichem son'io che con mia buona sorte / oggi mi travestii da pastorella; / piú non vedrai, Germinio, la donzella, / se a me non la congedi per consorte" ("I am Sichem, who, with my good luck, / today disguised myself as a shepherdess; / you will not see the girl again, Germinio, / if you don't give her to me as my wife") (3.6, p. 47). The biblical text does not speak of a ruse; this detail is either the playwright's invention, or she is familiar with an apocryphal tradition. For example, the *Pirkei De-Rabbi Eliezer* (*Chapters of Rabbi Eliezer*), a biblical commentary known in Europe in the sixteenth and seventeenth centuries in non-Jewish circles, claims that Sichem tricked Dinah, though not through disguise: "Because the daughter of Jacob was abiding in the tents, and she did not go into the street; what did Shechem, the son of Chamor, do? He brought dancing girls who were (also) playing on pipes in the streets. Dinah went forth to see those girls who were making merry; and he seized her, and he slept with her"; English trans. and ed. Gerald Friedlander (New York: Hermon Press, 1970), p. 287.

25. See Weaver, "Spasso spirituale," pp. 356–58.

26.

". . . Ahi dura sorte
che ad huom ci fa suggette pria che nate,
schiave a quello ci rende."

27.

Lice all'huom ciò che vuole;
tutt'a noi si disdice.
Sichem Dina furò con grande astuzia;
ei da naiuno è biasmato e solo a Dina
si dà la colpa. Quel ch'è vizio in noi
per gran virtute a lor sempre s'ammette.

28. Alessandro D'Ancona, *Origini del teatro italiano* (Turin: Loescher, 1891; rpt. Rome: Bardi, 1971), 1: 270, n. 8. See also Carmelo Musumarra, *La sacra rappresentazione della Natività* (Florence: Olschki, 1957).

29. Cod. Ricc. 1413, ff. 172–83.

30. On the Sibyls, ancient prophetesses subsumed by the Christian tradition, see Josiane Haffen, *Contribution à l'étude de la Sibylle médiévale: Étude et édition du Ms. B.N., F. Fr. 25.407, fol. 160v–172v: Le livre de Sibille* (Paris: Annales Littéraires de l'Université de Besançon. Les Belles Lettres, 1984). The Apatisti were known for their game entitled the Sibillone. Could this use of sibyls be in part an homage to the Academy?

31. The card game is probably French in origin and is known in Italy from about the fifteenth century. The name may derive from the expression "Je l'ai." See David Parlett, *Oxford Guide to Card Games* (Oxford: Oxford University Press, 1990), p. 90.

32. Michelangelo Buonarroti, the younger, *Le Mascherate*, act 2, scene 5, in *Opere varie in versi ed in prosa di Michelangelo Buonarroti, il giovane*, ed. Pietro Fanfani (Florence: Le Monnier, 1891), pp. 147–64. I thank Danilo Romei for this reference.

33. "quasi tutta la fatica consiste nel rappresentare e non nel comporre . . . a me conviene e comporre e rappresentare," f. 1v.

34. The convent of San Girolamo maintained many connections, not only cultural, with the secular world. For example, the nuns invested their dowry money in businesses in the Old Market—they owned a shop that sold fish, another pastry—and they were the custodians of the money box of the Gate of San Giorgio. They lent their dowry money at interest, especially to other communities, on a fairly regular basis, if on a small scale, operating somewhat like a bank.

35. ASF, *Corp. rel. soppresse* 96, filze 12, cc. 129r–130r, 13, ff. 181v–182r, 197v, and 14, ff. 180v–201r, texts by Gabriella Angiola Baldovinetti, Raffaella Vanni, and Maria Laura del Buono.

36. Cod. Ricc. 2974, vol. 3, published in an abridged edition by Cesare Guasti in the *Calendario pratese del 1850*, anno V (Prato, 1849), pp. 53–101.

37. ASF, *Corp. rel. soppresse* 96, filza 15, f. 182r.

Craig A. Monson

13. The Making Of Lucrezia Orsina Vizzana's *Componimenti Musicali* (1623)

Elsewhere in this volume Elissa Weaver describes the case of the convent writer Maria Clemente Ruoti and her interaction with the literary world of the Accademia degli Apatisti, beyond the cloister wall in Florence. I, on the other hand, should like to look at a somewhat comparable musical figure, Donna Lucrezia Orsina Vizzana of the Camaldolese convent of Santa Cristina della Fondazza in Bologna, the only Bolognese nun known to have taken the decidedly public step of publishing her music, a single collection entitled *Componimenti Musicali*, which saw the light in 1623.[1] As my title implies, I limit myself largely to what may have gone into the making of her style. I hope to suggest how her work reflects, not only the artistic influence of her immediate monastic environment, but also the richly changing musical world beyond the convent wall, which, theoretically, she should scarcely have known. Perhaps it may even reflect, indirectly, the activities of a Bolognese *musical* academy that she could never have joined herself. A detailed discussion of how Lucrezia Vizzana made what she heard her own must await another time and place.

Lucrezia Orsina Vizzana, like most nuns of her time, has remained little more than a name to us. Had she been drawn less to the arts and letters and more intensely to expressions of piety perhaps it might have been otherwise. Significantly, although the Bolognese seventeenth-century amateur historian Count Gasparo Bombacci, carefully set down the exemplary life of Lucrezia Vizzana's aunt, Donna Flaminia Bombacci—the only Benedictine nun in Bologna to have died in odor of sanctity before the mid-seventeenth century, who for twenty-two years spent her nights in constant prayer in the chapel of Santa Cristina with only brief periods of rest on bare boards—he makes no mention at all of Donna Flaminia's distinguished musical niece in his family history.[2]

Lucrezia Orsina Vizzana's life therefore can only be pieced together from widely scattered scraps of information. Her mother, Isabetta, had come to her marriage with Ludovico di Obizo Vizzani in October 1581[3] from the moderately illustrious Bombacci family, active in the silk trade. Isabetta Bombacci was the eldest survivor of the twelve daughters of Giovanni di Antonio Bombacci, *gonfaloniero del popolo* in Bologna in 1570 and *anziano console* three years later.[4] This number may not have been all that extraordinary for upper-class families, and the fates of the twelve were certainly quite typical. Six of Giovanni Bombacci's daughters died in infancy; another lived long enough to marry but soon died in childbirth. Of the surviving five, only Isabetta Bombacci married, and after bearing at least three sons and two daughters, expired before the age of forty. Isabetta's four remaining sisters all became nuns, no fewer than three at the convent of Santa Cristina—where the trio outlived all their other siblings by ten to thirty years.[5]

The future composer Lucrezia Orsina Vizzana was born to Isabetta Bombacci and Ludovico Vizzani on 3 July 1590. It is not clear when she entered the convent of Santa Cristina, though she was there at least by age eight, and in her late teens she and her older sister Verginia claimed to have been in the convent since their earliest childhood.[6] Santa Cristina was the obvious choice for offspring of the Bombacci and Vizzani families, for they had already established strong family ties within its walls. Around 1600 there were no fewer than three Bombacci sisters in the convent already—one more than was deemed prudent and normally permitted in post-Tridentine Bologna.[7] Two of the three Bombacci sisters subsequently served as abbess of the convent and played singular roles in the history of the institution.

Lucrezia and Verginia Vizzani claimed to have become nuns in 1598. This date probably marks the time they were accepted, and agrees closely with the date when their father lent the convent 5,900 lire for a term of four years. Lucrezia and presumably Verginia received their habits around 1602, when Verginia took her late mother's name, Isabetta, and probably professed at age sixteen. On 5 December 1606 Ludovico Vizzani canceled his loan of seven years before, and the convent in turn absolved him of the dowries and furnishings of his two daughters, perhaps in anticipation of an impending group consecration of nuns, following the Roman pontifical, scheduled for September of the following year. In March of 1607 the twenty-year-old Isabetta and the sixteen-year-old Lucrezia petitioned the Sacred Congregation of Bishops and Regulars in Rome for permission to participate in this lavish ceremony, only held every ten years or so, despite the fact that neither had reached the age of twenty-five. Isabetta's request was finally granted, but Lucrezia had to wait for the next *Sacra* six years later, when in 1613, after further repeated petitions, the Congregation of Bishops granted her dispensation, although Lucrezia was still twenty-two months short of the requisite age.[8]

Having settled his daughters in Santa Cristina, taken care of their dowries, and agreed to provide thirty lire a year for the upkeep of each, Ludovico Vizzani had discharged his paternal obligations in the customary way. By 1610 their father had married an Elena Zani. The premature deaths of their brothers further weakened the remaining links to the Vizzani and to their father, who (not surprisingly) ignored his daughters in disposing of his own estate. After Ludovico Vizzani's death in 1628, it took several years of litigation in Bologna and ultimately in Rome for Donna Lucrezia and Donna Isabetta Vizzani to reclaim a portion of their mother's dowry from the illegitimate grandson their father had legitimized shortly before his death and made his sole heir.[9]

Having entered Santa Cristina in her earliest childhood, Lucrezia Vizzana would scarcely have known the world beyond the convent walls. The world she had entered, however, would have to be called one of the best of all possible monastic worlds in Bologna. By the early Seicento Santa Cristina had become one of the wealthier, more exclusive, and most artistically distinguished of Bologna's monasteries for women.[10] Catering to Bolognese noble and patrician families such as the Bolognetti, Bottrigari, Pepoli, Malvezzi, and Vizzani, as well as aspiring families of slightly lower rank such as the Bombacci, it remained out of reach of what the nuns themselves called "ordinary" women. Around 1620 the thirty-eight professed nuns were served by no fewer than fourteen servant nuns, a ratio that in fact struck ecclesiastical authorities as overly luxurious.[11]

Some members of the convent, who tended to call each other "Donna" rather than "Suora," and referred to the convent as the "collegio" rather than as the "monastero," aspired as much, perhaps, to the arts and letters as to the religious life, or saw nothing incongruous about the intermingling of the two, in a way that had characterized male members of their order at various periods.[12] During Lucrezia Vizzana's girlhood the convent underwent a substantial rebuilding and expansion of its external church, underwritten by various nuns, who also provided it with as many as nine lavishly decorated altars.[13] An elegantly decorated convent necrology at Santa Cristina, now known only from eighteenth-century copies, was designed, not only to record the pious ends of those sisters who had achieved "good deaths," but also to commemorate the artistic and intellectual accomplishments of others with interests in those directions.[14] Significantly, one of the longest encomia in the collection is to Donna Lucrezia Orsina Vizzana.

How did this little girl not only learn music, but learn it so well that she also came to compose and even to publish her works? At first sight it might appear that the times were totally inauspicious for such a prospect. In 1598, the year of Lucrezia's acceptance, for example, Alfonso Paleotti, who had succeeded Cardinal Gabriele Paleotti as archbishop of Bologna, began to republish earlier decrees forbidding outside music teachers to teach in the convents of the city, thereby provoking a stream of convent petitions to the Congregation of Bishops in Rome for exemptions to the rule. But between 1598 and 1610 the uniform response "Nihil" awaited repeated petitions for outside music teachers, however aged or godfearing, from several Bolognese convents.[15]

At Santa Cristina, however, there seems to have been no shortage of musical talent already within the convent, on which the young Lucrezia Vizzana could have relied. Her most probable mentor would have been one of her mother's three sisters, for young girls were commonly entrusted to the care of their aunts upon entering Italian monasteries, and this still remained the practice at Santa Cristina, at least during Lucrezia Vizzana's youth. One of her aunts, Camilla Bombacci, in fact turns out to have been a musician. At her death in 1640 at the age of seventy, Donna Camilla was remembered in the convent necrology as "first organist, and three time mistress of the novices, and subsequently abbess." In 1623 the current abbess suggested Camilla Bombacci for the post of *maestra del choro*, though Donna Camilla ultimately ended up as abbess instead.[16]

But Camilla Bombacci was in fact only one of several talented musicians at Santa Cristina during Lucrezia Vizzana's formative years. Chief among them must have been Donna Emilia Grassi, clearly the dominant musical force at Santa Cristina in the early Seicento. In 1599 Emilia Grassi received the dedication of Adriano Banchieri's *Messa Solenne a otto voci*, presumably underwritten by her family. It is worth taking a look at this dedication by the garrulous Olivetan composer, for what it tells us about Emilia Grassi and also about music at Santa Cristina:

> On the day when the feast of the Glorious Saint Christina was solemnized, finding myself in the church of Your Reverence while First Vespers was being sung, and hearing with great pleasure the harmonious concerti of voices, organs, and various musical instruments, directed with most exquisite sentiments of devotion, I endeavored to learn from a musician, my particular friend (who was present there) who was the head of these concerti; and from

> him I learned it was Your Reverence. And justly he further added that in addition to your other most honorable qualities you are highly skilled both in singing and playing, using all [these talents] for the praise and glory of our Blessed Lord. . . . I desire no other reward, only that on occasions when you perform [these concerti] you and your dear sisters would remember to pray God for me in your devout and holy prayers.[17]

Donna Emilia Grassi definitely served as *maestra del choro* for most of the second decade of the century and into the 1620s. After her death in 1633, during her second term as abbess, she was remembered fulsomely as "adorned in the principles of all musical instruments which she played so well that she was second to none."[18]

Two years after the appearance of Banchieri's collection, on the other hand, another nun from Santa Cristina, Donna Adeodata Leoni, received the dedication of the *Secondo Libro de' Motetti*[19] by the fellow Camaldolese, Gabriele Fattorini, sometime organist of Faenza cathedral. The dedication by Don Donato Beroaldo, "Monaco Camaldolense," suggests that the motets had been gathered for publication specifically at Donna Adeodata's behest. Within the next five years the singing nuns of Santa Cristina were the object of a third dedication, this time Giovanni Battista Cesena's *Compieta con Letanie*, which like the previous two consisted of works for eight voices. The dedicatory letter by the Venetian publisher Giacomo Vincenti, which marvels at the divine musical *concerti* at various Bolognese convents and singles out those at Santa Cristina in particular, suggests that the standards admired by Banchieri had not diminished.[20] Finally, in 1613, the year of Lucrezia Vizzana's consecration, Ercole Porta, organist of the collegiate church of San Giovanni in Persiceto, dedicated his *Vaga Ghirlanda di Soavi e Odorati Fiori Musicali*, a more diverse collection of motets, psalms, and *falsobordone* settings in simple, hymnlike chordal style, for one to five voices, to Donna Cleria Pepoli of Santa Cristina. It is surely significant that of some ten musical collections dedicated to convent women in Bologna and the immediate area between 1582 and 1675, no less than four were dedicated to nuns from Santa Cristina, all within a fourteen-year period that would have to be regarded as Lucrezia Vizzana's "formative years."

Thus Santa Cristina della Fondazza was apparently well supplied with talented musicians of its own, from whom the young Lucrezia Vizzana might have gained inspiration and learned many details of her art. There is an additional problem, however, in attempting to explain the nature of her work. Vizzana's music belongs to the *stile moderno*, which had found its way into Bolognese church music only during the fifteen or twenty years before the publication of her *Componimenti Musicali* in 1623.

Example 13.1. Lucrezia Orsina Vizzana, *Usquequo oblivisceris me in finem?*

A number of her motets seem especially self-conscious in their adoption of the new expressive traits of the novel solo idiom. The intensely expressive *Usquequo oblivisceris me in finem?* (Example 13.1) is one such work, serving up one or more examples of all her favorite musical gestures: the delicately virtuosic ornamentation at each of the first two cadences; the transposed

Example 13.1. (cont.)

repetition of phrases for rhetorical effect, most notably at the opening; the disjunction between phrases caused by beginning a new line of text on the chord a whole-step below the cadence of the previous phrase, clearly at bars 19 to 20, and probably also at bars 5 to 6.

Two other gestures are particularly arresting, however. The first involves the expressively jolting juxtaposition of two major chords a third apart, obviously at bars 25 to 26 (B-flat major versus G major), and possibly also at bars 6 to 7, which can successfully be harmonized C major versus E major. More unusual and most striking of all is the bold leap away from the suspended vocal D against the bass E-flat for expressive effect at bar 14, a notable violation of the time-honored rules of sixteenth-century counterpoint. All these features, including the boldest of them, reappear in greater or lesser profusion throughout Vizzana's collection.

How then, could Lucrezia Vizzana have learned this modern idiom? She and all of her potential nun music teachers at Santa Cristina had left the musical world outside the cloister at the crucial time when music was beset by significant changes. When Ludovico Viadana's immensely popular *Cento Concerti Ecclesiastici*, that temporal landmark of the new monodic style in sacred music, first appeared in Venice in 1602, for example, Lucrezia had already been behind the convent wall for at least four years while her possible nun music teachers such as Camilla Bombacci or Emilia Grassi had been cloistered for at least fifteen. One wonders when and how distinctly they first heard the echoes of the newer style also reflected in Lucrezia Vizzana's own motets. Clearly, the church hierarchy would generally have offered scant encouragement to any open attempts to keep up with these changing musical styles, at least to judge by the Congregation of Bishops' response to a petition dated 1606 from three modern-minded singing nuns at the convent of San Biagio in Cesena:

> Sister Felicita Stellini, Sister Anna, and Sister Armellina Uberti . . . all considerably versed in music, and desirous to study how to sing some spiritual motets *alla Romana*, humbly request that you permit Canon Manzini to come once or at most twice to the public parlatorios to explain and teach to the above-mentioned nuns the way they are sung . . . in the presence of the Abbess and the appointed chaperones.[21]

This request met with the inevitable response: "Nihil."

Yet, despite similarly severe restrictions in Bologna, the evidence suggests that music from the outside world could be heard, and increasingly did find its way inside the walls of the more musical convents such as Santa Cristina; resourceful nuns already had years of practice in finding ways to work within and around episcopal prohibitions. Beginning in 1605, for example, the Congregation of Bishops began to relax its previously emphatic prohibition concerning performances by outside musicians at convent festivities in Bologna, over the strenuous and repeated objections of

Archbishop Alfonso Paleotti.[22] During the next few years the convents of Corpus Domini, Santa Catterina, San Guglielmo, San Bernardino, Sant'Orsola, Santi Vitali ed Agricola, and Sant'Omobono, one after the other, all requested and received permission to bring in musical outsiders for feast days and funerals in their external churches.

Evidence suggests that such outside musicians also came to perform at Santa Cristina, on which occasions the musical nuns could have experienced the newer musical styles of the early Seicento. Most appropriately the echoes of such new music should have reached their ears only faintly, through the grated window above the high altar or through the one in the side-chapel of Santa Cristina. Evidence reveals, however, that musical nuns found better ways not only to hear but even to see outside performers. After a pastoral visitation of 1623 it was reported that the raised organ rooms, one on each side of the high altar, accessible only from the nuns' inner chapel, had windows not only facing the high altar but also directly facing the external church. These windows were equipped with screens that were movable and perforated in such a way that the nuns could see into the nave. Furthermore, there was also another spacious "choir" at the opposite end of the public church, above the doors, with very large grated windows through which the whole of the external church could be seen,[23] including the *cantoria*, just beyond the grates, where outside musicians presumably would have performed.

Evidence also suggests that the nuns not only could hear, but also could study the scores of new music. It is hard to imagine that the dedicatees of the musical prints of Banchieri, Fattorini, Cesena, and Porta never set eyes on the collections dedicated to them, which they or their families probably had paid for. Nuns from other Bolognese convents definitely owned volumes of music at exactly this time. An inventory from another of the most musical convents, Santa Margherita, reveals, for example, that in 1613 a Suor Emilia Arali owned seven books "to sing and play"—in addition to a spinet, a guitar, and a lute (the last two of which had been forbidden in Bolognese convents at least since 1580). Other inventories from Santa Margherita testify to the continued presence there not only of these instruments but also of clavichords, violins, and several trombones (the latter two also specifically banned in Bolognese convents for decades). In 1617 the nuns of San Guglielmo were also left a trunk full of vocal music by a benefactress.[24]

Furthermore, musicians and music teachers may have been repeatedly forbidden to visit convent parlatorios, but the nuns' own parents were not.

There would therefore have been little to prevent the Bolognese composer, wind-player, and esteemed music teacher Alfonso Ganassi[25] from visiting his daughter Donna Alfonsina, who had entered Santa Cristina around 1591.[26] Perhaps he presented her with music or passed along musical information. At Santa Cristina the introduction of such musical information or music books may have become especially easy. Although in 1623 Lucrezia Vizzana maintained that it was still customary to request the abbess's permission to send or receive anything *ex clausura*, other nuns admitted that the abbess no longer bothered to examine all incoming and outgoing mail as she should, and that there were no regular chaperones appointed to keep watch in the parlatorios.[27]

This all suggests that in the decade after Archbishop Alfonso Paleotti's death in 1610, episcopal vigilance around the convents must have relaxed. It is significant that the flood of musical petitions from Bolognese nunneries to the Congregation of Bishops in Rome virtually dries up after 1610. From a musical point of view, perhaps the most telling witness to this possible new laxity at Santa Cristina was the fact that from around 1615, at the instigation of Donna Emilia Grassi, Santa Cristina actually began to employ a regularly salaried, unauthorized *maestro di musica*, Ottavio Vernizzi, the organist of San Petronio.[28] Church authorities would promptly put a stop to that practice when it came to their attention in 1623. This all suggests that despite episcopal prohibitions, ways could be found to nurture Lucrezia Vizzana's musical talents, at least from her mid-teens onward.

Having established that for Lucrezia Vizzana *clausura* may have been rather less restricting than episcopal prohibitions might at first seem to indicate, can one go so far as to suggest what music may actually have reached her within the cloister walls? Given the elusiveness of music's very nature, one can scarcely hope to rediscover from the musical language of Donna Lucrezia's own works what constituted her musical world to the extent that Carlo Ginzburg managed to recover many literary sources that shaped the cosmology of the sixteenth-century miller, Menochio, on the basis of his own words.[29] Nevertheless, the musical gestures of Vizzana's motets offer interesting clues which I would like to explore, as far as is possible in the space available, and with the disclaimer that my speculations must remain tentative.

Banchieri's *Messa Solenne* of 1599, dedicated to Donna Emilia Grassi, provides a plausible starting point, for Banchieri himself seems to have assumed that the nuns of Santa Cristina would perform these works. In this light it is intriguing to encounter, in the opening bars of the motet for the elevation of the Host from that collection, a four-voice work scored only for high voices, presumably with the nuns in mind, the expressive juxtaposition of two major chords a third apart (G major versus E major) on "dulcissime Jesu" (Example 13.2).[30] The same gesture can be seen in Vizzana's *Usquequo oblivisceris me* (Example 13.1), and was particularly favored by Lucrezia Vizzana, who introduces it in at least half of her own motets, sometimes several times in a single piece.[31]

By 1599 this musical device was common enough to have entered the general language of secular music, of course, particularly for expressive ends. One does not have to look far to find it in the later madrigal repertory, for example. It is safe to suggest, however, that the madrigal repertory is more readily available to us than it would have been to Lucrezia Vizzana. The gesture appears somewhat less commonly in the sacred repertory of the early Seicento, which Vizzana is more likely to have known. Banchieri had introduced it only three times in the whole of his 1599 *Messa Solenne*, for example. He comes to use it a little more liberally in his more diversified collections containing new-style motets for one or two soloists and basso continuo, such as *Gemelli Armonici* (1609), his *Vezzo di Perle Musicali* (1610), and *Nuovi Pensieri Ecclesiastici* (1613) (Example 13.2).

Of these collections, *Nuovi Pensieri* strikes the listener as most self-consciously modern, both by its title and by its contents, which employ many of the modern devices likewise common in Vizzana's works. This collection also happens to include a so-called Ghirlandetta of motets by five local organists, whom Banchieri describes as "amici ed amorevoli dell'Autore." Two of the names are already familiar to us. Ercole Porta dedicated his own musical collection to Donna Cleria Pepoli of Santa Cristina in 1613. Indeed, Porta's publication is even advertised by the publisher at the back of Banchieri's print.

The second familiar contributor to Banchieri's *Nuovi Pensieri* is Ottavio Vernizzi, specifically singled out by Banchieri as "cordialissimo amico dell'Autore,"[32] who, as we have seen, also served as the unauthorized *maestro di musica* at Santa Cristina during the second decade of the Seicento. Significantly, in roughly the same years when Banchieri was experimenting with the modern sacred style for one or two voices and continuo, Vernizzi himself published or republished three collections that included several works for a few soloists and continuo: *Armonia Ecclesiasticorum Concertuum* (1604), *Angelici Concentus* (1611), and *Caelestum Applausus* (1612).

Thus we find three musical friends, who all had connections with

Example 13.2. Instances of chromatic juxtaposition.

Santa Cristina, who all were experimenting with the *stile moderno* and exchanging motets in that style, and who were also publishing one or more collections containing such works between 1604 and 1613. Of these three composers, Vernizzi can most easily be placed on the musical scene at Santa Cristina over a period of years. Interestingly enough, of the three he seems to be the one to rival Lucrezia Vizzana in his preoccupation with the expressive juxtaposition of two triads a third apart, a device which appears in about 65 percent of his few-voice motets. Significantly, in 1623 the abbess of Santa Cristina remarked that as part of Vernizzi's duties the *maestro di musica* "composes some pieces to play, that is *canzoni* and the like."[33] It is thus quite plausible that he might have been the one to extend this musical circle to include, indirectly, his probable pupil, the talented student composer from Santa Cristina, who was trying her hand at similar works in exactly those years.

The motets of Vernizzi and his friends could not have represented the farthest boundary of Lucrezia Vizzana's musical world, however. Although all the other elements of her musical language have precedents to a greater or lesser extent in the new-style solo and few-voice motets of Banchieri and Vernizzi, Vizzana's most striking expressive motif, the leap away from a suspended dissonance in the vocal line, seems to find no place in the sacred works of these Bolognese organist-composers. This striking skipwise resolution remained much less common in the sacred repertory in general than the juxtaposed major chords mentioned earlier. Even Vizzana's Venetian contemporary, the so-called avant-gardist Giovanni Francesco Capello, whose harmonic idiom is generally much more adventurous than hers, particularly in its extensive use of chromaticism, introduces comparable leaps from suspended dissonances in only about a dozen of the more than 110 motets from his five motet publications.[34] By comparison, the device appears in six of the twenty motets in Vizzana's single collection.

Even in secular music such leaps from dissonances remained something of a rarity. They do turn up, interestingly enough, in Ercole Porta's secular collection, *Ore di recreazione musicale*, published in 1612, a year before his sacred *Vaga Ghirlanda*. Even here, however, the skipwise resolution only appears in the opening pair of pieces, *In un sospir'accolta* and *Ch'io mora? Eccomi pronto al morir*. Episcopal prohibitions aside, one cannot rule out the possibility that Lucrezia Vizzana's more extreme musical gestures had their origins in moments from Porta's secular *Ore*, clearly quite inappropriate for the cloister.

Such expressive text setting, whether from the likes of Porta or Vizzana, inevitably calls to mind Claudio Monteverdi, the most familiar and distinguished composer well known for the introduction of untoward dissonances in his works. There had been some precedent for Lucrezia Vizzana's attempts at expressivity in the monodic works from Monteverdi's *Vespers* published in 1610, including one identical use of her favorite leap from a dissonance in the opening monodic section of *Audi coelum*;

another example appears at the opening of a five-part *Christe, Adoramus te*, published by Giulio Cesare Bianchi in 1620. But even in Monteverdi's sacred works the most intense variety of skipwise resolution of dissonant suspensions turns up only rarely.[35]

The more common usages of this gesture occur not in Monteverdi's sacred works from the early Seicento but in his madrigals, particularly those of Book 4 (1603) and Book 5 (1605), and in the powerful and extremely influential *Lamento d'Arianna*.[36] From the two dozen or so similar passages in these works, only a few are illustrated in Example 3.

In a study of Monteverdi's influence on colleagues and pupils, Denis Arnold suggested that the introduction of transposed repetitions of text fragments for rhetorical effect or the resolution of a suspended seventh by a leap (the same expressive gestures we have observed in Vizzana's motets) in Claudio Saracini's *Seconde Musiche* (1620) reveal "the sincerest form of flattery," so much a reflection of Monteverdi's influence that they "require no comment."[37] Obviously, the question of similar possible influence becomes considerably more problematic when the imitator in question is not a noble Sienese amateur, active in the world, but a woman immured within a Bolognese convent. Could the cloistered Lucrezia Orsina Vizzana have learned this expressive language and other features of her style from Claudio Monteverdi? Could the idiom of the madrigals from his Books 4 and 5 somehow have served as a source for her own dissonant leaps, either directly or indirectly?

Monteverdi was no stranger to Bologna. Indeed, it had been the irregular dissonance treatment of madrigals from his Books 4 and 5, including one of those cited in Example 13.3, that had drawn the fire of the old-fashioned Bolognese music theorist and canon regular of San Salvatore, Giovanni Maria Artusi.[38] The year after Artusi's second assault on what Monteverdi termed the *seconda prattica*, it was the by-now familiar Adriano Banchieri who in his *Conclusioni nel suono dell'organo* of 1609, having commented that "when the words in compositions call for breaking the rules, this must be done in order to imitate the word," went on to single out "the most gentle composer of music, Claudio Monteverdi . . . with regard to modern composition. His artful sentiments in truth are worthy of complete commendation, uncovering every affective part of perfect speech, diligently explained and imitated by appropriate harmony."[39]

More significant for our purposes, when Banchieri founded his musical academy, the Accademia dei Floridi, in 1614, he stipulated that the motet or sacred madrigal by Lassus or Palestrina, whose performance was required at each of the weekly musical meetings, could be replaced by "one

Example 13.3. Monteverdi madrigals.

of those madrigals by that most gentle of composers, Claudio Monteverdi, at present the most worthy Director of Music at St. Mark's Venice, which have been changed into motets by Aquilino Coppini, by request of the Most Illustrious Cardinal Federigo Borromeo."[40] Virtually all these Monteverdi madrigals-made-motets, which thus were heard at the musical gatherings of Banchieri and his friends, certainly including the likes of Ercole Porta and Ottavio Vernizzi, came from Monteverdi's experimental Books 4 and 5, and included all of those cited in Example 13.3. Not only

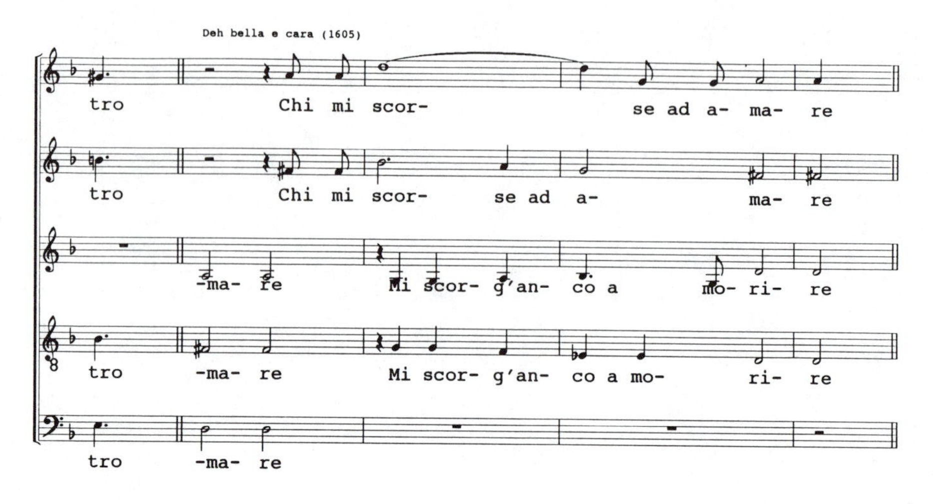

Example 13.3. (cont.)

did these works have an honored place in Banchieri's weekly academies, but their composer himself was even feted at a meeting of the group on the feast day of Saint Anthony of Padua in 1620, when Monteverdi was conducted to San Michele in Bosco by Banchieri and Girolamo Giacobbi, *maestro di musica* and colleague of Vernizzi at San Petronio.[41]

Monteverdi also seems to have had other, ongoing personal contacts with Bologna during these years. He had visited the city just the year

Example 13.3. (cont.)

before he was honored by Banchieri's academy to establish his musical son, Francesco, as a law student in the city. For two weeks in late January and early February 1619 the composer stayed with his son, who was received at the monastery of Santa Maria dei Servi—by an interesting coincidence, only about a five minutes' walk, around the corner and up the street, from Santa Cristina della Fondazza, where during that time the nuns might well have been preparing with Ottavio Vernizzi the music for the feast of the founder of their order, Saint Romuald, celebrated at the convent on February 7.[42] It appears that later in the year the young Francesco Monteverdi sang as a substitute at San Petronio, where he would surely have encountered Ottavio Vernizzi in his role as organist.[43]

Thus one can establish clear links between Monteverdi, Bologna, and the Banchieri-Vernizzi musical circle,[44] and demonstrate that the experimental madrigals from Books 4 and 5 were highly esteemed in that circle, at least in Coppini's more decorous motet versions, which would have provoked fewer blushes if they also found their way to the convent of Santa Cristina. At least some of Coppini's pious contrafacta had in fact been conceived with nuns in mind, for the 1608 collection bore a dedication to Suor Bianca Lodovica Taverna at the convent of Santa Marta in Milan.[45] It is very tempting to suggest that Banchieri or Vernizzi's greatest musical gift to the nun composer Lucrezia Orsina Vizzana, who obviously could not have joined them at the Accademia dei Floridi, would not have been to present the convent with any of their own attempts at the *stile moderno*, but to introduce Lucrezia Vizzana to the music of Claudio Monteverdi.

At this point, an additional, less illustrious figure reemerges, however, to offer a closing link in this putative chain of influence. It is that third and most elusive member of our trio of Bolognese composer-organists, Ercole Porta, off in the Bolognese suburb of San Giovanni in Persiceto. In 1620 Porta published a large and typically diverse compendium, entitled *Sacro Convito Musicale*. The works in this later collection turn out to be more self-consciously modern than Banchieri's or Vernizzi's—or, indeed, than Porta's own earlier, more tentative *stile moderno* pieces, dating from before the founding of the Accademia dei Floridi. The solos and duets reveal a boldness of harmony and flights of ornamentation that must reflect Porta's own encounters with the works of Monteverdi in the intervening years. And in a half-dozen of these motets we find Porta's own experiments with Vizzana's boldest musical gesture, the leap from a suspended dissonance, as illustrated in Example 13.4.

It would be tempting to imagine that Porta turned his attention to such skipwise resolutions after hearing prepublication performances of Vizzana's more adventurous motets. But, as if to confirm unequivocally his debt to Monteverdi, Porta actually borrows, reworks, and resets one of Coppini's contrafacta texts in his 1620 collection:

Monteverdi/Coppini	*Ercole Porta*
Ure me Domine amore tuo,	Ure me Domine amore tuo
quam [sic] fecit amor mori,	quem [sic] fecit amor mori
incende me, hoc igne	incende me, hoc igne
subiice cordi meo facem tuam	subiice cordi meo face tua
O IESU amore tuo,	O Iesu amore tuo
liquescere me velis,	
fugiat omnis amor mei a me,	
Iam fervent mihi propter te me dullae	
O IESU amore tuo,	
anima mea languet	languet anima mea
iam rapior amore tuo dulci.	iam rapior amore tuo dulci.

No such musicological "smoking gun" emerges to confirm unequivocally whether it was the Monteverdi madrigal-motets or the Monteverdi style as filtered through Ercole Porta that most directly helped to make Lucrezia Vizzana's musical style. But a fascinating motet, *Sonet vox tua in auribus cordis mei*, a kind of exordium to her collection, in which Lucrezia

Ex. 4. Porta, O dulcissime Jesu (1620)

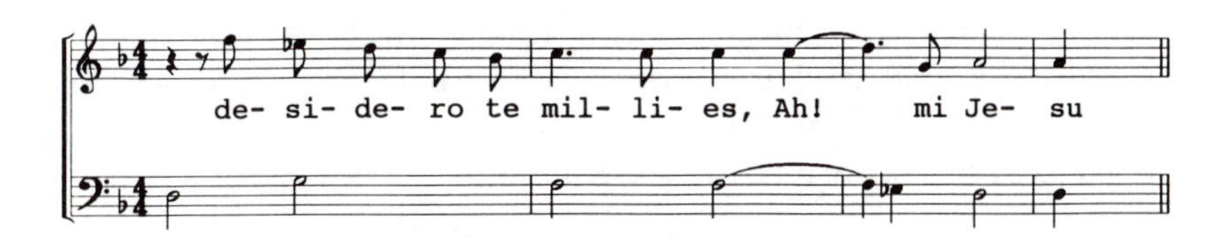

Porta, O Domine, salvum me fac (1620) [tenor tacet]

Porta, Corda Deo dabimus (1620)

Example 13.4. Ercole Porta's use of leaps from suspended dissonances.

Orsina Vizzana in effect presents her musical rhetoric, if not her face, to public gaze, reads remarkably like a response to one of Porta's motets from 1620, *Surge amica mea*, a matter which I shall discuss elsewhere.[46]

What does emerge clearly, however, is that Bolognese experiments in the *stile moderno* were not limited to the better-known musical world around San Petronio, San Pietro, and San Michele in Bosco, but were also pursued discreetly behind cloister walls in Via Fondazza. Indeed, it is particularly intriguing to discover that some of the Bolognese attempts to adapt the boldest gestures of that style for sacred use turn out to have been created within the aesthetically "marginal" environment of the convent, by a woman who could have experienced that style only indirectly, illicitly, and at a distance. There can also be little doubt that Vizzana's motets reflect a broadening in convent musical practice to include both the lavish but not especially "modern" works characteristic of the Banchieri, Cesena, and Fattorini prints dedicated to nuns at Santa Cristina, and the more overtly modern musical idiom for solo voices and basso continuo, which came to characterize the nuns' own performances for the rest of the century.

The appearance of Lucrezia Vizzana's *Componimenti Musicali* early in 1623, a decade after the flurry of modern publications by Banchieri, Porta, and Vernizzi, and a decade after the last of the four collections dedicated to the musical nuns of Santa Cristina, effectively marks the end of the most musically illustrious period in the history of the convent.[47] After 1623, though she lived for another forty years, Bologna's only publishing musical nun never again ventured into print. Whether she continued to compose is impossible to say. Still, we are lucky to be able to glimpse as much as we can of her musical world, a world that was intended to be so emphatically private. On 1 January 1623 Lucrezia Vizzana dedicated her works to her fellow nuns at Santa Cristina, the fifth and final such dedication they would receive. It was a fitting choice, for it was the special nature of the hidden world they shared which helped her creativity to flower in ways that would have been largely impossible for her beyond the convent walls in Via Fondazza.

I should like to thank Monsignor Niso Albertazzi, abate parroco di San Giuliano in Bologna, for granting me permission to visit the church of Santa Cristina, which has been closed to the public for many years, and Signor Gianluigi Panzacchi for his help and many kindnesses during my visits to the church. I am also indebted to Padre A. Ugo Fossa, prior and librarian of the Monastery of Camaldoli (Arezzo) for permission to consult manuscripts in the library of the order. I should also like to thank the Camaldolese hermits at the Hermitage of the Immaculate Heart, Big Sur, California, for their hospitality during the time I spent working in their library.

Notes

A complete copy is preserved in the Civico Museo Bibliografico Musicale, Bologna. A second copy, missing the canto secondo, survives in the Biblioteka Uniwersitecka, Wrocław.

2. Bologna, Biblioteca Universitaria (BUB), Ms It. 3856, pp. 133–36. Donna Flaminia's sanctity is singled out in Antonio di Paolo Masini, *Bologna Perlustrata*, terza impressione (Bologna: Erede di Vittorio Benacci, 1666). See Gabriella Zarri, "I monasteri femminili benedettini nella diocesi di Bologna (secoli XIII–XVII)," in *Ravennatensia IX: Atti del convegno di Bologna nel xv centenario della nascita di S. Benedetto (15–16–17 settembre 1980)* (Cesena: Badia di Santa Maria del Monte, 1981), p. 347. To this day Flaminia Bombacci is remembered in the menology of the Camaldolese order on 28 September: "V. FLAMINIA BOMBACE monaca (+ Bologna 1624), austerissima, ricolma di pazienza, di carità, di umiltà, dormì sempre su nude tavole; sperimentò prodigiosamente l'assistenza dell'Angelo Custode, spesso predisse il futuro, lasciò alcuni mirabili scritti ascetici" ("The venerable Flaminia Bombacci, nun (+ Bologna, 1624), most austere, full of patience, of charity, of humility, she always slept on bare boards; she experienced the assistance of her guardian angel, often predicted the future, left some admirable ascetic writings"). See D. Anselmo Giabbani, *Menologia Camaldolese* (Tivoli: De Rossi, 1950), p. 59.

3. Bologna, Biblioteca Comunale dell'Archiginasio (BCB), Ms. B901, p. 373.

4. BUB, Ms. It. 3856, pp. 98, 103, 122; the sixteen *gonfalonieri del popolo* ruled in civil and criminal matters concerning the common people of Bologna; the eight *anziani* rendered judgments in minor civil and criminal cases.

5. BUB, Ms. It. 3856, pp. 75–76, 122. Fecundity must have run in the family; Isabetta Bombacci's great-grandmother Lodovica had borne no less than twenty-four children (p. 133). For Margaret King's comments on wealthy women's tendency to bear unusually large numbers of offspring, see her *Women of the Renaissance* (Chicago: University of Chicago Press, 1991), pp. 2–4.

6. These details are gleaned from Bologna, Archivio Arcivescovile (hereafter cited as AAB), Reg. Batt. 1590–1592, f. 74v, and from petitions in Rome, Archivio Segreto Vaticano, Sacra Congregazione dei Vescovi e Regolari (ASV, VR), posizione 1607, lettere A–B.

7. Other family members have been retrieved from the Vizzani sisters' dowry agreement, Bologna, Archivio di Stato (hereafter cited as ASB), Notarile, Belvisi Giulio, Prot. 8, f. 379r, and from the dowry agreements of Ludovica

(Donna Flaminia) Bombacci (ASB, Notarile, Rusticelli Annibale, Prot. 9 [1578], f. 77r), Isabella Bombacci (ibid., Prot. 11 [1580], f. 141r), and Camilla Bombacci (ibid., Prot. 3–33 [olim Prot. 18 (1588)], ff. 113r–114v). A "Messer Zuan Bombizo," credited with the foundation of the illustrious Camaldolese monastery of San Michele di Murano in Venice, is linked to the Bolognese Bombacci by Valerio Zani. See BCB, Ms. B3758, "Osservazioni Istoriche del Sig.r Conte Valerio Zani sopra l'Arbore Genealogico de' SS.ri Conti Bombaci Nobili Bolognesi, e Patrizij romani Colle loro varie Derivazioni, e Allianze."

8. For the dowry arrangements, see ASB, Demaniale 51/5009 (Santa Cristina), ff. 1v and 2v, and ASB, Notarile, Belvisi Giulio, Prot. 8, ff. 378r and 379r. For their requests regarding the *Sacra*, see ASV, VR, posizione 1607, lettere A–B, posizione 1613, lettere B–F, Reg. Regularium 8 (1607/08), f. 55v, and Reg. Regularium 14 (1613) f. 132r.

9. Proof of Ludovico Vizzani's remarriage appears in BCB, Ms. B700, no. 150, and ASB, Notarile, Sturoli Ventura, Prot. 1, f. 2r, dated October 21, 1610, where "Elena d[e] zanis" is named as Ludovico Vizzani's wife. For the legitimization of Angelo Michele, son of Dionigio di Ludovico Vizzani, by Ludovico Vizzani and the subsequent litigation with Lucrezia and Isabetta Vizzani, see ASB, Famiglia Banzi, busta 8, nos. 104–8. Interestingly enough, in 1639 Angelo Michele agreed to pay the dowry of his sister, Valeria di Dionigio Vizzani, who entered Santa Cristina, professed, and took the name Donna Maria Clorinda (ASB, Demaniale 20/2881 [Santa Cristina], no. 15/V). Donna Maria Clorinda and her aunt, Donna Lucrezia Orsina, seem to have struggled for decades to obtain the yearly support due them from Angelo Michele (see ASB, Demaniale 35/2896 [Santa Cristina], no. 4/H.H).

10. On the history of the convent of Santa Cristina, its architecture and art, see Roberta Zucchini, "Santa Cristina della Fondazza: Storia Architettonica e Storico Artistica," Tesi di Laurea, Università di Bologna, 1987–88; and Ugo Capriani, "Chiesa e Convento di Santa Cristina della Fondazza in Bologna: Ipotesi di Ricerca e Recupero," Tesi di Laurea, Università di Bologna, 1987–88. I should like to thank Dottoressa Zucchini and Dottore Capriani for providing me with copies of their theses, and for many other kindnesses.

11. In 1618 the Congregation of Bishops had refused to permit the nuns of Santa Cristina to admit another servant nun because the ratio was already 43 to 13 (ASV, VR, Reg. Regularium 21 [1618], f. 242v).

12. On the early Camaldolese love of learning, see M. Elena Maghieri Cataluccio and A. Ugo Fossa, *Biblioteca e cultura a Camaldoli, Dal medioevo all'umanesimo* (Rome: Editrice Anselmiana, 1979). On the Camaldolese in later centuries, see Giuseppe M. Croce, "I Camaldolesi nel Settecento: tra la 'rusticitas' degli eremiti e l'erudizione dei cenobiti," in *Settecento Monastico Italiano*, ed. Giustino Farnedi and Giovanni Spinelli (Cesena: Badia S. Maria Del Monte, 1990), pp. 203–70.

13. It is significant that Santa Cristina is the only convent for which Carlo Cesare Malvasia's *Le pitture di Bologna* (1686) provides the family names of the nun patrons of virtually every altarpiece in the external church. See Malvasia, *Le pitture*

di Bologna 1686, ed. Andrea Emiliani (Bologna: Edizioni Alfa, 1969), pp. 266 [181]–268 [183]. (Bracketed numbers refer to the modern pagination, which does not always agree with the facsimile pagination. Some pages contain only the editor's modern commentary, and therefore include only modern pagination.)

14. Bologna, Biblioteca Arcivescovile, Libreria Breventani, Ms. 64. An eighteenth-century transcription by Baldassare Antonio Maria Carrati appears in BCB, Ms. B921. See also Camaldoli, Biblioteca del Monastero, Ms. 1087.

15. For a discussion of the abiding attempts by Gabriele and Alfonso Paleotti to control convent music, see Craig Monson, "Disembodied Voices: Music in the Nunneries of Bologna in the Midst of the Counter-Reformation," in *The Crannied Wall: Women, Religion, and the Arts in Early Modern Europe*, ed. Craig Monson (Ann Arbor: University of Michigan Press, 1992), pp. 191–209. See also Gian Lodovico Masetti Zannini, "Espressioni musicali in monasteri femminili del primo Seicento a Bologna," *Strenna Storica Bolognese* 35 (1985): 193–205.

16. "*1640* 6 xbre d[onn]a Camilla Bombaci d'anni 70 organista prima e tre volte M[aest]ra delle Novizie indi Abbadessa" (BCB, Ms. B921, p. 50). For her nomination as *maestra del choro*, see AAB, Misc. Vecchie 820, fasc. 2 [Processo, 1622–23], f. 14r. Lucrezia Vizzana could also read and write Latin (see BCB, Ms. B921, pp. 50–51), which she might have learned from another aunt, the saintly Donna Flaminia Bombacci, who was also well versed in the language (see BUB, Ms. It. 3856, p. 134; see also Camaldoli, Biblioteca del Monastero, Ms. 652, ff. 19r–20r).

17. "Ritrouandomi il giorno nel quale si solennizaua la festa della Gloriosa Santa Cristina nella Chiesa di V. Reuerentia, mentre si cantaua il primo Vespro, & sentendo con mio molto gusto, gli armonici Concerti di voci, Organi, & varij strumenti Musicali, guidati con soauissimi affetti di deuotione, procurai sapere da un Musico mio particolar amico (che iui era presente) chi era capo di detti Concerti, & dal detto fui raguagliato esserne V. Reuer. & meritamente (disse) soggiungendomi, che oltre le altre sue honoratissime qualitadi, esser lei si nel cantare come al sonare molto intelligente tutto servendosene a laude, & gloria d'Iddio Benedetto . . . altro in ricompensa non desidero, solo che concertandogli all'occasioni, lei insieme con le sue care sorelle habbino in pensieri pregare Iddio per me nelle sue deuote & sante orationi." Adriano Banchieri, *Messa Solenne a otto voci* (Venice: Ricciardo Amadino, 1599).

18. For Emilia Grassi's tenure as *maestra del choro*, see AAB, Misc. Vecchie 820, no. 2 [Processo, 1622–23], f. 14r. "In primo Anno secundi trienij obiit maximo casu dolore Soror Nobiliss.ma huius Mon.rii Abbadissa D. Emilia ex Ill.ma Familia de Grassis integritate maximo profund.e Virtutum ornatissimaque pricipue in Instrumentorum omnium Musicalium pulsatione ita excelluit ut nulli seconda fuerit" (BCB, Ms. B921, p. 5).

19. Published in Venice by Ricciardo Amadino, 1601. A copy, missing the canto primo part, survives at the Archivio del Duomo in Vercelli. I thank Robert Kendrick for bringing this collection to my attention. Fattorini was in fact also among the very first composers to apply the monodic style to sacred music. See Christopher Wilkinson, "Gabriele Fattorini: Rival of Viadana," *Music and Letters*

65 (1984): 329–36. The monodic music appears in Murray E. Bradshaw, *Gabriel(e) Fattorini "I Sacri Concerti a Due Voci" (1600)* (American Institute of Musicology Miscellanea 5 Early Sacred Monody, vol. 2) (Neuhausen-Stuttgart: Hänssler-Verlag, 1986).

20. *Compieta con Letanie che si cantano Nella Casa di Loreto, et Motetti a Otto Voci, di S. Gio: Battista Cesena* (Venice: Giacomo Vincenti, 1606).

21. "D. Felicita Stellini, D. Anna, et D. Armellina Uberti . . . tutte alquanto versate in musica, desiderose d'imparare à alcuni mottetti Spirituali alla Romana supp^{no} humilmente le SS:^{rie} VV Ill^{me}; che voglino conceder licentia al Con'ico Manzini di detta Città, che possa andare una volta sola, ò due al più alli publici parlatorij per discorrere, et insegnare alle sud^{te} monache il modo, come vanno cantati . . . con l'intervento dell M're Badessa et delle deputate Ascoltatrici" (ASV, VR, posizione 1606, lettere A–C).

22. See Monson, "Disembodied Voices," passim.

23. AAB, Misc. Vecchie 820, fasc. 2, "Visitatio localis Ecclesie et Monasterij Monialiu[m] .S. Christine. Bonon." It appears that the remedies demanded after the visitation of 1623 were only partially successful, for after Archbishop Girolamo Boncompagni's pastoral visitation of 1654 he decreed "Alle finestre delli Organi si levino li Cartoni, e vi si ponghino tavole permanenti" ("The cardboard [covers] for the organ windows should be removed, and permanent flats should be installed") (BUB, Ms. It. 231, no. 1, ff. 8r–8v).

24. For the inventories from Santa Margherita, see ASB, Demaniale 51/3918 (Santa Margherita); for the musical bequest at San Guglielmo, see ASB, Demaniale 80/814 (San Guglielmo), entry no. 21.

25. See Gaetano Gaspari, *Musica e Musicisti a Bologna* (Bologna: Forni Editore, n.d.), pp. 170–75.

26. ASB, Demaniale 31/2892 (Santa Cristina), f. 128r.

27. ASB, Demaniale 48/2909 (Santa Cristina), especially f. 11r.

28. AAB, Misc. Vecchie 820, fasc. 2 [Processo, 1622–23], f. 15r.

29. Carlo Ginzburg, *The Cheese and the Worms: The Cosmos of a Sixteenth-Century Miller*, trans. John Tedeschi and Anne Tedeschi (Baltimore: Johns Hopkins University Press, 1980).

30. Banchieri also introduces the device, again for expressive effect, in the Creed at "ex Maria Virgine." It appears for coloristic effect in the *Te Deum* at "tibi coeli et universae terrae."

31. Interestingly, the juxtaposition of third-related chromatic chords represents the most striking feature of her style singled out in Jerome Roche, "Orsina, Lucretia," in *The New Grove Dictionary of Music and Musicians*, ed. Stanley Sadie (London: MacMillan, 1980), 13: 874.

32. Banchieri's description of Vernizzi as "cordialissimo amico dell'Autore" calls to mind the remark from his 1599 dedication, when he had spoken of "A musician, my special friend (who was present there)", "un Musico mio particolar' amico (che ivi era presente)." Perhaps Vernizzi had been the musician present with Banchieri for first Vespers of Santa Cristina, who had revealed to him the details of musical practices there.

33. "V'è anco Ottavio Vernitio Mastro della Musica ch[e] scrive delle cose

da sonare cioè, Canzoni et simili" (AAB, Misc. Vecchie 820, fasc. 2 [Processo, 1622–23], f. 15r).

34. On Capello, see Jeffrey Kurtzman, "Giovanni Francesco Capello, an Avant-gardist of the Early Seventeenth Century," *Musica Disciplina* 31 (1977): 155–82. Leaps from dissonances turn up in three motets from the *Sacrorum Concentum* (1610), in five from *Motetti opera quarta* (c. 1612–13), and in four from *Motetti in Dialogo* (1613). I thank Professor Kurtzman for kindly allowing me to examine his transcriptions of Capello's complete works. There is nothing to connect the biographically elusive Capello with Bologna, although one cannot rule out the possibility that Vizzana might have had a chance to examine copies of these publications. The rhetorical transposed repetition of a leap from the seventh at the opening of her *O si sciret stultus mundus* offers an interesting parallel to the opening of Capello's *Tristis est anima mea*.

35. Isolated examples appear as early as the *Sacrae Cantiunculae* and the six-voice mass, however. See Hellmut Federhofer, "Die Dissonanzbehandlung in Monteverdis Kirchenmusikalischen Werken und die Figurenlehre Christoph Bernhard," in *Claudio Monteverdi e il suo Tempo Relazioni e Comunicazioni*, ed. Raffaello Monterosso (Verona: Valdonega, 1969), pp. 464–66.

36. For Gary Tomlinson's exploration of Monteverdi's own experiments with the leap from a suspended seventh, and the composer's increasing sophistication in its use, see Tomlinson, *Monteverdi and the End of the Renaissance* (Berkeley: University of California Press, 1987), p. 121.

37. Denis Arnold, "Monteverdi: Some Colleagues and Pupils," in *The New Monteverdi Companion*, ed. Denis Arnold and Nigel Fortune (London: Faber and Faber, 1985), pp. 115–16. Saracini's collection was dedicated to Monteverdi.

38. Of the substantial literature on the Monteverdi-Artusi controversy, particularly useful is Claude V. Palisca, "The Artusi-Monteverdi Controversy," in *The New Monteverdi Companion*, 127–58. See also Tomlinson, *Monteverdi and the End of the Renaissance*, pp. 21–30, 106–9; also Suzanne Cusick's fascinating interpretation of the gendered rhetoric of Artusi and Monteverdi, "Gendering Modern Music: Thoughts on the Monteverdi-Artusi Controversy," *Journal of the American Musicological Society* 46 (1993): 1–25.

39. *Adriano Banchieri Conclusions for Playing the Organ (1609)*, trans. Lee R. Garrett, Colorado College Music Press Translations 13 (Colorado Springs: Colorado College Music Press, 1982), pp. 50–51.

40. Quoted in Denis Stevens, *The Letters of Claudio Monteverdi* (Cambridge: Cambridge University Press, 1980), p. 211, which also summarizes the Monteverdi-Banchieri contacts. Banchieri printed the statutes for his academy in his *Cartella musicale* (Venice: Giacomo Vincenti, 1614). For a full translation of them, see Clifford A. Cranna, Jr., "Adriano Banchieri's *Cartella Musicale* (1614): Translation and Commentary," Ph.D. dissertation, Stanford University, 1981, pp. 25–36. Amid the contrafacta by Monteverdi, Coppini had also included one by Banchieri, who thanked him effusively for doing so in his *Lettere Armoniche* (Bologna: Girolamo Mascheroni, 1628; rpt. Bologna: Forni, n.d.), p. 121.

41. See Giuseppe Vecchi, *Le accademie musicali del primo seicento, e Monteverdi a Bologna* (Bologna: A.M.I.S., 1969), pp. 73–92, for a discussion of Banchieri's

academy and Monteverdi's contacts with it. See also Stevens, *The Letters*, pp. 211–12. The primary information regarding Monteverdi's contact with Banchieri and his academy derives from Banchieri's two letters to Monteverdi included in *Lettere Armoniche*, p. 141, with the second letter added in the appendix to the new edition of 1630.

42. The anniversary of the translation of Saint Romuald's body to Fabriano was 7 February. A *Libro, nel quale vengono notate diverse Memorie attinenti al Camerlingato*, dated 1728, which records the customary chapel expenses, includes the note, "A di 7 Febraro. Festa del nostro P.S. Romualdo Il Monas[te]r[o] fà Cantare la Messa Aparata" (ASB, Demaniale 26/2887 [Santa Cristina]). The same expense book also includes the feast of Saint Romuald on June 19. In 1666 Antonio di Paolo Masini had also indicated that it was customary to celebrate the feast on 7 February (*Bologna Perlustrata*, p. 225). On the other hand, the feast is not included in Baldassare Antonio Maria Carrati's transcription of the calendar/necrology from Santa Cristina (BCB, Ms. B 921), which does include Saint Romuald's feast on June 19. The Camaldolese breviary of c. 1580 includes the propers for the feast of Saint Romuald on June 19, and also those for the feast of his translation on November 29; but the feast of the translation is entirely absent from the calendar at the beginning of the breviary. See *Breviarium monasticum secundum Ordinem camaldulensem: nunc recens reformatum, summaque diligentia emendatum et excusum* (Venice: Johannes Variscum, [1580]), ff. 60v–63r and 154v–156v of the Proper of Saints. Monteverdi could not have attended the celebrations, since a letter to Alessandro Striggio, dated 9 February 1619, indicates that he had just arrived back in Venice. See Stevens, *The Letters*, pp. 143–44.

43. Monteverdi's younger son, Massimiliano, also studied in Bologna during the 1620s, taking his degree in medicine in 1626. The details of the Monteverdi sons' stays in Bologna appear in Vecchi, *Le accademie*, pp. 80–82, 91 n. 88; see also Stevens, *The Letters*, pp. 142–44, 211–14, 240–43.

44. Aquilino Coppini had also been in contact with Bologna in the years immediately after the Monteverdi-Artusi controversy. In 1609 he had written to Vincenzo Cavalli of Bologna, inquiring after Artusi, "who lashed out at the divine Claudio Monteverdi's music, and published something from the Cavaliere Butrigarius [Bottrigari] aimed against him." Quoted in Claudio Sartori, "Monteverdiana," *Musical Quarterly* 38 (1952): 406.

45. See Margaret Ann Rorke, "Sacred Contrafacta of Monteverdi Madrigals and Cardinal Borromeo's Milan," *Music and Letters* 65 (1984): 175. I thank Professor Rorke for lending me her copies of the Coppini prints, and Robert Kendrick for originally calling my attention to the link between Coppini's collection and Milanese nuns.

46. Craig A. Monson, *Disembodied Voices: Music and Culture in an Early Modern Italian Convent* (Berkeley: University of California Press, forthcoming 1995).

47. It is another interesting coincidence that when Lucrezia Vizzana's motets saw the light in 1623 it was not from the presses of Giacomo Vincenti, who had dedicated the 1606 collection to the nuns of Santa Cristina, or from the local Bolognese presses of Giovanni Rossi, who had published Banchieri's *Nuovi Pensieri* and Ercole Porta's collection of 1613, but from those of the Venetian publisher

Bartolomeo Magni, who between 1619 and 1628 published one sacred, four secular, and one pedagogical work of Banchieri. See Andreas Wernli, *Studien zum literarischen und musikalischen Werk Adriano Banchieris (1568–1634)* (Publikationen der Schweizerischen Musikforschenden Gesellschaft, serie 2, vol. 3) (Bern and Stuttgart: Paul Haupt, 1981), pp. 221–29.

Robert L. Kendrick

14. Four Views of Milanese Nuns' Music

Music in the female monasteries of Milan boasts a long tradition; its documentation begins with the Ambrosian chant Office for the feast of Saint Victor, produced in 1327 for the Benedictine house of San Vittore in Meda.[1] Other manuscripts, such as the now sadly mutilated antiphoner written in 1360 for the Benedictine foundation of Santa Radegonda in the city, testify to the ongoing practice of music.[2] But the first evidence for nuns' polyphony is found in the episcopal strictures on music making, as well as the more positive evidence of organ building, both of which begin to appear in the diocesan records around 1550.

For instance, the sumptuous organ constructed by Gian Giacomo Antegnati, for the Monastero Maggiore, in 1554 testifies to the centrality of music in the elaborate decorative plan of the house's double church (after 1500, nuns' churches in Lombardy were typically built with an external church [*chiesa esteriore*] for the laity and a monastic church [*chiesa interiore*] for the nuns).[3] Antegnati's contract specified the organ's impressive size and location in the internal—not external—church, thus requiring that nuns be its players.

The public renown and patrician prestige of nuns' music in Milan was a central issue in the aesthetic and pastoral debates over the form and value of sisters' performances, debates held over two centuries from both outside and inside the claustral wall.[4] Music in these monasteries would be described by enthusiastic visitors as late as the 1770 musical tour of the English critic and composer Charles Burney.[5] Over the course of the seventeenth century, above all during the tenure of Archbishop Federigo Borromeo (1595–1631), the performing skills of Milanese nuns would lead to some fifty dedications of single motets or entire editions.[6] But is was precisely the public nature of Milanese monastic music that would also contribute to its place among those items of nuns' behavior which some archbishops, starting with Carlo Borromeo (and his individual and radical interpretation of the Council of Trent's decrees), would want to restrict and even banish entirely, in line with their ideas of monastic enclosure (*clausura*) for nuns.

In this essay, I shall simply outline four different perspectives on nuns' music, as heard across the wall that divided the double churches of female monasteries. Three of the views are exemplified by a visit or encounter, each with a particular female monastery with their varying order-specific and social traditions. Although none gives a complete account of sisters' music making, they serve to highlight the differences of post-Tridentine practice even in such an ostensibly conservative center as Milan, the largest diocese of the seventeenth-century Catholic world.

One important view of what nuns' music was and was not supposed to be is found in the visitation of 12 February 1571, paid by Carlo Borromeo to the Rich Clare house of Sant'Apollinare in the southwest quarter of Milan.[7] It is important to place this episcopal intervention in the context of Carlo's ongoing efforts to install strict *clausura* and "reform" daily life in Milanese monasteries.[8] The efforts as a whole had begun vicariously—literally through vicars—even before his 1565 arrival in Milan. Carlo's ideas and practice for the reform of these institutions, such as the struggles over his model project at the Angeliche house of San Paolo, represented a decisive break with the public, political, and sanctoral traditions of Milanese female monasteries in the later Middle Ages. Carlo had obtained papal bulls from 1566 on to visit—that is, reform—the leading female cloisters of the city, whose membership was drawn largely from the urban patriciate. This visitation to Sant'Apollinare should therefore be seen as a test of strength between Carlo and the urban aristocracy who heavily influenced the monastery.

As was standard, the archbishop and curial officials took depositions from individual nuns, heard testimony, and later issued rules for the monastery. Music played an important role among the abuses that Carlo was concerned to correct, although it was far from the only infraction. The deposition of Suor Buona highlights its role:

> When I was to be confirmed as mother of this convent, there came here the Padre Commissario [Carlo's vicar], who told me that Suor Clementina had asked him for a visitation permit for Messer Giovanni Antonio the organist, who taught the said Suor Clementina to sing and taught Suor Angelina Serafina to play [keyboard]. He came also to tune the keyboard of Suor Angela and the organ.[9]

The depositions of several other nuns—including Suor Michaela, Suor Paola Hieronima—also mention that Messer Giovanni was admitted once a year with a permit (*licenza*) issued in 1568, that he gave written music lessons (*per cartella*) inside the monastery's walls, as well as the fact that the nuns fed him on his visits. Carlo's orders for the monastery, including punishments of eighteen different nuns, dated 30 March 1571, also detail some of the irregular musical behavior of several sisters:

> Suor Geronima Caterina . . . will say penance every Saturday in the refractory for three months for her errors, as noted in the record of this visitation, namely having possessed madrigals and amorous sonnets and not having watched the parlor as was her duty . . . Suor Angela Serafina will be deprived of the veil for three months, and will be relieved of her duties as organist, nor can she regain this office for six years.[10]

Suor Angela was also to ask pardon for her offenses every Wednesday for six months, and was deprived of active voice for three months. Furthermore, Carlo ordered:

> The large harpsichord should not remain in her room, but somewhere else in the monastery, nor can she play it or any other instrument, nor sing polyphony for three years.[11]

Suor Clementia was punished not for her singing but rather for having spoken to outsiders without *licenza* and for having accepted gifts, as well as for having fed Messer Giovanni Antonio during his pedagogical visits. Indeed, despite the fact that the first diocesan synod of Carlo's tenure, the famous 1565 meeting largely prepared by Nicolò Ormaneto, had outlawed public performance of polyphony and had restricted the use of instruments inside female monasteries, Carlo did not punish the Clarissans for music making per se, but rather for their infringement of the more universal bans on the importation of men without a *licenza*, and above all for their feeding Messer Giovanni Antonio.

Carlo's visit points out a number of things about musical life at Sant'Apollinare. First, the sisters obviously enjoyed a high level of music making, including secular music, keyboard playing, and if the description of Giovanni Antonio's teaching "per cartella" is to be taken in its normal sense, possibly also composition lessons. But the willingness of the nuns to import Messer Giovanni after his permit had expired also testifies to the fragile nature of music education in their institutions. One or two nuns, like Suor Clementina, themselves cloistered at age eighteen, were responsible for the music making in the whole foundation, including teaching novices and performing music.[12]

In the case of Sant'Apollinare, Messer Giovanni remains an elusive figure. No musician by that name is recorded in the account book of the Duomo, or among the musicians who contributed to motet and madrigal anthologies in Milan. But a 29 November 1568 petition in the Milanese State Archives for a patent does detail the discovery by a certain Giovanni Antonio Brena of a harpsichord that could be retuned by various intervals.[13] This figure may well have been the teacher at Sant'Apollinare: his petition shows that he moved in the circles of the urban patriciate from which the house drew its members. And, as a musician of that circle, he would have had no responsibilities toward Carlo and his ideas of monastic reform. Finally, his invention of a retunable harpsichord would have been of great use for performance of mixed-voice polyphony under the conditions of all-female choirs in such institutions as Sant'Apollinare. This is further strengthened by the records of Carlo's visitation, which note Messer Giovanni's tuning of the instruments, probably not the routine tuning needed on a daily basis, but quite possibly some kind of annual tuning to a suitable pitch. Indeed, a later, similar scheme for returning harpsichords is found in the 1606 keyboard ricercars of G. P. Cima, which collection is dedicated to the first nun whose compositions have survived, Caterina Assandra of Pavia.[14] Further afield, the 1672 treatise of the Bolognese theoretician Lorenzo Penna, *Li primi albori musicali*, contains similar transposition instructions and is also dedicated to nuns.[15]

Carlo's visit to Sant'Apollinare also points up the fact that it was precisely polyphony—in the parlors but also in the double churches for Mass and Vespers—that drew archepiscopal wrath for its attractiveness to the outside world. The importation of men as teachers, and of outsiders in general as an audience, was perceived as a danger to convent life. Indeed, one of Carlo's vicars in 1578 would express his position on the place of music inside *clausura*:

> Playing the organ at some monasteries of the more reformed nuns is not considered necessary, and so they have not wanted to build organs in their churches . . . and often the organists and singers of polyphony tend to be the least disciplined and least spiritual.[16]

We do not know what became of the music making of Suor Clementina or Suor Angela in the immediate aftermath of Carlo's visit. The long-term effects, however, remain open to question, since two different nuns at Sant'Apollinare received musical dedications in the latter half of the seventeenth century, and a 1728 list of duties calls two nuns "maestre del canto figurato."[17]

Indeed, one might question even the short-term effects of Carlo's reforms, given such documents as a 1593 order from the curia of his immediate successor, Gaspare Visconti, forbidding the importation of male music teachers—precisely the Clarissans' offense—into the model foundation of Santa Cristina, an Ursuline house founded just nine years earlier under the auspices of Carlo himself.[18]

A second view of nuns' music is exemplified by the radically different approach of Carlo's cousin, successor, and custodian of his cult, Federigo Borromeo. One key source for Federigo's support and encouragement of music in female monasteries is his voluminous correspondence with individual nuns in his favored institutions—the Humiliate foundation of Santa Caterina in Brera and the Augustinians at Santa Marta above all. Federigo's devotion to the administration of the entire diocese meant that his visits to these monasteries were sometimes more epistolary than physical. But numerous sermons preached to nuns survive as well, and along with the letters reveal his concern with the spiritual, physical, and intellectual well-being of the sisters.[19]

Unlike Carlo, and indeed many other prelates, Federigo clearly considered this well-being to include music making. One source for this is Federigo's three volumes of correspondence with Suor Angela Confaloniera at Santa Caterina in Brera, dating from the last decade of his life, 1621–31, and preserved along with Federigo's other writings at the Ambrosiana. But the prelate's sermons (*ragionamenti*) also provide an insight into his view of the devotional and spiritual effects of female monastic music. For Borromeo, the key to these effects was not so much musical style (although the prelate, along with some Milanese composers, criticized overelaborate ornamentation that served to mask the rhetorical effect of the text) as much as the internal qualities of devotion and humility appropriate to the "most select portion of Christ's flock," the position of nuns, in the prelate's view.[20]

It is also clear that these traits accorded well with the key points of Federigo's spirituality, whose synthesis of the *devotio moderna* with Ignatius Loyola's ideas of internal dialogue stressed simplicity, self-examination, and reflection on divine love as manifested in such key texts as the Song of Songs.[21] A *ragionamento* given to nuns, probably at Santa Caterina in Brera, or Santa Marta (both of which houses were jurisdictionally subject to the archbishop, and both of which were quite active musically), takes the Assumption of Mary as a starting point for some twenty-five pages of the archbishop's philosophy of music:

> Today the Church sings "Assumpta est Maria in caelum, gaudent Angeli," and to accompany the angelic song we should say something about spiritual music . . . and we will speak of the things necessary to make good music, the first being . . . a good voice, the second being the composition . . . but the third, and most important, is the *affetto* . . . that the composition of the music be appropriate to the words. . . . But the perfection of music derives not from the composition, or from any artifice, but from the manner of singing and from the *affetto* of the singer.[22]

Federigo's emphasis on *affetto* and simplicity for nuns' music underscores the formative influence of Filippo Neri and the Oratorians on his pastoral philosophy. Federigo's views on nuns' music stem directly, on the one hand, from his Platonic-Pythagorean synthesis of music in the system of the world, which considered earthly music to be a pale but important reflection of heavenly music. On the other hand, his unusual encouragement of practical music making can perhaps be traced to his desire to open up every path for the individual Christian to God, including that of music, and even to his gender-differentiated and gender-equal epistemology. In his pastoral treatise *De ecstaticis mulieribus et illusis*, the archbishop posited that women were more open to both true and false mystical experience than were men; Borromeo saw music making as a preparation, in the case of at least one female mystic, for authentic (divinely inspired) ecstacy.[23]

If Carlo's and Federigo's policies exemplify two divergent approaches to nuns' music from the standpoint of episcopal authority, an entirely different perspective is offered by the accounts of visitors to Milan, the third view I present here. As mentioned, the laudatory travelers' reports on the performances of Milanese sisters would last almost up to the Josephine suppressions in the late eighteenth century. If archepiscopal decrees reflect ideas of spirituality and pastoral practice, the travel descriptions stem largely from visiting secular aristocracy, and reflect the world of courtly Milan as well as that of the city's patriciate.[24]

In addition, the locus of the reports tends to differ somewhat. Federigo had been concerned with houses under direct episcopal jurisdiction: but visiting dignitaries tended to hear music, above all for Sunday Vespers, in the principal Benedictine foundations (or more precisely, in their exterior half-churches) subject to the more permissive male regulars of the order, not the archbishop. In the seventeenth century, these included: the Monastero Maggiore (to 1626), Santa Radegonda, and Santa Margarita, three of the largest female monasteries of the city. But a 1624 account of the Grand Tour of the Polish prince Ladislav Wasa includes the mention of a musical ensemble during Sunday vespers at that house which was a focus of Carlo's reforms, San Paolo.[25] Similar reports at this and other houses stem from a Medici chronicle forty years later, to be mentioned presently.

The travel accounts are often associated either with major events in the city's life—such as the 1598 and 1649 visits of the bride of the reigning Spanish Habsburg—or with the festivities, musical and other, for the more routine visits of other worthies. The descriptions begin with the rise of urban panegyric literature around 1600, and are also reflected in the local guidebooks to the city, such as Girolamo Borsieri's 1619 supplement to Paolo Morigia's *La nobilità di Milano*, which describes the famous singer Suor Claudia Sessa at the monastery of Santa Maria Annunciata (a house of Lateran Canonesses), and in the later guidebooks of Carlo Torre and Serafino Latuada.[26]

In terms of specific information, these accounts are often, perhaps necessarily, disappointing. There is no discussion, for instance, of exactly what kind of music, or which pieces, were performed at a given Mass or Vespers. Nor can we infer information as to the performance practice of music, for example the specific use of instruments, or how choirs of nuns might have sung music written for mixed—that is, high and low—voices.

But the accounts are almost formulaic in certain frequent features. One is the remarkable, heavenly effect of nuns' music making, to which visitors refer again and again as inducing ecstacy. This kind of description may have to do with the widespread perception of the cloister as an Earthly Paradise, whose inhabitants performed the music of the angels. This concept, found in Federigo Borromeo's writings as well as in other authors, could only have been enhanced by the actual circumstances of performance inside the double church—an at least theoretically invisible group of singers on the other side of a wall, with a timbre of purely high voices unlike anything else to be heard in Seicento Milan. In light of the universal problems with boy sopranos and castrati mentioned by composers and theorists in Lombardy, the high pitch levels of female monastic choirs represented quite literally the only sonic prefiguration of the angelic choirs to which Federigo often referred.[27]

Yet the palpable corporal presence of nuns is borne out by the accounts of the most important visitors, for whom music and conversation in the external parlor after Vespers was almost invariable. Indeed, the sheer quantity of curial restrictions on parlor music testifies to its ubiquity. One of the most informative travel accounts is that of the 1664 visit of

Cosimo III de' Medici, Grand Duke of Tuscany, to Milan. There exist two separate versions of his travels "in Lombardia," that is, to Bologna, Ferrara, Mantova, Venice, Brescia, and Milan—one a less polished account written by Filizio Pizzichi, one a more formal court chronicle by Cosimo Pria.[28] Cosimo was something of a fancier of nuns' culture, and the travel diaries record his hearing a virtuosa nun singer at the Monastero degli Angeli in Brescia, as well as music in female monasteries in Venice and Mantova. Cosimo's visit of 25 June 1664 to Santa Radegonda in Milan, by this time the most famous—and infamous—musical monastery in the city, takes up two pages of Pria's account:

> He went to hear Mass at the Benedictine nuns of Santa Radegonda, nuns noble, rich and skilled, especially in music, in number some 140 . . . they have made such great progress, especially in music, that they have perfected themselves in both instrument playing and in singing like any good *professore* [professional musician].[29]

There follow several lines deleted in pen, the only excision in the carefully produced account. Pria remarks on the division of the musicians at Santa Radegonda into two competing *truppe*, that is, choirs of singers and instrumentalists, and then continues his narrative after Vespers were completed:

> At the open door of the monastery, [Cosimo] talked at length with them . . . in the presence of the Abbess, who was also pleased by the idea, the nuns brought out their instruments, and sang *ariette*, lasting more than a good hour.[30]

Obviously, Cosimo's special status, as head of a state in alliance with Milan, afforded him privileges and extraordinary treatment at the monastery. But this account, written essentially as Medici propaganda, tells us through its silence as well. For the only legible words under the penstrokes of the deletion are: "the archbishop . . . that they never obey his interest." It was precisely in the 1660s that the nuns of both Santa Radegonda and Santa Margarita ran afoul of the strict, Roman-trained Archbishop Alfonso Litta, who succeeded, at least temporarily, in banning polyphony at Santa Margarita and Santa Radegonda entirely. It would seem that the original narrative mentioned Litta's strictures, and that the passage was then excised from the final version so as not to offend the powerful prelate. Cosimo's visit highlights the conflicting influences on female monasteries and their musical life: Pria's passage, the only long description of music in the entire travel narrative, testifies to the quality, size, and noble backing of Santa Radegonda's singers and players, the largest musical establishment in Seicento Milan. But as we have seen a century earlier with Carlo's visit to Sant'Apollinare, a strict prelate like Litta could contest the independence and musical life of even the most patrician monastery.

So far, the three views I have presented have all been from outside, across the dividing wall of the double church, or through the grates of the parlatorio. I would like to conclude by considering what Lombard nuns themselves might have thought of music, and what role it might have played for them. Several other chapters in this volume address this issue, perhaps the central historiographic question for our consideration of cloistered women's worldview and culture in early modern Europe. But the evidence from Lombardy for nuns' own views of the purpose and effect of music is fragmentary.

The enormous pressure of such occasions as Carlo Borromeo's visit to Sant'Apollinare can hardly have provoked anything but the most defensive of formulations on the part of his interlocutors. It is perhaps best to return to the Federigo Borromeo correspondence, and to sample one sister's expressions of the spiritual role of music in daily life, as written to a prelate extremely supportive of music making.

Suor Angela Flaminia Confaloniera of Santa Caterina in Brera seems to have received her musical training after her profession vows; her letters testify to her understanding of divine music, and its relations to earthly sound, echoing Federigo's words as well as common musical aesthetics of the time:

> Dearest Father, the first effect of this divine melody is to enrapture my soul to God, the completion of this melody . . . to hear in these parts [voci], one distinct from the other, such consonance, and to hear [the music's] soprano, and all the other parts, is so different from [earthly] voices.[31]

A later letter to Federigo, from around 1630, provides more concrete information about music at the monastery:

> The situation is this: there is a nun here, who is the one who taught me how to sing and play. She is the sister of Signore Antonio Rusca. This nun knows how to compose, and she has composed a lot of motets. Her brothers are going to get them published and want to dedicate them to Your Excellency as a sign of gratitude appropriate to her as well as for the benevolence you

> have shown our monastery. These compositions have been highly praised, and I believe that monasteries will like them. And since this young woman is very spiritual [molto spirituale], I believe they have been composed with great fervor [con molto spirito], and so she would like to dedicate them to you, because there is no one whom our monastery loves more than you.[32]

What music "con molto spirito" might have meant to a nun in Santa Caterina must remain a mystery, since the 1943 bombing and fire at the Ambrosiana destroyed the only known copy of Suor Claudia Rusca's *Sacri concerti a 1.2.3.4. e 5.*, published in Milan in 1630.[33] But if Suor Confaloniera was not simply engaging in hyperbole, hardly a quality that Federigo valued highly, this letter would then seem to confirm that nuns did consider some music to embody ideas of spirituality and to be suitable for their institutions.

I would like to conclude this chapter with another example, this time a musical one, of nuns' own philosophy of music. Example 14.1, excerpts from the first section of the motet *Cari musici*, opens the *Motetti a 1.2.3.4.*, published in 1691 by Donna Bianca Maria Meda of the ancient Benedictine monastery of San Martino del Leano in Pavia.[34] Unlike any Lombard motet collection of the later seventeenth century, Meda's print begins with a piece that is an apostrophe to musicians about music; more precisely, a call, at least at first, to *refrain* from music in favor of divine contemplation:[35]

> Cari Musici, cum grato silentio voces comprimite
> suspendite sonos, cantare cessate,
> et contemplate dilecte Jesus amores;
> non me turbate, no, no, amante
> armonici chori, cantare cessate.

In one sense, *Cari musici* takes up a common poetic conceit of the seventeenth century, that of the ultimate fallibility and unsatisfactoriness of earthly music compared to the music of divine contemplation and celestial harmonies awaiting the saved individual soul. Yet it hardly seems an accident that this is a favorite point in Federigo Borromeo's thinking as well; it is found in his *ragionamenti* to nuns as well as in his Christian-optimistic explication of the natural world, the *Tre libri della lauda divina*.[36]

At the same time, the renunciatory message of the aria text seems contradicted by Meda's careful crafting of the music, with its opening imitative ritornello, sustained first note in the voice, long descents in the

Example 14.1. Bianca Maria Meda, *Cari musici*, measures 1–38.

Example 14.1. (cont.)

melodic line from successively higher pitches (e″, f″, g″, a″), virtuoso vocal leaps, and abrupt swings between the keys of A minor and C major.[37] And indeed, after a first strophic aria on the delights of Jesus' love, the central recitativelike section reverses the poetic conceit, calling on the heavenly choirs to sing after the singer has heard the voice of her heavenly spouse, and reaching its climax on a long high g″ (Example 14.2):

> Ah, quid dico? anima ingrata
> in silentio taciturno;
> amores sponsi audio sepelire,
> ah, non tacete, no, no,
> o voces canorae, non tacete.

This is then followed by the second strophic aria of the motet, concerning the human impossibility of loving Christ in silence ("Amare et silere / cor, tentas impossibile"). The piece then closes with a typically florid—but rather harder-won—"Alleluia" section, commonly found in late Seicento Lombard motets.

In one sense, Donna Meda's motet falls into the Seicento tradition of music about music, singing about singing.[38] More precisely, it is music about nonmusic, singing about the ultimate unsatisfactoriness of earthly music until the recognition of divine benignity sanctifies human longing and singing. It thus seems reasonable to view the piece as Meda's proem to her own collection, a motet that reflects her own view of music's role in leading the listener to the contemplation of unheard, eternal celestial harmonies. And through the voices of female monastic singers projected over the wall of the *chiesa interiore*, nuns like Meda could thus reclaim their public sanctoral role that all Carlo Borromeo's visitations had failed to erase.

Perhaps it is precisely this tension between earthly and celestial sound that marks all four views of music in the female monasteries of Milan. From the dangers to Carlo's reforms associated with music at Sant' Apollinare, to the patrician prestige of Santa Radegonda's Vespers, from the humble but intense mysticism of Federigo's views on music, to the family ties of music at Santa Caterina, this short conspectus of perspectives on nuns' music seems to underline the traditional, almost magical, view of music's power. In addition, points from other authors in this volume—Federigo's passionate pursuit of specifically female mysticism are reminiscent of John Coakley's ideas about male alienation in Trecento mendicant thought—recur in the Milanese evidence as well.

Example 14.2. Measures 66–80.

The philosophies of music summarized here also point up the intellectual distance of early modern Europe from post-Enlightenment thought. The "transcendent" connotations of nuns' music for its listeners, and the clear association between music making and female rapture, highlight the dangers of imposing anachronistic interpretations on these essentially ritual and symbolic phenomena. Above all, the aesthetic views for and against nuns' music in Milan underline the centrality of that art and its most famous practitioners in the worldview of a fissured yet intellectually unified culture quite different from our own.

Notes

1. Now preserved in Milan, Biblioteca Trivulziana, codex 509; see Caterina Santoro, *I codici medioevali della Biblioteca Trivulziana* (Milan: Biblioteca Trivulziana, 1965), p. 110. Although the house itself was located in the town of Meda, some forty kilometers north of the Lombard capital, its monastic population was overwhelmingly Milanese; the abbess had seigneurial rights over the region into the Ducento (see Leandro Zoppé, *Per una storia di Meda* [Meda: Comune di Meda, 1971]).

2. Archivio Storico Diocesano, Novara, sign. A2; see E. Dahnk Baroffio, *I codici liturgici dell' Archivio Diocesano di Novara* (Novara: Associazione di Storia Ecclesiale Novarese, 1978), p. 7. My thanks to Monsignor Angelo Stoppa for his help in my examination of this manuscript.

3. For this architectural form in Lombardy, see Liliana Grassi, "Iconologia delle chiese monastiche femminili dall'alto Medioevo ai secoli XVI–XVII," *Arte Lombarda* 42 (1964): 131–50. The contract between the nuns of the Monastero Maggiore and Gian Giacomo Antegnati is dated 4 September 1554 and preserved in the Archivio di Stato, Milan (ASM), Fondo Religione, parte antica, 2147. A transcription may be found in Robert Kendrick, "Genres, Generations, and Gender: Nuns' Music in Early Modern Milan, c. 1550–1706," Ph.D. dissertation, New York University, 1993, Appendix. For the best summary of the church's decorative scheme, see Giovanni Battista Sannazzaro, *San Maurizio al Monastero Maggiore* (Milan: A cura della parocchia di Santa Maria alla Porta, 1992); on the organ see Sandro Boccardi, "L'ultimo restauro all'organo Antegnati," in idem, pp. 205–6, and Boccardi's notes to a recording using the instrument: Frescobaldi, *Fiori musicali*, Astrèe E 8714 (1991).

4. For archival and repertorial studies of female monastic music in the diocese, see Kendrick, "Genres, Generations, and Gender."

5. For Burney's visit to the Humiliate house of Santa Maria Maddalena (al Cerchio), see Percy A. Scholes, ed., *Dr. Burney's Musical Tours in Europe* (Oxford: Oxford University Press, 1959), 1: 77.

6. These are listed in Kendrick, "Genres, Generations, and Gender," Appendix 2.

7. The documentation is preserved in the Archivio Storico Diocesano, Milan (ASDM, formerly Archivio della Curia Vescovile), sezione XII, "Ordini Religiosi e Congregazioni," vol. 64, fasc. 2; most of the documents have been published in Paolo Sevesi, "Il monastero delle Clarisse in S. Apollinare di Milano (documenti, secoli XIII–XVIII)," part 5, *Archivium Francescanum Historicum* 19 (1926): 76–99. My citations are from the ASDM manuscripts.

8. On this effort as a whole, see P. Renée Baernstein, "The Birth of the Counter-Reformation Convent: The Angeliche of S. Paolo in Milan, 1530–1630," Ph.D. dissertation, Harvard University, 1993; and Danilo Zardin, *Donna e religiosa di rara eccellenza: Prospera Corona Bascapè, i libri e la cultura nei monasteri milanesi del Cinque e Seicento* (Florence: Leo S. Olschki, 1992), esp. pp. 41–56.

9. "Quando io dovevo esser confirmata madre di q*ues*to convento, come fui, uenne qua il P*adre* Comm*issar*io ap*ostoli*co p*er* effetto, et mi disse che suor Clemen*tin*a gl'haueua dimondato licenza di poter far uenire in conuento M*esser* Gio*vanni* Ant*onio* organ*is*ta che insegnava à cantare ad essa suor Clemen*ti*na et a sonare a suor An*ge*la Serafina, et qu*est*o p*er* far accomciare l'istrum*en*to di suor Ang*el*a Serafina, et l'organo," ASDM XII, vol. 64, f. 204.

10. "Suor Gerolama Caterina . . . dica sua colpa ogni sabbato in refettorio per tre mesi delli diffetti commessi, de' quali consta nel processo di questa visita, per haver tenuto madrigali et soneti amorosi, et non haver custodito il parlatorio com'era obligata . . . Suor Angela Serafina stia per tre mesi senza il uelo. Sia priua dell'ufficio di organista, nè si possa rimettere a questo ufficio per sei anni," ibid.; also in Sevesi, "Il monastero delle Clarisse," pp. 86–87.

11. "L'arpicordo grande non stia in camera sua, ma altrove in conuento, nè lei possa sonar su quello, o altro instromento, nè cantar per tre anni canto figurato," ASDM XII, vol. 64, f. 204.

12. The disputes over visitation permits (*licenze*) for male music teachers, and over nuns' teaching each other and their girl lay pupils (*educande*), would last into the eighteenth century. For some documents on the matter from across Italy, see Gian Lodovico Masetti Zannini, *Motivi storici dell'educazione femminile*, vol. 1 (Bari: Editorialebari, 1980), chap. 5.

13. The petition is reproduced and transcribed in Guglielmo Barblan, "La vita musicale in Milano nella prima metà del Cinquecento," in *Storia di Milano*, (Milan: Fondazione Treccani degli Alfieri, 1961), 9: 853–95, at p. 888.

14. Giovanni Paolo Cima, *Partito de ricercari e canzoni alla francese* (Milan: Tini and Lomazzo, 1606), pp. 73ff. (a modern edition, with an unreliable translation of Cima's instructions, is found in *Corpus of Early Keyboard Music*, ed. Claire G. Rayner [n.p.: American Institute of Musicology, 1969], vol. 20).

15. Lorenzo Penna, *Li primi albori musicali* (Bologna: Giacomo Monte, 1672), Book 3, chap. 19: "Del suonare vna, ò due, ò tre, ò quattro, &c. Voci più baße, ouero vna, ò due, ò tre ò quattro &c. Voci più alte"; the 1672 Bologna edition of this work has each of its three books dedicated to a different nun in Parma.

16. "Che il sonar' de organi presso alcuni monasterij di monache più riformate non è tenuto di tanta necessità di modo che sin qui non hanno voluto erigere organi nelle lor chiese et le organiste et cantore di canto figurato spesse volte

sogliano esser le manco disciplinate et manco spirituale," letter signed "vicario delle monache," c. 1578, ASDM XII, vol. 48, f. 65.

17. The documents are found in ASDM XII, vol. 64. Carlo's attempt to regulate and ultimately to ban female monastic polyphony seems to fit into his project of "social disciplining" as defined by the ecclesiastical historian Paolo Prodi in "Riforma interiore e disciplinamento sociale in San Carlo Borromeo," *Intersezioni* 5 (1985): 273–85; Prodi draws on the concept of *Sozialdisziplinierung* in early modern Europe as outlined by the writings of Gerhard Oestreich.

18. The letter from the (unnamed) vicar general, dated 22 October 1593, is in ASDM, XII, vol. 74, fasc. 4.

19. Borromeo's writings and letters are preserved in the Biblioteca Ambrosiana (BA); I thank Louis Jordan for his help with these sources.

20. A selection from the prelate's voluminous correspondence with nuns is found in Carlo Marcora, "Lettere del cardinal Federico alle claustrali," *Memorie storiche della diocesi di Milano* 11 (1964): 177–424. The quote from Borromeo's *vicario delle monache* which refers to the idea that "Essendo le Vergine a Dio consacrate la più illustre porzione della greggia di Cristo" can be found in ASDM XII, vol. 49, f. 19.

21. There is no satisfactory modern treatment of Borromeo's thought; for the best overview, see Paolo Prodi's entry in the *Dizionario biografico degli italiani* 13 (Rome, 1971), 13: 38–39; and for the prelate's aesthetics, see the important study by Pamela Jones, *Federico Borromeo and the Ambrosiana: Art and Patronage in Seventeenth-Century Milan* (Cambridge: Cambridge University Press, 1993). My thanks to Benjamin Westervelt for his ideas on Borromeo's policy.

22. "anco canta la S*an*ta Chiesa: *Assumpta est Maria in Celum gaudent Angeli*; adunq*ue* p*er* accompagnar' il canto dell'Angeli diremo qualche cosa circa la musica spir*itua*le . . . et diremo di quelle cose che si ricercano p*er* far buona una musica . . . dico adunque che la p*rim*a cosa che si ricerca p*er* cantar bene è la buona voce; la 2.a è la compositione . . . ma la 3.a et quella che più importa è l'affetto . . . che la compositione del canto sia conforme all'affetto delle parole . . . la p*er*fettione della musica la qual non nasce dalla compositione del canto ne da alcuna arteficio, ma dal modo del cantare et dall' affetto de colui che canta," from "Dell'Assontione della B.V.," BA, F. 4 inf., ff. 359ff.

23. The chapter entitled "De Canto, et de Sono" in Book 4 of this treatise (Milan, 1616) concerns the role of music in inducing rapture on the part of several of the female mystics whom the prelate supported; the most notable, and most musical, of these was Caterina Vannini of Siena, of whose musical preludes to ecstacy Federigo provides several accounts in the treatise.

24. A convenient summary of Seicento travelers' accounts is provided by the essays in *"Millain the Great": Milano nelle brume del Seicento*, ed. Aldo de Maddalena (Milan: Cassa di Risparmio delle Provincie Lombarde, 1989).

25. This visit, along with a stop on the 1612 Grand Tour of Jan Sobieski, is noted in the Polish and Latin travel diaries transcribed in *Podróż królewicża Władysława Wazy do krajow Europy Zachnodniej w latach 1624–1625 w świetle ówczesnych relacji*, ed. Adam Przyboś (Kraców: Wydawniectwo Literackie, 1977), pp. 240–41.

26. Excerpts from the printed accounts may be found in Jane Bowers, "The

Emergence of Women Composers in Italy, 1566–1700," in *Women Making Music: The Western Art Tradition*, ed. Jane Bowers and J. Tick (Urbana: University of Illinois Press, 1986), pp. 116–67, at pp. 125ff.

27. A number of Lombard musical editions, among them Giovanni Ghizzolo's 1622 *Messa e salmi* and Ignazio Donati's 1623 *Salmi boscarecci*, provided instructions for the downward transposition of soprano parts if competent (male) sopranos were not available. For contemporary views of nun singers as prefigurations of the angelic choirs, see Angelo Berardi, *Ragionamenti Musicali* (Bologna: Giacomo Monte, 1681), pp. 109–10; and Costanzo Antegnati's dedication of his 1592 *Salmi à otto* to the singers of San Vittore in Meda (Antegnati's preface notes the "eterni e perfettissimi concerti de chori Angelici nel Paradiso, come sò che voi fate").

28. The accounts are preserved in Archivio di Stato, Florence, Mediceo Principato, filze 6382 (Pizzichi) and 6383 (Pria), and are summarized in Giulia Calvi, "I Toscani e la Milano barocca," *"Millain the Great,"* pp. 169–90.

29. "[Cosimo] Andò a sentire Messa alle Monache Benedettine della Chiesa di S*an*ta Rodegonda Monache Nobili et Ricche virtuose, e partic*ularmen*te nella Musica, sono di n*umero* circa 140 . . . hanno fatto progresso tanto grande, che si sono perfezionate nel Suono, che nel Canto come qualsivoglia bravo professore." carta 50r. Pria, "Relazione del Viaggio-fatto del Ser.mo Sig.re Principe Cosimo Terzo di Toscana L'Anno 1664," ASF, f. 12a 63183, carta 504.

30. "et alla Porta aperta del Monistero, fece lungo discorso con loro . . . et alla presenza della Madre Badessa, che se ne compiacque ancora lei, fecero uenire li Strumenti, e cantarono Ariette . . . che durarono sopra una grossa hora," ibid.

31. "P*ad*re mio car*issi*mo, la prima cosa che fa questa melodia [è che] rapisce l'anima in Dio dove troua il compimento di questa musica, si sentono poi queste uoci, una distinta dall'altra, ui è una consonanza . . . che vi è soprano, e tutte le altre parte, ma sono tante diferenti le uoci," undated letter to Federigo, G. 8 inf., ff. 159v–160.

32. "La cosa è questa; che vi è una Monicha, et è quella che à insegnato à mi a cantare e sonare, et è sorella del Sig*no*r Antonio Rusca. Questa monicha sa comporre, e cosi à composto asai motetti, e gli sor fratelli gli fano meter in stampa, e gli vogliono dedicar à V. S. Ill*ustriss*ima per signo della gratitudine, che a Lei conuiene auere, per la beniuolenza che mostra al nostro monasterio. Questa compositione è stata molto laudata, e credo che sarà di gusto alli monasterij e come questa Giouana è molto spirituale, credo che siano composti con molto spirito; e cosi uorebe dedicarli a Lei p*er*che il nostro Monasterio non à persona che più ama di Lei," undated letter to Federigo, BA, G. 8 inf., ff. 469v–470r.

33. According to the 1684 biographical list of Santa Caterina's members ("Biografia delle monache umiliate di S. Caterina di Brera," Biblioteca Ambrosiana, Ms. Trotti 453, written by an anonymous nun, ff. 13v–14), Rusca was born in 1593, received music instruction before professing vows, and died in 1676.

34. Bianca Maria Meda, *Motetti a 1.2.3.4., con violini, e senza* (Bologna: Pier-Maria Monti, 1691). *Cari musici* is scored for high voice (*canto*), two violins, and basso continuo. According to the sources summarized in Alessandra Veronese, "Monasteri femminili in Italia settentrionale nell'alto medioevo: Confronto con i

monasteri maschili attraverse un tentativo di analisi 'statistica,'" *Benedictina* 34 (1987): 406, the house was founded in the ninth century.

35. The text of the opening aria might be translated as: "Dear musicians, withhold your voices with pleasing silence, suspend your sounds, stop your singing, and tenderly reflect on Jesus' love; no, do not disturb me from loving, harmonious choirs, but cease your singing."

36. For a discussion and edition of this latter work, see Alessandro Martini, *"I tre libri della lauda divina" di Federico Borromeo: Ricerca storico-stilistica* (Padua: Editore Antenore, 1975); on music, see Book 1, chap. 3, "Delle creature," ibid., pp. 227–28.

37. On a broader level, this seeming contradiction between meaning and form recalls Walter Benjamin's classic distinction between "sound" and "script" in seventeenth-century German tragedy, *Ursprung des deutschen Trauerspiels* (Frankfurt am Main: Suhrkamp-Verlag, 1972), pp. 227–37. For some other applications of this distinction, see Eric Chafe, *The Church Music of Heinrich Biber* (Ann Arbor, MI: UMI Research Press, 1987), p. 127; and idem, *Tonal Allegory in the Music of J.S. Bach* (Berkeley: University of California Press, 1991).

38. For an excellent introduction to the "metamusical" secular cantata, see Margaret Murata, "Singing about Singing, or the Power of Music Sixty Years After," in *In Cantu et in Sermone: For Nino Pirrotta on his 80th Birthday*, ed. Fabrizio della Seta and Franco Piperno (Florence: Leo S. Olschki; n.p.: University of Western Australia Press, 1989), pp. 363–82.

Notes on the Contributors

John Coakley is Associate Professor of Church History at New Brunswick Theological Seminary, New Brunswick, New Jersey.

Mariateresa Fumagalli Beonio-Brocchieri holds the chair of medieval philosophy at the Università degli Studi, Milan.

Katherine Gill is Assistant Professor of the History of Christianity at the Yale Divinity School, New Haven, Connecticut.

Robert L. Kendrick is Assistant Professor of Music at Harvard University, Cambridge, Massachusetts.

E. Ann Matter is Professor of Religious Studies at the University of Pennsylvania, Philadelphia, Pennsylvania.

Craig A. Monson is Professor of Music at Washington University, St. Louis, Missouri.

Catherine M. Mooney is Assistant Professor of History at Virginia Commonwealth University, Richmond, Virginia.

Antonio Riccardi is a poet and an editor at Casa Editrice Mondadori, Milan.

Ann M. Roberts is Associate Professor of Art History at the University of Iowa, Iowa City, Iowa.

Anne Jacobson Schutte is Professor of History at the University of Virginia, Charlottesville, Virginia.

Karen Scott is Assistant Professor of History at De Paul University, Chicago, Illinois.

Carolyn Valone is Professor of Art History at Trinity University, San Antonio, Texas.

Elissa B. Weaver is Professor of Italian at the University of Chicago, Chicago, Illinois.

Gabriella Zarri holds the chair of Modern History at the Università degli Studi, Florence.

Index of Modern Authors

General Index

This book has been set in Linotron Galliard. Galliard was designed for Mergenthaler in 1978 by Matthew Carter. Galliard retains many of the features of a sixteenth-century typeface cut by Robert Granjon but has some modifications that give it a more contemporary look.

Printed on acid-free paper.